# The Complete Guide to

# New Zealand

# SMALL BUSINESS

Everything you need to know about buying, running, selling or growing a small business in New Zealand — and everything in between

## - Bob Weir -

A catalogue record for this book is available from the National Library of New Zealand

Published by RJ Weir Ltd

www.pinpointbusiness.co.nz

ISBN : 978-0-473-74243-0

Book cover, font, and illustrations by Anca Belu

## Table of Contents

# ABOUT THIS BOOK

## What this book will do for you

The goal of this book is to help you build a successful business, where success may mean something very different for you than it does for other business owners. If you want to remain a solo business or small, this book is for you. You may want to increase the size of your business from a non-employer to an employer. I will guide you on how to do that. If you want to embark on a path to significant growth, there is information here for you. You may want to buy a business or sell your business. We will discuss these processes.

I will cover most aspects of what you will come across in the small business world in New Zealand. It may not cover everything, but it will touch on a huge amount of relevant information.

## You can read it all, skim, or select a topic

When I read business books, I often skim, looking for key points to meet a need I have at that time. While you can read the book from cover-to-cover, it also allows you to go to the topics of greatest need.

I have broken the book down into relevant chapters, and then many subheadings within each chapter. This will assist you in jumping to the topics most relevant to your small business journey.

> I have also pulled out points I'm keen to emphasise. These are highlighted like this and include the pointer symbol.

# Big business references - they are relevant

You may be small. You may have limited capital, tight cash flows and be balancing a raft of roles. However, this does not mean you can't approach your business with the same professionalism, passion, and tools that a larger business does.

While you are best to avoid some of the high-cost bureaucratic processes big business needs to follow, there is still a great deal you can learn from them both the good and the bad. I have drawn on proven processes in both the small and big business world.

# Kiwi business cases - I'll discuss many

There is much we can learn from the successes and failures of other New Zealand businesses. I will cover many examples throughout the book. Often, the best thing you can learn about a business may not come from a business like yours. It may come from a different business, in a different industry, or one that is significantly larger than your own. The lessons we can learn can come from very diverse sources.

---

### *Kiwi and other business examples*

Throughout the book, I will cover many business examples, including successes and failures. I refer to startups, long-standing businesses, small businesses and large corporates. There are many Kiwi examples. You may have heard of them, so hopefully you are better placed to relate to their success or failure. I also reference key research or other case studies that reinforce a point I am making.

**They will appear in boxes like this.**

---

One always takes a risk when celebrating how good any business might be.

In the 1980s, the USA based energy company **ENRON** was the trendsetter and a poster company in finance and energy. The business community could not get enough of them. However, legal authorities later discovered that they were committing fraud on a grand scale and the company collapsed. **Kenneth Lay**, the chair, and **Jeffrey Skilling**, the CEO, both ended up in jail and sixteen other people pleaded guilty for crimes committed at the company.

Closer to home, **Allan Hubbard** purchased **South Canterbury Finance** in the 1950s. It was one of the most respected second tier lenders in New Zealand for decades. Even as the Global Financial Crisis was at its peak, many regarded it as a safe bet. Soon after, it collapsed and became New Zealand's biggest corporate failure, costing New Zealand taxpayers about $1.5 billion.

**Jim Collins's** 2001 book *"Good to Great"* sold over four million copies, making it one of the most successful business books of all time. In it, Collins used the example of eleven large, listed businesses in the US to argue how he believed a good company could become great. It was the must-read business book at the turn of the century and the volume of sales showed the strong acceptance the business community placed on his suggestions.

Sadly, of the eleven businesses, one went into liquidation. Another, **Fannie Mae**, faced repeated charges and fines for falsifying earnings results from 2002 to 2006.[1] It was also at the centre of the subprime collapse that triggered the Global Financial Crisis in 2008. **Philip Morris** produces cigarettes, and I discuss the **Wells Fargo Bank** prosecution later in the book.

Within 10 years of the book's release, this group of companies was underperforming the stock exchange. [2,3]

Therefore, there is every chance I may sing the praises of a great Kiwi business who, sadly, after I put pen to paper, may face hard times or, through many circumstances, cannot live up to their current standing. I guess that is the reality of business. It does not weaken my enthusiasm to point out Kiwi success stories, and there are many. I hope I do not put the writer's curse on any business I single out in this book. Instead, I hope they only achieve greater success.

# What this book won't do for you

## It won't give you all the answers

Many self-help books offer you the world. This one doesn't. Business doesn't work that way. Your business may be small, but you operate in a large, complex world. The circumstances your business faces are not the same as those faced by equivalent businesses. Your business is unique. This book helps you simplify your world and to understand the reality of where you operate.

Hopefully, this book will answer many of your questions. If not, please ask someone for help. You deserve to get an answer, as there is no such thing as a bad or dumb question, not when it's about your business.

> *"Like the* 'right to remain silent' *is the right to ask a question and expect a reasonable answer. You then not only learn from what you observe but learn from others."* **- A Cherokee saying.**

## It won't make decisions for you

As this book will highlight, you need to surround yourself with the best advice you can afford. It will also outline the mental limitations we all share, as we all possess imperfect brains and can make very imperfect decisions. You will need to seek advice. Just be sure those giving you advice know what they are talking about and that they have your best interests at heart. Have faith in your own ability and don't fear making your own decisions. No-one knows your business or has the passion for it like you do.

## It won't help you control the uncontrollable

Too many business owners can become overcome with a victim mindset, blaming factors outside their business for issues they face. Consider the *Serenity Prayer* when you feel like the victim of external factors that are affecting your business that you cannot control. I will discuss how to maintain an awareness of such factors. However, the focus of this book is on what you can do, not what others can do to you.

> *"God, grant me the serenity to*
> *Accept the things I cannot change.*

*Courage to change the things I can;*
*And the wisdom to know the difference".*
**-Alcoholics Anonymous version of Reinhold Niebuhr's**
**Serenity Prayer**

## It won't create more hours in your day

While I hope this book will allow you to get far more out of your business, it can't create a longer working day for you. If you want to bring a sustainable change to your business, you need to plan and set aside time to bring about that change. Continuing to do what you have always done will only produce what you now have. If that is not good enough for you, make the time to do something about it.

## It won't keep you up to date

As soon as any author puts pen to paper and offers advice to small business owners, laws and rules change. While I have done my best to ensure the information provided here is practical and useful, you need to consider what may have changed between when I wrote things down, when you read these words, and when you come to act on those words. This is no more common than with tax law.

I hope this book will give you a good steer on what you need to do, but if the details are critical to you in any area, make sure you seek the right expert to ensure you have the latest and most accurate data and information.

## It won't replace expert advice

The small business world can be complex, and you need to know so much. This can become overwhelming. I've attempted to cover as much information as possible here to guide you. No matter the detail I've provided, nothing will replace expert advice specific to the challenge you may face at a specific stage in your journey. There are many places within the book where I recommend you seek such advice. Even if I don't explicitly state this, it's always implied.

You should never underestimate the value of advice from someone who knows what they are talking about. Likewise, be cautious about taking advice from pretenders.

*"Opinions are like assholes. Everyone has one."*
— **Simone Elkeles.** American young adult author.

Fantastic advice from experts is likely to cost you. Failing to seek good advice when the risks are high could be far more expensive.

# CHAPTER 1

## INTRODUCTION

## DOING BUSINESS IN NEW ZEALAND

It's so pleasing to see you are taking the time to improve your Kiwi business or that you want to learn more about running a business. Perhaps you have never owned or run a small business and are considering it. I love to see owners of small businesses achieve the success they seek and deserve.

## We rank amongst the best

New Zealand is one of the best countries in the world to start and run a business. Let's look at some statistics that back this up:

- **Transparency International** ranks us third, only behind Denmark and Finland, as the least corrupt countries in the world.[1]

- We are ranked the fourth most peaceful country on the **Global Peace Index.** [2]

- We are ranked fourth in terms of **gender equality**. [3]

- The **World Bank** ranks us first as the easiest country to do business (out of 190). [4]

- The **World Justice Project** produces an index that combines factors like corruption, open government, human rights, security, civil and criminal justice. New Zealand ranks 8th on their rankings.[5]

- We are ranked first as the **easiest country to set up a company**. This measures the number of steps (we have only one), the time it takes (less than a day), the capital needed (we don't need any), and whether it differs for men or women (it's the same for both). [6]

If you just want to start a business on your own, you really don't need to do anything - you can start as a sole trader anytime you want.

# We are a big country — really!!

When you look on a world map, you will see our country tucked away in the bottom right-hand corner. The enormous land mass that is Australia is to our west, and the Pacific Ocean is to our east, so we look tiny.

If Kiwis are asked, it is likely they will say New Zealand is small. But this is not completely the case.

Our largest city, Auckland, with a population of about 1.7 million in 2024, would rank as the fifth largest city was it based in the USA. It would be ranked within the top ten biggest cities in the European Union.

The land mass that is Singapore is barely larger than Lake Taupo in the North Island.

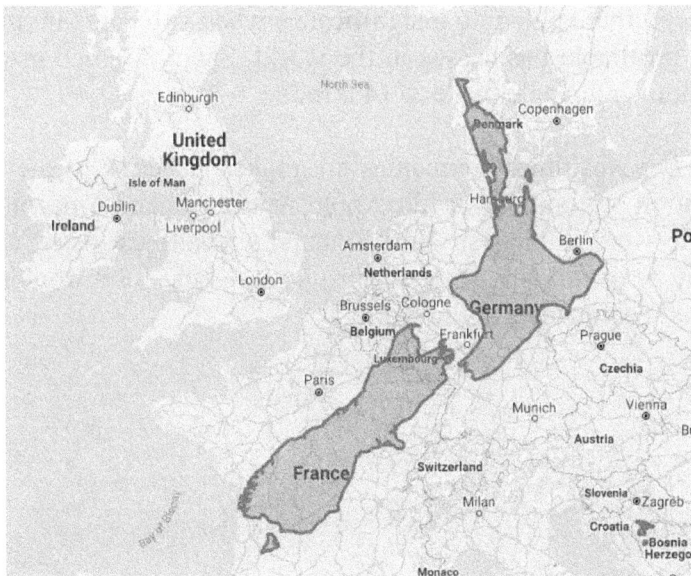

If you put a map of New Zealand over mainland Europe, with Wellington sitting just above Munich, Cape Reinga would be in Denmark. and Invercargill would be very close to the Spanish border with France [7].

# But doing business here has its challenges

Unfortunately, in this big, beautiful country of ours, we only have about 5.3 million people scattered across our land. This puts us about 120th in the population rankings, just above Ireland and just below Norway.

We operate in a small marketplace. While we rank high on many measures, our economy is tiny, ranked 51st in the world.

We are isolated. The world map shows we are in the middle of nowhere. Wellington, along with Canberra, hold the top spots as the most remote capital cities on the planet.

Our biggest companies deliver healthy numbers, especially compared to those of us in small business. Fonterra's profit was around $990 million. Fletcher Building was $800 million, ASB Bank $1.4 Billion and Spark $830 million.

However, these pale into insignificance when you compare them with the most profitable businesses in the world. Saudi Aramco made about $247 billion, and Apple made $114 billion.

When the wealthiest companies are ranked in terms of their market capitalisation, it's companies like Apple, Microsoft, and Amazon who are among the world's biggest. New Zealand's wealthiest listed company, Xero, may be one of our greatest start-up successes, but it wouldn't make the top 1000 companies in the world [8]

# Some Kiwi small business statistics

If you have your own small business or perhaps you are looking to start one, great. Welcome to the family. We play a significant role in the New Zealand economy.

- There are over 560,000 businesses in New Zealand with 400,000, about 70%, having no employees. [9]

- Over 97% of businesses in New Zealand have less than 20 staff. These are called **Small to Medium Enterprises** or **SMEs.**

- These businesses employ 680,000 people, which is about 28% of all Kiwi employees.

These small business trends have not changed dramatically over many years. They are also very similar around the world. Our businesses are small. Really small. However, in terms of the number of businesses, there are more of us than any other sized business in New Zealand, and worldwide - and by a very long margin.

If you are in small business or want to start a small business, you will be part of a huge business community that is the fundamental backbone of the New Zealand economy.

# Why own a small business?

You no doubt have heard many people question why someone would own a small business. Perhaps you are still asking yourself the same question.

And it is an excellent question.

Owning your own business is not for the faint of heart. If you are currently employed and receiving a wage or salary, you can take comfort in knowing that money will be in your bank account every week, fortnight, or month, depending on your pay schedule. The job may or may not meet all your expectations, but at least the money keeps coming in.

If you are on a wage, you can tell people what you make every hour you work. You probably fill out time sheets to tell the boss where you spent that time.

When you own your own business, not only may there be little or no money coming in, there could also be periods where there is more money going out than in. There is also every likelihood you have put large amounts of your own money in the business, and even re-mortgaged your home to fund it.

When you own your own business, it can be scary adding up the hours you put into the business for the money you take out. It's likely at some stage in the life of your business your hourly rate will be well below the minimum wage.

So why would you do it? Why do so many people in New Zealand own a small business?

There must be a good reason because, as the statistics show, over 500,000 of us are doing it.

There are some excellent reasons.

Whatever happens in your business, it is yours. It is yours to make of it what you want. It is yours to grow, or change, or improve, sell, buy, or even close.

When you work for someone else, you are at the mercy of their decisions. You must follow other people's rules, procedures, and policies, even if they make no sense or you don't agree with them. Many of us have worked for some great people and in some great businesses. But we can also say we've worked for some real idiots, bullies, even sociopaths or narcissists - yes, the business world is full of plenty of bosses who are pretty ugly human beings.

If it's your business, you can't complain about the boss because that's you.

When you own your own business, you can pursue a passion. You can try things and you can decide to do things without asking for anyone's permission. You can experiment. You can employ people and change their lives. You can help a customer, a community, a society, even the world - plenty of people started businesses and changed the world.

I will assume if you are reading this book, you already own a business or are contemplating taking the step.

All I can say is good on you. You are amazing.

My aim in this book is to inspire you to take that leap and do it if it's something you've always thought about but have been afraid too. If you already have a business, my goal is to make it work more for you to bring you more satisfaction, even joy, and hopefully a reasonable lifestyle.

# What defines small business success?

You will often hear individuals described as *"successful businesspeople"*. But what does that mean, really?

The Oxford English Dictionary defines *"success"* as:

### *The accomplishment of an aim or purpose.*

The key thing to take from this definition is that success is based on achieving *"an aim or a purpose"*. As your small business is your own, only you can define what that aim or purpose is.

> *"Success is not final; failure is not fatal: it is the courage to continue that counts."* - **Winston Churchill.**

People very often define business success in terms of the size of a business, the amount of money it generates, the staff it employs, or the years it has been operating.

| | Success in your small business is defined by one thing and one thing only - YOU. |
|---|---|

Maybe becoming big is your goal. If that is your aim, that's great. Don't let anyone tell you otherwise. Whether big, tiny, or anything in between, defining success is very much up to you, the owner of your business.

# CHAPTER 2

## THE MOST IMPORTANT THING IN YOUR SMALL BUSINESS — YOU!!

Before I launch into all the mechanics of running a business, I must devote some time to the most critical thing in a small business - YOU, the small business owner.

I will devote some time in later chapters on the topic of understanding who you are, the limitations of your brains, and how we make decisions. For now, let's make sure at every step in our journey through this book, and your business, that you never lose sight of the importance of caring for yourself. Your small business is only one part of your life - it can't be everything.

To succeed in small business, as with any endeavour in life, you must take care of yourself and those that are dearest to you. This is not a soft consideration. It is the most real and brutal reality of business. If you do not place a high importance on this, not only will you suffer, but so too will your business.

Nothing will contribute more to reaching success in your small business than you. The more you grow in your understanding of yourself and the more you care for your own wellbeing, the greater the likelihood of achieving the success you seek for your business.

Your wellbeing comes before our discussion on business goals, strategy, marketing, staff, finances, or any other topic. You need to come first in your business' priorities.

You are the business' greatest strength. But you could also be its greatest threat.

Too often we apportion the success or failure of our business to external factors: the economy; the government; new laws; suppliers; our competitors; or unpredictable customers. Many factors external to your business could lead to your business failing to achieve what you desire. However, success or failure in business is nearly always driven by the owner.

Therefore, a book that discusses how to run a successful small business needs to detail how you might know, manage, care for, and nurture yourself.

Your wellbeing and happiness are likely to be tightly interlinked with the state of your business. Your ability to think clearly and to make wise decisions will depend upon a healthy state of mind. Your physical and emotional strength will help you battle through the tough challenges that you will inevitably face. You need to be healthy for the business to be healthy. When the business is healthy, your ability to manage stress and feel happy will be much greater.

The quality of your decisions will make or break your business. You don't have the luxury of relying on someone else to do this when you are not at your best. The quality of your decisions will decline when you are tired, stressed, unhappy, distracted, and not focused on the moment at hand.

Therefore, how you are going is not just a lifestyle consideration. It is fundamental to your small business achieving the success you seek.

# How stressed are you?

## What is stress?

The **World Health Organisation (WHO)** defines stress relating to our work environment as:

> ***The response we may have when presented with work demands and pressures that are not matched to our knowledge and abilities, and that challenge our ability to cope.***

Pressure in business will be unavoidable. This pressure may keep you alert, motivated, able to work and learn, and lift your performance, depending on your available resources and your personal characteristics. However, if that pressure becomes excessive or otherwise unmanageable, it will lead to stress.

Prolonged and severe stress can damage your health, relationships, and the performance of your business. Yet, the right amount of stress is quite stimulating. We experience this with those events that we're sometimes crazy enough to do, like bungy jumping, parachuting, or a rollercoaster ride. In these cases, the stress is transient, or you may frame the stress positively.

> Stress is a very personal thing. What affects you may have no impact on others in the same situation.

If two people are exposed to the same set of traumatic situations, one person may have vastly different emotional and mental effects compared to the other.

We may each interpret the common signs of stress in different ways. If you are pursuing something you love that brings you meaning, you are far more likely to be positive about how you deal with stress symptoms. However, in other circumstances, some of us look upon the stress symptoms as a serious threat to our wellbeing. Here, the impact of the stress becomes almost self-fulfilling as was shown in research carried out by the **University of Wisconsin-Madison** in 2011.[1] Stress affects your health and can reduce your life expectancy. It will also diminish your ability to make good business decisions.

If stress becomes severe or prolonged, take heed.

The major factor that determines your stress levels is not what exists in your environment, but what happens inside you, in your thinking. To understand this, you first need to recognise the difference between pressure and stress. We talk about pressure and stress as if they are the same, but they are not. Pressure is the external demand in the environment. Everyone has pressure in his or her work life. That is not stress. Stress is how people process that pressure in their minds.

Our response is a state of mind and is our perception of the event or circumstance. It may not reflect in any way the state of reality as it appears to everyone else.

## Why zebras don't get ulcers

**Robert Sapolsky** is a professor at Stanford University, and one of the world's leading neuroscientists and experts in stress. In studying wild baboon populations in Kenya, Sapolsky examined how prolonged stress can cause physical and mental afflictions in some animals and, more importantly, in humans.

Sapolsky explained the physical processes that occur when animals, including humans, experience stress. There is a release of the hormones, **adrenalin** and **glucocorticoids**. These hormones can have a range of effects on us. In the wild, when an animal faces real stress (i.e., being eaten), it focuses its attention entirely on survival.

In his book *"Why Zebras Don't Get Ulcers"*, Sapolsky discussed his view that animals such as zebras stress for short periods of time then recover back to their normal state almost immediately (e.g., after escaping a predator's claws). However, in more advanced animal structures, like baboons, where there is a natural pecking order in the group and the animals have more time on their hands, they can suffer ongoing levels of stress.

Sapolsky speaks of the stress humans suffer, which is often created from our own interpretation of reality. He calls it **psychological stress** or stress that is the *"invention of our minds"*, which may not come from a genuine threat.

Often, our stress responses seem (and most times probably are) very irrational. Not only do we get stressed amid actual events, but we also get stressed about the possibility that events may confront us - however unlikely.

> Robert Sapolsky believes we have evolved to be intelligent enough to make ourselves sick with stress.

We spend a lot of our time ruminating about what we did or didn't do in the past and we worry about what might befall us in the future. We have absolutely no control over either. We cannot alter the past or change the future, but we can get highly stressed and anxious about both.

Humans, and some primates, face severe and prolonged stress caused by psychological or social factors that in no way pose any actual threat to our lives, as would be the case in the wild.

We worry about future possibilities, whether real or imagined (e.g., *"My business might fail"* or *"I might stuff up badly")*. This is where the power of our mind overwhelms rational thought. We all know we can't change the past; but can only learn from it. We also know that we can't predict the future and have only a very limited ability to affect it. Yet we exhaust huge amounts of energy thinking about it.

We have the most control over what we are doing in the exact moment we are doing it. As we spend mental energy ruminating or worrying, we miss what's in front of us. In our business, that could be solving a critical problem, an idea to act on, a chance to help a customer or employee, or just enjoying the moment for no other reason than we are alive, well, and doing what we love.

## *What results from prolonged stress?*

Scientific research by people like Sapolsky and many others has shown that prolonged stress has real and measurable effects on our health, our life span and our performance. Here are some of the unfortunate results of prolonged stress: [2]

- Neuron damage affecting memory and learning.

- Reductions in sex drive.

- Weight gain.

- High blood pressure.

- Coronary heart disease.

- Sleep loss.

- Reduced immune function.

- Vulnerability to depression and other psychological disorders.

- Damage to unborn foetus.

- Damage to chromosomes leading to reduced life expectancy.

As you can see by these manifestations of stress, it's not something to treat lightly. It can have severe emotional and physical ramifications if allowed to go on unchecked. In short, stress can be deadly.

## How can you better manage stress?

How might you better manage stress as you work in your business? The key to this is **resilience**, which I will discuss a little later. No single "*cure*" exists for stress. Stress management is a whole-of-life issue and needs to be approached holistically. Stress is also a very individual experience, stemming from past learning, genetics, personality, temperament, our social standing, and our environment. As a result, quick fixes are unlikely.

The following are a few simple things that may knock the edge off your stress while you chip away at longer-term solutions and while you are building your resilience.

First, start accepting that you will face stress. Rather than considering it to be a weakness, become comfortable with the idea it will happen and then try understanding it. You may then be in a better position to manage it.

Here are some questions to reflect upon when you feel stressed:

- Do you acknowledge or realise when you experience stress?

- How does stress make you feel?

- What triggered that episode of stress?

- How could you avoid or distance yourself from those triggers?

When the stress comes and you can recognise it, there are some important steps you can take to manage the short-term. Breathing is the first simple response. Stop and note the surrounding things. Bring your mind back to the present moment. These steps can ease short-term stressors. Look later in this chapter at the further steps you can take to become more mindful and less stressed.

## "I don't think I'm any good at this": Our voice of self-doubt

I am confident that you (and everyone else of sound mind) have had unproductive thoughts in your business life. It can be all too common in business for us to face self-doubt when the cash is tight, when you've lost a customer, when you scolded a staff member or made what proved to be the wrong decision. The good news is you are not alone.

A business owner who never doubts themselves, believes they are always right and believes they always make the correct decision is likely to be arrogant, which is very dangerous in business.

Do any of these thoughts sound familiar?

- I really don't know what I'm doing.

- I feel like an idiot.

- I don't know what to do.

- I'm not smart enough to be doing this.

- Why do those guys find this so much easier than me?

- Why am I having all this bad luck?

And so on.

Much of our mental energy in business can be wasted on things we have absolutely no control over.

*"Most of life will unfold in accordance with forces far outside your control, regardless of what your mind says about it..... Eventually you will see that the real cause of problems is not life itself. It's the commotion the mind makes about life that really causes problems"*. - **Michael Singer** [3]

We all need to show ourselves a little compassion. These thoughts can become **hooks** that trap us in a pointless cycle. We are human. We will all have these thoughts. The key is to not get stuck on them. If you never have these thoughts, then that is also a concern. Overconfidence and arrogance in business can be very dangerous.

> Arrogance is very dangerous in business. Some of the biggest failures of New Zealand businesses arose from leaders who were arrogant.

When you experience these periods of self-doubt in business, don't fight the thoughts that come with it. We have little ability to control our thoughts when they come and go. They will come and go continually. The best we can do is accept them, acknowledge and observe them, and even make light of them: *"Hey, thanks, mind, but the 'I can't' thoughts aren't very helpful right now"*.

Thoughts are not facts. They are not you and they are not necessarily reality. You can't always believe everything you think. However, thoughts can have a powerful effect on what you feel and do. All too often, we allow unproductive thoughts to roll around our minds, over and over, potentially reinforcing something that simply isn't true. Yet, fighting them is a fairly fruitless exercise. The more you can acknowledge these thoughts, step back from them, let them pass and refocus on what you are doing at that moment, the better chance you have of not being absorbed by them.

Seek the counsel of friends, family, and colleagues when you experience self-doubt. Internalising these thoughts and attempting to address them ourselves may not end well.

# Key factors in becoming more resilient

Now that we've discussed stress and unproductive thoughts, what can you do to enjoy your business journey, not only when everything is going well, but more importantly, when it is not? There's no question that your small business will, at some stage, overwhelm you. It is how you handle those challenges that will determine whether you let them rule your life or whether you can take greater control of them.

How can you build your physical and mental resilience so that, when faced with a significant business challenge, you are better prepared to cope with it?

Resilience is a process, not a trait. It involves how you interact and negotiate with others, your world, and yourself. It denotes a way of moving on with a more positive outlook of your business amid adversity, trauma, and everyday pressure.

When faced with adversity, it will trigger past beliefs, which could cause a less-than-helpful response. Your ability to build your resilience gives you a greater chance of responding differently to future adversity.

As we've discussed, stress and wellbeing are different for all of us. Therefore, the way to build your resilience will also differ. Considering you can't do it all, focus on the areas in the list below that you believe will help *you* the most.

But it won't be easy because we are human, and we have lazy brains.

## *Our lazy brain*

Our brain is a powerful organ. While it takes up only 2% of our body weight, it uses more energy than any other human organ, accounting for up to 20% of the body's total energy use. Our brains are also extremely lazy. To conserve energy, our brains will choose the easiest option, the one requiring the least energy.

I'm sorry to say that you're wired to take the easiest mental path. Changing the way you behave and approach issues will not come easily and takes a lot of energy. So be kind to yourself. To achieve greater resilience, you need to take small, measured steps. Be selective about the changes you can realistically make. Reward yourself for small gains. And don't set yourself up to fail by attempting too many changes at once.

> *"Insanity: Doing the same thing over and over again and expecting different results."* - **Albert Einstein.**

Most of all, do something. You can't expect a different outcome if you keep doing the same things, as Einstein highlighted in his famous quote.

## *Things that make us more resilient*

### 1.    Relationships

Social relationships are vital to our fulfilment and happiness. People who have one or more close friendships are normally happier.

We don't just need relationships; we need close relationships. It doesn't seem to matter if we have an extensive network of close relationships or not. It's not the quantity of our relationships, but the quality that matters.

These are relationships with people where you are comfortable to share your personal feelings in complete safety. You can provide them with support and receive support from them. These relationships differ from having a circle of friends where the connections are more superficial. Being part of a large group in a party atmosphere is great fun and you should never underestimate these relationships. However, it is the deep, close relationships you should nurture and work on most. It is these relationships that will make you more resilient and happier.

During the times you face significant pressures when running your business, you might put your key relationships on hold, thinking that you don't have the time to devote to them. Your business is more pressing. Not only does compromising your relationships risk their survival, but it also makes you unhappy, which will affect your approach to business.

### 2.    Caring for others

Most people who care for others selflessly do so because of a genuine desire to help and improve the world around them. Whether this is volunteer work or simply giving a little extra, the act of caring for others will bring rewards for you.

From a business perspective, this could mean giving back to the community in a way that brings real meaning to you and your business.

A study by the **University of Exeter Medical School** in the UK compared the physical and mental health of a large group of people who volunteered with a group who did no volunteering. The results showed the volunteers had fewer instances of depression, greater life satisfaction, and a longer life expectancy. [4]

In their research and book "*Happy Money*", the **University of Exeter Medical School** and Michael Norton [5] showed that the more money people could give away to others, the happier they became. While I would not suggest you give away your hard-earned dollars freely, this does highlight that the act of giving can make you happier.

## 3    *Physical health*

You are healthier and feel better when you look after your body physically. Healthier people are happier people.

### (i)    Exercise and diet

The essential part that exercise and diet play in your health is very well documented by a vast array of experts. There's little benefit in me going into detail here. You've probably had people badger you about your level of exercise or your less-than-perfect diet at some stage. I won't force more guilt on you about burning off and restricting those extra calories or that additional glass of wine.

While I won't write too much on diet and exercise, it doesn't diminish its importance. When you decide on the rules that will guide how you run your business, do your best to fit in a little exercise and pay attention to what you're eating and drinking. It will make you feel better and happier, which will help your business.

### (ii)    Sleep

One other physical health issue critical to building your resilience is sleep. We are a society that has become very sleep deprived.

There is a range of scientific views on why the body needs sleep. **Russell Foster**, Oxford professor and sleep specialist, states that sleep has a vital role in restoration, energy conservation and, most importantly, consolidation of memories and the boosting of creativity.[6] Sleeping enhances our ability to be more creative and come up with new ideas compared with when we are tired.

*"Sleep is for wimps."* - **Margaret Thatcher.**

*"Sleep is a criminal waste of time and a heritage from our cave days."* - **Thomas Edison.**

Unfortunately, there is an almost perverse view and bravado from people like Thomas Edison and Margaret Thatcher that surviving on little sleep shows strength. It would seem these people succeeded on very little sleep. Even if that was the case for them, the scientific evidence clearly disputes this view.

Sleep is not an indulgence. It is critical for your ability to function, your mental wellbeing and your stress management. The more tired you are, the more stressed you get.

**Harvard and Berkeley Universities** carried out a study in 2007.[7] Two groups were tested, one with and one without quality sleep, using **Functional Magnetic Resonance Imaging (FMRI)** scans to see the impact on the brain. The results showed that sleep deprivation affects our emotional state, can make us irrational, and leads to poor decision-making.

A lack of sleep will directly affect your performance in business. It's closely correlated to the same drop in performance you get with alcohol consumption. Studies at the **Centre for Sleep Research** in Australia almost 20 years ago proved this.[8] Prolonged sleep loss can also have physical health effects, like increased weight.

How much sleep is enough sleep?

The Centre for Sleep Research states that there are individual differences in each of our responses to sleep loss. This may even be genetic. However, if we restrict sleep to fewer than **seven hours per night**, it will affect 80% of us. Unless you are confident that genetics puts you in the 20% group, aim for seven or more hours sleep every night.

What is critical is that you listen to your body. It is likely you will know when you are getting insufficient sleep, whether that's seven or more hours per night.

## 4.    Meaningful work and meaningful goals

Viktor Frankl, in his book "*Man's Search for Meaning*", about his time in a Jewish concentration camp, put forward a simple but powerful message. A person can survive almost any situation if they can find meaning in what they do.

> "*Everything can be taken from a man but one thing: the last of the human freedoms - to choose one's attitude in any given set of circumstances, to choose one's own way.*" - **Viktor E. Frankl** in Man's Search for Meaning.[9]

While you will see nothing as extreme as what Frankl experienced, it highlights the importance of finding greater meaning in your business if you want to achieve greater happiness and resilience.

This is central to the concept of your business having a core purpose. If you have a clear "*why*" for what you are doing, you are far more likely to achieve any "*what*" you may face.

> "*He who has a why to live can bear almost any how.*" —**Friedrich Nietzsche**.

Success for your business, as you define it, should be very much about achieving what brings you meaning. It's about fulfilling your core purpose, while fulfilling the business' core purpose.

It is much easier to lift yourself up from a setback when you are pursuing something you truly believe in and that brings you meaning.

> "*If you judge a fish by its ability to climb a tree, it will live its life believing that it is stupid.*" — **Albert Einstein.**

If you feel "*stupid*" within yourself, perhaps you have not assessed your true purpose or meaning, but are judging yourself by the standards of others.

## 5.     Hold true to your values

It can be very uncomfortable and stressful to be in an environment where people claim to work by a certain set of values, yet their behaviours contradict what they purport to believe. For example, a business states that *"We operate with integrity"*. yet employees mislead their customers, or *"We are respectful"* when you see people being treated poorly.

You may not be aware of your values and, therefore, struggle to understand why you feel so bad.

Your ability to enjoy the journey in your business will rely heavily on your ability to adhere to your values. In any situation, it is key to respond in a way that is in line with what is important to you and what you stand for.

## 6.     Keep learning

I'm sure you have experienced the positive feeling associated with learning new skills and the confidence that comes with a deeper understanding of something of interest, including your small business. The fact you're reading this book shows your desire to continue learning.

Research has revealed that continuous learning helps with goal setting and creating a sense of achievement. Studies by **Aldridge** and **Lavender** in 2000 [10] and **John Field** in 2012 [11] have shown that continued learning increases our:

- Self-confidence.

- Autonomy.

- Physical health.

- Capacity to cope with potentially stress-inducing circumstances.

- Self-esteem.

- Self-efficacy, or our belief that we will succeed in certain circumstances.

- Sense of control over our own lives.

Adult learning influences attitudes and behaviours that affect our mental wellbeing.

If you continue learning through your adult life, it will build your resilience.

## 7.    *Staying present and being in the moment*

I have made several references about how to manage stress and paralysing thoughts by pausing and refocusing on the present. People refer to this as **being mindful.**

Mindfulness has become a more widely used term in Western society. It has, however, been part of Eastern cultures for thousands of years. In our world, where a vast array of distractions and external stimulation saturates us, we often lose the moment. We can start operating on autopilot. Sometimes we just need to stop and smell the roses.

For those of you who have done meditation or some form of yoga, you will have a strong understanding of the concept of being mindful. However, these pastimes are not everyone's cup of tea. There are still some very simple techniques you can follow to become more present when you feel you are losing control or being overrun with stress or the thoughts rattling around in your head.

These are three techniques **Russ Harris** suggests in his book *"The Happiness Trap"*, [12] to bring you back to the present moment.

### (i)    <u>Take five breaths</u>

The breath is a great way to centre you when you are drifting off or feel you are all over the place. You can do it anytime and anywhere.

Take five slow, deep breaths. Breathe out as slowly as you can until your lungs are empty. Then let them slowly refill.

When you are doing this, focus on your breathing and nothing else.

Now look around you and notice what you can see and hear at that point in time.

### (ii)    __Drop anchor__

This one aims to connect with the surrounding environment. It's good if you are sitting in a room with other people and you feel your stress levels rising.

Plant your feet into the floor.

Push them down, noticing the floor beneath your feet.

Notice the muscle tension in your legs.

Now look around you and notice what you can see and hear at that point in time.

### (iii)    __Notice five things__

This exercise is excellent if you can briefly escape from your work environment to spend a few minutes in the fresh air.

Pause for a moment.

Look around you and notice five things you can see.

Listen carefully to five things you can hear.

Notice anything in contact with your body, like the wind.

Now consider all the things impacting on your senses.

The more you do simple little exercises like this, the more they become a habit and the more likely you are to feel in control of your immediate circumstances.

Some other simple yet powerful examples to becoming more mindful each day include:

- Pause when you have that coffee and really taste it.

- Close your eyes when you cuddle your child and really feel what it's like.

- Stop and feel the wind in your face when you walk outside.

- Think about the texture of the food you are eating at lunch.

- Pause from the work at your desk, close your eyes and take two slow deep breaths.

These are techniques that will help snap you out of autopilot. They will get you focused on what's in front of you and they take only a few seconds.

## 8.    *Gaining greater control over your situation*

There were two extensive studies carried out to understand health issues in the British civil service, one over a 10-year period from 1967 and one in the late 1990s. Researchers refer to these as the **Whitehall Studies**. [13]

What these studies showed was that the further an employee was down the hierarchical ladder, the less control they had over their work environments, caused by a perceived lower social status. This also effects people's health. These health issues included increased stress, higher levels of heart disease, obesity, and higher blood pressure.

Thankfully, as a business owner, you have less chance of feeling lower on an employment hierarchy. However, if you feel you are not in control of your business circumstances, you are likely to experience the same stress-related issues.

You are more likely to enjoy your business, reduce stress, and increase resilience if you feel in control. By considering all the aspects in this book, hopefully you can achieve control of many aspects of your business

# CHAPTER 3

# GETTING INTO BUSINESS - STARTING A NEW BUSINESS

Starting your own business by taking an idea and bringing it to life is probably one of the most rewarding experiences you can have in your business life.

One definition of a start-up is:

> *"A human institution designed to deliver a new product or service under conditions of extreme uncertainty."* - **Eric Ries,** The Lean Start-Up. [1]

This definition is more typical of tech start-ups seeking enormous growth and seeking large amounts of external funding. This may well be you. However, most start-ups are far less ambitious. There will always be uncertainty, but it need not be extreme, as this definition implies.

There are many reasons you may have started, or want to start, your own business. It may be to pursue an idea where you see a need or to create a job when no full-time jobs are available (as occurs in tighter economic times). It may be from the desire to achieve the independence brought about by self-employment or because you believe you can do it much better than your current boss. There are so many examples of people seeing a need, having an idea, or pursuing a passion that requires them to start a business. Whatever the reason, it is great that you've done it or are considering it.

## It can't be just about the money

If the reason you are getting into business is to achieve wealth, I'd ask that you continue with caution. Financial rewards are an outcome, not a purpose. While there are many examples of start-ups that delivered significant financial rewards to those involved, all achieved this through significant hard work and a preparedness to take risks. For every case where large financial rewards occurred, there are many more cases that under-delivered or even failed.

Start-ups of any type can take significant effort to become financially sustainable. Starting is easy. Making it last is not so easy. Far too many start-ups don't survive because the owners run out of energy or run out of money.

One of the greatest challenges in any start-up is accessing funds to get the business off the ground and then to keep it going, no matter how modest the start-up is. These funds are not only to cover product or service development but for the owner to live off, especially if they have given up a more secure income to pursue their dream.

Even a start-up that requires only a small amount of initial funds can still take many months to see sales. You need to ask yourself this key question. *"How long can I last without income?"* That first customer or sale is like winning the lottery, but you could be many months waiting for the first dollar and then many more months to get a stable income.

I cover a range of ways your business can attract external funds in later chapters. Whatever source of funding you choose, you need to ensure you can cover your costs to startup the business, meet commitments to funders, and keep food on the table. Otherwise, it could be a very short-lived business venture.

If you have established that you can satisfy these criteria, then we can get into the process of getting your business going and keeping it going.

# Some successful Kiwi start-up stories and some stats

Much of the literature you see on start-ups seems to apply to those tech ideas that go from nothing to multi-million even billion-dollar ventures. These are very rare, which is why they are called **unicorns**.

There are a range of New Zealand start-ups that experienced significant growth.

# Kiwi startup success stories

Here are a few examples you may or may not be familiar with. Most show individuals achieving the success they sought, with limited business skills, chasing an idea with little money behind them but a heap of passion, and a huge amount of hard work.

### 1. Navman

Sir Peter Maire started Navman, the car and marine navigation business, in his garage in 1986. Between 1993 and 2004, Navman grew into four business units: Marine Electronics, Car Navigation, Fleet Tracking and GPS Applications and developed over 400 products. At its peak, it had over 300 staff in New Zealand and was operating in over 40 countries. Brunswick Corporation, a North American business, purchased the firm in 2004 for over $100 million.

### 2. VEND

VEND is a Point of Sale (POS) software system for the retail market. It is a software as a service (SaaS), meaning it is internet based and is paid for with monthly subscriptions. Vaughan Rowell started VEND in 2010. It was one of the first Point of Sale systems in New Zealand to go on the cloud and the first to be accessible on an iPad. This allowed retail shops to do all their transactions on their smart device rather than using expensive cash registers. In 2021, the Canadian-based Point of Sale company Lightspeed purchased VEND for just under $500 million. Vaughan, with his partner Zoe Timbrell, also founded the Pam Fergusson Charitable Trust, named in honour of Vaughan's mother. The Trust aims to expose kids of all backgrounds to technology, like computer coding, robotics 3D printing, science and more.

### 3. SEEQUENT

Seequent started as ARANZ Geo Ltd in 2009, an offshoot of the private medical research business, Applied Research Associates NZ Ltd (ARANZ Ltd). It developed 3D geological modelling software which allowed those in the mining, hydro, geothermal energy, environmental, and civil engineering industries to make the unseen underground world visible.

This allowed these businesses to make better decisions. The sale of software applications around the world resulted in significant growth. In 2018, the company changed its name to Seequent as it expanded into a new broader range of global industries and markets.

They call a startup selling for $1 billion or more a unicorn, because they are extremely rare, especially in New Zealand. The NASDAQ-listed engineering and software company, Bentley Systems, purchased Seequent for $NZ1.45billion in 2021 [2]

Most people who start a business did not do so with the expectation of achieving enormous growth. Many don't even want growth. In 2023, around 70,000 businesses came to life in New Zealand. Only a tiny number of these will pursue and then achieve significant growth. In fact, most won't last. In 2023, 65,000 businesses disappeared. Of the businesses that started in 2018, less than 40% were still around five years later.[3,4]

Those inspiring startup stories of an owner in his garage selling for hundreds of millions are incredibly rare. Most startups are far humbler.

The type of businesses that come to life every year will be as diverse as your imagination will allow. There are so many start-up stories, and most are humble little businesses that won't become the next unicorn, but will bring someone an immense amount of joy and pride.

The key thing to take from this is you don't have to be highly intelligent, tertiary educated, experienced or have significant wealth behind you. What you must have is a passion for what you are starting - you need to really love it - and you need to be ready for a lot of hard work and persistence to help you through the tough days.

# The "Lean Start-up" process

If your start-up involves a new product or unique service, and there isn't a lot of readily available information about how it will go, you may need to think a little more carefully about how to proceed. The product or service may need a reasonable level of cash and your time to get it ready to sell. You will then need to do a lot more to market the product than would be the case for a business with a well-known product or service.

What if you invest a heap of time and money only to find it doesn't sell? What if your great idea proves of little interest to everyone else? How do you know what will and won't sell when the idea is relatively new?

Eric Ries, a then 34-year-old Yale graduate, developed a concept to address this challenge. His book *"The Lean Start-up"* took the traditional concept of **lean manufacturing** and applied it to the process of start-ups. His desire to write the book came from the failure of one of his former companies, successes in later companies, as well as his time with start-up incubators and venture capitalists in the USA.

The traditional lean manufacturing concept was born from Toyota's improvement processes in the 1930s. While lean defines a process to identify and then remove waste from a business, it is also a culture. While it can apply to any business, even small businesses, it is more common in larger, more complex process and manufacturing-based industries.

Ries applied the lean concept to start-ups in the following ways:

- Take smaller steps in your product or service development, testing and retesting the market as your product or service develops.

- Take a **Minimum Viable Product** (MVP) to some level of market release to gain feedback from customers before seeking perfection. This then allows you to revisit the product or service, fine-tune it and do a further validation.

- Fail often, fail cheaply, and avoid continuing on a path to disaster by powering on blindly. Eric Ries put this in terms of **Pivoting** (changing direction) or **Preserving** (continuing the same path) based on the incremental feedback you receive.

# Some practical realities of starting a business

There are many other less-than-sexy tasks you must do when starting your business in New Zealand. While it's great to get wrapped up in the new product, idea, logo design, shop layout`, new machinery or whatever the cool stuff is, at least put some of your energy into some housekeeping issues about your new business.

I cover all these topics in a lot more detail throughout the book. For now, just note some of the following and add them to the tasks you must consider as you move forward with the start-up process.

## *Funding your start-up*

You need money to start your business, and you need money to live off. Where is it coming from? The most common place is your own back pocket. Others would be unlikely to offer you money if you aren't prepared to stump up with some of your own cash. The question is, how much have you got and how much do you need?

If you need the startup to make a certain amount of money very early in its life, it will start putting immense pressure on you. There will be additional pressure to pursue work and customers that are not in keeping with your values. You may discount your pricing just to get work. You may work ridiculous hours and affect your health. This could cause irreparable damage to your brand, cause significant stress, and may see the dream of your start-up ending before it even has time to succeed.

Even if you have been involved in other business ventures and borrowed money, banks may not offer you any credit for your new venture, not even a credit card.

Strangers are very unlikely to want to invest money in your idea or passion. Others are only likely to invest in your idea when the venture is well advanced, and you have proven yourself.

Here are some suggestions to manage the financial pressures and to fund your start-up:

- Keep your full-time job and use your weekends and holidays to set up the business.

- See if you can go part time in your job or swap your full-time job for a part-time job.

- Seek some contract work while setting up your start-up.

- If you have a personal partner who is working (e.g., a wife or husband), see if you can live off one wage.

- Look seriously at your spending and see what you can cut back while starting the business.

- Consider what personal savings you can sacrifice to get the small business going.

- Consider borrowing money against existing assets. If you are lucky enough to have a second property, that is a great help. You can use your personal home but be careful you aren't, literally, betting your house on your business.

Unfortunately, owning our own home, let alone owning a second property in New Zealand, is becoming more difficult than it has ever been. Fewer people own a home now than has ever been the case over the last 70 years.[5] Therefore, borrowing against a property to fund a new business is becoming something that will be out of the reach of most people. Sadly, this is a harsh reality for the younger Kiwis getting into business.

If you only have modest funds to work with, then you must start with modest expectations and build up through hard work, or, as the saying goes, **sweat capital**.

I cover all your funding options in greater detail later in the book.

# Shoof and growing within your means

In the 1970s, the Waikato based couple, Geoff and Bev Laurent, were living a regular, young farmer's existence on Geoff's family farm just outside Cambridge. Geoff was share-milking for his father, and his wife Bev was nursing. Geoff, like his father, was a very practical and handy Kiwi who was always looking for simple solutions to the many problems he faced everyday he was farming. His first product, that won a New Zealand Fieldays award, was the "Trickler", a device that added sanitizer to udder wash water, to help reduce mastitis.

In 1973, they were looking to buy a new $400 lounge suite. Geoff proposed to Bev, "*Shall we buy the lounge, or shall we start a company and sell this thing?*" Bev, the strategist in the relationship, responded, "*Well, I guess the lounge suite can wait a bit, and it might be fun*". And so began their business journey.

Geoff continued to find and solve problems and won a few product awards at Fieldays along the way. They knew nothing about marketing, manufacturing, even sales, but pushed on regardless. Interest spread and the sales started trickling in.

By 1979 they had a good range of products and opportunity presented itself when the heavily protectionist Muldoon government started giving incentives to get Kiwi businesses selling overseas. Bev and Geoff saw this as both a business opportunity and a chance to see a bit of the world - even if they sold nothing. They went to a Royal Show in England and received strong interest for their products and received orders from businesses in the UK and Europe. They were now exporters.

A product Geoff conceived in the 1960s but didn't manufacture until the 1980s was the "*shoe-for-a-hoof*" to help repair damage to a cow's hooves. It was a simple aid that saw significant interest in the UK and Europe. It was this product that inspired the name they would thereafter be called - "*Shoof International Ltd*"

What their travels also showed them was the wealth of products in Europe that could prove to be an enormous benefit to Kiwi farmers. However, New Zealand was literally "*closed-for-business*" in the Muldoon era, making importing almost impossible. A change to a Labour government in 1984 and "*Rogernomics*" saw an end to this and Shoof began importing a wide range of products.

Bev continued as the strategist and visionary and Geoff, the detailed hands-on guy. As they grew, they always stayed within their means. They never sought external investors or shareholders and only borrowed as the business grew. They remained true to their rural family values as more staff joined them.

They operated out of their family farm outside Cambridge. As they grew, the facilities had to grow - but only ever in stages. The first building was in 1985. Then came extensions to the buildings, again in stages each year from 1990 to 2002, and only occurring as growth allowed. Their systems also grew as they grew, implementing the enterprise system called SAP in 2004.

With the continued growth, a further modern building upgrade occurred in 2010 on the same property. It was in this year Shoof Chile was born, followed by Shoof Australia in 2011 and then China.

Shoof was turning over tens of millions a year, had one hundred staff and operations in four countries. A far cry from their humble beginnings in 1973.

In 2023, they sold the business to a private equity firm for an undisclosed sum.

Throughout this journey, they remained true to their purpose of supplying products to help the welfare of farm animals and the farmer. They never overextended their debt beyond their means and remained sole shareholders. They shared their private gains with all their staff in bonus schemes. Their staff wanted success for Geoff and Bev because it meant success for them, and they were part of a successful business. Their employees stayed because they wanted to stay. [6]

*"A day to invent*
*A year to manufacture*
*The rest of your life to sell"* - Geoff Laurent

# *Your business' legal structure – and a NZBN*

We go into a lot more detail in the legal chapters on the pros and cons of different business structures. You may start simply as a **sole trader**. You may set up a **limited liability company** (LLC), which is a relatively simple process. A Trust is a means to protect your personal assets from your business activities. We will discuss this later.

These are all very common. Some help from your lawyer and accountant can sort these for you. There is a lot more detail on business structures in later chapters. For now, just make note of this as a priority you need to consider as your business changes.

If you intend partnering with another person, you will need to discuss openly what you both want from the business. This relationship will be critical to the success of the new venture, so you need to be frank and honest. If you are uncomfortable to have these discussions, which is a warning sign straight away, get a third party involved to challenge you both.

If you register as a company on the New Zealand Companies Office, they will automatically issue you with a unique **New Zealand Business Number (NZBN)**. While it's not compulsory, you can register for a NZBN as a sole trader. This will help identify you as a genuine business and make your business searchable. There are government websites where you can register. [7]

## Systems and processes

I will cover the importance of having excellent systems and processes in your business in later chapters. For now, consider the systems you will need from day one and whether you can expand these systems as your business grows.

If you are starting a small business, whether sole trader, partnership or limited liability company, you will need to set up some workable systems from day one, particularly to help manage your money. The sophistication of the systems you choose will depend as much on your budget as anything.

For now, just accept you are going to need them and plan to do something about them.

## GST registration and tax

If you are starting your first business, you need to decide if you will register for GST. If you do, you will pay the IRD the GST on any sale you make and you can claim back the GST on most things you purchase. Managing the GST requires a lot of administration. You are basically collecting this tax on behalf of the IRD, as it is not your money.

If you are not likely to make more than $60,000 in the year ahead, you need not be GST registered. If it's likely to exceed this, you have no choice. You must register for GST, whether you are a sole trade or a company. This has been the threshold since 2009. It is likely to increase at some stage in the future, so check at the time of applying.

You have the choice of paying your GST two monthly or six monthly. The former spreads your cash flow throughout the year. The latter requires less administration and is more suitable for smaller businesses dealing with small amounts of GST.

In the early stages of your business' life, especially if you are new to the process of GST, I recommend you get some help.

## *Employing staff*

If you intend employing people to help you with your startup, there is a lot to consider. Have a read through the chapter on staff. For now, you need to make sure they've got an Individual Employment Agreement and job description and ensure you've registered the person with the IRD.

# Marketing your start-up

All the mechanics of setting up a new business that we have mentioned are important. However, the greatest challenge is how you intend getting new customers to buy what you are offering. If you are starting a business with a fresh idea, you need to convince other people, so they become as enthusiastic as you. I cover marketing in more detail later, but here are a few key things to consider when you have no customers and are starting out.

- Be prepared to work very hard. No matter how amazing your new product or service is, you must put the effort in to get in front of the right people and authentically sell the idea.

- Be very clear who your ideal customers are.

    o Who is most likely to want what you are selling?

    o Are they male, female, older, younger, wealthy, middle class, live rurally or in a city, renters or homeowners, other businesses or retail customers?

- Once you are clear about who your ideal customers are, this is where you focus all your effort. If you pick up other customers other than your ideal, that's a bonus, but not a priority.

- Consider how you reach your ideal customers. Is in online, social media, websites, in person, through other businesses, brokers or agents?

- Consider your marketing budget. How much can you afford? Marketing spend can be a bottomless pit of cash, which very few small businesses have. Determine how much you can afford and then seek the options that have the greatest chance of reaching your ideal customers, at the lowest cost.

- Be prepared to try things and experiment. No one marketing strategy will be the perfect strategy. While you need to be patient with the strategies you choose, don't hang on to them if they are not working and costing you money.

It is worth considering your business' trading name, logos and some printed material like business cards. It is also worth setting up an online presence. Social media pages are the lowest cost options, but you may also consider a simple website that you can expand as you grow. How much time and money you spend depends on your available time and your budget.

## Don't procrastinate - have a go

One of the biggest hurdles to starting a small business is fear. It's the unease to take that first step and the fear of failing. Yes, you need to consider the worst-case scenarios (the *"What ifs…"* we discuss later). If you can survive these scenarios, then the rest is upside, so you simply need to take that first step.

Well done. You are now a small business owner. Welcome to the club.

# CHAPTER 4

# GETTING INTO BUSINESS – BUYING AN EXISTING BUSINESS

Buying an existing business may be a far more appealing option than a start-up. An existing business will have an existing market, customers, property, plant and equipment, inventory, and possibly employees. It will also, hopefully, start earning you an income from the day you buy it.

The challenge will be to choose the right business, knowing what you are getting, raising the money to buy the business and then being able to run the business once you have purchased it. Like anything, you will get what you pay for.

There are many stories of buyers finding quite a different business after they concluded the sale compared to what the seller offered them. As a buyer, you need to be careful about getting emotionally attached to a business, being overly keen to buy it, without really understanding what you are buying.

Before you look to buy a business, read the later chapter on valuing a business and on selling a business. It is very important you understand what the seller is trying to achieve so you can go into the process with your eyes wide open.

## Choose the right business for you

Before buying a business, you must be clear on the following questions:

- Why are you buying the business? Employment? Independence? Income? Lifestyle?

- What is your long-term goal following the purchase?

- What do you enjoy doing?

- What are you good and bad at that will affect your ability to run the business?

You should be cautious about buying into a business where you have limited skills or knowledge about that business. If the business requires specialist skills that you don't possess, you will be at the mercy of employees who have those skills.

You need to choose a business you will enjoy running. It's not much point having a business that may well be delivering good returns, but is one that does not motivate you and one you don't enjoy being a part of.

---

> **Visit all the business brokers in your region and tell them what you are looking for. The best business for you may never be advertised**

---

This is not a time for your emotions to drive your decision. While you need to be passionate about it, if you view the purchase through rose-coloured glasses, you could end up with significant regret. If you feel you are not being objective enough, call on some independent eyes.

## *This is not a process to do alone*

You need to set aside some funds to find, review, and then purchase the business. No matter how simple or small the business you are buying, you will still need to call on external expertise. Typically, consider using the following experts:

- A **business advisor experienced in buying and selling.** If you are buying the business through the seller's broker, then they are likely to ensure the process is robust. The critical thing to remember is that the seller's broker is representing the seller, who compensates them, and they only receive payment upon the completion of the sale. As such, they will have the motivation to get signatures on a sale and purchase agreement.

Whether there is a broker leading the process, seek the advice of someone who has bought and/or sold businesses before, especially if you never have.

- An **accountant**. This is to ensure you've considered tax issues and to review all the financials. You also want to ensure you get an accurate and complete set of financial accounts, not a set that the seller wants you to see. A good accountant will confirm this. Some accountants will also be able to assist with a valuation of the business. Just be careful. This is a specialised area and most accountants won't have the experience.

- A **lawyer**. This is to prepare and/or review all legal issues existing with the business and any agreements related to the purchase. You may also need help in setting up your own company structure for the purchase.

- Specific **technical experts**. They can help review the business if it has aspects that are unique to that industry.

Even if you are buying a small business and it's not costing you a lot, you want to get it right. You need to think through who can best assist you.

## Contracts and legal agreements

The seller is likely to require you to sign a **confidentiality agreement (or non-disclosure agreement, NDA)** before they allow you any access to their business. This will protect the seller from you handing this information to others, especially if you choose not to proceed with the sale.

Sellers usually want to keep the sale confidential so that their staff, customers and competitors don't know it's up for sale. You will need to maintain confidentiality, but you still need to get all the information you need to make a sound decision.

If the business is operating out of a physical address, it will probably operate under a lease. If the seller owns the property, you will need to find out if they will lease the property after the sale - unless the sale includes a purchase of the premises (which is not common). The lease agreement is a key document that you should get reviewed by a lawyer.

## *How much can you afford?*

You need to understand how to value a business and determine whether the offer in front of you accurately represents its worth. I cover valuing a business in later chapters and use accepted valuation methods. However, these methods only tell part of the story. Typically, they include some assessment of what similar businesses are being bought and sold for.

If a bank is funding the purchase, they too will have a view on the valuation. This is not an exact science. In the end, the only price that matters is the price the buyer and seller agree on.

---

Valuations are not an exact science. In the end, the only price that matters is the price the buyer and seller agree on.

---

If you are new to this process, do your homework, and get help.

As with any purchase, you will get what you pay for. It's essential that you're very clear on what you can afford. It is likely you will have to seek external funds to buy the business. The greater the amount of external funding you require, the greater will be the pressure on you to buy a business that will deliver the cash to pay off these loans. If you are required to access these external funds by securing them against personal assets, this will add pressure. For example, if it all fails, could you lose your house?

> *"If you can't afford it, you can't afford it."* - **My grandmother.**

If the business is service-based or includes limited stock, plant, equipment or other assets, it is likely to have a high level of **goodwill**, a

---

concept we explore in far greater detail later. While this is very common, it poses additional risks if the business fails, as there is nothing tangible to sell.

## *Caveat emptor - buyer beware*

You need to heed this long-standing legal term before buying.

The technical term for the process of investigating the business is **due diligence**. This is where you look carefully at all aspects of the business to ensure you know what you're buying. There is a more detailed list of items you should consider during due diligence later. You may wish to add to this list depending on your priorities and the specifics of the business.

You may not get access to the business' confidential information until you have agreed to a price and, if through a broker, signed the conditional sale and purchase agreement. Therefore, you will need to do as much research as possible before you can even get to due diligence. Search as much as you can for information that is publicly available.

This might include:

- How are other similar businesses being priced for sale? Check out TradeMe and the business broker's websites for similar businesses. (E.g., ABC Business Brokers, Link Business, NZ BizBuySell, Tabak Business Sales).

- Are you able to establish the brand exposure and reputation of the business?

- What are the perceptions of their brand?

- Are there any discussions or reports on the business on mainstream or social media?

- Check out the Companies Office website and search for the company. You can pay a small fee to access the list of securities listed on the **PPSR** (which we discuss later).

- If it's a business you can walk into and buy something, do this. What was the experience like?

- If they have a website, look at it.

Remember, if you signed a confidentiality agreement, you cannot discuss the business with anyone outside those listed in the document (typically your lawyer and accountant).

☞
> If you breach a confidentiality agreement the seller could take legal action against you.

The more detail you can find on the business, the more confident you can be in the price you negotiate.

# Buying a franchise

## What is a franchise?

Franchising is the practice where an established business (the franchisor) sells another person (the franchisee) the right to trade using their trademarks, systems, processes and experience. This is a widely successful business model operated by overseas franchises like McDonald's, and Subway, and Kiwi Franchises like Jims Mowing Service, Speedy Signs, Cookie Time, and many more.

Franchisees must operate the business under the franchisor's requirements (typically covered in a **franchise agreement**). The franchisee must pay fees to the franchisor. The agreement will define what the franchisor will provide to the franchisee in the way of systems, processes, training, and support.

If you're buying a franchise, the core principles do not differ from buying any business. You need to consider the same issues. There are, however, some advantages to choosing a franchise, especially if it's your first business.

These include:

- Entry into a business with an existing and well-recognised brand.

- Processes and systems that have been proven.

- Training and support.

- A more detailed record of past performance across several businesses within the franchise.

- An immediate network of other franchisees to refer to for help.

- The legal right to use an existing brand and systems.

- Purchasing power where the franchisor purchases on behalf of all franchisees.

- Existing marketing campaigns.

With these advantages will come restrictions that wouldn't apply in your own non-franchised business.

You won't have total control. There will be restrictions the franchisor lays down: including what products or services you can sell, how you sell, ingredients you use, equipment you buy, and so on. You may have to contribute to marketing campaigns. If you have innovative ideas to market or grow your franchise, the terms of the franchise agreement may restrict what you can do.

Before you commit to the purchase, you need to check if the franchisor will deliver what they say they will. Some franchisors may over-promise and then, after you buy, under-deliver. One of the best ways to establish this is to contact other franchisees in the same business.

Avoid the temptation to ignore the franchisor's requirements and do your own thing. If they have proven systems in place, you should follow them. If they don't meet your needs, discuss them with the franchisor before unilaterally changing them. You may be in breach of the franchise agreement.

As you are likely to be in this relationship for many years, you need to know as much as you can about the franchise owners. You want to know about their experience in franchising and in business.

You should not get a false sense of security that franchising is easy. Just because other businesses in the same franchise have been successful does not mean you will be successful. You must work just as hard and follow the same core business principles as any other business model.

## *Franchise agreement - key clauses*

This is a critical document that you need to read and understand. There is benefit in referring it to your lawyer.

These agreements will vary from franchise-to-franchise, but will include factors such as:

- The initial investment required.

- All franchise fees (upfront and ongoing).

- Penalties for breaching the agreement (e.g., late payment charges, trademark breaches).

- Duration of the agreement.

- Any geographical limitations on where you can trade.

- Obligations on and performance expectations for you.

- Obligations on and performance expectations of the franchisor.

- Stock to be included.

- The products and services you can and can't sell.

- Premises, leases and other equipment to be included.

- Your legal rights over intellectual property use (logos, trademarks, copyrights, patents).

- The process for the sale of the franchise. This might be more difficult than selling a business that was not part of a franchise.

- The process either party must follow to bring the franchise relationship to an end (**termination clauses**).

- Restraints of trade on what you can and can't do when you are operating the franchise and after you leave (periods where you can't open a directly competing business or employ people from the franchise).

- Dispute resolution procedures.

It is unlikely you will have a lot of scope to alter the agreement, especially with mature or long-standing franchises. This emphasises the need to fully understand the document, so you know exactly what you are getting yourself into.

## *Franchise fees*

All franchises will have to pay fees to the franchisor. The amount and form these fees take will vary from franchise-to-franchise. Ensure you're fully aware of all the fees and assess whether you believe they are good value for money. The key is less about the amount of fees, but more about what value they bring to your business. It is not uncommon for a franchisor to promise a high level of support at the time of purchase, but you find things are very different once you are in the business.

Fees typically involve an initial investment and then ongoing payments. The following are typical of what you will find in widely known international franchises. Smaller franchises are likely to bundle these into simpler fee structures.

Initial investment costs could include:

- Initial franchise fee.

- Property.

- Furniture, fixtures and equipment.

- Exterior signage.

- Opening inventory.

- Insurance.

- Training expenses.

- Legal and accounting.

- Opening advertising.

Ongoing fees could include:

- Royalty either as a percentage of sales (typically 3–10% of sales) and/or a fixed fee.

- Advertising fees.

- Equipment lease fees.

- Property lease fees.

- Insurance costs.

- Fee for use of systems.

## Downside of a franchise

If you already have a lot of experience running small businesses or want a lot of freedom to do what you want in your business, a franchise may not be for you. A franchise has the advantage of defined processes and systems, rules and ways to run the business and, thus, its proven performance. However, this will limit your freedom to do what you want, the products or services you offer, the pursuit of growth opportunities, who you market to and how you market the business.

If you want to end the franchise relationship and go it alone, you may incur significant costs to exit the franchise agreement, or the agreement may impose restrictions on what you can do.

If you are entering business with a desire to do different things, to experiment, to take risks, to have options to move in different directions, then a franchise is not a good choice.

## *What if you are the first franchisee?*

Every franchise had to start with its first franchisee. If you are buying into a franchise and you are the first, or among the first, it requires extra caution. To some extent, you are the guinea pig the franchisor will use to learn the trade.

If you are relatively inexperienced and need to enter a franchise relationship that is proven, well set up, and eases your shift into small business without significant risk, this may not be a good option for you.

If, however, you like what the franchisor is trying to achieve and see real potential, it might be an excellent opportunity. If you are the first or a very early entrant to the franchise, you are in a powerful position to negotiate a far more attractive and flexible franchise agreement. This could include:

- Easier exit clauses and the choice to go-it-alone.

- A lower purchase price.

- Greater freedom on product and service choices.

- More direct involvement with the franchisor.

# Due diligence

Due diligence is the process where you do as thorough an investigation into the business you are buying as you can. If a broker is leading the process, it is likely they will not let you see anything without a signed confidentiality agreement. This may still only give you access to a very basic level of information.

You may not get access to do a thorough review of the business until you have agreed on a price for the business. A seller, through the broker, needs to be certain you agree on the price, otherwise it is a waste of everyone's time continuing. Sadly, you may have to counter the seller's sale price after only seeing a minimum amount of detail about the business.

If you have agreed on the price, the seller will typically request you to sign a conditional sale and purchase agreement. You will now have access to everything. Make sure you run the sale and purchase agreement by a lawyer before signing. It should give you complete freedom to withdraw from the process for any reason you wish. When you sign this, it will include a due diligence period. Be sure this is enough time for you to carry out the due diligence, secure any funding, and get your lawyer and accountant to carry out any work they need. Typically, this is four weeks, but you could ask for more.

If the sale is being done without a broker, the process may not be the same or as formal. However, this does not lessen the importance of doing a thorough due diligence.

If you are looking to buy a franchise, the franchisor will probably have a set price and process they follow. You may have a limited ability to negotiate, but that should not deter you from doing due diligence and to walk away if you aren't happy.

## Due diligence checklist

Here is a list of things you should consider as part of the due diligence:

- Request a full set of professionally produced annual tax accounts, at least the last three years. Don't accept edited or abridged accounts. If the sale is mid-year, get the latest available set of accounts from the seller's accounting system for the current year-to-date.

- Review all the official GST returns for the last couple of years. They accurately define what the business has been earning.

- Assess what the owners are paying themselves, if it is consistent with market rates, and if it matches the figures used in the valuation.

- Determine what the owners' roles are. When they are gone, who will fill their roles?

- Assess if there are any costs that do not reflect market rates that will affect you after the sale. For example, the owners may not be paying rent on a family-owned property, but you will have to.

- Assess how reliant the business is on the owner. If they leave, will the business die?

- Review the systems being used to run the business.

- Assess the condition of any assets that the business relies on.

- Read all legal documents, contracts and agreements. Seek good legal advice on these. One of the most common and critical legal documents will be the lease.

- Establish if there are any outstanding legal matters relating to the business, for example, a WorkSafe investigation.

- Review any consents the business must adhere to or consents you will need when you take over the business.

- Do as much market research as you can to establish if past revenue will reflect potential future revenue.

- Ask for and review **accounts receivable** and **accounts payable**. Any money owed to the existing owners or owed by them to others is entirely their responsibility. However, if the current owners have a history of not paying their bills, that reputation will pass to you to manage. Creditors may also come seeking money the business owes them. While this is not your issue, it is not a good start to supplier relations.

- Ask for a profit and loss statement by month for a full year. This will allow you to assess seasonality, the good and the awful months. If you are taking over the business when it is coming into the awful months of the year, you will need to consider what additional cash you might need.

- Review the business' marketing activities. Ask them for any monthly analytics reports they may get. You could get an independent marketing person to assess the effectiveness of the business' website and online marketing.

- Review the key customers and suppliers and the percentage each is of the business' sales and purchases, respectively. If a few customers or suppliers make up all the sales, this could present a significant risk, as they may be loyal to the current owners.

- Get the details of all staff members in the business, what they are being paid and the rosters they are working. If you take over and are reliant on them, they are in a strong bargaining position to ask for improved conditions. Remember, the seller **can't breach a staff member's privacy**, so you are unlikely to get all their details.

- Confirm if any employees are **vulnerable employees.** The **Employment Relations Act** outlines the definition of these employees. They are typically the positions most often restructured by business owners. They have limited bargaining power, and businesses can easily undermine their conditions. Cleaners are the best example. If there are employees or contractors providing a service like this to the business, seek advice as they attract greater protections than other employees.

- Confirm if all employees have current visas that allow ongoing work in New Zealand. If they don't, it could create issues for you when you take over.

- Confirm how the seller wishes to handle their employees' entitlements. They could pay them out completely and you start afresh. This is the simplest option, but if employees lose any entitlements as part of the transition, they may have little incentive to stay on.

# How to negotiate the final deal

Many people view the skill of negotiation as a gift that some people have, and some do not. This is not the case. Negotiation is a process. If you enter a negotiation prepared and follow some key principles, you can position yourself well to negotiate a favourable outcome.

Here are a few of these principles as they apply to buying a business.

## Be prepared

Do all your homework on the business before negotiating a price. Check out the chapter on valuing a business. Get advice from your accountant, assuming they have experience valuing businesses. Do as much research on the market the business operates in, anything you can find on the business plus understanding any information provided by the seller.

The seller is likely to have included a price higher than what they are prepared to take, so your offer should be below this. Be careful putting too low and offer in. The seller could just walk away. If they stay in the process, they are likely to be seriously annoyed and will counter with another price and will be very unmotivated to assist in the handover.

## Understand the seller

Do as much as you can to understand the motives and needs of the seller. This is just as important as knowing your own needs and motives. Why do they want to sell? Do you sense they are under time pressures to sell? Is price the critical factor or is it something else? Ask as many questions as you can to learn as much as you can.

## Know your "BATNA"

There is a term used in negotiation called **BATNA**, which means the **Best Alternative to a Negotiated Agreement.** It defines the course of action you will take if the negotiations fail and the two parties cannot agree. As a buyer, you may simply walk away and move on to another option.

However, if you are not clear where this point is, you may walk away prematurely and miss out on a great deal, or you could get emotionally attached and continue when you should have walked away. You should also consider what the seller's BATNA is likely to be.

## *Be careful about time pressures*

Parties in a negotiation are most likely to make concessions close to the end of the process. The person under the greatest time pressure is likely to make the most concessions. Always be cautious about drifting outside your parameters just because the other party has set a specific date.

# Immediate priorities after the sale goes unconditional

Typically, there will be a period after the deal goes unconditional, that prevents either party from getting out of the deal, but the business is still owned by the seller and is their responsibility. The business becomes yours on the date of settlement. The period between the sale going unconditional and you taking it over **must at least cover the notice period of staff**. If you need more time than this, make sure you include this in the sale and purchase agreement.

There is a lot to do in this period, so you need to be prepared.

Use this period to get as many tasks as possible in place, so you can trade from the first day you takeover.

- Meet with all staff as quickly as possible as they will be very restless and uncertain. If you intend employing them, get contracts in front of them as soon as possible.

- Don't be surprised if the staff ask for a pay increase, especially if the former owners hadn't offered a pay rise recently.

- Send credit applications to all your key suppliers and set up accounts so you can purchase from them as early as possible.

- Make sure the seller passes over ALL the intellectual property required in the sale and purchase immediately after the deal goes unconditional. The sooner you get this, the more time it will give you to be ready to trade from day one.

- If the business uses cloud-based systems, you are unlikely to have them offered to you. You will need your own subscriptions and you will need to have these ready to trade. It is critical the seller hands over all the data from their systems so that you can load them into yours (e.g., **CSV files**). This would include customer, supplier, and product details, including all pricing.

- Get all your bank accounts in place and consider if you need an overdraft facility to cover all the initial cash flow demands.

- If the business offers retail sales via an EFTPOS facility, you will need a merchant account and an EFTPOS account set up for the business. Confirm if this comes with the sale or is something you have to arrange. The seller may ask you to take over their contract, which may be a reasonable interim option.

- You will need to change over ownership of all vehicles to your name.

- Many sale and purchase agreements require the seller to accompany the buyer on visits to key customers and suppliers. Make time for this and ensure it happens.

- You and the seller may decide to send out a joint notice that the business is changing hands. If this doesn't happen jointly, you will need to communicate as soon as possible to customers and suppliers. Some may have work in progress (WIP) that you need to continue with.

- There may be contracts, agreements, the lease, and car registrations that you take over that the seller has paid in full that you benefit from. (E.g., you take over the business mid-month when the seller has paid the lease for the entire month). This will require a calculation to compensate the seller.

- The seller needs to ensure they have released all the securities and guarantees registered over the company's assets before takeover. Make sure this is done.

- You will need to change over utilities (e.g., electricity) from the seller's name to yours so you have power, water, and gas available.

- Make sure the seller hands over all logins, passwords, door codes, and keys at handover.

- Set aside time to do a full stocktake as close to handover as possible. If there is a lot of stock, this could be a significant task, so ensure you allow enough time. Ask the seller for a detailed list of all stock so this task can be done.

- The lease and other contracts need to be transferred to you. Your lawyers will need to sort this before settlement.

- Your lawyer and the seller's lawyer should deal with transferring funds from your bank to the seller's bank, but make sure this is all in hand.

# ...and now it's your business

Congratulations. The money has passed to the seller, all the keys are in your hand, and you are now the proud owner of a business. The sale process may have left you exhausted, but hopefully, you are also feeling really excited about what lies ahead.

Get a good night's sleep, brush yourself off as now the small business journey really begins

# CHAPTER 5

# WHAT DOES STRATEGY MEAN FOR YOUR SMALL BUSINESS?

Whether you have just started your business, bought into one, or have been at it for some time, are you completely clear what you want from your small business? Do your customers know what you are all about? Do you and everyone around you understand what you stand for? What are your medium to long-term goals, for say, the next 3 to 5 years?

You will address all or most of these questions if you develop a strategy for your business.

There are some small business owners who formulate the strategy for their business with little or no formal process. It comes naturally to them. Others need a process to guide them. Whether your strategy comes to you naturally or you need to follow a more methodical step-by-step process to develop it, you need to make sure your team are very clear on what it is. If not, you will be all on your own delivering it.

Many small businesses often relate the word "*strategy*" to the military or big business. However, a strategy is just as vital for you as it is for any sized business.

The Oxford English Dictionary defines "*strategy*" as:

> ***A plan of action designed to achieve a long-term or overall aim.***

The concept of strategy was born out of the military. The word comes from its French (stratégie) and Greek (stratēgia) origins, meaning "*lead*" or "*generalship*".

The word "*strategy*" became commonly used during the Napoleonic Wars. Carl von Clausewitz, who studied Napoleon and his strategies of war, was one of the first to use the term. The concept has been around for much longer if one considers **Sun Tzu**'s *"The Art of War"* that he wrote around 400 BC. It only became common in the language of business in the 1950s and 1960s.

Columbia University's Willie Pietersen's definition of strategy, as it relates to business, is one of the simplest and most compelling I have come across.

> *"What gave birth to strategy was the need to respond to two inescapable realities: the fact that we have limited resources, and the inevitability of competition."* - **Willie Pietersen** Strategic Learning.[1]

The definition is as relevant to small businesses as it is to big business. No matter how big a business is, it will never have unlimited resources. Time, money, or people. It must make choices: first, **what it will do** to be successful; and even more importantly, **what it won't do**.

Every business exists to meet the needs of someone. Even not-for-profits, charities, monopolies and government departments serve the needs of someone. If they don't meet those needs, those they serve will go elsewhere - and there will always be an alternative.

Small businesses rarely take a long-term view; they have no strategy, no business plan, no exit or succession plan.

Your strategy needs to address some simple but critical questions:

- *"Why does your business exist?"* (What is your **core purpose**?)

- *"What does your business stand for?"* (What are your **core values**?)

- *"Where do you want your business to be in three to five years?"* (What are your **goals**?)

# What are the consequences of ignoring strategy?

Far too many small businesses fail while similar, but larger businesses live on. There are many reasons for this. One is that small businesses don't set aside enough time or put enough priority on their future. They lose sight of why they got into business or of the external pressures that may shut them down.

While larger businesses have the resources to monitor the external world, develop and then execute strategy, it is no less critical for a small business. Perhaps it is even more critical to small businesses, as they are less able to survive the external shocks that a large business can tolerate.

> *"Out there in some garage is an entrepreneur who's forging a bullet with your company's name on it."* - **Gary Hamel**, business writer.

There may well be someone forging a bullet with your company's name on it, or you might be the person forging the bullet. Or maybe both.

# Keep it simple - at least do the basics

I will go through a lot of details on developing and executing strategy. Every small business owner will approach developing plans for the future of their business differently. Sadly, many will do little or nothing. While you are reading through all these details, don't feel you have to use all or any of these processes. Many small business owners are very good at formulating very effective strategies for their business without doing anything formal.

All I would strongly recommend is that you are clear about what you want from your business now and in the future. If you want your staff to support you on this journey, you need to communicate this with them.

# Why does your business exist? – Your core purpose

The reasons someone chooses to own a small business will vary. Whatever the circumstances for going into your small business, there will be a core reason that drove you to be in this position. Sometimes, we enter the small business world with well-meant but misguided intentions. Perhaps if you knew what you know now, you may never have done it.

A few questions to ponder:

- What does your business offer you besides making a living?

- What gap in the market (no matter how small) would arise if your business no longer existed?

- Why is your small business' existence important to the people you currently serve or want to serve?

- Why does it exist?

- Why did you start it?

- What purpose does it fulfil?

- What meaning does it bring you?

In answering these questions, you are defining what many organisations describe as their **core purpose**.

## *The Golden Circle*

Simon Sinek, from his book *"Start with Why"* [2] explained the concept of a business' core purpose using his Golden Circle. Sinek found that most businesses describe their businesses from the outside of the circle inward.

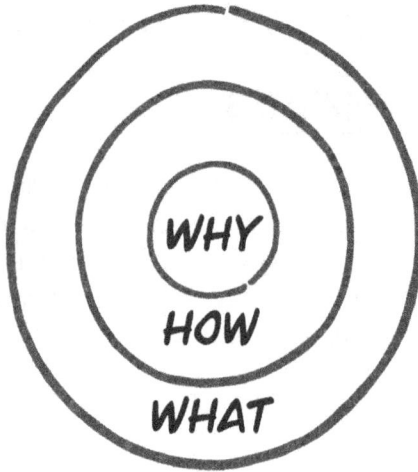

Let's use the example of a builder to highlight how the Golden Circle approach applies to describing a business' core purpose and how customers will relate to this.

The first is where the small business approaches this from the outside of Sinek's Golden Circle inwards. It shows a business that is clear about what they do, but not why they do it.

1. *What* : We build new homes.

2. *How* : We do the design and we use contract builders to manage costs.

3. *Why* : To complete your build on time and to budget.

If the same builder was very clear on their core purpose, which was to serve their customers, and were driven by this, they are more likely to approach this from the inside of the circle outward.

1. *Why* : Our business exists to see families in a new home that they love and never want to leave.

2. *How* : We work with you at every stage of the process to make it stress free.

3. *What* : We build new homes.

Your ability to prosper as a business is not just determined by what you sell. It is far more about what you believe, how your customers look upon you, and what value you bring to them. If you cannot establish your core purpose, it's likely customers won't understand it either.

Your small business' core purpose is the reason it exists. Do you know the reason your business exists? Why did you start it? Is that reason as strong now as it was then?

*"Purpose is what gives life meaning."* - **C.H. Parkhurst**, American clergyman and social reformer.

You may say it exists to make you a living. However, there are many easier ways you could make a living than owning a small business. Besides, why would your customers care about the money you want to make? If making a living or creating a job is your business' core purpose, you will soon run out of energy and your customers will see your business for what it is - a job for you.

If you are not clear why the business exists, what meaning you hope to gain from it, then it is unlikely you will last for long.

If you really look at your business and your motives, I doubt that money alone is your core purpose. Money is a necessary outcome of a successful small business. It is not the sole purpose it exists.

It is the core purpose that also inspires and continues to motivate you, your business partners, your associates and your employees.

# What do you and your business stand for? - Your core values

In business, you will rarely have a set of prescribed ways to behave or react in different situations. You have to make decisions with limited information. To do this, you need something to guide you on this journey, so you can make the best decisions, especially when those decisions are really challenging.

> *"The greatest help in meeting any problem with whatever courage is demanded is to know where you yourself stand. That is to have in words what you believe and are acting from."* - **William Faulkner,** American writer and Nobel laureate.

You need to understand what your business stands for. When your customers, your staff and others hear about you, what will spring into their mind? What is the moral compass that will guide you and your business?

Your core values describe what you and your business stand for.

The Oxford English Dictionary defines *"values"* as:

**Principles or standards of behaviour one's judgment of what is important in life.**

Values are the standards or principles that have a major influence on your thinking and behaviours. Often, the times we feel at our best are the times when we are living in accordance with our values. Values do not just relate to you in your personal life. The values of your small business will strongly reflect your own values.

The window into your values is through your behaviours, as these will be what your customers, employees and suppliers see. The values you display may influence decisions to buy from you, sell to you, or work for you. If you display behaviours that are inconsistent with your stated values, people will seriously question your authenticity.

It is very important that you take time to understand and accept your values. This is not just some abstract, feel-good concept. If you don't know what your business stands for, what will set you apart from anyone else? Why should customers become loyal to you if the basis of your business is superficial?

Values are not goals. Goals can change throughout the life of your business. Goals are something you can reach, tick off as you complete them, then set new ones. These goals may or may not be consistent with your values. For example, *"to be loved"* is a goal, yet *"to be a loving person"* is a value.

> Goals are time bound. Values are ongoing.

Values are not feelings either, although we tend to *"feel"* better when we are acting in accordance with our values.

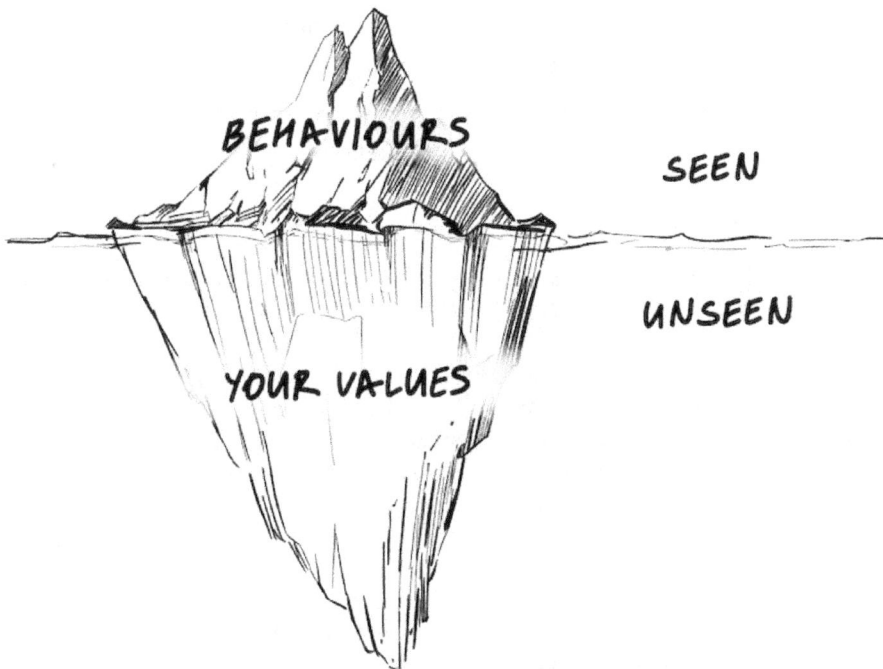

We could have a very wide range of values that we fall back on in different situations. Our values can change as we grow. Our values as a pre-school child will differ from those we would have as a parent.

What you need to do is narrow in on your three to five core values. These are the three to five values that stand out from all others. They are what you will never waver from, no matter what the circumstance. You may not know what they are, but they exist within you even if you have not established them yet. Understanding them will help you achieve the success you seek in your small business.

> *"Values aren't buses . . . They're not supposed to get you anywhere. They're supposed to define who you are."* - **Jennifer Crusie**, author.

## What are your values? An exercise.

Let's walk through an exercise to help you narrow in on what your core values are if you are unclear. Use this simple exercise to assist.

Scribble down your thoughts when you do this exercise. Writing them down will help clarify them, allow you to more easily sort through them, and provide a list you can refer to later.

---

### EXERCISE

#### Step 1

Consider a time in your working life when you felt at your worst because of circumstances within the work environment.

- What were you feeling?
- What was happening at the time?
- How were you being treated?
- How were people around you being treated?
- What words best describe this situation?

#### Step 2.

Consider a time in your working life when you felt at your best because of the circumstances within the work environment.

- Ask yourself the same questions.

#### Step 3

- Choose the words that best describe how you felt. What was missing in the first situation in Step 1 and what was present in the second situation? These will be words like "*courage*", "*honesty*", "*joy*", "*warmth*", "*creativity*", "*care*", "*accountability*", "*commitment*", "*decisiveness*", "*initiative*", "*strength*", "*knowledge*", "*service*", "*teamwork*", "*excellence*" and so on.

#### Step 4

- Group the words that mean the same thing together and choose just one word from each group.

#### Step 5

- Hopefully you are left with three to five words. These are very likely to be your core values.

---

# Convert values to behaviours

Unfortunately, if you settle on a list of words that you can relate to and you stop the process at that, it will mean little to anyone else. You have probably walked into many large organisations with values written up on a wall with words like "*integrity*" or "*innovation*" which are vague and could mean anything.

If you keep in mind the iceberg analogy, consider what behaviours you will see that reflect your values.

Here are a few examples from a range of businesses that I've come across over time:

- "*We don't do dirty*" - an air-conditioning installation business. The value of **cleanliness**.

- "*We will have fun*" - an airline, for its on-board attendants. The value of **joy**.

- "*Promise them everything, give them more*" - a painter-decorator. The value of **customer service**.

- "*Be accurate*" - a rural legal business. The value of **excellence**.

- "*Tell clients what's happening*" - the same legal business. The value of **transparency**.

- "*Yes, we can*" - a truck repair and maintenance business. The value of **commitment**.

- "*No dickheads*" - a chemical technology business. The value of **teamwork**.

These businesses chose the behaviours that reflect their values. Those in the business could relate to the words and knew what they meant. They were real and genuine.

## *Are they mission, vision, or values statements - or just pointless waffle?*

Many large corporates spend a lot of time creating elaborate statements to define their core purpose and values. Sadly, they often spend more time debating whether it should be called a vision statement, a values statement, a mission statement or some other title, then keeping it simple and focusing on what they really believe in. They then spend an inordinate amount of time playing with the words before they settle on something that most staff don't understand or don't agree with, and that only makes sense to those who wrote it.

Avoid those waffly, vague (and therefore meaningless) vision and/or mission statements. If you don't genuinely believe in the words on the paper, don't write them down and don't advertise them. It will only demotivate you and confuse everyone around you.

> If you truly believe in your purpose and hold true to your values, you should never have to write them down. Your actions will tell the story.

Share your stories, your thoughts and feelings on the business with your team. Discuss what you believe in and do it over and over, especially if you are growing and new staff are coming into your business. What matters most is your actions. If these contradict with what you are saying, then your words are hollow and pointless.

If you are very clear on what your core purpose and values are and you want to write them down, then please go for it and let everyone know. If you are clear, you won't have to spend much time on the process. They will flow off the end of your pen in minutes.

# Where do you want your business to be? - Your goals

A key part of the development of your strategy is defining what the long-term goals are for your business. You need to ask yourself:

- I know why I started my business, but where do I want it to go now?

- What is success for me?

- Knowing what I know now, what would my business be doing in three to five years' time?

- What is my exit plan when I decide to move on?

If you can establish your longer-term goals, you can then work back to a one-year and then even closer to, say, the next two to three months to define shorter-term targets and goals. Without a longer-term goal, you will simply drift along as the years fly past.

In a rapidly moving world, your goals will need to be reviewed and you may need to change your strategy as the years pass. Strategy and goal setting should never be static processes.

A word of caution. You want realistic achievable goals, not pipe dreams or wishes.

The popular literature will say you should shoot for-the-moon because you can achieve anything in business. By all means, stretch yourself. Make your goals audacious if necessary. However, be cautious of setting yourself up for failure.

If you can see a line-of-sight from your three-month and one-year goals to your long-term goals, then you are on your way. When opportunities present themselves on the journey and speed up achieving (or surpassing) your goals, that's fantastic. If your goals are measurable and specific rather than vague, then you'll be confident of reaching them.

## Generic business goals

While all businesses are unique, the strategies that many small businesses pursue are likely to be covered by one of several generic goals. These generic goals are a good starting point to help you define your specific goals. You may decide your goals are a combination of these generic goals.

The following are the common goals you will come across for small businesses, all of which I cover throughout the book:

- Starting a new business.

- Buying another existing business.

- Improving the existing business.

- Maintaining the business but making it more profitable.

- Growing the business.

- Selling the business - in part or in full.

- Being less involved in the business - by choice or through circumstance.

- Closing the business - by choice or under duress.

Every person entering a business should have at least some idea about how they will exit the business. You should have the end in mind at the beginning of the business' life. Yes, your views will change, or other opportunities or challenges could arise. As mentioned, strategy and goal setting are not static processes. Perhaps Mike Tyson explained how circumstances often shift your strategy and goals:

> *"Everybody has a plan until they get punched in the mouth."* - **Mike Tyson** Ex Professional boxer.

So yes, your plans or goals may cop a *"punch in the mouth"* along the way, but you must start with some sense of where you want your business to head and end. Then you can consider ways to manage the blows or opportunities.

On occasions, you'll need to make reasonably speedy decisions to take advantage of an opportunity. You also need to "*look before you leap*". If faced with a challenge or opportunity that is at odds with your goals, it is valuable to stop, pause and think before acting (especially where the decisions involve a serious level of commitment or risk). Also consider if the opportunity is consistent with your core purpose and values. If it's not, you need to tread carefully.

I've seen an unfortunate number of small businesses perceive something to be an opportunity they can't ignore, and grab it, only to find it has completely sent them on a course removed from their core purpose, values and goals.

---

## The business of doing a community good.
### Awakening the potential of rangatahi Maaori

Those in Aotearoa, New Zealand who struggle most to make it into the workforce are our young. This is most pronounced for those between 15 and 24 years of age. Within this group are those who are not employed, not in education nor are they in training. They have effectively fallen out of the system. This group of our young are, statistically, called NEET.

In Aotearoa, New Zealand, about 12.8% of our young fall into this category. [3]. This varies by regions across New Zealand and also between ethnicities. For Māori rangatahi (youth), the NEET is over 19%, which is double that of pākehā youth (8.6%).[4]

The reality for rangatahi Maaori is that difficult life and family circumstances, poor choices, or addiction to drugs and alcohol can put them out of step and in the wrong direction, where poor lifestyle choices are made. [5]

Addressing the challenges of disadvantaged Maaori youth is even more important considering they will be the future employees of Aotearoa, New Zealand. The Maaori population is growing and the average age of Maaori is 10 years younger than non-Maaori, so they are the future employees and small business owners of this country.[6]

Lizana Tuake grew up in Papakura South Auckland and moved to Huntly (Raahui Pookeka) with her whanau 15 years ago.

---

She experienced firsthand, the impact on the community when rangatahi fall out of the system that was never designed to meet their needs.

She was determined to break this cycle in her life and for others.

She was successful in earning a position in a large power company, where she would stay for over 15 years. As a young Maaori woman in a white, male dominated industry, she faced challenges and had to deliver above others to make her mark – and deliver she did.

Her roles in this large corporate taught her many skills and also allowed her to work closely with her community. The desire to do even more for this community was always there.

As opportunities to advance in this large business continued to pass her by, she decided to take her personal growth into her own hands. She paid her own way through an MBA, while being a mum.

While the comfort and security of such a business was hard to leave, she knew she wanted to pursue more, so left the company to work in an organisation helping with youth education. In 2018, she took a further step and started her own business focused on supporting kids from 15 to 18 to be more job ready. This was when OHO Mauri was born.

The skills she attained from her corporate life and her studies served her well in the small business world.

She set up OHO Mauri Solutions Charitable Trust. This would be the entity carrying out the programme, applying for all the funds from commercial and philanthropic businesses and government departments and also employs the 11 staff. Lizana wanted to protect her IP, to retain assets and build a business she could leverage, as well as offering a charitable service to those who need it the most. She achieved this by also setting up  OHO Mauri Solutions Ltd.

The Programme is grounded in the principles of cultural responsiveness and holistic wellbeing.  It weaves in work readiness, soft and life skills and work fitness and conditioning. Rangatahi then transition into meaningful pathways in either education, training and employment, backed with three years of pastoral care and support. The Programme supports all aspects of their whare tapa whā and is underpinned by data insights and tracking to ensure equitable and measurable outcomes for all.

Her business skills informed her that to attract sustainable support and the level of funding she needed to carry out her work, she needed to prove the Programme worked. Tracking performance of the Programme became as fundamental to the business as delivering the Programme. This has set her apart, as many charitable services struggle to provide funders hard-data to prove what they are doing is worth the investment. The success of the program can be proven through statistically sound data.

Lizana's and her team's success is now being sought after by other iwi organisations and communities across Aotearoa, New Zealand. Managing this success has become a challenge that many growing small businesses face. How to balance the passion for rangatahi she is helping while caring for what is most critical to her – her own whaanau?

> *"I had a hard pathway when I was in school. I didn't really know how to cope well in class. I got kicked out in year 10 for fighting and getting into a lot of bad stuff. I got put into a course but didn't really cope well and then got put into this course and found my way, making it easier in life now."* **Emily Katipa**. 16 year old OHO Mauri Graduate [7.]

# The power of SWOT

I do believe in using existing proven and straightforward business processes instead of creating them from scratch. One such process, to help prioritise your strategic direction, is **SWOT (Strengths, Weaknesses, Opportunities and Threats).**

Even if you have never used SWOT, it is probably a term you have heard before. Because of its overuse in the corporate world, SWOT has copped a bad reputation. Despite its image, it is still one of the most powerful tools to help execute strategy and a great tool for the small business owner.

There is some debate over who first came up with the concept. However, **Albert Humphrey** is most often credited with the idea. He led a research project at **Stanford University** in the 1960s and 1970s using data from many companies. The goal was to identify why corporate planning failed. The resulting research identified several key areas of failure, and the tool used to explore each of the critical areas was an initial form of what is now called a SWOT analysis.

## Face your "brutal realities"

Your business could face some brutal realities, both from within the business and externally to the business. However, this should not be at the expense of remaining positive about the future and maintaining the conviction to persist and achieve your goals.

I don't believe anyone has put forward a more powerful statement covering the balance between maintaining a positive attitude in the face of brutal realities than Admiral James Stockdale. He survived seven years in a Vietnamese prisoner of war camp.

> *"You must never confuse faith that you will prevail in the end - which you can never afford to lose - with the discipline to confront the most brutal facts of your current reality, whatever they might be." -* **Admiral James Stockdale** - The Stockdale Paradox.

While you won't face the same brutal facts as Stockdale did, you will need to consider the reality of your business' circumstances, both good and bad. You need to maintain a positive view of the future and then get on with it.

When completing your SWOT, be honest about your circumstances, including the brutal facts.

## Your internal focus

You first need to look within your business. In SWOT, the internal analysis considers your business' strengths and weaknesses.

- What **strengths** do you and your business possess that will help you deliver on your goals?

- What **weaknesses** are most likely to impede your progress?

This is the time to be brutally honest with yourself, which means not only accepting your weaknesses, but also not underselling your strengths. It may help to get a colleague or an advisor that knows you well to challenge you on some of these. You don't need a friend who is going to be nice to you.

## Your external analysis

There will be much going on in the outside world that will provide a vast array of opportunities for your small business. However, there will also be many things that could trip you up if you don't see them coming. We summarise these as the **opportunities** that exist now or in the future in the world outside the business and the **threats** external to the business that could have a serious impact on you.

There will be many of both - far more than you can determine and act on. Let's look at another proven and simple method to filter this information and prioritise the actions stemming from your review of the external world

## Porter's Five Forces - the external analysis

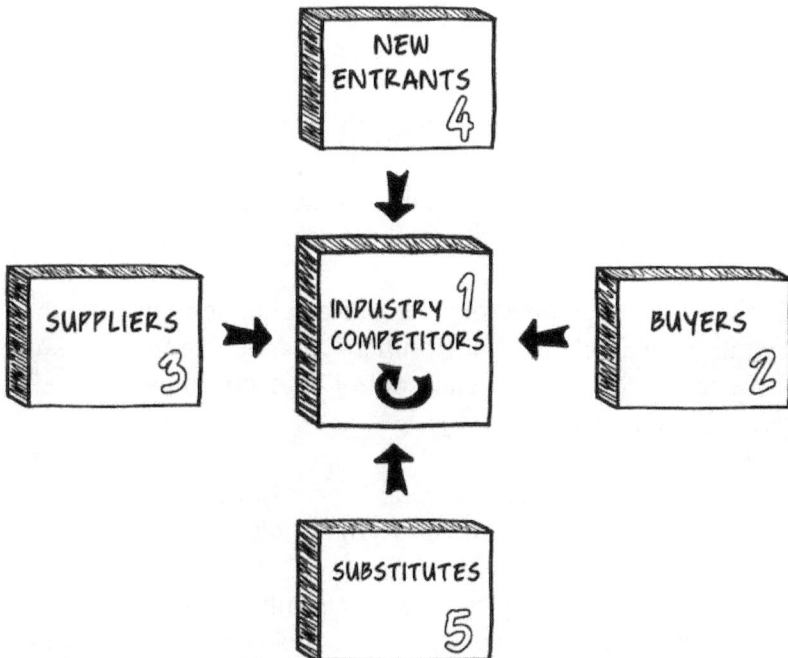

Let's break it down and see how you could apply it to your small business.

## 1.    *Existing competitors*

As a small business, you are likely to have many competitors, many of which could be much bigger than you. While your competitors should not overawe you, nor distract you from your own strategy, it is worth understanding who they are, what they are doing and what you might learn from them. You need to know what they are selling, where they are sourcing it from and who they are selling it to.

Their pricing is especially important if you sell similar products and services. You must decide on your own pricing and the margins you need to achieve to make your business viable. However, you can't ignore what their prices are. If you are substantially more expensive, and a customer can't see any value in paying more, then you are in trouble.

Understanding the following points about your competitors could prove invaluable:

- What makes them different from you?

- What marketing are they doing, and do you like it?

- How much are they charging for their products and services?

- What part of their business could you learn from and use in a way that aligns with your purpose, values, and goals?

Monitoring your competitors is important, but don't panic if they shift their strategy or implement new initiatives. You need to focus on your own strategy and what you can control, and not allow yourself to be distracted by someone else.

> *"Immature poets imitate; mature poets steal."* -
> **T.S. Eliot**. Poet and playwright.

Rarely is any idea completely new. Usually, ideas are influenced by what someone else has already done. If someone else, including a competitor, is doing something really well, learn from them.

## 2.    Your customers

I will discuss marketing and how you identify and reach your customers. This will be one of, if not the most important, part of your strategy.

**Without customers you have no business.**

Attracting and keeping customers is one of the most challenging parts of a business. You can never take your customers for granted. You should never stop looking for new customers and working on building loyalty with existing customers.

If you have a few large customers or a disproportionate reliance on one customer, your strategy needs to consider the risks of this.

Large organisations and government agencies can end a long-standing relationship with a small business in a heartbeat and it may have nothing to do with anything you did or didn't do. A change in a manager or key contact within the company can trigger changes in suppliers. Government departments may have to go to market and re-tender to meet policy, even if you have performed exceptionally well.

Your business could disappear simply because you rely heavily on one customer and that customer decided to go elsewhere. Your strategy needs to look at customer diversification.

## 3.    Your suppliers

It is likely you'll have a range of suppliers from whom you buy products or services. Given your size, you probably have little influence over larger suppliers and it's more likely they will affect you. If these suppliers raise their prices, alter their quality, cease to offer a product you rely on, or alter their service levels, you may find yourself stranded.

Look at those suppliers who could hurt you the most and consider what you would do if they failed to deliver what you want. It is rare that there would be absolutely no other option at your disposal. If there isn't, you will need to look at what you'll do if that supplier backs you into a corner.

If you source your products or services offshore, you can attract much better pricing and a much wider source of products. However, exchange rates, international freight and shipping, offshore political issues could all impact you.

Just as with customers, if you rely too heavily on one or a few suppliers, you face significant risk if you lose them.

If you believe a supplier is relying heavily on you for their survival, don't overplay your position. If they feel like they are being backed into a corner, forced to hold prices too low or meet unrealistic expectations, they could walk away. It's likely their strategy will look at ways to be less reliant on you.

## 4.    New entrants

There is every chance new people could come into your marketplace and directly compete with you. It's easy to start a small business in New Zealand. The barriers for similar competitors entering your marketplace could be quite low. If you are doing really well, it's likely someone else will see this and want a piece of your action.

Some new business may enter your market simply because they want to start a business for lifestyle reasons, having done no research and not realising that the market may already be overcrowded.

You may get no warning about new entrants. The key will be to maintain a level of oversight of your marketplace and be nimble enough to respond. The other critical point to remember is that, if you have loyal customers, they are unlikely to jump ship because someone else pops up.

## 5.    Substitutes

This relates to products or services that come out and make your offering redundant. You may well know the existing competition for your products or services and be comfortable you can compete. You may also be comfortable that you could survive a couple of new entrants. However, can you survive a business coming into the market that sells products or services that make yours irrelevant?

Businesses who processed photographs from negatives disappeared when digital photography took hold. The enormous growth in Artificial Intelligence will no doubt replace services offered by some businesses.

# Other external factors not covered by Porter.

Porter's Five Forces do not, however, consider some key external issues. Let's touch on these briefly.

## 1. Political or regulatory changes

Governments on all sides of the political divide come and go. Changes happen nationwide, and in District and Regional Councils in New Zealand. With this comes regulatory and legal changes that could benefit or damage your business. They could make business harder or easier than it needs to be.

As a small business owner, you are unlikely to have any political influence at all. Even the strongest lobby groups, with significant resources allocated to influence the political decision makers, don't get their way.

This does not mean you should do nothing. If your business has access to industry associations, look to join them. They may lobby on behalf of their members. If not, they may at least be aware of potential changes in the law ahead of time. If you rely heavily on government policies to attract revenue, consider the impact of potential changes.

## 2. Technological changes

The ongoing changes in technology could offer significant benefits or threats to your business. The pace of technological change hasn't slowed since the **Industrial Revolution.**

Horses became cars. Oil lamps became electric lights and air travel became accessible to everyone. Online marketing and the internet changed the world of advertising. Fibre optics and home automation have replaced traditional communication platforms. Personal computers, the internet, smart phones, home automation, e-commerce and the growth in artificial intelligence have seen significant change. There may be technology changes that are far less global in their impact but far more critical to your business.

Michael Porter's five-forces concept predates personal computers, the internet and now AI - and a long list of many other technological changes have come and gone and seen many businesses thrive and others die.

---

## Artificial Intelligence - the next internet?

In the time between researching the content of this book, putting pen to paper and getting it out to you, the pace of change in the world of Artificial Intelligence (AI) is moving so fast that it would become pointless to even attempt a discussion on it.

Many commentators are comparing it to the revolution that we experienced when we all gained access to a personal computer, or the internet became available to all of us.

OpenAI's development of ChatGPT has made this technology readily available to everyone, and even the novice can now get a taste of what AI can do.

Nvidia overtook Microsoft and Apple, to become one of the world's richest companies. Nvidia, founded in 1993 as a designer of chips for video game graphics, shifted into supplying hardware to power the AI industry in the 2020s. Within months of achieving this milestone, a Chinese competitor DeepSeek hit the market resulting in Nvidia experiencing one of the biggest single days losses in stock market history – over $US500 billion.

This shows how much interest exists in the AI market and how volatile and unclear its future still remains.

We must all monitor the progress of AI and what it might mean for small businesses.

All the big technology companies are increasing their focus on how to use and market AI.

How this massive growth and volatility in AI will present opportunities or threats for your small business is something only time will tell.

We must all monitor this and what it will mean for small businesses

---

## 3. Economic volatility

All of us, no matter our age, have seen good and not so good economic times. Even in the last 10 to 15 years, we have seen two of history's most extreme events.

From 2008 to 2010, the world's economies almost ground to a halt following the Global Financial Crisis (GFC).

The economic impact of the COVID-19 pandemic was still being felt in the years after the pandemic had passed.

While the next economic shock may not be a repeat of either of these events, we all know it will happen. When it occurs and how serious it might be will vary, but economic lows will happen. Similarly, we have experienced periods of strong economic growth, and we will experience them again.

As a small business, we have no ability to affect or change such events and have no control over them. We can only respond to them.

We always need to be considering the economic trends and adjust our strategies to either thrive or survive, depending on the situation. Good, well-run businesses will survive such events. These businesses will always ask *"What if…?"*. *"What if this robust economy falls, will we see it coming and can we respond to it?"* *"What if this weak economic environment picks up?* and *"Are we ready to maximise the opportunity?"*

## 4. Social changes

Social attitudes could provide both great opportunities and threats, depending on your business. You will have limited ability to influence these, but staying abreast of what is happening around your business will better prepare you.

The shift in attitudes to climate change and the environment are influencing people's decisions, particularly the younger generations. Banks are refusing to fund businesses like vaping. Some people won't invest if they believe their funds will support coal, oil and gas. Harassment and bullying can paralyse businesses, and settlements through the courts are now significant.

Many people have empathetic views on indigenous rights and a desire to right historic wrongs. Others strongly oppose this. The world of social media has allowed all such views to be aired without people being held to account for those views. Sadly, not everything that appears on such platforms reflects the truth.

When Simon Henry, the CEO of the New Zealand chemical company DGL Group, made derogatory and sexist comments about the chef Nadia Lim, in a one-on-one chat with a journalist, the response was extreme.

> *"I can tell you, and you can quote me, when you've got Nadia Lim, when you've got a little bit of Eurasian fluff in the middle of your prospectus with a blouse unbuttoned showing some cleavage, and that's what it takes to sell your script, then you know you're in trouble."* - **Simon Henry** CEO DGL Group.

His comments went viral, appearing on almost every online platform, in newspapers, and received extensive discussion on radio talkback. His comments caused the company's share price to drop by over $80 million in the immediate weeks after he made the comments. If he hadn't owned the company, it's likely the board would have sacked him.

If you slip up and do or say something that offends, your actions could quickly go viral no matter how small you are. Bad reviews could hit your website, social media pages and in blog discussions. Even if they are untrue and unfair, they could destroy your business.

---

> If we ignore social changes because we disagree with them or deny they are happening, we do so at our peril.

---

Should a bad review appear, you need to respond immediately and proactively. Should you make a mistake and if you said or did something you regret, admit it, own your words or actions and authentically say you are sorry and will do better. If it's misleading, correct it professionally. If you are in the wrong and you make excuses, respond aggressively or debate the issue publicly, it will only get worse.

Sometimes we must swallow our pride.

---

## Is this the death of traditional media - and societal change?

In April 2024, it was announced that after 35-years New Zealand's TV3 news and current affairs programs would end. Many in New Zealand's media expressed shock and concern. "It's a huge blow for democracy and a huge blow for the country" and "This is like going back to the 1970s for our democracy" [9]

There is, perhaps, no industry affected more by external forces than the media.

It is an industry that must be cognisant of technology changes, like newspapers to radio, to black and white television, to streaming and the internet.

Politics has a major effect on the industry. Television companies were government owned until TV3 was born in 1989. The industry has also had a history of heavy regulation and political interference.

Media also goes to the heart of our democratic life. Freedom of speech and an independent media are pillars of any democracy.

So, when major changes occur in the industry, the heightened emotions, the expressions of dismay, and shock by all those affected are not a surprise.

However, should these events really come as a surprise to the industry? For most observers, they have been coming for decades.

Perhaps the external force that has led to the greatest shifts in New Zealand media is the pressure of social change.

"Traditional broadcast platforms (TV & radio) still deliver the biggest audiences in New Zealand" [10] was the comforting headline for media traditionalists in 2014. While this headline put the industry at ease, the statistics behind the headline were telling a very different story. Large audiences were still watching these platforms, but they had been falling steadily since before the turn of the century.

In 2000, almost two-thirds of the time Kiwis spent watching television was on TV1 and TV2. By 2012, their viewing had declined to a little over 40%. [11]

---

This decline has continued, especially for the younger generations, who almost exclusively turn to digital sources for information. The over 60s kept the numbers up.

But by 2023, even they started deserting traditional media with most moving to digital. The desertion from traditional media to the digital world was most pronounced during the COVID 19 pandemic as more people turned to social media platforms to establish what was going on.

Young adults were spending more time watching TikTok than broadcast television and older viewers were turning to streaming services.

In the past, Kiwis trusted the traditional news outlets. This trust has been continually eroding.

All major news outlets have suffered drops in their trust ratings. Those of us who don't trust the news, or avoid it, do so because of concerns over its negativity, the impact that it has on our mental health, and what we perceive as political bias and opinion masquerading as news.

In 2020, 53% of Kiwis said they trusted the news. It was only 32% in 2024.[12]

While the expressions of grief and concern over the demise of journalism and traditional media may be very vocal, the social changes have been coming for a long time.

Whether right or wrong and whether they like it or not, the media outlet's customers, we the viewers, no longer want or trust their product in its current form and we continue to turn to other options - and we are doing it in droves.

# How to carry out and then implement your SWOT analysis

After walking through all these points, I hope you have a much better understanding of your small business and the world it operates in. I hope you have a clearer picture of the opportunities and threats in your external world. If not, spend a few hours in the newspapers, searching the web, and looking in industry newsletters and magazines to see if anything springs to mind.

How do you collate and use all this information to produce your strategy?

After doing your research, to establish your strengths, weaknesses, opportunities and threats, work your way through the following steps. It is even more effective if you can carry this out with someone else, even your team.

### Step 1

Put down the four SWOT headings (strengths, weaknesses, opportunities and threats) on a large sheet of paper.

### Step 2

Write down every idea that comes into your head under each heading. Keep going until you run out of ideas. Don't analyse or edit them just yet - just throw them down on the page.

### Step 3

Take a break, then come back and start grouping similar ideas together.

### Step 4

You don't need to do much more with your strengths. Note what they are and keep using them. However, your focus should now be on your weaknesses, opportunities, and threats.

### Step 5

Develop a single list with all the grouped items from the headings under weaknesses, opportunities, and threats.

### Step 6

Cross out any item over which you have no control. You may definitely want to monitor it, but if you can't do anything, leave it off the list.

**Step 7**

Now, reduce that list to just your top three to five items. If the list is too long, you simply won't get it all done. You must prioritise.

**Step 8**

Don't lose any of this information. It's too valuable to lose. What isn't a priority now may rise to the surface later.

You should now focus on these three to five priorities and build them into your strategy. If there are less than five, that's great. However, it is far more common that businesses have many more than five key things to do. Avoid a long list. You will not achieve them and may even set yourself up to fail and deliver none of them properly.

# Executing your strategy

We have now discussed the importance of formulating a strategy for your small business. The reason your business exists, the values you operate by and the goals you have set. We then used one simple tool to develop your top strategic priorities - SWOT.

However, this will mean little if you cannot execute that strategy. As you work your way through the remaining chapters of this book, start thinking about how you bring that strategy to life.

Your strategy is there to help you make choices. To establish what you will do and what you won't do. However, you will continue to face many priorities, many choices, and many paths you and your business could take. This could become overwhelming, especially with your limited resources.

## *What benefit does a business plan offer?*

A business plan adds specific targets you aim to pursue so you can deliver your five (or less) strategic priorities. Typically, it involves 12 months of operations and often it aligns with the tax year. It should summarise your strategy, define time frames, and be measurable.

Businesses tend to over-complicate the business planning process. It need only be brief and simple. In fact, a business plan should not be more than an A4 page. It should remain dynamic rather than a large document that collects dust on a shelf. It should also be visible, so you and your staff can gauge where you are on the journey and whether the journey is taking you in the right direction.

Some small business owners may be clear on the plan, but have it locked away in their thoughts. You may verbalise it with the rest of the business regularly, which is all fine, but don't be surprised if your message is forgotten, lost, or confused in translation. It's always best to write your plans down for your benefit and for the clarity of all those empowered to deliver it.

## Key performance indicators (KPIs), targets, and ratios

This term is commonly used in large businesses to describe the measures they will monitor closely. Financial ratios are one type of KPI. KPIs are often what a corporate manager's bonus is linked to. Banks often track ratios of large companies to ensure they can meet their lending requirements. They look at ratios and measures like debt-to-equity, liquidity ratio, free cash flow, and more.

I do not believe these are very helpful for a small business, but you need to know what measures best tell you if you are on track or falling behind on your journey.

Whatever you choose to monitor, it must be measurable and truly reflect what you need to do to stay on track. Vague measures or measures that are really difficult to calculate are likely to distract you from the important stuff.

Typical examples could centre around the sales per month. Leads generated and new customers gained. Cash in the bank. Positive feedback scores. Products manufactured. Near miss safety issues reported. And the list will go on.

## Budgets

I will discuss cash flow forecasts and budgets in greater detail in later chapters. For now, make sure you add a budget or financial plan that supports your business plan. There is not much point having an inspiring, elaborate business plan if you can't afford it.

## _Write up and then plan to review your business plan_

Don't get too precious about how you present the business plan to everyone. The key is it is clear, can be shared with the business, and most importantly, is brought to life and used.

Once you have the plan in place, review it, track how you are going, and adjust anything as circumstances arise. It's likely from the moment you complete the business plan, something will change, requiring you to adjust it or even completely rewrite it. This might be a monthly meeting with your business partner, advisor, accountant, or a trusted staff member.

# Even the basics is OK

As I mentioned at the start of this chapter, you don't need to use any of these techniques to develop an effective strategy for your business. These are proven methods businesses of all sizes, including massive corporates, have used for decades, so they work. They may not work for you.

If none of these methods excites you, that is perfectly fine. You may have your own proven methods to collate information about the world around you and how you decide on the future of your business.

However, all I will reenforce is how critical it is that you do something.

If you just roll along from month-to-month your business will end up somewhere. Whether it's where you want to be is a very different thing. Spend some conscious time thinking about what sort of business you want and where you want your business to take you.

# CHAPTER 6

## THE MIND OF THE SMALL BUSINESS OWNER

Everything covered in this book and everything you as a business owner do and don't do will be determined by what you put your mind to. How you decide and what decisions you make. How you take in information, process it, remember it, and then act on it. How you perceive the world you operate in and how you interact with others.

All this is determined through and by your brain.

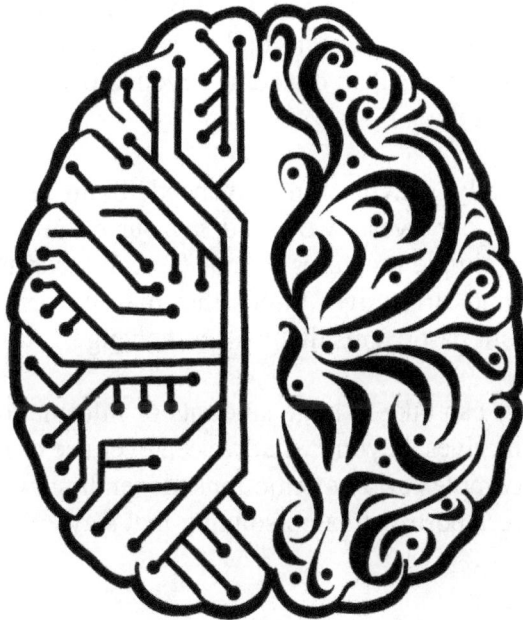

While this may seem self-evident, we rarely devote any time to understanding our brains, especially when the limitations of our brains could determine whether we succeed or fail in business - and in life.

Let's spend some time understanding how our brains work and why this is so fundamental to your business.

# The evolving brain

The evolution of the human brain has seen it triple in size over the last two million years. It is still on an evolutionary journey. While it has evolved, and has become more complex, our brains are far from a perfect creation. They have inherent limitations and inefficiencies.

Our brains are immensely complex and there is still much we do not understand about our brains, even though there is significant expertise devoted to neuroscience and psychological studies across the planet.

As humans, our brains allow us to enjoy many pleasures and joys in life that other animals will never experience. We can create and do things other creatures cannot. We can solve puzzles, talk, sing, feel, and love, grieve, and pursue our passions and dreams. In most cases, creatures with less-developed brains than ours don't even know they exist - they are not even self-aware.

Unfortunately, having an advanced brain also adds significant complexity to our lives - we could say our brain has burdened us with complexities simple creatures do not face. We can make ourselves sick with worry and stress over things that may never happen, and we can ruminate about past events that we can't change.

Our brains can take in huge amounts of information at every moment of our waking lives, beyond what we can ever use or remember. We have a wide and complex array of emotions, depending on who we are and our pasts. We were born with a personality that stays with us throughout our lives.

# Practice makes permanent

Each of the billions of neurons within our brains are connected to thousands of other neurons via a junction between the neurons called the synapse. Each neuron has thousands of synapses. While we don't know for sure how many neurons make up our brains, there are likely to be somewhere between 80 and 100 billion.

Therefore, there are trillions of connections in our brains creating a highly complex network of neuron paths. Our brain functions by transferring electrochemical signals between neurons. These trigger a series of actions and reactions. The number of neurons is the same in children as it is in adults. We are born with all the neurons we will ever have.

At birth, our neurons are sparser and more unconnected, and in the first two years of life, they connect rapidly as they take in new information. Every second, about two million new connections are formed in an infant's brain. By age two, a child has over one hundred trillion synapses, double the number in an adult.

They then reach a peak and have far more connections than are needed. At this point, the process of creating new connections is replaced by **neural pruning** - unused neuron paths are lost. As we mature, about half of our neural connections will be lost. If we don't use certain neural paths in our brain, we will lose them. [1]

Every time we learn an additional fact or skill, we change our brains in small ways. This process is called **neuroplasticity**. [2]

These chemical reactions or firing of these neurons in our brain are short-lived. To embed these new skills, we need to create structural changes in our brain - this takes much longer. If we do piano lessons one day, and come back the next day, we remember little or nothing about what was learned. When we learn a new language, we have to repeat words many times before they stick, and we remember them.

To learn the piano or speak a new language and create permanent change, we must repeat the process over and over - and over.

As we learn and evolve, change and grow, pathways are forged in our brains where the neurons are connected.

Complex skills are laid down in the brain after countless hours of deliberate training because our brain is a slow learner. Over time, such practice will result in these skills becoming so embedded that they are subconscious.

# Heuristics and biases

In our every waking moment, we are bombarded with huge amounts of information, far more that we need. We take in this information. Without knowing it, we are filtering it, ignoring most of it, filing some of it away in our memories, recalling past pieces of information, and then we act on it.

Our brains are lazy, so we subconsciously take shortcuts when we go through this process. These shortcuts are called **heuristics**. A heuristic is a mental shortcut that allows us to solve problems and make judgements quickly and efficiently.

Our brains were developed to help us survive, so we must filter information. We are all wired differently. Because of the shortcuts our brains must make, we often get things wrong, and we don't realise this is happening.

These shortcuts lead to biases. Some may be innocent, others more sinister and dangerous.

Our irrational minds are flooded with cultural biases rooted in our traditions, upbringing, and a lot of other subconscious factors that assert a powerful but hidden influence over the choices we make.

The importance of understanding our biases is not only to understand ourselves, but to understand how those around us may act in certain situations.

## Our blind spots

We have blind spots to the mental shortcuts we take and the biases we form. Blind spots are our tendency to recognise the biases in other people, but not in ourselves.

Unfortunately, we can be guilty of believing that our own view on things is accurate, even enlightened, and therefore the correct view. We may confidently judge other people's views, believing that they have biases and, therefore, are incorrect.

Consider this when you get into a debate over business, politics, religion or sport or in any debate where you stick steadfastly to a viewpoint - you may both be right and wrong.

# Examples of our many biases

The following are some very common biases that could affect any of us at any time and may impact our business. We should acknowledge we are all likely to be affected by these biases. Biases may seem self-evident when we are discussing them, but we may not be aware they affect us when we go about our daily lives. **Daniel Kahneman** and his close colleague **Amos Tversky,** through their years of research, identified many of these biases. Kahneman was the recipient of the Nobel prize in economics in 2002 for his work.

## *Attribution error - internal and external*

When things don't go according to plan, there are various ways we attribute the reasons for a less-than-adequate outcome.

When we observe others who have got things very wrong, we usually place the blame squarely with the people at the centre of the problem. This is called **internal attribution** - we attribute the problem to the person's decision making and actions.

It is too easy for people observing the actions of others to focus on the person more than on the situation they found themselves in.

We often explain world events as though the people involved in them had far greater control over than was the case. When bad things happen, we assume it's the fault of someone when it may have been out of everyone's control.

We don't have to go too far to find examples of this. I am sure we are all guilty of attributing blame for events in public life to politicians or blaming a sporting hero for a result that we were unhappy with.

On the flip side is how we attribute things that go wrong for us. Instead of holding ourselves accountable for our own actions, we may be tempted to place blame on external factors. This is **external attribution**.

Attribution errors can also occur when assessing things that have gone well.

When we see someone else do well, we may attribute this success to luck, being in the right place at the right time, rather than attributing the success to the person's skills or efforts. However, when we do well, we may attribute that success to our own efforts rather than luck.

## Representativeness and stereotyping

Throughout our evolutionary history, we have had to assess people quickly, especially strangers, to determine if they may be friend or foe. In doing this, we form views about a person knowing no details about them.

If we are introduced to someone and some pleasantries follow, such as where they are from, the job they have, a doctor, pilot, student, nurse, sports person, labourer, our brains will categorise these people. We form views about them based on a representation we have of them stored away within our minds. Hence, the term **representativeness**. We also commonly refer to this as **stereotyping**.

This can lead to some of the more sinister effects in our society, such as racism, ageism and sexism. We form false impressions of people based on their race, their age or their gender, knowing nothing else about them.

This can have major effects on our business. It will affect how we subconsciously view customers, employees, and business colleagues.

We would all love to believe we don't suffer from this bias, but we do. The challenge is to pause and challenge ourselves when we think this might be happening. Seeking an independent view also helps.

## Loss aversion

In business, we face risks that might provide the opportunity for us to gain something or to lose something, and we must decide whether to act on these. Unfortunately, when we compare or weigh up options, losses loom much larger in our thinking than gains do. We place far more importance and focus on avoiding losses than we do on achieving the equivalent gains.

The pain of losing is psychologically far more powerful than the pleasure of gaining the same thing. Since people are more willing to take risks to avoid a loss, loss aversion can explain differences in risk seeking versus risk aversion.

It may even go back to our evolutionary ancestors - losing a day's food would have been considered a greater risk than gaining one extra day's food. We are likely to fight harder to keep that day's supply than the fight to gain an extra day's food.

## The endowment effect

When we buy something, we are more inclined to hang on to it and put more value on it than before we owned it. If you queued for a ticket to a sporting event and paid a price for it you thought was fair, how much would you turn around and sell it for after you have got it? It's likely it will be significantly higher than when you lined up to pay for it. We possess the ticket and now put greater value on it.

People place a higher value on a good that they own than on an identical good that they do not own.

This reflects a type of loss aversion. It is called the **endowment effect.** We expect to receive more to give up a possession than what we were initially willing to pay to gain it.

Dan Ariely, in his book *"Predictably Irrational"*, puts forward the following view of why we exhibit this tendency:

> *"Why? Because of three irrational quirks in our human nature. The first quirk is that we fall in love with what we already have ... The second quirk is that we focus on what we may lose, rather than what we may gain ... The third quirk is that we assume other people will see the transaction from the same perspective as we do." -* **Dan Ariely**, Predictably Irrational. [3]

## Optimism bias

We can suffer from comparative optimism - the belief that we are less likely to experience negative events and more likely to experience positive events than other people.

We are biased toward more optimistic outcomes for ourselves than others. The "*it will never happen to me*" mentality is one way to describe this thinking, when statistics show a different outcome is likely.

When asked how good a driver we are (especially men), most of us believe we are above average - when we can't all be above average.

If you were to ask a couple on the eve of their wedding if their marriage will last, I doubt many will say "*no*" when we know how high divorce rates are.

Sometimes this optimism bias might work for us, such as the decisions to get into a small business - a little naïve optimism is probably essential.

In entering a new business venture, optimism is important. If we weren't optimistic, it is likely very few businesses would ever come to life.

Where optimism bias can be dangerous is where we ignore the warning signs about risks that could befall us, and we ignore some obvious facts or realities that pose risks we must consider. Sometimes businesspeople want to implement an idea or project so much, being certain it will succeed, that they fail to heed the warning signs.

Daniel Kahneman described how optimism bias can afflict businesses.

> *"When forecasting the outcomes of risky projects, executives too easily fall victim to the planning fallacy. In its grip, they make decisions based on delusional optimism rather than on a rational weighting of gains, losses, and probabilities. They overestimate benefits and underestimate costs."* -
> **Daniel Kahneman** [4]

## *Hindsight bias*

We are all aware of the saying that hindsight is 20/20 - basically we can assess events after they happened with complete clarity, but not so before they occurred. Unfortunately, this is a common bias that we get trapped by, especially in business.

We are prone to blame decision makers for decisions that worked out badly. We often give them little credit for successful moves that appear obvious, but only after the fact. When the outcomes are bad, we often blame those who made the decision. We believe they should have seen what we now know is very obvious - forgetting that it was far from obvious before these people made those decisions.

We can also be guilty of chastising ourselves over our decisions once we know the consequences, with hindsight. You need to be cautious of this, as you can't go back on your decisions. You must decide and just deal with the outcomes as best you can.

This can also be the case when we make decisions, and everything goes well. We should not assume that getting it right in that situation will transpire the next time. Prior to the decision being made, the outcome was anything but certain and a range of factors had to fall into place for the outcome to have come to fruition. Those factors may not have gone as planned and the outcome may well have been different.

Don't discount the role luck may have played in the outcome, either good or bad

## *Anchoring*

### <u>TEST</u>

How many countries are there in Africa?

(Hint: Decide if it's more or fewer than 65 and then pick a number.)

In many situations, people make estimates by starting from an initial value that is adjusted to get the final answer. The initial value, however it comes to us, anchors us and influences the answer we settle on.

If you knew the answer in the above test about Africa, the hint should have had little impact on you. However, if you did not know, there is every chance simply presenting you with the hint influenced your choice. There are many similar tests researchers have done that reinforce this bias.

By the way, there are 54 countries in Africa.

We can be influenced by information that we first receive when making decisions, if we feel that information might be valid. The anchor and our intuition can combine to see us accept this information and then we make a final decision based on that information without doing the analysis.

This is a very important bias to consider when going into a negotiation.

If you go in unprepared and have not done your homework, be very careful if the other party puts an offer to you. If it does not scare you away from the negotiation altogether, you may well be subconsciously drawn in. All subsequent discussions about the offer will move around the original anchor, and that may ultimately be bad for you.

## *Availability heuristic*

If someone asks us to determine the likelihood of an event occurring, we will delve into our memories. The most recent and easily retrieved information, rather than what the correct information might be, will influence our response. The easier the events spring to mind, or the more mentally available they are to us, the more likely that will be the answer.

After we hear about a series of earthquakes on the news, it reminds us to re-look at whether we have fixed objects in our homes to prevent them from falling. A friend suffers a heart attack scare, so we run off and get that long-overdue check-up. We hear about a spate of shark attacks in Australia and feel more vulnerable when we jump in the sea on our Christmas break.

In each case, the risk was no different before or after the information came to us - it is simply now more available.

The opposite applies when the same information fades and becomes less available.

As the availability of the event fades from our memories, our inclination to forget it happened increases, and sadly, it gets repeated.

The book *"This Time is Different - Eight Centuries of Financial Folly"*, by Reinhart and Rogof [5] covers examples of this. They describe how countries like Greece defaulted on their debt during the Global Financial Crisis, but when they looked back, Greece had defaulted often over the centuries. It would seem they never learned from past failures and continued to repeat them for centuries.

As the pain diminishes, and old habits take over, we repeat the same mistakes - over and over.

## Confirmation bias

This is one of the best-known biases, but sadly is also the one that we all too rarely recognise.

Over many years, we have formed opinions, views, or beliefs about different things. When we come across information that aligns or confirms this view, we can often use it to reinforce an existing view, while ignoring information that may undermine or counter that view. We are basically looking at the world through our internal filters and not with the open mind we would like to think we are.

Good examples of this include impassioned debates around religion, sport and politics and, sadly, our views on race.

Different people can be confronted with the same information, but use that information to confirm or refute a preconceived view of the world. A simple example is that all youths wearing hoodies must be criminals - which we reaffirm after seeing a hooded youth rob a dairy on the evening news.

## Framing effects

Let's say you are on the operation table about to be anaesthetised for, hopefully, a lifesaving operation. The surgeon leans over, smiles and says,

> *"You have nothing to worry about. I have done this simple operation a hundred times, and it has been overwhelmingly successful with 95% coming out fine."*

A little nervous, I would say.

But let's suppose the doctor frames the comment in this way:

> *"You have nothing to worry about. I have done this operation a hundred times but, unfortunately, five people died."*

More nervous?

This is a regular challenge when responding to news, for example, when the news presents an accident in terms of lives saved versus lives lost.

Advertisers regularly use the framing effect to present information in a manner that influences how viewers interpret that information about the products they are promoting. Why they say 95% fat free instead of contains 5% fat.

We can believe that we are too clever to be fooled by such things. However, we are and perhaps we want to forget the 5% fat and enjoy the 95% guilt free.

In many cases, having the same information provided to us in different ways may be inconsequential. However, to others, it could completely alter the meaning of the information being presented.

If we processed information with complete rationality, we would treat these situations in exactly the same way - but we don't.

Unfortunately, the shortcuts our brains take and our inbuilt tendencies to be irrational mean we will continue to misinterpret information depending on how it is framed and how our internal processes interpret the information.

The loss aversion bias highlighted that loss looms larger for us than the equivalent gain. Therefore, we will frame information that is presented in terms of a potential loss differently than the same information framed in terms of a gain.

## *Affect heuristic - the emotional response bias*

This bias relates to the **affect** something has on us - how it triggers emotions. The way information is presented, and the content of that information, affects different people in different ways - and therefore individuals develop biases.

Different words, images, or objects will have a different impact on us. If I said, *"lung cancer"*, *"car crash"* or *"depression"*, it would likely produce a response of discomfort or even dread, especially if you, or someone close to you, were affected by one of these events.

---

If, however, I said *"hug"*, *"mother's love"* or *"warmth"*, these are likely to produce feelings of affection. The word *"father"* to someone from a loving relationship will produce a unique response to a person abused by their father.

This bias is one that is affected by the emotional responses within us.

This mental shortcut is a bit like our filter for the *"goodness"* or *"badness"* of the information we receive and then filter - usually subconsciously, as with most of our mental filters. As with all the mental shortcuts, this filter leads to judgements upon which biased decisions can result.

As Robert Zajonc, the social psychologist, put it:

> *"There are probably very few perceptions in everyday life that do not have a significant affective component. We do not just see "a house": we see "a handsome house", "an ugly house", or "a pretentious house"* - **Robert Zajonc.** [6]

When someone is asked why something affected them or why they made a certain decision, they can struggle to explain why. Often, we make judgements without consciously knowing why we made them. Why did we like that house and not the other house? Why did we feel that way about that stranger? Why did that conversation affect me so much?

# Reducing the impact of our biases

The biases detailed above are but a small sample of the many shortcuts we take and have been identified and researched over many years by people like Kahneman, Tversky, and many more.

We could not survive each day if we did not take these mental shortcuts. We need to take in information and rapidly respond to it, and we do so without being conscious we are doing it.

The examples I've discussed above are typical of those that will impact business owners and the decisions they make.

The first step in managing the negative effects of biases is to accept that we are imperfect and that we take mental shortcuts. As a result, we have biases we may not even realise exist.

We need to be aware of these limitations. While we are gifted, innovative, talented and much more, we are still human, and we need to be cognisant of this. We also need to be kind to ourselves in accepting our humanity. We will get it wrong.

When the implication of a decision is significant on the business, on you, or other people, it is worth stepping back and asking yourself the questions: *"Are there any biases at play here?" "Am I being objective?"*

It is also worth deferring to those we trust and whose advice we are comfortable to take. These are people prepared to be honest with us rather than nice to us - remember, **NICE** stands for **Not Interested to Care Enough**.

# CHAPTER 7

# HOW WE MAKE BUSINESS DECISIONS

We discussed how our brain works and the shortcuts our brains take in getting through the day. These shortcuts lead to biases that affect our decisions. Success or failure in business depends on the decisions we do or don't make.

We take in a large amount of information every day. We filter most of it, encode it, sleep on it, remember some of it, forget most of it, incorrectly recall it, and process it so we form judgements and then decide.

All the biases we discussed, what we remember and what we forget, what information we take in and what information we ignore all impact the quality of our decisions. It's not surprising that we get so many decisions wrong.

Considering all these factors working against us, how might be we improve the quality of the business decisions we make?

## Everyday decisions

Every day in our business and our lives, we must make decisions. Most we do with no thought or analysis - we just make them and get on with our day. What to eat for breakfast? What to wear? What route to take to work?

However, we often need to make decisions that pose far greater effects on our businesses, and which may require deeper thought. Mergers and acquisitions. Taking on significant debt. Moves into new markets. Taking on or dismissing staff. Buying new assets. Agreeing to a significant contract.

Our colleagues, customers, suppliers, our staff and all those who interact with our business will make decisions that may or may not affect us.

# We time travel

Each decision involves our past experiences and the present situation. But unlike most other species, we decide based on predictions of the future. We are effectively time traveling.

Before we decide, we consider past experiences, present needs, and jump out in the future to assess what the longer-term impacts of our decision might be. We mentally time travel all the time. We simulate different outcomes to generate a mockup of what our future might be. Mentally, we can disconnect from the present moment and voyage to a world that does not yet exist.

Such a skill is unique to humans.

# Rational decisions - what are they?

In your business life, you will have likely been told that to make good business decisions, you must think rationally and make rational decisions.

> Running a business is intensely personal, as our lives, our self-esteem, and our families could depend on it.

We need to reconsider the view that decision making should be rational, especially as our brains are not wired that way.

Let's spend some time asking what it is to be rational and ask what a rational decision is and why this often-incorrect assumption about rationality has been fundamental to economics, markets and business for centuries.

## What is it to be "rational"?

The *Oxford English Dictionary* defines *"rational"* as:

> **Based on or in accordance with reason or logic.**
> **Able to think sensibly or logically. Endowed with**
> **the capacity to reason.**

For centuries, economic theory has held the view that businesses, markets and economies operate because people make rational decisions.

The mathematician **Daniel Bernoulli**, born in 1700, proposed that business and investment decisions are based on the **utility** associated with the decision. What material gains or losses will be associated with the decision?

Utility has formed the basis of economic and business theory ever since. Basically, the economic utility of a good or service is assumed to influence the demand, and therefore the price of that good or service.

Sounds true and, in the main, is the basis of the economic theory of supply and demand.

**Rational Choice Theory** forms the basis of economic theory. The central assumption of the Rational Choice Theory is that decision makers have logically consistent goals and, given these goals, choose the best option. It assumes those deciding are *"unboundedly rational"* [1]

This theory assumes that when people face choices, they will choose what delivers them the greatest benefit (utility) or satisfaction. It also assumes that being rational means decision makers are self-interested individuals.

However, this is very often far from the truth.

# Economics and human behaviour

In more recent decades, there has been a growth in the acceptance of **behavioural economics** or **behavioural finance**. This brings the irrationality of human beings and our innate psychology into consideration. It challenges past theories that economies, markets and businesses are driven by rational decisions made by rational people.

---

There is a growing view amongst economists and academics that we do not decide based on the historically accepted economic theories. People base their decisions on a wide mix of emotional, irrational, and altruistic reasons that may not aim to achieve the greatest financial return.

> *"We usually think of ourselves as sitting in the driver's seat, with ultimate control over the decision we make and the direction our life takes; but, alas, this perception has more to do with our desires - with how we want to view ourselves - than with reality."* - **Dan Ariely** [2]

# When deciding, we compare - it's relative, and it's irrational

When we are making decisions, we more often do it by comparing the relativity of different options. We don't always have an absolute view of the value of something in our minds. We compare the relative advantage of one option over another option before we make a final decision. This is another short-cut or heuristic and, as you'd imagine, it often ends up pushing us to the wrong decision.

Our decision making is relative and influenced by context. When choosing from alternatives, we can't help but make comparisons between options that are put in front of us. This can be to our detriment.

Our brains are wired to look for change, for patterns, for differences.

In a workplace, we will form a view of our value to the business based on our pay packet relative to other employees. We may have no information on what others are earning and feel quite happy. How would you feel if you then found out you were the lowest paid in the office but felt you worked the hardest?

Another example of relativity in decision making is how we compare the price to gain something versus the cost to go without.

For example, assume you know the price of a Big Mac is about $8. If I offered you a Big Mac for $13, your decision to buy it is likely to be a resounding *"no"*. Why would you? Now say you were on a long-haul budget flight for about 15 hours, and you arrived on the plane hungry. You had plenty of cash in your pocket and all you could buy were Big Macs and they cost $15 each. I dare say the relative value of the Big Mac has now changed and you probably wouldn't hesitate at paying the money - and you might buy more than one.

---

## Bread machines, popcorn and the decoy effect

Chuck Williams started Williams-Sonoma, a store focused on high-quality cookware, in Sonoma California in 1956.

In the 1990s, they introduced bread-making machines to their product range. The product was a novel concept, but Williams-Sonoma considered, through market research, that it would have strong sales potential. They put the machine on sale for a sale price of $275, which was deemed to be good value.

Sales were disappointing.

Rather than abandoning the product, they tried a different strategy.

Williams-Sonoma put a slightly better bread-making machine on sale with a few more features but at around double the price of their base model. This was well above what it was worth. They had no interest in selling the more expensive model. The store used the more expensive option as a **decoy** to give customers something to compare with.

This saw a significant increase in the sales of the $275 option.

Coffee outlets, and movie theatres selling popcorn are another example where businesses use the **decoy effect** in their sales strategies to take advantage of our irrational decision making.

Let's say you walk into the theatre and want a box of popcorn. You aren't overly hungry and know a box of popcorn isn't that good for you. You have two options. Chances are you'll buy the $5.00 box.

1.  Small  =  $5.00
2.  Large  =  $8.75

Now, let's say there were three options.

---

1.      Small   =       $5.00
2.      Medium =       $8.00
3.      Large   =       $8.75

Suddenly, the $8.75 box looks like good value. For only an extra 75c you can get a large box. And what the heck, you haven't been to the movies for months, so you get the large box.

The seller wants you to buy the more expensive option. This option is competing with the cheapest option for your purchase. The middle option is the decoy to push you toward the option the business wants you to buy.

You are looking to buy a computer, and a computer business presents you with three options. You are really struggling to choose. It is likely, in the absence of other information, that you will choose the middle of the three options. You compromise, which is why this is also sometimes called the compromise effect.

This method of marketing has been used to sell coffee, items on a restaurant menu, wines on a drinks list, online subscriptions, computers and many more.

Which item is the decoy may vary depending on the situation.

# Emotions and business decisions

As we have discussed, we are not rational beings. This means we can't ignore the emotional effects on our decisions. Past experiences, fear, memories, and more, influence our decisions. There is a growing view by researchers that emotions can improve the quality of our business decisions rather than worsen them. [3]

It's likely others in business will have told you to remove emotions from the decisions you make. How often have you heard the statement **"This is a business decision, it's not personal"** which implies its free from any emotion? Sadly, this is very often not the case, especially when we are so emotionally invested in our businesses.

Our emotional responses inform many of our decisions because that is what emotions do - to appraise and summarise an experience and inform our actions. Emotions are not sophisticated or precise, but their speed makes up for what they lack in sophistication and precision.

Our emotions will drive the decisions we make, and our success may depend upon our ability to understand and interpret these emotions.

During critical decisions about the business, we may feel anxious, stressed, and uncomfortable. These are signs we need to consider. Emotions can undermine and mislead our decisions as well.

> *"Emotions powerfully, predictably, and pervasively influence decision making."* - **Jennifer Lerner** et al. [4]

When a person responds to an emotionally significant event, their brain automatically searches their memory for related events, including the emotions that accompanied those events. If the feelings are pleasant, they motivate actions and thoughts expected to reproduce those feelings.

We'd like to think we can divorce ourselves from this process, but we can't. Rather, we need to embrace the emotions, but caution against spontaneously responding if the decision could have significant ramifications.

## *Emotions versus being emotional*

When we discuss emotions here, it is not implying that you should make critical business decisions if you are experiencing heightened emotions like anger, fear, grief, or sadness. If you feel overrun by such emotions, it may be a good idea to pause, calm down and avoid making any significant decisions.

If we are prone to these reactions on a more regular basis, we should consider strategies and the guidance of those we trust to get some distance between the heightened emotion and the decisions we might otherwise make while in that elevated emotional state.

The decisions we make while in an emotional state may have nothing to do with why our emotions are elevated.

For example, in getting ready for work after a terrible night's sleep, you have a battle getting the kids to school. You leave home angry and frustrated. Traffic is heavy, and a few people cut you off in traffic. By the time you get to work, you are not in a very pleasant frame of mind. The first decision you face is dealing with a customer complaint. In your heightened state, you decide to push back. *"To hell with them."* When you finally calm down, you regret your actions. Your anger had nothing to do with that important customer you just lost.

# The science behind, and risk of, going with your gut

Daniel Kahneman, in his book *"Thinking, Fast and Slow"* [5] described how our brains function based on two different types of thinking. One is intuitive or fast thinking, and the other is the slower, analytical thinking.

Let's do a little test to show this.

---

**TEST**

Without doing any written calculations, write down your answer to the following:

If a bat and a ball cost $1.10 together, and the bat costs $1.00 more than the ball, how much does the ball cost?

---

Your immediate answer is likely to be 10 cents, but somewhere in your thinking is an element of doubt.

Surely it cannot be that simple. It's not.

Our intuitive thinking process jumped to the immediate, seemingly simple answer. If instead we had drawn on our analytical thinking and ran some basic maths, we would have realised the answer is not 10 cents, it is 5 cents.

If the ball is 5 cents, the bat is $1.00 more, it must be $1.05. That means $1.05 + 5 cents = $1.10.

When we make decisions without applying the slower analytical parts of our brain, it's likely we are making what we often call **gut decisions**. They are fast, take less effort, and are usually the most common type of decision business leaders and business owners make.

Analytical and reasoned decisions require us to look outside ourselves, referring to others or to more information, statistics, data, or research. Gut decisions occur within us, so the answers need to be found somewhere from within. Our internal knowledge, experience, and past emotional events will guide us.

There is a very important caveat on gut decisions we need to contemplate.

Gut decisions based on deep and detailed experience or extensive training are often better than those based on analysis. However, if we have no experience, we need to be extremely wary about making gut decisions without seeking advice or doing some analysis.

> If you have no experience and make a gut decision on a critical issue for the business, it may be no better than a guess.

We need to challenge this intuition. This does not mean procrastinate and do nothing. It means pausing and challenging ourselves before taking the leap.

# Gut decisions by experts under extreme pressure

Gary Klein, a research psychologist (and critic of Daniel Kahneman's views on biases), did extensive research on the real-life decisions people make in high-pressure situations. He called his work **Naturalistic Decision Making** because it related to observed decisions in natural environments rather than in laboratory tests. [6]

He studied people making critical, even life or death decisions, such as firefighters, military personnel, pilots and astronauts.

These people are making snap or intuitive decisions, with minimal information, with shifting goals, no procedures, under significant time pressure, and with potentially serious, even life-threatening consequences.

While there is no question these experts make these decisions using their intuitive mental processes, and are gut decisions, they are based on years of experience and training. These experienced decision makers recognise patterns, and they don't compare options. They evaluate an option by imagining how it would play out.

Klein's work showed that expertise primarily depends on tacit knowledge, not on rules and procedures. He challenged that in these situations, gathering more information may not reduce uncertainty. In fact, he found that performance seemed to suffer when experts gathered too much information. This uncertainty could result from inadequate framing of data, not just the absence of data.

Michael LeGault, in his book *"Think"* stated that:

> *"Critical scientific reasoning almost always involves a component of intuition, and intuition is almost always informed by experience and hard knowledge won by reasoning things out."* - **Michael LeGault.** [7]

If you face a serious or critical situation in a business where the stakes are high and you have significant experience, more than anyone around you, trust your gut and decide. However, if you have little or no experience, or are feeling uneasy, I'd strongly advise you to apply some critical thinking to the problem. Seek expertise and think the problem through - this may not be a wise time to go with your gut - and then hope for the best.

# Fatigue, stress and the impact of wellbeing on decisions

If you are not at your best, if you are stressed, lack sleep or are unwell, the quality of your decisions will suffer.

The more decisions we make, the more energy-depleted our brains become. We become mentally fatigued. We can suffer from **decision fatigue**. The more decisions we make throughout the day, the harder each one becomes for our brain, and our brain tires and looks for shortcuts.

This can also mean our willpower becomes depleted, further diminishing the quality of our decisions.

Jonathon Levav and his colleagues observed the decisions made by judges on parole boards. The research reviewed over 1100 parole decisions and explored if the decisions had any patterns associated with them. The most striking pattern was the reduction in positive decisions in the latter part of the day, after the judges had made many decisions during that day. The judges were getting tired, and the easiest option was rejecting the parole application. [8]

> *"Research suggests that making repeated judgments or decisions depletes individuals' executive function and mental resources which can, in turn, influence their subsequent decisions".* **Jonathon Levav** et al. Stanford Graduate School of Business.

No matter how rational and focused we try to be, we can't make decision-after-decision without paying a biological price.

It's different from ordinary physical fatigue; we are not as conscious of being tired and low on mental energy as we are when we are physically fatigued.

You could become more impulsive, lose your self-control, and give in to the easy options. You could also simply avoid deciding.

Our willpower and our self-control are not unlimited resources.

How frequently, when we are mentally drained, have we succumbed and indulged in that extra glass of wine, or that ice cream that we had been so disciplined about avoiding when we felt content

# How can we make better decisions?

Embracing the reality of our limitations is crucial for making better business choices. Achieving success in business hinges on our ability to acknowledge and remember these limitations when making critical decisions.

Below, I summarise some of the key things to keep in mind when making important decisions:

- Our brain cannot process everything. You won't remember everything, and you will take mental shortcuts. Write things down.

- Consider the implications of your significant decision. Don't sweat the small stuff, but if the implications for the business are significant, pause and seek the counsel of others.

- Don't be afraid to listen to your emotions. How does the decision make you feel?

- Recognise what you have experience with and what you don't. When you have little or no experience, you need to be careful about making important decisions without advice and analysis.

- Apply **advocatus diaboli**, which is the Latin term for the Devil's advocate. This was an official role given to people to argue against why a person should be canonised (made a saint). This could be a trusted advisor.

- Accept when you are tired, stressed, or have been required to make many decisions. If you make significant decisions when you are like this, they may prove unsatisfactory - or you may simply avoid making any decision.

- Build rules, processes and systems into the business that will guide everyone, at least for the repetitive processes that occur. Read the chapter on operations.

- Be clear what the strategy is for your business - why does it exist, what does it stand for and what are the goals for the business? The clearer you are on these, the easy it will be to decide what you will do and what you won't do.

# CHAPTER 8

# MARKETING FUNDAMENTALS — THEY HAVEN'T CHANGED

We can discuss many business topics to help you succeed in business. However, if you can't attract and keep customers, you don't have a business, no matter how good every other aspect of your business is.

> "When it comes to marketing, what you want is unimportant. It's what your customer wants that matters. And what your customer wants is probably significantly different from what you think they want." - **Michael E. Gerber** [1]

You must know who your ideal customers are. You need to put yourself in their shoes and then implement the marketing that meets their needs.

☞ | Marketing is ALL about customers.

## What does marketing mean to you?

When I ask small business owners what marketing is to them, I get very different responses. Typical answers include it is *"advertising"*, it's *"a web page"*, it's *"promoting my products"*, it's *"cold calling"*, it's *"selling"*, and so on.

The American Marketing Association defines "*marketing*" as:

> **The activity, set of institutions, and processes for creating, communicating, delivering, and exchanging offerings that have value for customers, clients, partners, and society at large.**

Your business is being marketed, whether you do so consciously. Every time you discuss your business, sell a product or service, or come in contact with the world around you, the marketing of your business is happening. How well you are being marketed and how people receive your marketing is quite a different thing.

Marketing is a process that anyone can develop, and then deliver for their business, no matter how small they are. It's not a concept that requires a unique creative gift. As the definition above states, it involves communication. When I say communication, it is breaking through the noise and reaching those you wish to communicate with, namely your customers, either existing or new.

For many small businesses, with little or no experience in marketing, pushing their products, services, and entire business can be daunting. You may feel quite excited about the prospect of putting yourself out there, promoting what you do, what you sell, and chasing potential customers. However, you may also feel petrified about the whole idea of doing this and find selling yourself and your product or services a really uncomfortable process.

Many hate networking or cold calling. Getting customers is hard work. Therefore, as a small business, when you get a customer, it is so rewarding. And so important you look after them.

# Who are your ideal customers?

If you are going to devote your limited marketing resources to anyone, it should be on those you believe to be your ideal customers. This is not a one-off process. Your customers' habits and needs will change; the products and services you offer may change. If you are an established business, you must continually assess what your customers are saying and what they want or need.

Start by establishing as much information as you can about your ideal customers so you can choose the best and lowest cost methods to reach and engage with them. Here is a range of things you might consider:

- How old are they?

- Where do they live?

- What income might they have to spend?

- What do they read, watch and listen to?

- Where do they spend their free time?

- Where do they like to buy products? Online, in supermarkets, high-end shopping centres or small shops?

- How might your product or service improve their day-to-day lives?

- Where do they congregate?

- Are they another business or are they a household?

And so on.

# What makes your business different?

To an uninitiated customer, your business may look exactly the same as your competitors. What you sell or what you do might appear identical. You may be one of a dozen plumbers in a town. You may be a small accountant in a place with many other accountants.

What makes you different from these businesses? Why would a customer choose you rather than one of the many other businesses that do what you do? Can you answer the following question if asked by a potential customer?

> Why should I use you rather than your competitor?

This is a critical question that you need to answer without hesitation. If you can't answer it, how can you expect a customer to see it and choose you?

This is called your **point of difference.** Can you clearly distinguish what sets you apart from other businesses like you? Have you got a unique selling point? When people hear your business' name, what will spring into their minds?

If your only point of difference is price, you need to be cautious. As a small business, the depth of your finances is unlikely to sustain an attack from a larger business keen to steal your customers. Your point of difference needs to offer something that builds loyalty. Price is only one factor in the decision to buy from you. A focused and differentiated message has a better chance of breaking through the clutter and being remembered. Revisit your purpose and your values because this is part of what makes you different from others.

This differentiation is more likely to see you attract and keep more loyal customers, as you offer them something special that your competitors don't.

## What is your "brand"?

Typically, when someone mentions the word "*brand*" many people consider a business' logo. However, your brand is far more than this. Seth Godin defines a brand as:

> *The set of expectations, memories, stories and relationships that, taken together, account for a consumer's decision to choose one product or service over another.*

---

As with marketing, you are creating a brand around you and your business, whether you are doing it consciously. People will form a view of you and your business based on how you hold yourself, how you interact with them, what you say and what you do.

It is also an issue if no-one knows or recognises your brand. Being invisible is not good for business.

We discussed your point of difference. This is very much tied to your brand. When someone thinks of you or your business, or sees your business name or logo, what thoughts come to their mind?

Your brand is intangible. You cannot touch or hold it. It exists only in the minds of your customers. However, you present your brand to the world in the collateral material you use. Your logo, trading name, catch phrases, colours and so on. When existing customers or potential customers see the things that represent your business, what will come to mind?

> Brand is not a logo. Brand is an emotional attachment. It's how you make people feel. It's the experience you create.

There is a close link between your brand and your core purpose. The way you and your team behave around customers, suppliers and other external parties will contribute to the brand they perceive. The logo simply identifies you. What people feel about you and how they want to engage with you will depend on your brand, not the logo.

It is simple things that form in people's minds like *"Don't call those guys; they never call you back,"* or *"That lady tells a great story about her business, but that's not how she delivers her service,"* or *"Those guys were amazing, so good to work with."*

You will have a reputation. You have no choice about that. Where you have a choice is what kind of reputation you want and what efforts you put in to develop that reputation.

As the owner of a small business, your personal brand and your business' brand are so related that they could well be the same thing.

In their book *"The Human Brand"*, **Chris Malone and Susan Fiske** [2] discussed two factors that contribute to your small business' brand. They are your warmth and your competence.

- **Warmth** will be judged by assessing whether you are kind, friendly and good-natured; whether you appear sincere, honest, moral and trustworthy; whether you possess an accommodating orientation; whether you are perceived as being helpful, tolerant, fair, generous, and understanding.

- **Competence** is judged by assessing whether you are efficient, capable, skilful and clever enough to successfully carry out your intentions towards your customer in either the services you offer or the products you provide. Contributing to competence are your strengths, resourcefulness, skills, creativity, and intelligence.

The warmth you show your customers and your competence to deliver the product or service reflect your business brand.

The challenge of brand is being able to measure how your brand is viewed in the marketplace. There are organisations who can measure what people think of your brand, such as Tracksuit. Sadly, these are out of the reach of most small businesses.

You won't have money to get extensive reports prepared on the awareness and attitude to your brand. However, if you deliver a great experience, look after your customers, protect how all your brand collateral is presented, then it will only create positive views of your brand and your business.

## *Your trading name versus your company name*

You may have tried to register your business on the **Companies Office**, but the company name you wanted may have already been taken. You could call your business after your name - Mary Smith (2024) Ltd. The company name is not that important to your marketing. What is important is your **trading name**. This is the name you use in the wider world.

Some small business owners don't want the outside world to know who the shareholders and directors of the company are. They choose a company name that bears no resemblance to their trading name.

The only thing to keep in mind is to not choose a name that conflicts with anyone else in the market. They may have a registered trademark. If so, it may have the ® symbol next to it. However, just because you don't see the symbol, don't assume it's not registered. Even if no one has registered a name or symbol, if the business has been using the name for a while, it may give them the right to it ahead of you.

Besides, why choose a name that will conflict with someone else? You want to distinguish yourself.

When choosing the name, make sure it is easy to understand, makes sense to customers, and if possible, will give you a better chance of being found with online searches. If you're struggling to find the right name for your business, there are handy AI powered tools like **Namelix.com** that can help.

I will discuss **keywords** and **Search Engine Optimisation (SEO)** elsewhere in the book. If you can find a name that might rank well in online searches and meet the business' key messages, then that's perfect. However, this may not always be possible.

One last point. Be careful using trading names that are gimmicky or use deliberate misspellings e.g., *"Kwick"* instead of *"Quick"* Research has found that people look upon these with some scepticism and while they might be unique, people will misspell them in searches, may take a second or two to understand them, and it might turn them off altogether [3].

# The Four Ps of marketing

Before I get into the specifics of what you can do to reach your customers, let's look at some basics of marketing.

**Edmund Jerome McCarthy** put forward in his 1960 book *"Basic Marketing - A Managerial Approach"* [4] his view that there are four fundamental variables that marketing needs to consider. These are the

Four Ps of marketing. McCarthy's concept, while over 60 years old, is as relevant today as it was then.

The Four Ps are:

1.  PRODUCT
2.  PRICE
3.  PLACE
4.  PROMOTION

Over the last few decades, people have refined and added to these Four Ps including Positioning, People, Process and Packaging. However, the original Four Ps are still an excellent place to start when considering your marketing strategies.

## *1.    Your Product (or service)*

People don't buy your product or service; they buy the benefits it brings to their lives. These benefits can come in many forms.

There is a saying in marketing that sums this up *"People don't want a drill, they want a hole, they just need a drill to make it"*. So, benefits, rather than the product or service, should always be your focus.

If your product or service does not help or solve your customer's issues or problems, then you will really struggle.

In his book *"Buyology"*, **Martin Lindstrom** [5] discussed the challenges faced by businesses trying to establish why people make certain purchasing decisions. Most of us struggle to really pin down the basis of some of our purchasing decisions. We don't really know why we choose to buy one item or brand over another. We are often very poor at understanding our own actions and then explaining them. This may make it difficult for you as the seller of a product or service to predict what your customers are likely to do when they probably don't know themselves.

Lindstrom says that tests using **Functional Magnetic Resonance Imaging (FMRI)** which monitors brain activity, demonstrated that our purchasing decisions (as with most of our decisions) are not driven by rational thought processes, but by our emotions.

> When we choose to buy one product over another it is very often an emotional decision. And we often can't accurately explain why we made that decision.

This challenges the idea that asking potential customers what their actions might be, using market research, will answer your questions. As a small business owner, you are also unlikely to have the resources to carry out any sizeable research. The best and lowest cost option may simply be to get the product out into the market as inexpensively as you can and see what the response is. You can continue to revise and adjust your offering based on the response.

## 2.     *Your Pricing*

Determining the price for your product or service can be a challenge, especially for a start-up, when you are selling a unique product, or you are selling your time. There are a few important things to consider in pricing:

- Is your product or service unique?

- How important is pricing in differentiating you from others?

- What are your closest competitor's prices?

- What does it cost to produce or purchase your product or service?

- What value does the customer believe they are receiving from your product or service?

### a)     *Unique product or service*

If you are confident your product is unique or offers something for your customers that no-one else can offer, you're in a powerful position to push your prices up. You still need to be cautious that you are not becoming excessive in your pricing. If you exceed the value the customer believes they are getting from your product, they may simply choose to go without.

It is also very unlikely that any product or service you produce will remain unique for long. Even if you have protected the intellectual property of your product or service, if it's in demand, someone may replicate it and eat into your market.

### b)    *Price versus loyalty*

As a small business, it is very unlikely you will ever be able to compete with bigger businesses solely based on price. They are likely to have much deeper pockets and the capacity to undercut you and even run at a loss to strangle you. Instead, offer more than price so you can build up strong loyalty with your customers.

If you do this, it is far less likely that customers will move if a lower cost option comes their way. Businesses that compete solely on price are really only selling a commodity: a product or service that has no distinguishing difference except price; where people will simply go to the seller who offers the best price.

### c)    *Competitors' prices*

Every customer will have a point where their loyalty is tested if the price difference with your nearest competitor is too great. If your product or service is not unique, you ought to monitor the pricing activity of your nearest competitors. While you may not follow their price changes, you at least need to know where you are relative to them.

It's also worth remembering that you may believe your competitor is the store down the street. It may actually be the business on the other side of the world selling into your region via the internet. Spend some time online determining who all your competitors are.

### d)    *Cost of making or buying your product or service*

There is little point in reducing the price of your product so much that you are not making money selling it. While this would appear to be self-evident, far too many small businesses don't fully understand the cost involved in producing each of their products or services, or the cost of buying and shipping the products. This will mean their sales prices may not deliver sustainable margins.

I will discuss the concepts of fixed and variable costs and gross profit and margins in much greater detail in later chapters. For now, you need to consider what it costs to produce or buy each individual product and the additional fixed costs (or overheads) that you have (for example, your rent).

If you make short-term decisions to lower your prices based on competitor behaviour, you could find yourself in a lot of trouble. You may well sell more and appear to be making more money, but by the time you take out all your costs, you might not be in great shape.

### e)     *Price versus value*

There is a view that the price you charge customers should not reflect the cost to produce the product or service, but the value it adds to the customer. The key point to remember is the value the customer gains will be subjective. The only relevant consideration is what the customer perceives to be the value. This can be difficult to gauge, especially since decisions by customers are not always rational.

## 3.     *Your Place*

When Edmund Jerome McCarthy first put forward the concept of the Four Ps in 1960, the internet was still over 30 years away. He was referring solely to bricks and mortar. These days, your place may be solely online, a building, or both.

The internet offers your small business access to markets that 25 years ago would have been beyond your reach. However, there are still a huge number of small businesses who operate solely out of a physical location.

Even before the COVID-19 lockdowns hit and saw many of us working from home, many small businesses operated out of their homes. This is a great option as it costs you nothing and may work well with your personal life. It's not a great idea if you have a growing number of staff, stock to manage, workshop requirements, and traffic and customer movements. You might find you get a complaint from a neighbour and then your local council might step in if you are in breach of a district plan or are breaching traffic movement rules.

Your choice of location may have been determined by factors other than what best suits your business. The town where you live, where your kids go to school, where your family is located, where your husband, wife or partner works. You may well have purchased a business whose location was beyond your control.

Even with these restrictions, there are still many factors you should consider if you have some ability to decide where you intend setting up your business. Here are a few considerations.

- **Customers**. The most critical consideration about the location you choose is reaching your customers. There's not much point being in a location that's convenient for you if it's inconvenient for your customers.

- **Costs**. Most businesses can't purchase the property they operate from, but must lease a property. Consider what you can afford in lease fees, outgoings and any work you need to do to change the property.

- **Lease conditions.** Make sure you understand the lease terms if you are, like most small businesses, renting a property. If it's a long-term lease, it provides certainty. A short lease is good if you want to exit for larger or different premises or a better location. It could be a significant risk if your location is critical to your business, and the landlord has the ability under the lease to ask you to leave.

- **Space and capacity.** If you choose inadequate space to save costs, it could prove to be a false economy, especially if your goal is growth, and you are tied to a longer lease.

- **Competition**. Depending on your business, you may wish to locate next to competitors, to feed off their customers, or as far away as possible.

- **Suppliers**. If you are heavily reliant on certain suppliers and their speed and availability of response, you may need to be nearby. Otherwise, you may just need to consider freight inwards and outwards.

- **Staff**. If you have employees, you may need to consider their needs.

- **Brand image**. If you have an image you want to portray, your location may enhance or undermine this.

Where you have the option to choose your location, do your homework. Getting it wrong could be very costly and if it involves a longer-term lease, you may be stuck.

> Most importantly, ask yourself what location will best serve your customers and make it easy for them to find and engage with you.

If you are already in a location, but you are not satisfied with it, the decision to move may be a critical one. It is most likely to be a trade-off between the increase in sales you hope to achieve and the costs to move. If your current location is restricting your business from achieving the purpose you have set and the goals you want to achieve, you should seriously consider a move, or be left with regrets of what might have been.

## 4.      *Your Promotion*

This is the "P" that most people associate with marketing - promoting your product or service through some form of advertising.

I cover this in far greater detail in that chapter. The challenge is deciding what form of promotion best meets your needs, as you can't do it all, but the choices are endless.

# Then came more "P"s of marketing

Over the years, the marketing industry has evolved and with that, more "P"s have been added. Some now talk about the Seven "P"s of marketing. The three additional "P"s are **People, Packaging, and Process**.

- **"*People*"** relates to the choices you make when you recruit or assign existing staff to customer relation or sales functions. These roles are not suitable for everyone.

  Some marketing specialists also add customers to the list of "*People*" who are critical to a business?

- **"*Packaging*"** relates to how you present your product. Is it consistent with your brand and does it appeal to your ideal customers? Does it align with your customer preferences?

  There are many variables in packaging that might be important for your business. Consider these examples:

  - Safe and secure (**Amazon**),
  - Helps the product last longer (**Anchor milk**),
  - Sense of occasion (**Apple**),
  - Environmentally friendly (**Body Shop**).

  What would your customer expect from your packaging?

- **"*Process*"** is the end-to-end connection between your business and your customers. This covers the process from the moment a potential customer searches for you, interacts with your website, calls you, walks into your shop, or emails you, and finally buys your product or service.

  Whatever all these connection points are, they need to be helpful to your customers. I touch on this further when we discuss websites and the systems and processes you implement in your business.

# Another important "P" of marketing - Positioning

Another "P" of marketing, which is probably as important as all the others, is your **positioning** in the market. This further defines what you are about and who your customers are.

Your positioning relates to where you sit in the market relative to your competitors.

- Is your offering a lower cost option relative to competitors, targeting the budget conscious customer?

- Are you in the high margin, quality market where those you are appealing to are prepared to pay a premium?

- If you offer a service, is it focused on quality, even if it means you lose out on jobs because others undercut your price?

- Do you offer great service but at a much lower price than larger, more expensive, existing businesses?

> Whatever your position is in the market you need to be crystal clear on what you stand for, what your purpose is, and who your ideal customers are.

# The Marketing Funnel

As far back as 1898, **Elias St Elmo Lewis** [6] developed the concept that a customer's journey starts first when they discover you exist, then learning about you, then contacting you, purchasing off you, and hopefully coming back again. His model was called the **AIDA model,** after Attention,

Interest, Desire, and Action. It is also called the Purchasing or **Marketing Funnel.**

Lewis described the process a salesperson must lead a potential customer through in order to achieve a sale. He believed this was a linear process, from one step to the next, the steps being Attention, Interest, Desire, and Action.

Even after over 120 years, these principles still apply.

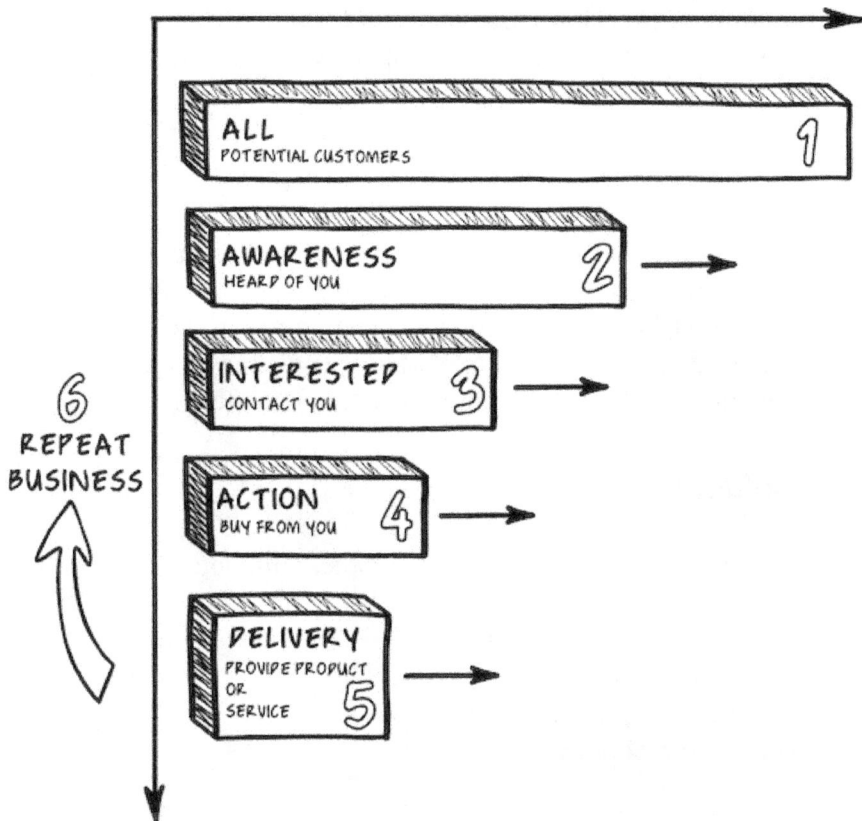

Let's take this concept and expand on it a little, as it relates to your small business and the entire marketing process, not just a one-off sale.

Consider the funnel for your business as a graph like that shown in the figure above. The impetus of your marketing efforts is described in each bar of The Marketing Funnel.

## Column 1.    "All".

Identify all your potential customers. Anyone who could use your product or service in the area you are selling. This could be a huge list.

## Column 2.    "Awareness"

Even though a very large number could use your product or service, it's likely most have never heard of you. Find the best way to engage with these potential customers at a budget you can afford so they have at least heard of you. This is represented by Column 2, which is much smaller than Column 1.

## Column 3.    "Interested"

Once they have heard of you, attempt to spark enough interest so they contact you now or at a future date. Some sort of **call to action** will assist in getting them to contact you (e.g., *"Contact us for a discount"*). This is Column 3. Many people may have now heard of you, but will they do anything with that knowledge?

## Column 4.    "Action"

Hopefully, if they call you for a quote, with an enquiry. walk into your store or visit your website, their experience is such that they buy from you. Unfortunately, this is not always the case. That is why Column 4 is smaller than Column 3. The percentage of sales represented by Column 4 relative to enquiries (Column3) is called your **conversion rate.**

## Column 5.    "Delivery"

After all this effort, to gain a customer, do everything you can to deliver the product or service as best you can. It has cost you too much time and money to guide the customer through the funnel only to under-deliver and disappoint them.

## Arrow 6.    "Repeat Business"

If you do a great job, the hope is the customer will use you again and also refer you to others. This then increases each column thereafter and hopefully that continues.

## *Tracking the funnel - tracking leads*

A process many businesses follow is to track the numbers of people in each step of the funnel.

While the ultimate measure of success in marketing is sales, the focus needs to be more on all the stages of the funnel that lead to a sale. If the number and quality of the possible customers making their way into the funnel are increasing, the sales will come.

The leads you are getting could come from phone calls, emails, meetings with potential clients, website visits, exhibitions, or networking sessions. Capturing and tracking these leads is invaluable.

If a lead turns into a quote for work, this is the next stage of the journey through the funnel.

Finally, how many of these quotes were successful?

If you are tracking leads, enquiries, quotes and finally sales, you can track your conversion rates.

You may have a record of winning half the quotes you submit. Alternatively, you might expect about half those who come into your shop or onto your e-commerce website will buy something.

Different methods of marketing g will deliver different conversion rates. The quality of leads from an email campaign will be low, typically 2-5%. However, a well developed online marketing campaign with well-researched keywords and SEO will deliver much higher conversions, but also costs more per lead.

The more you track each step in the funnel, the more confident you will become about where the best leads come from and what your conversion rates are likely to be.

For example, if your marketing gets you in front of 200 people, experience has shown you that around 10 are likely to contact you. You have also found that of these 10 people about 5, or 50%, will buy something. If each sale delivers a profit of $100, it means that if you generate 200 leads, you should deliver $500 in sales. If the cost to get those 200 leads exceeds $500, then that marketing was not good value for money. If, however, your average sale was $1000 then it was money well spent.

If you are busy and don't have the time to keep your marketing efforts going, it means your leads will drop. If you are tracking leads and you are finding they are falling, for any reason, it gives you prior warning of a potential downturn in future sales.

Clearly, these trends will move around, but the more you track your leads, the more confident you can be about the value of your marketing and the amount of future sales. If you are achieving the same leads but the sales are falling off, it will prompt you to explore why and shift your efforts.

This is where a great **customer relationship management** (CRM) system is really important. This information could be critical to establishing what your forward sales volumes are like and getting prior warning if customer patterns are changing.

---

### FIRST TABLE
### Humble beginnings and a simple idea

Mat Weir and his family once visited a small French restaurant in Queenstown that was offering a '*locals secret*', a 50% discount for early diners. The restaurant aimed to attract customers during its quietest period and create an atmosphere that would draw in more diners as the evening progressed. Mat, who had been building websites since he was fifteen, saw the potential to scale this simple idea into an online marketplace.

In September 2014, he launched First Table in Queenstown.

His initial success came with ten partner restaurants in Queenstown, a town known for its high concentration of dining venues. Mat noted in hindsight that it was the perfect place to launch the concept because of the ability to reach a critical mass quickly as word-of-mouth spread. While Auckland has become a significant market for First Table, had he discovered the idea there, rather than Queenstown, it would have been a much tougher place to launch.

---

The First Table model allows restaurants to sign up at no cost, aside from offering a 50% discount on the food bill for two to four people for an otherwise empty table. Diners pay a small booking fee to access the offer.

The idea quickly took off in Queenstown, and Mat set off across New Zealand in a campervan. By day, he visited restaurants to pitch the idea and learn what resonated with owners and managers. In the evening, he coded and then drove to the next city.

He initially engaged a few part-time salespeople on commission, but this approach achieved little, as they were not fully committed. Mat realised he needed to hire dedicated employees to join him on his journey.

The concept continued to gain momentum, and Mat saw the opportunity to expand internationally. He flew to the UK and connected with an ex-Queenstown resident and loyal First Table customer, eager to support the journey. Together, they began signing up restaurants across the region. After a few weeks in England, Mat boarded a plane back to New Zealand. By the time he landed, the UK website was live and ready to go, marking the official launch of First Table in the UK.

First Table's success lay in its ability to act swiftly and adapt to new markets – something larger businesses cannot achieve.

Mat bootstrapped First Table's growth from day one, never seeking outside investment. While this is a characteristic of many New Zealand start-ups, and demonstrates an ability to grow within one's means, investors need to be confident start-ups can maximise the benefit of any money they invest in the business.

In 2023, First Table sought equity funding through Snowball Effect. The large subscriber base and broad appeal of First Table attracted strong interest, raising over $3.5 million, with Invest South and Mainland Angel Investors as the major contributors.

By 2024, First Table had partnered with 2,200 restaurants across New Zealand, Australia, and the United Kingdom, and over 1.7 million people had created a First Table account. With a global team of around 40 staff, Mat continues to seek new opportunities in the hospitality industry to help diners discover the best restaurants and deals.

# CHAPTER 9

# REACHING YOUR CUSTOMERS — ADVERTISING — THE OPTIONS KEEP CHANGING

While the fundamentals of marketing have been around for over a century, the methods of reaching and engaging with customers have changed significantly during that time.

The choice of methods to advertise is significant and continues to grow. While your small businesses will have a limited marketing budget, your issue is not the amount you spend on advertising. What is critical is that the advertising you choose delivers the value you expect. It you are spending a lot and it is delivering high-quality leads which then turn into customers and sales, then it is money well spent.

There is a table in the Appendices of this book that provides details of the traditional advertising options to consider and what the pros and cons are of those options.

Let's explore how the world of advertising has changed for business and what options may be most appropriate for your business.

## The changing face of advertising

Over the decades, even the centuries, businesses have been looking for ways to promote their products and services through advertising in whatever medium was available.

The first newspaper in this country was The New Zealand Gazette, that started in 1839. Since then, many newspapers have come and gone. The New Zealand Herald was born in 1869 and continues to this day.

In this era, businesses had few other options to advertise, and customers had few other outlets to get their information about the world. The newspaper was pretty much their only choice. So, if you read the newspaper, you would likely see the advertisement.

Radio was first broadcast to Kiwis in the 1920s, with advertising only allowed from the 1930s. This presented another medium that businesses could use to force themselves in front of customers. The golden years of radio were from the 1930s to the 1960s. When radios started appearing in motor vehicles, radio advertisers had a captive listener. This is still the case today, and is why radio remains a viable, if not high-cost, option for small businesses.

New Zealand was slow to adopt television compared to the rest of the world. It came in the 1960s. Television advertising came soon after. Television would dominate our lives for the next five decades. Those who could afford the costs to advertise on TV had an almost guaranteed audience. For most small businesses, it was well out of reach.

In recent years, the growth of digital television, such as TVNZ+, is bringing more accessible advertising options for small business. Digital television will be lower cost and allow more targeted advertising. While it is in its infancy in New Zealand, growth in this medium seems inevitable. It should allow more affordable options for small businesses to use television advertising.

These traditional advertising options were all that existed in the marketplace for decades until the internet was born. With this came an explosion of options that small businesses could use to reach a huge audience for a relatively small investment.

Social media advertisements were relatively inexpensive. Google AdWords allows a small business, with some clever choice of keywords, to drive traffic to their website for cents-per-click.

The internet has now created a proliferation of choice not only for the small business advertiser, but the consumer. This has occurred while the traditional methods of advertising also remain.

While paper-based newspapers are dying, all news outlets are now online. The NZ Herald continues to rank in the top five most viewed websites in the country and is the number one Kiwi based website that is searched (only offshore websites like Google, Facebook and YouTube rank ahead of it).

While free to air television is also under treat with declining numbers, it remains a powerful medium for those who can afford it. Add to this the growth of streaming channels and television remains a choice for those big brands with the budgets.

Even the simple billboard that once provided a single image has been replaced by electronic billboards that provide multiple images every hour, day, and night.

Your small business is now overwhelmed with choices on where to put your meagre marketing budget. Your potential customers also have a huge choice of the medium to turn to get their information. This makes the challenge of reaching your customers increasingly difficult.

If you decide on social media as your outlet of choice, which platform will you choose? Facebook, TikTok, Instagram, X (Twitter) LinkedIn, WeChat, WhatsApp? If you choose AdWords campaigns, will you be able to force your message through the enormous volume of websites who may not be a competitor, but are competing for the top three spots on a website search?

What this all means is you have an increasing volume of choice on where you spend your marketing dollar, but your customers also have an almost infinite choice of options where they spend their time, whether online or through traditional media options.

This means the importance of being crystal clear on the fundamentals of your customer has never been more critical. Understanding the basics is so important. You must truly understand your purpose and what you stand for. You need to be razor sharp on defining your position in the market, your point of difference and your ideal customers.

> It has never been more critical to understand who your ideal customers are and how you can serve their needs. Only then have you any hope of choosing the advertising that has the best chance of success.

If you choose a medium to advertise, you can't sit still. Things continue to change. Your marketing efforts must include time to research what works.

And even more challenging is staying abreast of what your customers want and need.

# Advertising trends - the growth of digital and decline of TV and newspapers

The **New Zealand Advertising Standards Authority** keeps track of the trends in advertising in New Zealand. This provides a clear picture about where we have spent our advertising dollars over the last 10 years.[1]

The total spend on advertising has increased from $2,177 million in 2012 to $3,389 million in 2022, an increase of a little over 50%. However, in that period, the spend on digital marketing has increased from $366 million to $1,778 billion - an almost five-fold increase. This is about 52% of the total spend on all advertising, and this has increased from 16% in 2012.

In this period, the amount spent on radio has fluctuated but remained about the same, between $250 and $275 million. While these statistics don't explain why radio is holding up, having captive audiences while driving, especially in peak hour traffic, is a contributing factor.

Television and newspaper advertising have both been declining almost every year over this period. This is in terms of both the amount being spent and the percentage of the total spend. In 2012, advertisers spent over 25% of their budget on newspapers, coming second only to television, where they spent 28%. In 2022 newspapers had dropped to just over 6% and television only 15%.

Therefore, even though the online world is getting more dispersed, with more choices, it is the dominant place to promote your business. For small business it remains the most cost-effective option to advertise and reach customers.

# Online marketing

Putting aside its challenges, online marketing is still the most cost-effective and powerful option for small businesses.

It offers your business unprecedented options to reach customers and markets that would have been totally out of your reach 15 to 20 years ago.

Online marketing also offers very detailed analytics about who has interacted with your business. As you can track all the actions by online users, you can receive quick and accurate feedback on what marketing has worked and what hasn't. You can see what pages people have visited on your website, how long they stayed, where they came from, what order they visited and so on. This is one of the most significant advantages of online marketing over traditional forms of advertising for small business. In the past, you would not have had the resources to research the effectiveness of your advertising campaigns that online marketing allows.

The growth of online marketing and sales has brought about an enormous industry of marketing companies to support small businesses.

I do not intend to cover the details that would allow you to implement your own Google Ads campaign. I won't tell you how to design your webpage, or your LinkedIn, Facebook or Instagram profile.

My aim here is to guide you towards the best mix of marketing options to align with your goals for the business and to provide you with some principles to develop your online presence.

If you are a heavy online and social media user with strong IT skills, then there is an endless supply of material to help you develop your own online presence with minimal external help (e.g., Digital Boost). [2] If this is not your forte, there are many options available to get the help you need, hopefully at a price you can afford. I am certainly the latter of these groups and have called on the support of website developers and social media experts to guide me.

The pace of change is likely to outstrip your knowledge and if you are running a business, you simply won't have the time to build that knowledge and then implement the marketing you will need. So, you will probably need to continue seeking external expertise.

Don't underestimate the amount of work maintaining a high-quality online presence might take. Once you have built a website, entered the social media world, or blogged, you are unlikely to see much of an increase in sales from day one. It's not that simple. You need to make ongoing efforts to connect with your potential customers. It may take many connections with a potential customer before they act, connect with you, and then buy from you.

As with all your marketing efforts, you need to be selective, as you can't do it all. You will also need to be prepared to try things and fail. It's no longer possible to bet on one form of marketing, even one form of online marketing. Things change, so you need to keep trying new ways to reach potential customers. At least if it's online, the cost of failure is far less than other traditional marketing options.

## *The importance of your online content*

The key purpose of the content you put online is to attract and keep customers by providing them with relevant and valuable information. Whether you use written information, diagrams, illustrations, video or audio, it must add value. If done well, the content can also tell a story about your business. It can also be a **call to action** for those watching or reading the content. Educate the viewer, and perhaps alert them to your product or service to improve their situation.

The development of high-quality online content is called **content marketing**.

One challenge of content marketing is that it may require you to volunteer a lot of free information. However, if the reader gets value from that information, it raises your perceived competence. If the quality of your online content is high, it will increase the trust readers have in you. They are more likely to visit again (and again), if done well, essentially giving you permission to engage with them.

In developing any content, first stop, and ask yourself if that content will genuinely help a potential customer. Is it interesting, unique, even humourous? They, like you, are very time-poor. If you are solely plugging your business and what you are providing adds little value or interest, you can't expect a significant result.

> **Does your content answer the questions your ideal customer is asking?**

If you're stuck trying to work out what content to create, try making a list of common questions that your customers ask you. Then review your website to see how well you answer those questions.

Unfortunately, developing great content takes time. One of the most powerful forms of content is video. Unfortunately, even the most basic forms of video take time to produce. If you want to provide informative *"how-to"* videos, especially if they entail editing, it can chew up large amounts of time if you do it yourself.

## Your website

There were 5.03 million internet users in New Zealand in February 2024. This means 95.7 percent of the total population is online. [3]

There are also about 400 million websites around the world. [4]

With this much traffic, building your website could simply be like putting a small sign in the middle of the Amazon jungle and hoping people find it.

While a website is now almost a given for any business, it requires effort to make it work for you. It needs to fit in with your business' broader strategy. It may be the only connection between you and potential customers, so it needs to reflect well on who you are, what you stand for, and your point of difference.

Get clear on what you hope to achieve from your website.

If your business is local to a small region and most of your customers come through word-of-mouth or from a demographic with low internet use, you may not need to invest significant effort in a website. However, if you rely heavily on it to attract new customers and sell to them online, expect to devote more time to achieve the reach you are seeking.

## Do you build a website yourself or seek help?

This is a decision only you can make and depends on your computer literacy. In saying that, there are far more platforms available now that allow business owners to do it themselves. Web-platforms, like **Squarespace, Rocketspark or Wix**, allow businesses to build their own websites. Even more sophisticated platforms like **Wordpress**, one of the most widely used around the word, can be modified by a small business owner without any specialist skills, with some basic training.

Even if you don't want to build the site yourself and you get a web developer to do it for you, it's really important that you can change the website whenever you want. The more you add fresh information to the site the better. You don't want to be calling, and paying, your web developer every time you want to make minor changes.

You may well have the skills and the interest to do it yourself, but most small business owners won't have the time. Quality web development takes time and experience. It may well be better value to engage a web developer than distracting you from the business.

## Getting on page one of Google

Your website may be there simply to validate who you are with customers who already know about you. However, it could be your primary tool to reach and connect with all potential customers. In either case, you should still apply some simple methods to increase your chances of being found.

If the primary reason for your website is to attract customers and entice them to follow your marketing funnel through your website to where you make a sale (either online or through your physical store), you will need to think in far more detail about how to develop your website.

**Search Engine Optimisation** (SEO) techniques and the requirements to be found change continually. Maintaining expertise in the best SEO techniques requires specialist knowledge.

An important part of your website and other online content design is understanding the keyword searches people are using. Keywords are the individual words, or the string of words people are typing into a search engine to find the information they are after. With the increase in verbal searches, these keywords could be different to those typed into a computer or mobile device. With the growing use of artificial intelligence tools like ChatGPT, it is unclear how this might change search techniques.

If you understand these keywords, you can build them into all your online content, especially your website. There are free tools online you could use to do keyword research, like **MOZ.com**. [5]

Some techniques to increase your chances of forcing your way up the rankings are:

- Choose keywords throughout your website that are most likely to be what a person will choose when looking for what you are selling.

- Where possible, create pages for your website that are targeted at one specific keyword.

- Include the keyword in the page header, page description, main heading and in subheadings where relevant.

- Use keywords in natural phrasing and use them a lot throughout the webpage.

- Provide high-quality content on your website. Make it information rich and valuable to your target customer.

- Update your content regularly with new information.

- Give all your web pages descriptive names as Google often displays search results as a link to the page title.

- The more interconnected your website is with other websites, the more highly ranked it is likely to be. This is called **backlinking**.

- The more highly ranked the website that refers to you is, the better your ranking will be.

- When connecting with other websites, use hyperlink titles that are descriptive and consistent with your target keywords.

- A well-designed website with well-organised pages will rank more highly.

- The more popular your website becomes, the higher ranked you will become.

Remember, search engines like Google change their processes all the time and the online world is very dynamic. You need to keep reviewing and refining the best techniques so that potential customers can find your website.

I believe even if you are an expert, you should still turn to external people, at least to offer you an independent set of eyes on your website design. If this is your primary method of connecting with current and future customers, you need to do it really well.

## SEO, UX, UI and other website jargon

In the world of website design, there has been a level of tension between the developers focused on driving people to your website and designers who want a site that is easy to use and really helpful. I have discussed SEO. It is of little use having an amazing website that no one can find. You need great SEO built into the design coupled with really effective paid advertising campaigns.

**UX** or **User Experience** and **UI**, **User Interface**, are concepts that relate to the design of the website. It describes how it's laid out, how easy it is to navigate, the choice of buttons, colours, page layouts and so on. If a user, who will hopefully become a customer, finds your site and then really struggles to find what they want, you will quickly lose them.

Therefore, a great website design considers both SEO and the experience a user will have when they find the site.

If you are new to these concepts and website design, before going live with your new website, get a few people to use it.

The concepts of UX and UI become even more important if you have an e-commerce website. After the user finds the site and navigates around it, your hope is they become an instant customer and enjoy the experience enough that they pull their credit card from their pocket and buy from you.

We discuss e-commerce websites a little more when discussing sales.

## Mobile devices

With the rapid increase in mobile devices, it is now almost certain a customer will use their mobile device to search.

With six million phones in New Zealand, we have more smart phones in this country than people. [6]

A customer is most likely to make a spontaneous purchasing decision from their smartphone. When designing your website, you must consider making it mobile and computer friendly.

Most good website platforms now incorporate both desktop and smartphone design. Make sure you know what every page on your website will look like on both a desktop and a smart phone before finalising the design.

> Google now determines their Search Engine rankings based on the mobile performance of the site – not the desktop

If your website doesn't perform well on a mobile, it will struggle to show up on a Google search.

## Permission marketing

Seth Godin, in his book *"Permission Marketing"*, put forward his view that, in the online world, businesses need to move away from traditional marketing techniques to **permission marketing.**

A business normally forces its way into your life through a TV or radio advertisement, an internet pop-up or banner, billboard or any of the many approaches we are used to seeing. This is called **interruption marketing.** The hope for a business using this technique is that the interruption will catch the customer's attention and result in them taking some action. The billions of dollars that go into advertising are usually based on this technique.

Seth Godin believes we should do more to get the permission of potential customers to start a relationship with us. Over time, this will hopefully lead to sales.

The idea is to get potential customers to give you their contact details so you can build a relationship with them. Most customers will protect these details (a little like they protect their wallets.) and are unlikely to hand over their details unless they feel they are receiving something in exchange. In your online activity, you can offer future customers something of value to gain their details and permission to interact. This could be good quality free information, or the chance to win products or services.

While traditional interruption marketing remains important, you're likely to have much greater success if you can build a relationship with your potential customers so they want to use you, rather than pushing yourself on them. Besides, you will need to spend significantly more to produce sales through a prolonged interruption marketing campaign.

## *Email marketing*

Another powerful form of online marketing is email marketing. This is where you engage directly with existing customers or potential customers using email communication. While you can do this on an email-by-email basis, there are some excellent email marketing tools on the market that can send large numbers of emails automatically. They also provide detailed information on the success of an email campaign.

One of the most popular and free systems, at least for a basic level of use, is **Mailchimp**. There are many others.

Many website platforms have email marketing as an add-on feature, like **Squarespace**. There are also some very sophisticated platforms (e.g., **Infusionsoft**, by Keap**, Salesforce or HubSpot**) that allow a highly automated level of email interaction with users.

The digital systems that allow you to collate customer information and communicate electronically are called **customer relationship management (CRM)** systems.

Choosing the right CRM follows the same criteria you would follow to choose any system. I cover these in the chapter on operations. Some

**Enterprise Resource Planning systems** or ERPs, which are more sophisticated SaaS software systems, have CRM systems built into them. Consider this when choosing your SaaS.

Email marketing allows you to personalise communication, direct people to your website, your Facebook page or other social media site. You can offer deals or simply provide high-quality content that you believe will benefit the reader.

I am sure you have been on the receiving end of emails that serve no purpose other than to fill up your inbox. No matter how good the quality of your email is, most people will delete it without even looking at it. You are only likely to get 2 to 5% of those you contact responding to the emails in the way you wish. However, you can send out hundreds of emails in the one **email blast,** at no cost, increasing your chance of a higher **click though rate** to your website or social media page.

As with any online interaction, it needs to be of value to the reader.

Another very important requirement of email campaigns is ensuring the customer, or their email system, does not treat your emails as spam. If those receiving your emails report them as spam in their email account, your CRM could block you from sending further emails to potential customers. If you are using email marketing software for bulk emails, they may remove you from their site. Worse still, you could be in breach of the law.

New Zealand's **Unsolicited Electronic Messages Act (UEMA)**, also called the **anti-spam law,** covers the requirements around electronic communications, including the sending of spam emails. Under this law, you cannot use harvesting software, or other means, to get email lists to send bulk email blasts if you have not received permission from those people to do so.

A few key questions to ask when sending emails, to reduce your chances of being considered spam:

- Did the recipient of the email give you permission to engage with them?

- Do they know why you are engaging with them?

- Have you authenticated who you are?

- Can the recipient opt out of emails or unsubscribe from further emails (as opposed to reporting you as spam)?

- Is any of the information misleading?

An important point to remember it is the receiver of the email who decides if it is spam, not you. You may feel what you are providing is extremely useful and of high quality. If the recipient doesn't agree with you, they could report your emails as spam.

So consider what you are sending and whom you are sending it to so you can make the most of your email marketing.

## *Social media*

The growth in social media has been extraordinary. Almost five billion people, or 63% of the world's population, use social media. They also use multiple platforms. [7,8] Almost all the research shows that the use of social media will remain strong and needs to be factored into a small business' online marketing strategy.

In 2024, 78.7% of the New Zealand population were using social media [9.] So, it's safe to say that nearly every adult in this country is or has used social media.

There are many social media options you could choose to reach your customers. This list represents the world's most popular social media platforms. WhatsApp and WeChat are not as widely used in New Zealand as the other platforms.

Social media is changing continually. In the past, people only used it for personal communications. Now, it is a major place to do business.

| SOCIAL MEDIA | START DATE | APPROX NUMBER OF MONTHLY ACTIVE USERS WORLDWIDE |
|---|---|---|
| FACEBOOK | 2004 | 3.05 BILLION (NZ 2.95 MILLION) |
| WHATSAPP | 2009 | 2.78 BILLION |
| YOUTUBE | 2005 | 2.49 BILLION (NZ4.24 MILLION) |
| INSTAGRAM | 2010 | 2.04 BILLION (NZ2.15 MILLION) |
| WECHAT | 2011 | 1.32 BILLION |
| TIKTOK | 2016 | 1.2 BILLION (NZ 1.65 MILLION) |
| LINKEDIN | 2003 | 424 MILLION (NZ 2.5 MILLION) |

The core marketing principles are just as relevant to social media as any other marketing media. You need to know your customers. This will influence which social media site you favour and how you use it. As with any online content, make sure it adds value to your customers and raises their view of your competence and trustworthiness. Who are you trying to reach? What do you want to tell them? What is your point of difference?

Engaging short videos are one of the most consumed forms of content on social media. [10] While many of us waste enormous volumes of time watching pointless, quirky videos, from a business perspective, content without a purpose is unlikely to work. High-quality content has been, and remains, very important.

Many small businesses choose social media as their only source of online marketing. A key consideration with this is determining how much freedom and control you want over your online presence. Remember, if you use a social media platform, the site dictates what you can and can't do. If you develop your own website, you have complete ownership and the freedom to manage how you interface with your customers.

Many small businesses use both, with each medium being a means to link to the other. If you have the resources to do this, having both a website and a social media presence is far more powerful than one alone.

You should choose the social media that best meets your customers' needs. If you can achieve this using many sites, you are unlikely to have the time to be active on every site. Therefore, choose the site (or sites) you are most familiar with and enjoy being on the most.

As with all your marketing efforts, review what is working and what isn't, and be prepared to change course.

## *Blogs*

**Blogs** (short for **web logs**) are another low-cost means of sharing valuable content online. They are also an excellent place to get views from other business owners in similar situations to you.

You can provide blogs through a vast range of small business forums. Social media sites like LinkedIn allow you to enter blog discussions with like-minded people. There are many websites and blog sites devoted to small business.

As with social media, blogs should be a way of providing useful content to potential or existing customers. Once they come to your social media page, you can direct them to your website.

If you offer good quality information in your blogs, it will hopefully trigger discussions or debate. It may not lead directly to more customers, but it will increase people's awareness of you, will lift your credibility with peers, and may lead to referrals.

## *Online advertising*

Kiwis are big users of online advertising, and we draw in a lot of money from our online activities. Total digital advertising revenue in New Zealand grew by 4.3% year-on-year, reaching $2.112 billion in 2024. Almost half of this revenue (47%) comes from website searches. Social media advertising generates about 10% of the revenue. [11]

If you are a big user of the web, social media platforms, and apps, you will be aware of the wide range of methods advertisers use to get an advertisement in front of you. The sophistication and use of your online data to find you is extensive, if not a little scary.

While many of these adverts will be very annoying to you as an online user, it does not mean you should avoid using them to get in front of your own customers.

Before deciding on an online, paid advertising strategy, consider the principles of your marketing. Also consider combining traditional and online method for campaigns, assuming your budget allows, as one could support the other.

**MediaWorks,** who still run several radio stations, sold out of their television interests in 2020 and diversified into outdoor advertising (for example, billboards and the back of buses) and online advertising. When they run a radio campaign, they encourage businesses to run a parallel online campaign. This means that when people hear the radio commercial, and then do an online search, it will drive traffic to your website. If there is no online presence, the person's search, triggered by the radio commercials, may simply pull up a competitor's website and drive your potential customer to them. Ironically, your expensive radio campaign may help a competitor more than you.

The most popular online advertising media is Search Advertising via **Google Ads** (formally called **AdWords**). This is based on a **pay-per-click** (PPC), meaning you only pay when someone clicks on the advertisement. To push your Google Ad to the top of searches, you need to choose the best keywords. The cost of these words is determined through an auction - the most popular keywords cost the most.

Keep in mind that those you are competing with for keywords and, therefore, the means to score high in searches may be unrelated to your business and not be an actual competitor. If you are in a highly searched business sector, your online competitors could be enormous companies, with deep pockets, meaning keywords are very expensive.

For example, a keyword like *"best mortgage rate"* is likely to have a lot of competition and be very expensive. Banks will be prepared to spend a lot to get one click, and they have the budget to do so. They only need to get one mortgage signed up to gain a significant financial return on these clicks.

Google Ads were originally just the sponsored website link that appeared at the top of a search. You can now choose from a wide range of **Google Ad** options to promote your business, including **Google Shopping**, **Google Display**, **Google Videos**, **Performance Max** and more.

Determining the right mix for your business can be a matter of trial and error, but specialist digital advertising companies should be able to help you narrow down to the most effective campaign types to avoid you spending on channels that are unlikely to deliver a good return for your money.

Advertisements on social media sites such as LinkedIn and Facebook can also be a cost-effective option. [12]

The advantage of this type of advertising is that you can tailor campaigns to target particular audiences. You can also gain detailed insights into the success of the campaigns.

There are a range of tools you can use to establish your keywords. However, most small businesses turn to the experts to help develop Google Ad and social media advertising campaigns.

If you engage a marketing business to manage your online advertising, make sure you understand what they can deliver and ensure it meets your needs. You need to be sure you know what you are getting for your money. Typically, those providing these services will charge a fixed management fee per month to set up and monitor the campaign, as well as setting budgets that are used to cover the costs per click.

While you need a reasonable time for the advertisement campaign to work, typically at least three months, if they are not delivering, review the campaign and try something different. This process can't be static. It needs to be reviewed and refined.

## Some tips on logos and colours

While your brand is far more than a logo and a trading name, the imagery you use is still very important. You can spend a lot of money getting logos designed. However, there are plenty of people who will do it for a small investment. You may also have a go at a logo design yourself, which is more achievable with AI tools like **Looka.com.**

Keep in mind you need to ensure your images and logos do not conflict with other businesses. These businesses may or may not have registered their trademarks.

Ensure the imagery has no hidden meanings. Sadly, people have designed logos only to find others, look at them and see something very different to you - and it may offend or be inappropriate.

Colours also have meanings. There has been a significant amount of research done on these meanings. This is typically called **Colour Theory** [13]

These are a few examples of what different colours mean:

- **Red**: energy, passion, excitement, and urgency
- **Orange**: friendliness, warmth, and enthusiasm
- **Yellow**: optimism, clarity, and happiness
- **Green**: growth, health, and tranquility
- **Blue**: trust, reliability, and professionalism
- **Purple**: creativity, luxury, and wisdom
- **Pink**: femininity, romance, and sweetness
- **Black**: sophistication, elegance, and authority
- **White**: purity, simplicity, and cleanliness. [13]

It is worth creating a palate of logo and colour options, presented side by side. Get a few other people to give you their opinions. Even throwing them on a social media post and asking for strangers to help you select isn't a bad idea. Websites like **Coolors.co** can be very useful in helping you to create a colour palette for your brand.

# Your brand rules - never break them

Once you have settled on your trading name, logos and colours, collate all this information in the one document. Get the codes for the colours you chose. These will typically use a **colour coding standard** like **RGB** or **HEX** (e.g., HEX#371616 or RGB 55, 22, 22)

Make sure that you or others always follow your brand rules when producing marketing material. This could be in emails, on business cards, letterheads, vehicles, clothing, social media, websites and more. While your brand is more than this, it is still what people see and it needs to be consistent every time.

## Word of mouth - the most powerful marketing of all

I will discuss a vast array of options you can use to market your business. While all can assist, no marketing is more powerful or gets better conversions or leads than word-of-mouth.

> We act on the recommendation from someone we trust far more than we will from any marketing campaign, no matter how good it is.

This is the case no matter how slick your marketing campaigns might be. We will even listen to the referral of a stranger ahead of a business' marketing messages. How many of us have chosen a tour, a hotel or a business based on a Google ranking, other star rating or written feedback provided by people we have never met?

Doing an amazing job is the best way to build word-of-mouth. If you don't and your customer leaves unhappy, no amount of marketing can undo the damage a bad review will cause.

The ultimate marketing strategy every small business seeking to achieve is one that sees all their work coming from referrals and word-of-mouth. The conversions from an enquiry to a sale will be higher than any other marketing you do. It is also the lowest cost marketing there is - it's free.

The challenge you will have, especially if your business is relatively new, is that the word is not out there anywhere near what you need, and not enough people know about you. That is why you must resort to other forms of marketing - and hope, over time, that if you keep doing an amazing job for your customers, the business will come in.

> The most powerful marketing you will ever do, without fail, is doing a great job for your customer - every time

# Influencer marketing

With the growth of the internet and social media platforms, has come the growth of **influencer marketing**. This is where someone on a social media platform we follow recommends a product or service. Because we follow these people, even though we don't know them, we are more likely to respect their advice. If they have used a product or service and like it, you are also likely to choose it.

Therefore, influencer marketing is like another form of word-of-mouth marketing.

There is a perception, which is perhaps justifiable, that all influencers are young, attractive people pushing beauty products. The growing reality is very different, including in New Zealand. Influencers exist in all demographics. Older people, sports people, musicians, disc jockeys, former actors, journalists and more. A quick visit to the website of one of New Zealand's leading talent agencies, **Johnson & Laird**, will give you an idea of the influencers they represent and what they can do for you. This organisation was originally there to act as agents for entertainers. Now these same entertainers are offering businesses access to their fan base to promote their products.

An influencer may choose not to promote your product or service as your brand may not align with theirs - no matter what you are prepared to pay.

The influencer doesn't need a huge list of followers to be beneficial. While it helps, it's the quality of the followers and whether their followers are your ideal customers. You may only need a few people to act on the influencers' advice and purchase what they are promoting to make it worth your while.

If influencers are being paid to advertise a product or service, they need to show that is the case. Failure to do this is a breach of the **Advertising Standards Authority (ASA).** There is a long list of breach notices, listed on the ASA's website, of influencers who advertised a product without telling people they were being paid to do so.[14]

The influencer usually decides the process by which they promote your product or service, not you. For example, if it's by video, they will probably want to develop the video as they see fit. There may be restrictions on how the influencer will let you use the material after they have finished their campaign, if you can use it at all.

Finally, while influencer marketing is growing, it remains a minor player in the online marketing space. It is worth considering it as the costs are not prohibitive, depending on the influencers' reach. It would be wise not to use only this form of online marketing, but to use it as a part of your broader marketing strategy.

## Analyse what worked through customer feedback

No matter what methods you use to market your small business, you need to consider how you track what has worked. With traditional marketing, you may have to ask customers when they first engage with you how they found you - newspapers, paper drops, radio and so on.

It is likely the customer may not recall how they came to contact you, but it is always helpful to ask.

It is also worth finding some simple ways to get feedback from customers about how good your product or service was and what you could do to improve it. This could be through online survey methods (like **Survey Monkey**), or simply by talking directly with your customers.

Many times, the best feedback is unsolicited, and people will often do this as a rating on your website. Sadly, they can also add less than flattering feedback if you let them down.

## Some proven feedback metrics

There are some simple yet proven feedback methods many organisations use to get customer feedback. Most of us are busy and rarely feel motivated to give feedback unless there is some benefit for us or it's extremely convenient. These are a couple of methods widely used.

### 1.    Net Promotor Score (NPS)

The NPS is a market research metric that is based on a single survey question. Many businesses have used the Net Promoter Score across the planet for the last 20 years. It is likely a business has asked you to complete a NPS after you used their services or purchased their products.

*"How likely are you to recommend <this brand> to a friend or colleague?"*

The answer is a simple score of 1 to 10. "10" is *"Very Likely"* and "0" is *"Not at all"*.

We then group those who responded as:

- **Promoters** score 9 to 10. They are loyal enthusiasts who will keep buying and will refer it you others.

- **Passives** score 7 to 8. They are satisfied but not enthusiastic and are vulnerable to move to competitors.

- **Detractors** score 0 to 6. They aren't happy customers who could damage your brand with negative word-of-mouth.

Subtracting the percentage of Detractors from the percentage of Promoters yields the Net Promoter Score, which can range from a low of -100 (if every customer is a Detractor) to a high of 100 (if every customer is a Promoter).

### 2.    Customer satisfaction (CSAT)

A **customer satisfaction (CSAT)** survey customers also asks customers one simple question:

*"How satisfied are you with <organisation>?"*

Answers range from 1 to 5, with 5 being *"highly satisfied"* and 1 being *"highly unsatisfied"*.

Alone, these surveys don't explain which customer is satisfied or dissatisfied. As a result, surveys such as these should always include a request to provide information asking the customer to explain why they answered the way they did. This tells you why someone was unhappy, so you know what to improve or stop, but also why they liked you, so you know what to keep doing.

**Survey Monkey** is a simple, low-cost software option to do surveys. If you want to seek more detailed feedback, you can ask as many questions as you want. However, unless the customer is highly motivated to praise you or just as motivated to criticise you, they may not waste their time, unless there is something else in it for them. Shorter surveys will get answered at much higher rates than longer ones, so where possible, keep them to less than a minute to answer.

# Networking

The word *"networking"* is often misinterpreted. Some people look upon it as wining and dining or rubbing shoulders with people we'd prefer not to hang out with. However, for small businesses, networking is one of the most powerful ways to share experiences, pursue referral work and build up a circle of like-minded business allies. It's important that you purposefully build time into your calendar to network if you believe it will get you in front of ideal customers.

Networking could also include getting out and seeing all your customers and your suppliers.

When networking, always ask yourself: *"Is this networking session helping my business?"* This will save you precious time networking in less effective places. There may well be people you enjoy meeting with for a coffee or a drink. Such social outings are great, but if it's not benefiting your business, it's just a drink, not networking. Enjoy it for what it is - time with friends.

You may feel it is awkward meeting with other people when their motives are solely to chase business. Some of us are also uncomfortable with overtly selling our business, or even talking about it. Remember, the people you are networking with are there for the same reason as you and probably have the same challenges and interests.

Small business networking comes easier to some than others, but the good news is you can practice and improve your networking skills. With time, you will become increasingly comfortable and see the significant benefits networking can bring.

Always carry your business cards with you. If you are new to networking, start with some simple goals. Aim to meet one new person. Give them your card and get their card. As you do more networking, you'll get more cards and hand out more cards. Never throw these cards out until you've transferred them into your CRM. You never know when that contact could be valuable.

## *Networking groups*

There are many structured networking groups throughout New Zealand. Some will be locally based, some are at a national level, and some are international. They may cover specific types of businesses, be open only to members or to any small business that wants to attend.

An example of an international business networking group is **Business Network International (BNI)**. There are over 150,000 members worldwide in this network.

Others include the **Chambers of Commerce,** the **Retail Association,** and the **Franchise Association**. You can also attend exhibitions and conferences.

If you look around your town or city, there are sure to be similar groups that meet to improve their businesses.

# You can't do it all — it's time to choose

If you are reading through the above list and feeling overwhelmed, I apologise. I fully understand that you will not have the time and certainly not the money to implement even a few of the above marketing initiatives. I have simply presented many of the options that exist.

Choosing the right marketing and advertising strategy for your small business must start with the basics. If you are now very clear on your core purpose, your values, your goals, and your ideal customers, you will be much better placed to decide on the marketing that will work for you.

You need to focus on the customers you want to attract and what they need. Then select the marketing methods that are likely to deliver the best results at the best price. While patience is necessary to establish what works, don't be afraid to try new options. If you found one method worked well, keep doing it.

# CHAPTER 10

## SELLING TO YOUR CUSTOMERS

You've got the business up and going. Your marketing has attracted interest from potential customers, which is great. Well done. This is half the battle won.

However, it is of little use if the customer walks out of your shop, never returns a call after you sent them a quote or bounces off your e-commerce website before making that purchase.

Most small businesspeople I have met say they hate the concept of selling. The comment that is all too common is *"I am no good at sales"*. This statement depends heavily on what your personal experiences are as a customer and your perception of what a salesperson is. Too often when we hear the word *"sales"*, the image of the hard selling used-car salesperson, or television shopping program springs to mind. This is where you feel you are getting something you have no interest in forced on you. It's that feeling that the salesperson has no interest in what you want but is solely interested in selling what they want to sell so they can get their commission.

We need to re-frame this view of *"sales"*, especially as they apply to doing business in New Zealand.

## Kiwis don't do bulls..t very well

The success in selling or the style of sales that work can have a lot to do with the culture of the place where the sales are being made. If you are lucky enough to have travelled the world, you will understand what I mean.

Kiwis are not too patient with people putting on a show when trying to sell them something. We see through *bullshit* pretty quickly. Kiwis don't do gloss, glamour and insincerity very well. We like people to be straight with us, with no frills. We like honesty. Kiwis don't tip, and we rarely haggle. We like a good deal, and like paying less, but will pay what is fair if we can see it. If you are selling in New Zealand, keep this in mind.

If your market is offshore, it is worth understanding what works in that culture.

No matter the outlet you are selling from, remember the most critical things in selling. Sales is about understanding the customer's needs, and doing everything you can to help fulfil their needs.

☞ | Sales are not about talking. Sales are about listening.

# You are not selling - you are helping and serving

When a customer walks into your store, calls you, or emails a request to you, they have a need they want met or a problem they want solved. Your priority is understanding what their need or problem is. Very often, a customer will come to you believing the solution they are seeking is one thing, but what they really need is something quite different, so **now is the time to listen**.

After listening, ask open questions to explore the need. Open questions start with the four "*W*" s or the "*H*". **What, where, when, who, and how**. *"How can I help you?" "What is the problem you are trying to solve?" "Where have you gone for help so far?" "When do you need this delivered?" "Who are you buying this for?"*

If you actively listen and explore, you will be in a much better position to come up with a solution that meets the need. People want to be listened to. They would not have come to you if they didn't have something they needed.

> You are not selling you are helping. You are listening not for the purpose of responding but for the purpose of understanding.

No one will know what you can do to help a customer more than you. No one will have the passion for the product or service your business is providing more than you. If you believe in what you are doing and love what you are doing, you don't need to sell. People will see that. If you listen, understand and genuinely believe what your business does can help the customer in front of you, then you are an exceptional salesperson.

If you use old-fashioned brute force sales techniques to sell a product or service that does not solve the problem or meet the need, don't expect to see that customer again. Also, don't be surprised if that customer shares their experience more widely, including on your website.

If, after listening and asking questions, you realise you can't help with the product or service you are offering, admit it. You may point the person to someone or somewhere else that could help. You may not have made a sale this time, but that person won't forget the experience. When they need what you are offering, they are likely to come back, whether it's tomorrow, next week, or next year.

## You still have to close the sale

Closing out the deal may well be the least appealing part of the sales process. You have listened intently and understand the customer's needs and are confident what you offer meets that need. You've built a good rapport and feel the customer has a level of trust in you. But just when you are certain you have the sale over-the-line they start to show indecisiveness or doubt. They may feel some guilt and talk themselves out of the sale, even though you know they want to buy.

The customer may use a few typical excuses not to buy, and they may not be true. *"I need more time to think about it". "I think it's too expensive". "I need to check with my wife".* They may not be under any time pressure, you know it's the best deal they are going to get, and it's likely their wife doesn't care or has already agreed. They just use these excuses to walk away from making that final decision.

This is where you need some methods to close the deal. It is these methods that most of us struggle with and typically don't enjoy. We feel like we are pushing someone to do something they don't want to do.

You might close the deal by offering a call-to-action so they act now. *"Sale ends this month"*. *"This is a limited only offer"*. *"If you buy now we can fit your install in next week"*. *"If it's price, I can see what else I can do"*. *"I'm happy to leave you for a moment so you can chat to your wife"*

You might walk them through the reasons you know they came to the point where they are so close to buying. *"Bob, remember that you said you always wanted this"*.

If you are sending out a final proposal or quote to close the deal, make it easy for the customer to accept it. Many quoting software packages have an *"Accept Quote"* button on the the quote. Don't just send the quote and make no effort to communicate. You are giving the customer too much opportunity to walk away from a sale you are confident meets their needs. Tell the customer that you will follow up, when you will follow up, and then make sure you do. *"Bob, you said you needed to recheck dimensions before accepting. Im calling to see how that went as I'm confident we can make it work"*.

If you don't follow up the person may set the quote aside and forget about it as the desire to act has passed and they've moved on.

# Customer service - it's simple but is too rare

We are all customers, and we can all quote examples where we experienced superb customer service and where we experienced really poor customer service. Even though we all know what wonderful service is, too many small business owners do not deliver excellent customer service. Many businesses include *"Customer Service"* as a core value, yet don't live up to their own expectations.

Customer service is not about the big things. It's about the small things and many are really obvious, yet far too many businesses don't do them.

Here are some tips:

- Listen. Don't assume you know what the customer wants. Often the customer doesn't know what they want.

- The most important customer is the one standing in front of you. It's not the one on the phone that is ringing, or the one in the queue looking impatient, or the regular who walked in.

- Use basic phone etiquette. State your name, your business and be upbeat when you pick up the phone.

- Return ALL your missed calls. Once the customer in front of you has gone, then return the call.

- Do what you say you will do. Don't make commitments you can't fulfill.

- Set realistic expectations. Customers respect this. If you can't do something, don't say you can and then disappoint.

- Turn up on time. Your customers are also time poor, so respect their time.

- If you can't turn up on time, call ahead. We all understand life throws unexpected things at us.

- Take your shoes off before walking into someone's home. You are there to work. They live there.

- Be polite, be helpful, be kind.

- Most customers are great people who just want help. Enjoy helping them.

- Smile. Say hello. Show interest in the person. You might meet a new, interesting person and besides, it makes the customer feel special.

- If a customer looks flustered, unhappy even angry, empathise and do your best to explore what the problem is and calm the situation.

Finally, make sure your staff are also doing these things. Not much point if you are the only person in the business doing it.

# The customer is not always right

While you should do the best you can to meet a customer's needs, you should never tolerate abusive or anti-social behaviour, nor should your staff be subjected to it. No sale is worth that. If you have done your best and the customer is not reciprocating with respectful behaviour, you can sack them as a customer. Politely tell them you no longer want them as a customer, and they should go elsewhere and not return, as you won't serve them.

Respect begets respect.

# Handling complaints - they are a gift

You will never get it right every time, but hopefully you'll get it right most of the time. When you get a critical review, an unpleasant phone call, a disgruntled customer, look upon it as a gift. Perhaps, initially, you won't see it that way. However, if someone is really unhappy, you'd much prefer to hear about it than for it to be festering out there and knowing nothing about it.

When you get the feedback, you can do something about it, and you can learn from it.

> In business it's not about whether you make mistakes. It's about how you deal with those mistakes

If an unhappy customer confronts you, the first thing to do is take the heat out of the situation. Acknowledge their concern, even if you don't agree. Then work though the problem with them, seeking a solution.

- Listen. Allow the person to get their frustration off their chest.

- Empathise. You will have been in their position at some stage so you can relate.

- Determine what their requirements are. Seek the solution that would address their concern.

- Is it reasonable? Keep in mind that the customer is not always right. But sometimes you need to play the long game. You may have to give something to get the customer back.

- Follow up. Before you depart the conversation, check what you are committing to do. Then do it and check back in later.

Often, showing interest in a customer's concerns and addressing them will result in far more satisfaction and appreciation than getting it right the first time.

## Cognitive limitations and too many choices

All human beings have a limit to their cognitive capacity to take in information and process it. **Cognition** is a general term covering our mental processes, including attention, memory, language, and knowledge.

In 1956, **George Miller** quantified our cognitive capacity in an academic paper. His research found what he called *"The Magical Number Seven, Plus or Minus Two"*. [1]

He asked his subjects to pay attention to several items, memorise them, and then repeat back what they could remember. He kept finding that across a wide range of tasks, the number seven kept popping up as a limit on human recall. His paper established that the limit to our information processing was seven items, plus or minus two. Some of us may manage nine and some of us only five, but on average it's seven.

In short, understand that when you face many choices and new information, there will be a limit to how much of that information you can absorb and process.

Consider the experience when you go into a new restaurant, and the waitress hands you a menu that feels a bit like being handed a novel and has so many food and wine choices your head is spinning. It can even be stressful. You may feel like asking someone else to decide for you. Compare this with the fine dining experience, where you have only a few choices. Meat, chicken, pork, fish or vegetarian. Better still, there is a *"trust the chef"* option.

---

## The Jam Experiment and too many choices

In her book "*The Art of Choosing*", Sheena Iyengar outlined her research on how people make choices and what impacts on the quality of those choices. She carried out wide research.

One of her simple experiments was carried out in a large delicatessen called Draeger's Market based in the Bay area of San Francisco. The store offered a huge variety of products. It offered 15 types of bottled water, 150 types of vinegar, 250 types of cheeses, 300 flavours of jam, and much more. Such choice was one of their points of difference, of which they were very proud. This created a lot of consumer interest and attracted a lot of people to their stores. Iyengar's research set out to determine whether this level of choice translated into sales.

Iyengar set up a tasting stall with jams near the storefront.

In the first test, there were almost 30 flavours that customers could choose to sample. This large selection attracted most of the people before they entered the store. They were asked to taste as many jams as they could. They typically stopped tasting after only two jams. If they liked a jam, they could go to the store shelves and buy their selection from the 300 flavours at a healthy discount. Unfortunately, most got to the jam shelves, became confused, and debated the merits of a choice for up to 10 minutes. Less than 5% ended up buying anything.

In the second test, there were only six jams that customers could choose to taste. In this case, customers again still only tasted two jams. However, when confronted with the large selection, they were far more confident in their final choice, selecting

---

it almost immediately. Of the customers who had to choose from six, 30% made a purchase and were also completely comfortable with that choice when interviewed later.

While Draeger's continued with their strategy, because it attracted huge numbers of people, they had to assist customers in narrowing their choices to convert the browsing into sales.

The Jam Experiment showed that we love to be offered many choices. We find it fascinating. However, if we are confronted with too many options, we feel obligated to spend more time choosing. We then either decide not to choose, because it's too hard, or have an uneasy feeling that we made the wrong choice, even if the choice met our needs.

> *"When people are given a moderate number of options (4 to 6) rather than a large number (20 to 30), they are more likely to make a choice, are more confident in their decisions, and are happier with what they choose."* - **Sheena Iyengar,** The Art of Choosing [2]

☞ Keep in mind when presenting what you are selling to customers. Help them choose.

# Selling online - Trends in New Zealand

Offering your customers the opportunity to engage and buy from you online is becoming more essential than ever, and the trends would show this is not changing. Statistics are testament to this.

> *"New Zealand is the 42nd largest market for e-commerce with a predicted revenue of US$7,500 million by 2024, placing it ahead of Portugal. Revenue is expected to show a compound annual growth rate of 4.9%, resulting in a projected market volume of US$9,079.6 million by 2028, with an expected increase of 6.5% in 2024."* **Ecommerce Data Collection Agency (ECDC).** [3]

New Zealand's overall economy ranks below 50th in the world, so the above statistic shows we buy a lot online.

Online sales in New Zealand are more effective for some industries than for others. The ECDC research shows that technologies, fashion, hobby and leisure, groceries, home wares, and DIY are the highest. Interesting is that **Countdown** (or Woolworths) groceries are the biggest single online seller in New Zealand - a trend that started during COVID-19 and is likely to continue.

No matter the current statistics, as they will change, if you sell to customers, it would be foolish not to consider where online selling fits in with your business strategy.

## The COVID-19 effect

The isolation that came with the COVID-19 pandemic saw a historic drop in traditional sales in New Zealand but a significant increase in online sales. [4][5]

The COVID-19 pandemic normalised the processes of remote selling, with terms like *"click-and-collect"* becoming mainstream. We are now very comfortable to buy our groceries online, as the Countdown statistics show. There will always be a role for selling through **bricks and mortar** outlets. While naysayers argued online sales would see the death of physical shops, it has not occurred. While online sales are growing massively, statistics also show they still only made up about one tenth of total sales in New Zealand. [6]

People are far more comfortable to purchase online and if you operate through a physical location, you should also seriously consider a combined online sales strategy.

## Online sales do not always meet customer needs

Sadly, it's not always a great experience buying online, as most of us could attest. Finding your way around an e-commerce website can be a simple experience or a very unpleasant process, depending on the website. The ease of payment may vary and then what turns up on your doorstep, if it turns up at all, may not be what was expected. We are also unclear in New Zealand what our rights are when online sales go wrong. [7]

The online experience starts with your website design, and specifically the e-commerce side of the design.[8] We've already discussed the importance of UI and UX on websites. These are even more important if you want a customer to part with their hard-earned cash.

## Online sales and the challenge of freight

While it is really important to develop a great online website that makes life easy for a customer, it is not always this that affects the customer's e-commerce experience. Often it is the challenges around shipping. There are some unique challenges with freight when people buy from your e-commerce site.

When the customer reaches your cart, you want them to continue and purchase. If they got this far, they are a motivated buyer, and you don't want to lose them. Ideally, if what you are offering is what they want, you want them to pay there and then. If you cannot offer a price, including freight, but indicate you will get back to them, that may be enough to turn them off going ahead and they leave the website.

Remember, there are ways of tracking bounce rates from your cart page. Ask your web developer if you can get a report.

# Some simple tips to assist in your day-to-day business' life

You need to always be on the lookout for how you can make your day-to-day activities easier and more efficient. If you are doing something that annoys you, and you find yourself doing it often, it's a good place to start.

You may also need a fresh set of eyes to see the inefficiencies you come to consider as normal. Someone who asks: *"Why are you doing it that way?"*. They could see something that you have become used to, which makes no sense to anyone else.

All small business owners are busy. The secret is being busy doing the important stuff and not doing stuff that adds little value and drives you crazy.

Here are a few tips that may help to improve a day in your small business' life:

- **Wasted time:** On occasions, pause and keep track of where you spend your time. If you are service based, how many hours are you billing and how many hours attract no revenue? Are you wasting too much time doing things that add little value?

- **Monitor the dollars:** By the time you finish this book, you'll be sick of hearing me talk about monitoring your cash. No apologies will be forthcoming on this point. Cash is your lifeblood, so keep an eye on it as often as you can. Inefficiencies and wasted time cost money.

- **Remember your personal rules:** When we talked about YOU, I highlighted the need to set a few basic rules to ensure you are looking after yourself. These will be different for everyone. Whatever yours are, do your best to stick to them. Whether your rule is turning your phone off after 6pm, picking up the kids, going to the gym, going for a walk, put a priority on it.

- **Monitor your inventory:** What's happening with your inventory? If it's rising or falling abnormally, it may give you an early sign of the health of your business. If it's sitting around, it means you have good money you could use elsewhere. I will explore inventory management in more detail later.

- **Track your KPIs:** While this term may be more appropriate in a corporate environment, whatever you call them you need to track the things in your business that are critical to your success When you set these indicators, consider only those that make a real difference and only those you can measure. Keep a regular eye on them, observing how they are trending and whether they are improving. If not, why not?

- **Talk to your customers:** They are what will decide your fate. Keep in touch with them in the easiest way you can. If something annoys them, or they see ways to improve, listen.

- **Talk to your staff:** Even if there are only a few of you, talk to each other. Catch up regularly so you all know what's going on.

- **Spend time on the business:** This is the point where I say you need to devote a little time and thought to working on the business, not in it. Set aside a little time each month for this and ask, *"How and where can we improve?"*

- **Look out for waste:** Any materials or time that add no value to the business or your customers is waste.

- **Keep the place tidy:** If you work in a mess, it is likely your business will be a mess, or staff and customers will assume it is. Good housekeeping also makes the workplace safer.

- **Plan and schedule activities:** Do some planning, weekly or monthly, to keep you and your team focused on the priorities.

- **Implement and use good systems and processes:** I will get to this.

- **Celebrate your successes:** You may frequently find yourself and your team being too busy to reflect on how well you're going. Fit in a small amount of time to celebrate your successes. You deserve it. Enjoy them.

# Time - your most precious resource and how to manage it better

The most valuable and precious thing you have and can give to another person is your time. Yet, as small business owners, you may not manage the use of this valuable resource as well as you could. There will never be enough hours in the day when you own a small business.

Just as you have to make choices when deciding your business strategy, you must make choices about how you prioritise your time.

Successful time management is about prioritisation. The most important priorities are those that deliver on your goals and your core purpose. They may not be those urgent tasks that swamp you every day. You need to consider short-term urgent priorities and also longer-term important priorities.

Once you know your priorities, consider what in the following list is most relevant to you.

- **Be decisive.** It is better to decide with the best information you have than to wait until everything is clear and you miss the opportunity.

*"It is even better to act quickly and err than to hesitate until the time of action is past."*

—**Carl Von Clausewitz,** 18<sup>th</sup> century military strategist.

- **Don't procrastinate.** Procrastinating chews up huge amounts of time, increases your stress, and will affect your small business. Identify when you are doing it. If it is an unpleasant task that you hold off completing, then it will only be there tomorrow.

- **Avoid interruptions.** If you need to get important tasks done without interruptions, then dedicate time to complete them away from the distractions.

- **Avoid multi-tasking.** We often hear people boast about being good multi-taskers. Avoid multi-tasking. There is no prize for doing a lot of tasks poorly rather than one task really well.

- **Set deadlines and stick to them.** Learn to set deadlines for tasks and then finish them. Sometimes simply finishing a task, irrespective of its impact, is a reward in itself. Expect others to do the same.

- **Manage your emails.** Emails are one of the easiest methods of communicating in business, but can be overwhelming. Take action on each email. Delete them if they add no value. Act on them immediately, whenever you can. Be brief. People don't like long emails so no point writing long emails they won't read. Maybe a phone call is a better option then an email?

- **Write things down.** Some people have the gift of committing things to memory and then recalling them. Unfortunately, most of us don't, especially if we are experiencing mental overload. Write those important and urgent things down so you remember them. There are many smartphone apps to help with this. This could become your to-do list.

- **Use a calendar or weekly planner.** This is important for you and any members of your small team. You could share your calendar. There are also many time sharing and scheduling apps you could use.

- **Be punctual and expect punctuality.** If you are sloppy getting to appointments, it will tell all those around you that time and discipline are not important to you. If people are late, don't reward them by waiting for them. Reward those who are on time by starting the meeting on time.

- **Manage social media.** Differentiate what is important time being spent on Facebook, LinkedIn or other social media platforms for the business versus the time spent on entertaining gossip or silly videos - and, therefore, a waste of time.

- **Networking versus social catch-ups.** Networking brings more customers or strengthens partnerships and is important. Likewise, a social catch up may be an important rule for your wellbeing. Know the difference and make sure your networking is helping your business, not wasting your time.

- **Control the controllable.** It is important to stay informed on what is happening in the outside world and how it might affect your small business. However, don't get hung up on external issues that you cannot control or even influence.

- **Build routine and habits.** The more you get into habits like those above, the easier they will become. The routine and habits on the little things free you up for the important, innovative, and even fun things.

- **Be responsible. Be disciplined.** Once you commit to any or all of the above points, be responsible and stick with them. If you consider the outstanding performers in any field, it's their attention to detail and discipline over the long term that helped them achieve their success.

## Exploring "lean" processes

**Lean manufacturing** processes have been around for a long time. They became part of the culture in the Japanese car industry, particularly Toyota, soon after the Second World War. The Japanese captured this in the word, Kaizen, meaning *"changing for the better"* or *"continuous improvement"*.

At its simplest level, those using lean aim at finding waste in a business process and then eliminating that waste. More importantly, is building a culture where everyone continues to look for wasteful or inefficient steps in their processes and then removes them.

Manufacturing businesses, like the car industry, are where lean has added significant value. However, the principle of understanding business processes from end-to-end, looking for waste in those processes, and developing ways to remove that waste can apply to any type of business. Waste is anything that is not **adding value** to your business.

In his book *"The Factory of One"*, **Daniel Markovitz** [1] defines something to be **value-adding**-when:

- The customer will pay for the activity
- The activity transforms your product or service, and
- The activity is done correctly the first time.

## *Process mapping*

The first step an expert in lean processes will do when they arrive at a business is stand back and observe the way things are done. They will then draw up the details of the process or processes on a process map. This is an illustration that shows every step in the process, where decisions are required and who is responsible for each step.

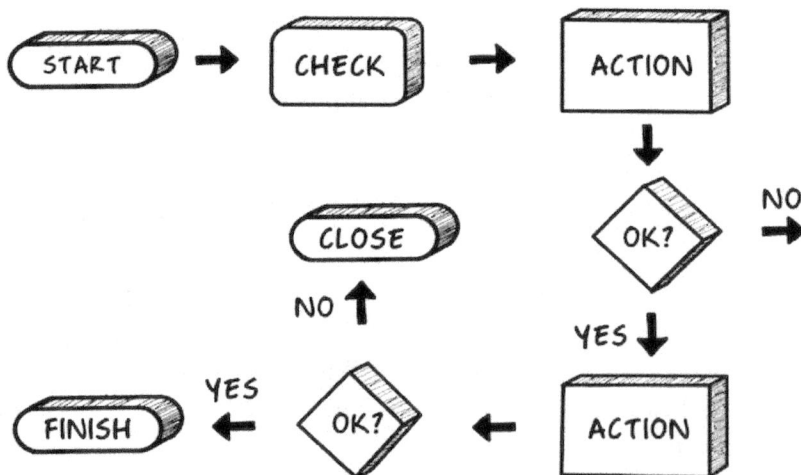

Most small businesses are pretty good at removing wasteful or pointless steps in the way they work. We simply cannot have overly complex or bureaucratic processes. However, all small businesses will have waste. Identifying that waste and then allocating the time to do something about it is the challenge.

Often, we can be so used to doing something a certain way, we are blind to the opportunities to do it better. When we see a way to improve, the effort to change can be so great, and our time so limited, that we put up with it, hoping to deal with it when time allows, which never comes.

## *Five-S*

A lean technique called Five-S represents a way to consider and manage waste. In Japanese, these five S-words are **Seiri**, **Seiton**, **Seiso**, **Seiketsu** and **Shitsuke**, which translate in English to **Sort**, **Straighten**, **Shine**, **Standardise** and **Sustain**.

In simple terms, this would typically include:

- Finding a place for everything and keeping it tidy.

- Clean up your desk, office and workshop, and keep it clean.

- Keep on top of your filing and throw out things that add no value.

- Standardise things you do often either through training, procedures, or systems, so they deliver the same outcome every time, no matter who is doing it.

- Encourage your team to look out for waste and not to be afraid to ask, *"why are we doing it this way?"*

- When a good idea comes up, try to act on it. People will stop suggesting things if nothing ever happens.

# Logistics - getting supplies into the business and products out

If you are quite small, you may source the products and materials you need locally. As you get bigger, and the diversity of your needs grow, you will probably look much further to get the best products and raw materials at the best prices.

You may also want to diversify your options, so you are not reliant on a single supplier. As such, your supply chain becomes a critical consideration for growing your small business.

Likewise, if you must ship your products to your customers and remain competitive, this is also an important process to understand and get right.

## *Freight within New Zealand*

I touched on this when we discussed e-commerce sites. There are a wide variety of shipping options within New Zealand. Courier businesses, like **NZ Post,** offer online pricing options and pick up and drop off services. Some freight companies specialise in bulk haulage, others do palletised deliveries, some containers and some do it all. There are also companies that only transport within a limited geographical area while others do nation-wide freight.

Some small businesses may just buy an appropriate vehicle and do the deliveries themselves.

In short, there will be a way to have supplies delivered to your business and freight businesses who will ship whatever product you require to anywhere in New Zealand. This is not the challenge. The challenge is doing it at a competitive price that does not wipe out all your margins and makes you uncompetitive. In short, shop around, talk to a lot of freight companies and do the sums before settling on one. You may well decide to use a few freight businesses.

Another key consideration is how much of your freight costs to absorb and how much you pass on to your customer. If you decide to offer free freight, it will be very attractive and simple for your customer, but you really need to know your pricing and margins to ensure you can make this work financially.

Other options include offering free freight for larger orders, where the volume of the sale covers the freight. Check out what competitors are doing and what is acceptable practice in the market you operate in to get a sense of what your customers will be expecting.

No matter the choice you make, you need to really understand your costs to buy or manufacture the product, your pricing and your margins before deciding. A poor choice could see all your margins wiped out by freight.

## *Importing*

While many small business owners are nervous about importing, it is very achievable even for small businesses. New Zealand's market is small, with a limited choice of products and suppliers. While for many small businesses this is adequate, many of us need to look further afield to continue offering our customers choices and to continue competing. Offshore suppliers offer an enormous range of options you will never get in New Zealand.

There are many parties shipping large amounts of small retail items into New Zealand everyday through businesses like **Amazon** and **Temu.** Many small businesses can use such channels to access products for their business. However, when you need larger volumes of raw materials or products for your business these options will be inadequate.

Australia is an obvious first choice to consider importing larger volumes. They are our second biggest trading partner [2], are nearby so easy to connect in person with, and there are no language barriers.

We import most from China, but we do, however, import from just about every corner of the globe.

If you are considering importing in larger quantities, it's not without its risks and there are several things to consider.

Remember, exporters want to sell. Park any biases about countries and any perceptions others may have given you. Only take advice from those that have experience in the markets you are looking to trade with and ignore the ill-informed and the naysayers.

Nothing beats visiting the people you intend buying off, especially if getting it wrong could really hurt your business. If you are only importing small amounts or the risks are low, an overseas trip may not be justified. However, I would be reluctant to buy off any overseas supplier where there is a lot at stake unless others you know well have used them and can vouch for them or you have met them and explored the facilities they operate from.

You should also confirm the legitimacy of the companies you are looking to deal with. Depending on the country you want to buy off, services exist to do foreign company searches, so do your due diligence.

One of the key parties to bring on board to work with you is an experienced freight forwarding company. These guys are specialists in international shipping. They will coordinate all freight between other countries and New Zealand, and can organise internal freight in both countries. They can also deal with all customs requirements.

Many overseas exporters may have large **Minimum Order Quantities (MOQ).** Some will only sell in 20- or 40-foot containers. These orders are called **Full Container Loads** or **FCL**. However, such volumes may be out of the reach of many importers. Some suppliers may be prepared to sell in smaller quantities, like pallets. This is called **Less than a Container Load,** or **LCL.**

Typically, the shipments will have fixed shipping costs and fixed customs charges. As such, the more you can get into an order, the better the cost per item purchased will be. Also discuss with your freight forwarder and supplier where the responsibility for the goods passes from the supplier to you. It could be ex-works, namely from the supplier's factory or it could be at the port, which is called **Free on Board** or **FOB.**

Another major challenge is arranging payment. If the supplier has no history with you, they may ask for full payment prior to releasing the goods. Others may ask for a deposit before manufacturing the goods and then won't release all the paperwork for you to unload the products until you have paid them in full.

Options exist where a third party holds the money until you have received the goods and are happy with everything. This is called **escrow**. **Alibaba**, the world equivalent of New Zealand's TradeMe, offers this service, as well as listing an endless choice of products and supplier details to help connect buyers and sellers across the globe. Whether you use this service will be a balance between the risk of losing the money to an unscrupulous seller, and the cost of the service.

Finally, make sure anything you import complies with New Zealand requirements. The last thing you want is having your product banned for non-compliance, leaving you with a lot of products you can't sell.

## *Funding your imports*

One challenge with importing for a small business is the size of the payments required and the delays between when you have to pay, when the products arrive, and then the time to sell those products. Managing these cash flow challenges will be central to making the importing strategy successful or not.

Turning to traditional funding arrangements such as an overdraft is a legitimate option. In many cases this may be sufficient to cope with the swings in cash. However, the major lenders offer more tailored options for importers, like **trade finance.**

This is a material decision that involves risks. As such, you need to approach it in the same way as any other risk or decision to borrow money.

## *Stock and inventory*

No one wants to hold inventory (stock). It's money sitting on the ground. If it's perishable, it will need to be stored correctly and you will need to turn it over quickly. It requires warehouse space, with the associated costs. We'd all like to operate on the traditional Japanese system of **Just-in-Time** developed by Toyota in the 1970s.

However, as your business grows, as you face longer lead times, especially if importing, carrying inventory becomes essential. You may also have to produce more than your customers have ordered to manage the costs of production and to ensure you can meet demand. Sometimes you may do this in quieter periods rather than have staff sitting idle.

No matter the reason, as you grow, you are likely to have to carry inventory.

If your business has inventory, you need to manage it. This takes discipline and an attention to detail. If you don't do this, and it gets out of

---

control, you could be leaking cash all over the place and not even realise it.

Here are my tips for keeping your stock under control:

- **Get an inventory system.** This must meet the needs of your business. There are basic systems (like that offered within Xero) and more specialised systems. Refer to the discussion on choosing the right system.

- **Use the system.** While it is one thing to implement a system, it is pointless if it's not used all the time or is not used correctly.

- **Only place orders through your system**. That rushed phone call to get something quickly is a habit you need to stop.

- **Check all stock when it arrives**. This should be done against a packing slip, to pick up any errors from the supplier. Make sure they provide packing slips. It's standard practice. Only pay them for what's delivered and make sure their invoices match the packing slip, as well as checking pricing.

- **Store the stock well.** This ensures you can access it easily and safely and it is where it is supposed to be. This is where you could apply some lean processes.

- Only allow products to be taken out of stock **if they are linked to a sale, job number** or whatever system that links inventory to sales. Allowing people to grab something in a hurry and sort it later creates a mess, because most people never *"sort it later"*.

- **Keep your product details up to date especially prices**. Some suppliers provide the ability to connect their catalog to your system or provide catalogs to be uploaded to your system from a spreadsheet or file. This is a key consideration in choosing your system.

- If you don't have a system to track stock, **plan regular stocktakes.** If everyone used your system well, you may only need occasional spot checks of key stock items. You can plan at least one full stocktake for the end-of-year accounts.

- If you find errors, damaged or missing stock, **do stock adjustments immediately and often**. Big errors may mean you don't have the stock when you need it, or you could order stock you don't need. Also, big errors will flow through to your financials.

Another key consideration in making sure your stock is correct is the impact it has on the profit (or loss) and tax. If your stock has grown considerably over the year, not only will it have sucked up significant cash, but it will also have a big impact on profitability and tax.

I will go through this in more detail when we discuss the profit and loss statements.

# Buying, renting or leasing plant, equipment or vehicles

Your small business may have very little need for plant and equipment. Perhaps a personal car in the business may be all you need. For others, especially in the trade, building and construction industry, even if you are a small operator, you will require plant and equipment.

This is where you will have to decide if you hire the equipment as you need it, buy the equipment, or to lease it.

Kiwis have traditionally wanted to own their plant and equipment, but leasing could be a genuine alternative to consider.

When starting out, if the work is inconsistent, and you only need equipment sporadically, consider hiring it. This could be **wet hire** where the equipment comes with the operator, or **dry hire** where you are only hiring the equipment.

As time goes on, if you are hiring it more often, there will be a point where it will make sense to have full-time access to the plant, equipment or vehicles.

We discuss later in the book the danger of using your own cash to buy plant. It can suck up all the money you need to pay all the other monthly bills. It is more likely you will need to borrow money to pay for the equipment.

Shop around for the best asset finance deal. The equipment seller, asset finance companies (like **UDC Finance**) or the banks will offer different options. Some lenders will be happy to lend solely for this purpose and secure the loan against the equipment. You may not need to have any other accounts or lending with them.

The key considerations will be the interest rate and the term of the loan.

It is rare to get finance that would extend beyond five years. Lenders want you to pay these assets off quickly. If the equipment is second hand, you may still find funders, but the repayment term may be shorter (say three years) and there might be higher rates reflecting the higher risk. Basically, if you default on the loan, the lender will take the equipment off you. It will be harder for them to on-sell older equipment.

The downside of owning the equipment yourself is not only that you have to finance it, but you also have to sort all the maintenance, repairs and registrations. Plant and equipment, unlike property, will depreciate. Factor in additional maintenance as the equipment ages. You will eventually need to have the financing available to replace the equipment.

Leasing is also an option.

If you are leasing, you don't own the asset but pay monthly fees to have exclusive use of the equipment or vehicle. These monthly lease payments are tax deductible. If you own the vehicle, only the interest on the loan is tax deductible, but not the principal repayments. The party leasing to you will sort all maintenance of the vehicles, relieving you of this hassle. There are different leases. Sometimes you will take ownership of the vehicle after a specified period or the lessor will replace the old vehicle with new vehicles.

A lease may end up costing more in the long run. The advantage is it gives you greater certainty of cash flows, as the fees will be fixed. You are also not burdened with debt and capital costs when the vehicle needs replacing.

If you have an existing fleet of vehicles, plant or equipment, a lease company may look to buy the vehicles off you and then lease them back. This is a good option if you need to get your hands on cash now at the expense of spreading cash payments for the lease in the future. It also releases you from the headache of managing a fleet of vehicles.

The decisions to hire, buy or lease will be determined by doing your maths, comparing the cost of one option against the after. Make sure you consider what is and isn't tax deductible, as this will affect the decision. Don't get too hung up on whether you do or don't own the equipment or vehicle. The other consideration is the time and effort to maintain the equipment.

# Systems to improve your daily operations

Most small businesses that I come across could use better systems and processes. This is especially the case for businesses with longer standing owners, people who are not very computer literate, or owners reluctant to change historical practices. Others want to improve their systems but don't know how or see a huge amount of work to change. While plenty of businesses have survived on paper-based or other old systems, it is getting much harder to do this in the current business world.

With the variety and power of small business software packages and apps on the market, there is no reason your small business cannot access relatively low-cost, high-quality software systems. If chosen well, they can solve many day-to-day issues, provide repeatability and remove waste. There has been an avalanche of software packages and business apps coming onto the market over recent years, and this is likely to continue.

The discussion on too many choices in previous chapters is very relevant here. I see many businesses throw their hands up in frustration trying to find the right system and end up doing nothing.

The most valuable systems are those that replace repetitive but necessary actions, collect important business data for decision-making, and remove the need for you to do anything you particularly dislike.

If you already have a solution for managing your day-to-day operations and are happy with it, you may not need to change anything, just because there's a better option out there. However, keep in mind what your future needs might be. Your current system may quickly surpass its use-by date and it doesn't hurt to be prepared for this.

Most systems that are available are **software as a service (SaaS)**. They are cloud based, involve monthly subscriptions, and are automatically updated as upgrades occur. This differs from the past where you purchased a software package, downloaded it onto your hard drive, and purchased upgrades over time.

In the last 10 to 15 years, the market has been flooded with a huge choice of SaaS systems.

# Some all-too-typical signs you need a better system

To assess your need to change or install a new system, as well as choosing something suitable for your small business, I've listed some very common issues people face in small business when their systems are not working for them. If you can relate to these points, then it may be time to shop around.

- You are unsure if your labour costs are correct, and if the jobs being quoted will actually make you money.

- You have no ability to establish the gross profit on each job to establish which were profitable.

- Inventory is coming in and not being received into stock and taken out without recording the movement. There is also no way to establish the amount of stock without a stocktake.

- You have very little traceable history on your customers and no way to communicate with them after a sale.

- Your planning is not great and each week your schedule is derailed by reactive work or unforeseen problems.

- The quality of your products or services is inconsistent, leading to customer complaints.

- Your accountancy costs are excessive at year-end because of the time to pull everything together.

- You have limited ability to track cash flow and the profitability each month as you don't know where the money is going.

- You waste time and effort reconciling invoices each month with prices for materials and labour being incorrect.

- Costs are not being allocated to the right jobs or the correct cost codes.

- Invoices are taking too long to pull together, are being sent out too slowly and you re being paid late.

- Invoices and packing slips from suppliers are not being collected and you are paying them late.

- No leads are coming into the business from your marketing efforts, or when they arrive, you miss them so they are not actioned.

- While you know what your financial results are at the end of each month, you can't explain why they are what they are.

...and I could go on....

If any of these apply to you or if you could add a few more of your own issues to the list, perhaps it's time to look for a good system so you can find better ways of doing thing

> No matter the system you use, it must save you money, make you money, or improve a customer's experience. It is just a means to that end.

---

# Choosing the best SaaS for your small business

I am unapologetic about strongly recommending every small business use a SaaS in their business. While I am old enough to remember slide-rules before calculators existed, punch cards and paper records before accounting software, I am not the slightest bit nostalgic. There will be a SaaS system on the market that would help every business.

However, where I am very empathetic is in the challenge faced by small businesses in choosing the best option and, even more so, finding the time to implement a new option. This is a genuine challenge and is normally where things go awry.

The big guys will often implement an **Enterprise Resource Planning** or **ERP** option. These allow a large company to do everything across the entire business in the one system. They may require some customisation of the software. While these allow a business to cover all aspects of the business, they can be very expensive. As a small business owner, you may have to pick more affordable options that may not do everything you want but may be infinitely better than what you currently use.

Let's discuss how to make the selection of a new system a little easier.

## *The first system you'll need - accounting*

While there should be a SaaS system that will replace most of your small business functions, the priority is making sure you have an accounting system. I would not recommend any business of any size to operate without this. The only consideration is which SaaS best suits your accounting or bookkeeping requirements

In New Zealand, the system most small businesses will turn to is **Xero**. It is a Kiwi business and has changed the software accounting landscape with over 270,000 subscribers in New Zealand. Xero does small business accounting extremely well and that may be all you need. However, its strengths in other areas are not so good and you will probably need other SaaS systems to integrate with Xero.

**MYOB** is also popular in New Zealand, has more built-in functions, and is more suitable for bigger small businesses.

---

There are many other systems on the market, but these are the most popular choices I have come across in New Zealand.

Before making a choice, consider your total business needs, as other systems may have an accounting, general ledger, as well as other functions critical to your business.

## Short listing the best options

I would never attempt to list the SaaS systems now available. I have used many, but that still only represents a small fraction of what's on the market. It's unlikely you will find a complete review of the systems you are considering in one place to guide you through your decision process.

However, there are some key things you can do to simplify the process of short listing a system or systems and then deciding which one to go with.

Here are a few tips:

- Establish what operational issues you are trying to solve before you look at solutions.

- Develop a list of features the system absolutely must have and other features that are nice to have.

- Ask other people in similar businesses what they use.

- If you already are using a system that you are happy with, for example Xero, consider Add-Ons that integrate into that system rather than starting from scratch. Many SaaS systems integrate into a range of other systems. This is one thing Xero does very well.

- Ask your accountant or advisor for some input.

- Spend some time online reading software reviews and blogs. Even if you don't use Xero their list of Add-Ons is extensive and lists SaaS options by the function they perform. (But be warned, the list is huge).

- Most software providers will have free trial demos and online videos. Spend a bit of time watching these. If they don't have such information, I'd steer clear as they are likely to be immature and a better option will exist.

- Contact the provider's help desk with questions and ask for a demonstration. If they don't help and don't have a local presence to help you decide, drop them off your list.

- Decide how easy the software is to use. If it is not user-friendly, move on. There is no reason these days to choose systems that are not user-friendly.

- Make sure you know all the costs and what currency the software is charged in. Many are in US dollars.

- Look at systems that have a strong local presence. There may be excellent overseas alternatives, but with little or no local support, it could be an issue when you need help. Larger software providers manage this through strong online and phone-based support.

- If you are likely to need two or three systems across the business, check whether they can easily integrate and work together. For example, does your payroll system talk to your accounting system? Does inventory information feed into your financial software? Does time sheeting access materials information from inventory?

- If you have three of more systems to implement, start looking at larger ERPs. For example, a business may need job scheduling, payroll, accounting, and inventory. An integration between two systems is fine. Three of more is getting messy.

- However, don't go for a sophisticated system if you don't need it. It could get costly.

- Be realistic. No system will do everything you need. Just make sure they do the absolute must haves.

# Implementing a new system

The biggest challenge for small businesses is not the choice of the system but allowing sufficient time and resources to implement the system correctly.

Many businesses start using a system with inadequate effort set aside to implement it. This could cause an even worse outcome than staying with the old, inefficient system. The reason this is so common is that implementing these new systems well can take significant time, cost money, and sometimes require specialist skills. It can suck up a huge amount of your staff's time when they don't even have time to do their existing job.

Even if you pay outsiders to set up the system, you must have internal expertise to use it after it's in operation. The best way to get these skills is to be heavily involved in setting it up.

If you cannot see a solution to these challenges, I would be very wary about implementing a new system until you have the time and money to do it.

Here are some tips and thoughts on how to implement a new SaaS system.

- Before making any commitment to a new system, scope out what work is required to implement it.

- Treat the implementation of the new system as a project - it needs a budget (money and time), and a schedule with milestones. The most critical milestone is when it goes live and replaces the existing system.

- Allow people uninterrupted time to devote to the system's development, even if it is a day-or-two a week. You may need some temporary labour to cover your staff to allow them time to do this.

- Avoid implementing in your busiest seasons of the year. Delay the work until your quieter periods.

- Understand the limitations of the new system. No system will be perfect. Don't shoot for perfection if it adds limited value and takes significant effort to implement.

- Get your staff involved in the implementation throughout. You may only require their views on what is necessary to make their lives easier. It may be necessary for staff to implement some aspects of the software or to check data. For others, it may be training. Having everyone's support is very important.

- Do as much work offline as possible and allow the existing system to operate as long as is necessary.

- Remember the saying, Garbage In means Garbage Out. If you must enter a lot of data in your new system, like customer and supplier lists, product details, pricing and so on, make sure you check the data before entering it. Many call this data cleansing. Again, do this offline.

- Stage the implementation. If you can implement just part of the total system, ensuring it works well, and then implement the next stage, it will be better than implementing everything in one go and then having to fix a new mess.

- The better SaaS providers will offer implementation support. Use every moment on offer from them.

- Make sure everyone knows how to use the new system and how you want it to be used. If staff hate it, can't use it, or you have not trained them, they will work around it - and you will face more problems.

- Don't go live with the new system until you are comfortable. If you are not ready, delay.

- Once you go live, make sure the system is being used as you intended and note any issues - no implementation will be mistake free.

- Keep improving the system as you use it. Once it's implemented, persist with it. It will only get better.

# CHAPTER 12

## HOW TO EMPLOY AND KEEP THE BEST PEOPLE

Most businesses in New Zealand are sole proprietors and don't employ people, and many never want to employ staff. There are about 400,000 non-employee or solo businesses in New Zealand, which is about 70% of all businesses. [1]

However, if you are a solo and have a desire to grow, you will need to employ staff.

It's unlikely that anyone you employ will have the passion for your business that you do. You may find managing people hard work - it can be. Employees can also become a high cost for you. This could be a stress you don't want or need.

A fear of employing staff could be a major stumbling block to your growth or even your survival. Success, particularly in service-based industries, is often restricted by the number of hours you can work. To make more money, you have to work harder and longer or employ more people.

Employing the right staff and then looking after them, in a way that gets the most out of them, is critical, and one of the most challenging aspects of owning and running a small business.

## Remember the human in human resources

Often the Human Resources profession forgets the most critical part of what it does - to look after people. It's an area of business that can get overrun with the pressures of process. Recruitment, equal opportunity, remuneration, performance management, employment relations laws, and payroll are examples of processes that are required in any business when staff are employed, including small businesses.

It is important you don't lose sight of the most important fact about your staff. They are people with their own weaknesses, strengths, goals, and desires. Your staff will have their own life issues and could bring these issues to work. They are likely to have a different temperament from you. They will have unique personalities. Different situations will stress them. Their diversity could be an enormous asset or a major headache.

While you must be conscious of following the right processes, don't get swamped by them at the expense of treating your staff as human beings.

You must select the right people, manage your expectations of them, and not condone unacceptable behaviours. If you get the right person through the door, look after that employee. Treat him or her with respect. Remember your values. Your staff will scrutinise your behaviours more than anyone. Keep front of mind that you are human too. You don't have to know everything, and you will make mistakes. Admit this to your staff, as they will respect you for it.

Most of all, be yourself.

Having other people working beside you and sharing in your business can be hugely rewarding.

# Your culture - they stay because they want to

Getting good staff is difficult. When you get someone who is great for your business, you want to keep them. As the business grows and you take on more people, the challenge only increases. If you get a great group of people and things are going well, business will be so much easier.

But what can you do to keep these people, grow the business further and continue with a great team?

It's about your culture.

Perhaps an overused word, but it is why people will join your business and it is why they will stay or leave.

*"Culture matters. How management chooses to treat its people impacts everything for better or for worse."* - **Simon Sinek.** [2]

How you pay people is important, but it's not the only reason people stay. If money is the only reason they are staying, you may have a bigger problem - this is often called **golden handcuffs**. They are only their for the money and it's unlikely their heart will be in it.

People will more often stay because of the culture within the business. How the environment they are working in makes them feel. That they are part of something bigger. That they feel worthwhile and you treat them well.

You, as the owner, set the culture of your small business. If you struggle to get people and, more importantly, you are losing people, be brave enough to ask if it might be the culture you have developed that is contributing to this.

# What motivates staff?

The culture that exists within your business will motivate or demotivate people. We are all motivated by different things. What motivates one person may seem irrational to another. To get the best from people in a business, you are looking to motivate them, so they give their best.

*"The term motivation refers to factors that activate, direct, and sustain goal-directed behaviour. Motives are the "whys" of behaviour - the needs or wants that drive behaviour and explain what we do. We don't actually observe a motive; rather, we infer that one exists based on the behaviour we observe."* - **Dr Jeff Nevid**, Professor of Psychology, St John's University. [3]

As a small business owner, you cannot make another person do anything. We would like to think we can control others, but we cannot. We can only control **what we do**, and **what we say**. We'd like to believe we can also control **what we feel** and **what we think**. Sadly, we cannot even control our thoughts and our feelings. Thoughts come and go. Some will be good and some bad but we can't control them. Feelings come and go based on our reactions to the outside world.

So if we can only control what we do and what we say at any point in time

> If all we can control at any point in time is what we say and do, not even what we think and feel, how can we hope to control what others do?

Motivation is also a very personal thing. Both **extrinsic factors** and **intrinsic factors** motivate us.

**Extrinsic motivators** come from things outside us, like rewards, money, trophies, feedback from others, social acknowledgement.

**Intrinsic motivators** are those things that come from within us. These are activities we do because we love doing them. We are not looking for any external recognition for them. They bring us pleasure or contentment.

The challenge with motivating our staff is that they are all different. Applying pay increases across the board, praise, feedback, or other extrinsic motivators may work for some, but not for others. It may be very difficult to assess the intrinsic motivators for staff - they, like many of us, may have difficulty understanding their own motivations.

In his book *"What Makes Us Tick"*, psychologist and social researcher **Hugh Mackay** [4] describes the desires or motives that drive all of us. He did not ask people what motivates them to establish this list. Typically, we can't always articulate what our desires or motives are. We are not always rational, so we may say one thing yet do another - and then we may attempt to rationalise why we did what we did.

Mackay's research highlighted that we may be motivated by one or more of the following list at different times and under different circumstances. He also highlighted this is by no means a complete list.

## 1. *To be taken seriously*

As a unique individual, we desire recognition and acknowledgment. We all want our voices to be heard as authentic and worthy of attention. We can't bear to be overlooked, dismissed, or belittled. Being looked upon as trivial, having our views disregarded or being made to feel our opinion doesn't matter, can be very damaging to our self-esteem. Not being taken seriously feels like the ultimate insult, and insults fester. Our desire to be valued is universal, but its intensity varies between individuals and at different times of our lives.

## 2. *To have "my place"*

Knowing where we came from, where we belong, and places where we feel physically and psychologically safe are important to us. These are places we consider to be our own, whether at home or in our work environment. It could simply be our work desk. It takes time to be comfortable, to feel safe and then for that place, work or home to draw out the best in us.

## 3. *To have something to believe in*

Over the centuries, many people believed in greater beings, a god or gods. Over time, our beliefs have broadened. We also need to believe in what we do. We might believe in the business we are part of, or simply believe in the team we are a member of.

If these beliefs run deep, it can be immensely powerful - for good or bad. Such beliefs need not be rational, if those having that belief see it as fact or knowledge. To the non-believer, the believer looks irrational.

If staff genuinely believe in what the business is doing and our actions and behaviours reinforce that, it can be very powerful.

## 4. *To connect*

We are social creatures. We need to engage and communicate with other people. While we need to get on with work and not sit around chatting all day, people need a level of social interaction.

The **Hawthorne Experiments**, which were carried out at Western Electric's factory at Hawthorne in Chicago, in the late 1920s and early 1930s, demonstrated this.

The experiment aimed at observing the productivity in a work environment when researchers made different changes, like lighting and working hours. Researchers concluded it was not the changes in physical conditions that were affecting the workers' productivity, but that someone was actually concerned about their workplace. The experiment also provided opportunities for the workers to discuss the changes and the effect that communicating in groups had on them.

## 5. *To be useful*

We all know how devastating it is to our self-esteem to be called useless, especially by someone whose view we value. All people want to be of use, to add value. Even the laziest person rises to the occasion when there's an opportunity to prove themselves.

Most people are decent human beings - we want to help others in need. Most of us, when asked, are helpful; some of us don't even wait to be asked. We often do things for others with no thought of a reward or even recognition for ourselves. Clearly, not everyone is like this. Sadly, some people exist solely to serve themselves.

## 6. *To belong.*

There are aspects of what makes us human that are part of all of us that have developed through our evolutionary journey. One is our need and desire to be part of a group. Our ability to socialise, cooperate and use our collective to overcome the physical limitations we have that other animals do not. While the world has changed, this need has not.

Human beings are as socially interdependent now as they have ever been. While introverts may gain energy from being alone, our default position, as humans, is still to be together. We love to meet to talk, to work, to eat and drink, to socialise. We love to go to concerts, movies, sporting events or the theatre with someone. We need to belong, and a lack of belonging is distressing.

Individuals who are isolated in our society can find it very distressing and damaging to their mental health. This is no different in a business. Staff want to belong. They want to build relationships with the owners and other staff members. If they never develop these relationships and become isolated, they will probably underperform or leave.

## 7.  *To be in control*

We like to have, or at least feel like we have, control over our circumstances. Having no control over our situation can be very stressful.

Too often we want to control others, which we can't. All we can control is what we say and do at that moment in time. When we cannot get others to do what we want, we can become very frustrated. Rather than trying to control staff, we need to empower them, so they feel in control of what they do during their workday. This will build greater ownership for their work.

## 8.  *To have something happen*

We want to see things happen through action rather than words. While we may not always like change and may not agree with the things happening around us, people like to see things getting done - we do not enjoy boredom. We enjoy movies and entertainment because things are happening. There is action and something going on.

We do like some level of stability and ritual in our lives, and we can resist change when it is thrust on us. We resist change where we have no control over it. However, we are a species that has continually acted to improve the world, and the pace of the change and the actions we take to bring it about are unending.

Staff will be far more motivated when the business is actively doing something and achieving results. We all get frustrated when we hear people say they intend to do something, then never follow through.

Nothing will assist in finding what motivates your staff more than getting to know them. One size will never fit everyone. The more you know about those who work for you, the better will be your chances of finding the motivators that get the best from them for their benefit and your business.

# Maslow's hierarchy of needs - as relevant now as in 1943

In 1943, **Abraham Maslow** introduced his famous theory that human beings are motivated based on a hierarchy of needs. [5]

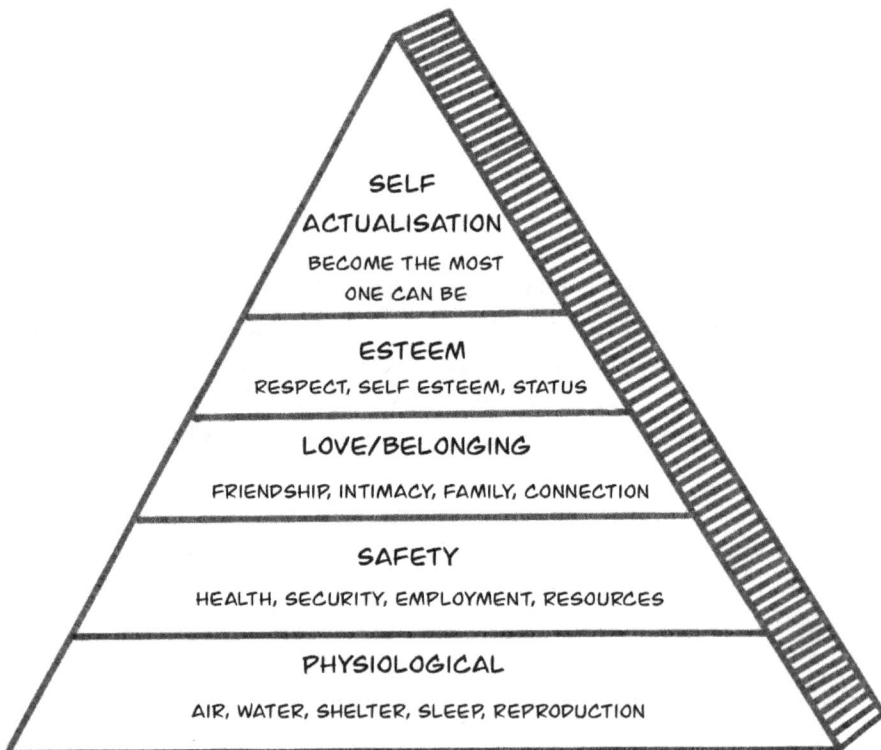

SELF
ACTUALISATION
BECOME THE MOST
ONE CAN BE

ESTEEM
RESPECT, SELF ESTEEM, STATUS

LOVE/BELONGING
FRIENDSHIP, INTIMACY, FAMILY, CONNECTION

SAFETY
HEALTH, SECURITY, EMPLOYMENT, RESOURCES

PHYSIOLOGICAL
AIR, WATER, SHELTER, SLEEP, REPRODUCTION

We are not likely to be motivated by a higher-level in Maslow's hierarchy unless the lower needs are being met. The need to be loved and to belong will not be a need if we aren't able to feed ourselves, don't have clean air to breathe, or believe our lives are in threat.

The same applies to the way you remunerate people. If you pay your staff at a level that does not allow them to meet their basic living needs, then they are less likely to be motivated to achieve greater things.

Therefore, while money is not a great way to increase people's motivation, if it is too low, it will demotivate them. The goal is to reward people fairly so they can meet their personal needs. This will hopefully mean money stops being a factor, so it is other factors higher on Maslow's hierarchy that are driving motivations.

# Selection and recruitment processes

The first and most critical step in building a team of people in your business is recruiting the right staff. Small business owners often spend very little time on the recruitment process when it's one of the most important business decisions they must make.

## Short-term options to find staff

There are a wide range of external experts you can engage to help you when necessary. The good thing about using people in this way is it's a short-term cost where you can pursue the exact skill you want at the time you need it. You can also stop it when you don't need or can no longer afford it.

You may well require support over a longer period, but only for a few hours each month. For example, you may wish to get someone to manage your accounts at the end of the month. Rather than employ a full-time person, you may engage a service provider who can do this for you. They will charge a higher hourly rate, but you don't have any of the work that comes with employing someone.

Likewise, you could use **labour hire businesses** to employ an apprentice or a trades person.

These types of short-term relationships are always easier to end than they are for permanent employees, especially if things are not working out.

## Permanent employees

If you're growing, you will need to look seriously at employing staff. These could be full-time, part-time, or casual employees.

Often, small businesses put too little time into employing the right people.

The legal aspects of the employment process can be frightening for some small business owners, so they avoid recruiting. If they have the wrong person, they may tolerate poor performance rather than face the risk of personal grievances, legal issues, and unwanted costs and distractions from their business.

Owners can struggle to understand why their employees are not as devoted to the business as they are and build unrealistic expectations. Many don't articulate what they expect of their employees, cannot give them useful feedback, or do not assess their performance frequently enough.

While there are no guarantees with people management, some key principles will minimise the pain of getting it wrong. We discussed a lot about how we tick as human beings in previous chapters and what motivates people.

The following discussion will help manage the legal and procedural processes when employing staff.

## Position descriptions, Individual Employment Agreements and staff handbooks

Before you advertise for a new person, you need to form a very clear view of what role you need, and what you want in the person who fills that role.

- How clear are you about the details of the role you want to fill?

- What are you able to pay and is it enough to attract candidates?

- What, other than salary, makes working with you attractive?

- What minimum skills must they have?

- What minimum qualifications must the person have?

- How many years of experience do they need to bring?

You will then need to prepare a **position description** for the role (also called a **job description**). This is not only a requirement, but it will clarify the role for the candidate and could also be very important should a dispute arise in the future. This will help clarify what you want from the role and the person who finally fills it.

You must also develop an **Individual Employment Agreement (IEA)**. This is the over-riding legal document covering the employment relationship. If you do not have a template prepared, there are government websites that offer excellent tools to help you build an IEA at no cost. [6]

If you have some specific concerns or want to use different clauses, seek legal advice. You should never edit a standard clause provided to you by an expert or government department without seeking a legal opinion. If an issue or dispute arises, non-standard clauses will create problems and may not be enforceable.

I won't list all the clauses you need in and IEA, but here are a few that warrant particular emphasis:

- Ensure you cover **confidentiality** so a staff member does not take your key information to a competitor.

- Consider **restraints of trade** for key senior staff if you fear they could leave and take your customers or staff with them. You need to draft these carefully if they are to be enforceable.

- You should always include a **90-day trial** clause.

- **Employment Protection Provisions** are required and apply if you sell the business in part or in full.

- Detail your expectations around **health and safety**.

- Include **dispute and termination** clauses.

The **position description** should cover the following as a minimum:

- Job title.

- Pay range.

- Key accountabilities of the role.

- Minimum requisite qualifications.

- Desirable but non-essential skills.

- Any **financial delegations** (what the person can spend without asking your permission).

- Any personal attributes that the person in the role must show.

You should offer short-listed candidates a copy of the position description before any interview. You only need to provide an IEA to the successful candidate after you verbally offer them a position.

You do not need to include all the tasks an employee needs to carry out in the position description. It should be more high level. You want some flexibility so you can discuss other tasks and activities with your employees without having to update the position description each time.

It is also advisable, if your business is growing and more staff are being taken on, to produce a **staff handbook.**

You can't cover all the policies and procedures in the IEA or position description. A staff handbook applies to everyone and can include all those things not covered in agreements. Topics typically include personal use of vehicles, lunch and meal breaks, clothing requirements, smoking, training, key health and safety expectations, codes of conduct, drug and alcohol rules, and any other key expectations for anyone working in the business.

If you decide to have a staff handbook, you should provide it with the IEA and position description to new employees for their signature. If you need to update the staff handbook, you will need to re-circulate it, so everyone knows what has changed.

> The position description and IEA must be signed **BEFORE** the employee starts any work with you. If they come out even for a day's work as a trial, they are employed

Some clauses in the IEA, especially the 90-day trial clause, may not be enforceable if a staff member has started work with documents unsigned.

## Finding, short-listing, and interviewing candidates

There are several methods you can use to reach out to potential candidates. The type of person you are seeking will influence how you advertise. Consider the candidates and, just like customers, think about how best to engage with them. Online recruitment sites like **SEEK**, **TradeMe Jobs** and **Student Job Search** are common. Social media sites are also very popular.

You can go to a recruitment company to do the short-listing for you. This is usually not cheap but may be appropriate for a more senior, specialist, or management role. You should shop around to find the best recruiter for you. If you find a recruitment company you are happy with, they can become a very beneficial advisor for your business should you grow.

If you have the option, interview two or three candidates. It helps if you have another person with you to get a broader perspective and to avoid subconscious biases, as we have already discussed. When asking questions, get the candidates to offer specific examples where they showed the skills and behaviours you are looking for. An example question might be, *"Tell me about a time you disagreed with a fellow employee or boss and how you resolved it."*

The key to an interview is not to catch people out. You want them to feel comfortable so they will be their true self. Many people may have never been in an interview. Others may perform badly in an interview environment but be an exceptional candidate. Cater for the position. For example, hands-on, outdoor roles may attract people who are not good in an interview.

You may also need to get people to demonstrate their technical skills during the selection process if they are applying for specialist roles.

Always ask for work **references** and follow up on them. Don't rely on written references, as they could have been written by anyone. Speak directly to referees. If candidates can't provide references, ask them why not, as it could raise some suspicion. While candidates will normally only give you references that are likely to be positive, it is surprising what you can discover if you ask referees some probing questions. One question to always ask a referee is *"would you employ this person again?"*. The answer will tell you a lot.

Depending on the role, you may also wish to do additional checks on the individual. This could include their criminal history, driving status (especially if driving is essential for the job they will do), and even creditworthiness. It is likely you will need to gain the applicant's permission to do these checks.

Pre-employment **drug and alcohol testing** is becoming more common. You need to ensure your IEA is very clear about your drug and alcohol procedures. If you want to have a workplace free of drugs and alcohol, your procedures could vary from a simple policy statement with no other actions through to a detail program of random drug and alcohol testing. Be very clear about this in your employment documents, policies and procedures, as it is a controversial issue and a staff member could challenge it. This may be one to run past and employment law expert if you are unsure.

Employing close friends and family is very common in small businesses and can be very effective. However, it's not without its challenges. You don't want the stress of the business to damage an existing relationship. If you are recruiting close friends or family, you need to be clear on the needs of the business and the boundaries of the relationship.

> Remember, if the candidates are not right for you, don't employ anyone. Start looking again. The cost of getting it wrong is too great.

You may struggle to find any suitable candidates. This could put your business under pressure. If you fail to attract the right person and have to start the recruitment process again, it is time consuming and expensive. However, getting the wrong person could be even more painful.

# Set clear expectations from day one

If you have done your reference checks and are happy, and if the candidate has accepted the position and signed the position description and IEA, they are ready to start.

The clearer you can make your expectations known to the new employee, and the earliest you can do this in the relationship, the better. It could remove a lot of heartache later and most new staff members want to know what's expected of them.

These could be very high-level expectations or quite detailed. How detailed may depend on the balancing act between sufficient clarity and not scaring off a potential employee after being overrun with what they may see as petty rules.

Here are a few examples:

- A cafe owner makes it clear to new employees that staff cannot take food for free but are welcome to buy food at cost price.

- An electrician tells new staff they must be at the office every morning at 7 a.m. for a safety and planning meeting.

- A new receptionist is told how to answer all phone calls to support even the most difficult customer.

We discussed the benefit of developing a staff handbook. Even if the new staff member has signed it, going through it with them after they start will be helpful.

Some businesses also have **induction check sheets**, which include a list of things that need to be sorted when the person starts. It is also a handy reminder for what you need to go through with new staff, in case you get busy and forget. Simple things like getting all the paperwork signed and filed, ordering clothing, getting a copy of licences for filing, providing computer passwords and logins, making sure they have a set of keys to open the business, going through safety procedures like evacuations and so on.

You should reinforce your business values and how important they are to you. You may find an employee meets the requirements of their job description but behaves in a way that is at odds with the values you hold dear.

# Rewards and compensation

While your work may motivate you, and you may also extract meaning and pleasure from it, you still need to make a living, as do your staff. As Maslow put it, we need our basic needs to be met first. We need to be paid enough money to at least lead a basic life, get the kids through school, buy or rent shelter over our heads, and enjoy some basic pleasures in life.

All of us will have a very different view of what we feel we are worth versus what we are paid. Nothing can bring out irrationality in us more than establishing our value in terms of some material measure - namely money.

Businesses can only pay what they can afford, with staff wages often being the single biggest financial expense for any business of any size. You also need to ensure you pay fairly and with some recognition of the value society and the marketplace puts on certain positions.

It is worth considering some of the biases and irrationalities that exist within us that will influence how we respond to what we are paid.

As human beings, we can't help but compare. When deciding, we like to compare one option against another before choosing. Nowhere is this more relevant than when we are looking at how much we are paid. We compare ourselves against other measures to establish if we feel we are paid fairly. We compare with other employees, other similar businesses, other professions, and other industries.

The way human resource professionals appraise people's roles, and then attach a salary to that role, is all based on comparisons. We look at the job, compare it with a basket of similar businesses in the same industry, and come up with a salary. This process does not consider whether a police officer is more valuable than a doctor, the CEO of a company, or a person helping the homeless. We may all struggle to accept why one person is paid a huge amount while another, who we feel is far more worthy, is paid far less.

## Performance pay schemes

Often businesses use incentive schemes, bonuses, commissions or other performance pay processes. If done well, they can drive behaviours that support the business - they can benefit the employee and the business.

However, there are many situations where businesses do not implement these processes particularly well, and they drive perverse behaviours that damage the business.

The danger with rewards is that it shifts from **intrinsic** to **extrinsic rewards**. People may not do their job because they love doing it or believe in it, but because they are motivated by the reward.

---

### *More money doesn't mean better performance.*

One would think that a CEO making many millions of dollars would feel happy about their salary, considering many of their staff, who contribute to the company's success, earn a fraction of that pay.

Human irrationality in establishing our financial worth, was demonstrated when CEO salaries were made public in the USA in 1993 by federal securities regulators.

---

Regulators felt such transparency would make boards think twice about paying excessive amounts to CEOs.

Sadly, the opposite occurred. CEOs started comparing their own salaries and bonuses with their counterparts. Before the release of salaries, they were satisfied; however, they demanded increases when they could compare - "*Why am I paid less than that CEO?*"

When performance pay systems are put in place, and not thought through well, they can deliver very perverse behaviours.

A few examples:

- The American bank, Wells Fargo had a class action taken against it by customers in 2017 to the tune of $US110 million. This was because staff opened about 2 million fake bank accounts. This occurred because staff were set unrealistic performance targets for bringing new clients into the bank, which was only measured by new accounts being opened.

- In 2015, Kathmandu was forced to apologise publicly for mistakes in the CEO's bonus scheme. The company suffered a significant fall in earnings, but the mistake still saw the CEO do much better come bonus time.

- Many factors contributed to the demise of Dick Smith. One was the incentive scheme suppliers offered the company. The company was offered very healthy rebates for buying more stock. This saw the business purchase far more stock than it needed. The rebates could be put into the financials to improve the short-term performance of the business, which was the CEO's incentive. Unfortunately, Dick Smith built up huge stock levels that it could not sell.

We respond to incentives. The important thing to remember is that they are the right incentives and drive the right behaviours.

If you feel the pay levels are fair relative to the market, and you have decided not to put in other payment schemes, there are many other non-monetary or social-based factors you can use that could be low cost and extremely effective incentives. This is where you need to know your staff.

Staff members may be at different stages of their lives and be motivated by different things. Some may want more free time. Others may want as many hours of work as you can give them to pay off their mortgage. Some just like to be told they are doing a great job, while others may like to be pampered with an occasional gift.

If you are considering a performance pay scheme, think this through carefully. These schemes, if poorly designed, could drive the wrong, even perverse, behaviours. You could find you are paying your staff extra when they did not deliver what the business wanted.

> Never forget that it is often the little things that can make the difference with staff more so than the large financial incentives.

# Regression to the mean and long-term staff performance

Daniel Kahneman, from his time assisting the Israeli Air Force, debated with a commander about his practice of chastising the cadet pilots when they performed badly. He also questioned why the commander never acknowledged them when they performed exceptionally well.

The basis for the commander's actions was that when he praised the pilots for exceptional and above average performance, they would typically follow up with a lesser effort, yet when he berated them for a below average performance, their next effort was much better.

Kahneman argued that the reason for this was simply that the pilot's flight performance over time would drift back to their normal levels of performance or return to the **mean**. When they had a terrible day, chances were this would not continue for long before they returned to their average performance. When they had an exceptional day, its likely it wouldn't last, and they would fall back to a more normal level of performance.

We will typically operate on either side of the mean, regressing back to that mean. If we continue to practise, build our skills and experience, the mean will slowly lift over time, but from day-to-day we are likely to oscillate around the mean.

The shifts away from our mean are likely to have elements of luck. Instilling fear through criticism is unlikely to encourage better performance. If it does, it may have nothing to do with the criticism but have more to do with the staff member just having a better day.

A professional golfer has those days where every ball drops and the next day nothing goes well. The skill of the golfer should keep them near their handicap, but some days, good or bad luck will push that player away from this. A significant focus on practice and increased skill and fitness will see their handicap improve, but this takes time, as the body and brain must adapt.

So, keep in mind, your staff member may not be at their best for many reasons and berating them for a bad day may not help much. Consider what their mean performance is. If that mean is normally above expectations, be patient when they have a bad day as they will return to their above average performance

If their mean is consistently below expectations, that is a quite a different issue requiring a different response, which I will get to.

# If you can't afford it, you can't afford it

It is far more common for a small business owner to want to pay their staff more than they are being paid. The opposite situation, where an owner refuses to pay a staff member more, is often less common. You know the pain of being short of staff or employing the wrong staff. You hate the thought of losing someone who is really good simply because you can't pay them enough.

Unfortunately, you won't be able to afford to keep throwing money at people to keep them.

Continuing to use money as a motivator can prove very expensive and can often prove rather futile as, in the long run, it is unlikely to change people's behaviours. No doubt they will take more money if offered (most of us would), but whether it changes any behaviour, and whether it will make them stay for the right reasons, is a very different thing.

## Know what you legally must do

The two key pieces of legislation that cover the relationship between you and an employee are the **Employment Relations Act 2000** and the **Holidays Act 2003.** While you must comply with them, as with any laws, you will never know all the details, but there are some basics. The position description and an Individual Employment Agreement (IEA) are the two key documents which will ensure you are complying with these Acts.

The **Holidays Act** is a hard set of laws to understand and comply with. Many people struggle to get this right and can find they face a situation where they did not follow the rules correctly and end up owing their staff large amounts of unpaid leave. Even the experts struggle with it. Many payroll systems will say they comply with this act, but these systems are only as good as the information you put into them.

Issues arise when people work on public holidays, accumulate sick leave, work part time, or variable rosters. How you accrue annual leave can create confusion. Leave entitlements can also grow into a significant financial liability if staff aren't taking their leave. You need to manage this.

These are a few key **legal requirements** you need to know. These do change, so check out what the requirements are when you are completing the documents.

- **Minimum wage.** You cannot pay anyone below the **Minimum hourly rate**. This gets lifted from time to time to keep pace with living costs. Find out what it currently is and ensure you are paying your employees this amount or more.

- **Living wage.** This is a voluntary wage level that is defined and describes what a person should make to live a reasonable life. It is typically above the **minimum wage**. Many employers strive to deliver this. However, many small businesses can't afford to pay this amount. It is not compulsory, but staff will know what it is.

- **Minimum wage rates for young people**. Typically, the minimum hourly rate for young people or people on a youth training scheme will be lower than the rate for adults.

- **90-day trials.** Different political parties have different views on trial periods. In recent years, businesses with less than 20 staff could include this clause. Changes have come and gone, allowing all larger businesses to use them or exclude them. As of 2024, all businesses could include them. Always include these clauses in your IEA if the law allows it. I will discuss why shortly.

- **Rest and lunch breaks.** You will need to provide your staff brief breaks through the day, typically 10 minutes, plus their meal breaks.

- **Annual leave.** Your staff become entitled to annual holidays, public holidays, sick leave, bereavement leave, parental leave and other types of leave if they meet certain conditions. They are entitled to four weeks' annual leave after 12 months of continuous employment.

- **KiwiSaver.** For any staff member over 18 years of age you will need to contribute 3% of their salary to KiwiSaver.

If you are unsure of what your legal obligations are for your staff, seek good advice. If you get this wrong, you may lose a valuable staff member. It could end in a dispute, and it could cost you money, time, and a lot of emotional energy.

# Managing and dealing with poor performance

It is very unlikely if you own and operate a small business for many years, and employ staff, that you won't face a staff performance issue at some stage. When you do, it is also very unlikely you will enjoy dealing with it. No one does. It is probably one of the worst things a small business owner will face and most of us want to ignore it and hope it goes away.

Unfortunately, when staff are not meeting your expectations, the worst thing you can do is ignore it and do nothing. You will simply condone unacceptable behaviours that will start being considered acceptable and you will have to live with them.

If the performance issue is minor and just a one-off, you may make a note in case you see it again. If it happens more often, your response could be as simple as a quiet word reminding the person of your expectations.

If the issues continue or worsen, you may need to increase the action required. It's important you document every stage of this process. This could become vital information if the situation worsens. You can easily dispose of the information if things turn around. Such documentation need be as informal as a few notes scribbled in your diary.

> The actions you take will depend on your style, your relationship with the person, the person's possible responses, and the specifics of the issue. **The worst action is no action**.

If the behaviour continues, and softer approaches are not working, or an event occurs that is very serious you will need to act. If people are hurting your business and showing no signs of responding to the expectations you've set, then you can't allow this to continue. This can be particularly damaging to your small business, especially if you only have a few staff.

## When you must remove a staff member

If you believe you have taken all reasonable steps and you can see no path forward other than removing the person from the business, then it's time to seek some advice. Don't get so paralysed by a fear of grievances or legal action that you go no further. Even if you follow the best possible process, you may still face a challenge.

Consider the risk and damage of keeping the staff member against the risk of them challenging you if you dismiss them. Sadly, you may prefer to face the latter risk compared to keeping a destructive person who simply doesn't fit.

Likewise, this is where your emotions could be running high, and your intuition is screaming out to act, and get rid of the person as quickly as possible.

Take a breath and pause.

> Take a breath. Walk away. Calm down before you act no matter how serious the issue. Don't become part of the problem.

You don't want to become part of the problem. This is the time to pause. Reacting prematurely and getting this process wrong could prove very costly, financially, emotionally and on the culture of the business - not to mention on your mental health.

The best way to limit the risk of legal action is to get good advice from an employment law specialist - someone who has dealt with many cases before. It will cost you, but the support you will get will be more than worth it, even if you have done it before. Every person is different, so every case will be different.

The more you can document before you get to this stage, the better. If things turn nasty, the more facts you can present, examples, timelines, and other details, the better.

As the employer, you need to show that you have acted in **good faith** throughout the process. The legal process will not look fondly on employers who do not appear to act appropriately during these processes. Remember, while you want the person gone, for the stress and heartache they have caused you, they are still people, and you need to respond respectfully, professionally, and lawfully.

# Removing a person for poor performance

This is not a simple or easy process, so prepare yourself for what is coming. I will keep saying it - **seek advice,** but here are the key steps to consider, some of which I've already highlighted:

1.  Document everything from the moment you feel a dismissal is even an outside possibility.

2.  Inform the staff member as early as possible how they have not been meeting your expectations.

3.  When discussions get more serious, you should offer the person the option to have someone with them as support.

4.  You too should have someone with you to document discussions and back you up if debate occurs later.

5.  You need to give them the opportunity to respond and explain their side of the story.

6.  After taking their response into consideration, be clear about what they need to do to meet your expectations. Document this, and ensure they understand this, even if they don't like it.

7.  You need to show that you have given them a reasonable chance to correct what they have been doing.

8.  If the person does not meet what you have agreed, you cannot dismiss them **unless you have clearly stated that their inaction could cause the loss of their job**. You must be explicit that this is a possible outcome.

9.  Be very careful with statements like, *"if you don't leave, I will dismiss you"*. If the person then resigns voluntarily, the employee could argue that it was a **Constructive Dismissal**. The employee felt they had no option other than to resign.

10. If it is clear the person will not or cannot change, then you can proceed with dismissal.

11. You must ensure you pay the person any outstanding entitlements, including their notice period and holiday pay.

12. Remember, the staff member is well within their rights to lodge a personal grievance if they are not happy, even if you are sure you have done everything correctly.

> Please seek legal advice. If you do not follow the correct process, you could face legitimate legal challenges and hurt a lot of good people

## *Performance versus redundancies*

There are cases in a business' life when you may have to remove staff because of genuine redundancy reasons. These could include a loss of major customers or contracts, downturns in market conditions, shifts in the strategy for the business, or a partial or full sale of the business (which we discuss in more detail later).

All may mean that the positions of one or more staff members can no longer be justified. If your business cannot sustain positions without putting the survival of the business at risk, you may have no choice but to let people go or restructure your operations.

This can be an emotionally challenging process, even more so than dismissal, because you may have to let people go who are good people who have done nothing wrong.

The following are the minimum steps you need to follow for redundancies:

1. Develop a document outlining the business reasons for the redundancies, what positions will be affected and what options there are for staff. **This document should not be a final decision**. You must present it only as an option while seeking feedback from staff on alternatives.

2.    Discuss your option(s) with staff and face up to all their questions before leaving it with them. This is their jobs at risk, so the least you can do is take all their questions on the chin, no matter how uncomfortable they may be.

3.    You should leave this document with staff for a reasonable period so they can seek their own advice, consider alternatives, ask questions and provide feedback. How long this period should be could depend on the size of your business, the staff affected and the complexity of the changes. A week would be the minimum.

4.    When you receive all their feedback, you need to consider it thoughtfully. Your staff are not stupid. If they realise you are simply going through the motions and had no intention of considering their views, then your risk of grievances will escalate. Besides, who says what they come back with may not be valuable and provide alternative solutions.

5.    If this does not change your need to let people go, and there are no alternate positions available in the business that they could fill, then you will need to give them notice that their position is redundant. They can either work out their remaining notice period (as defined in their IEA) or you could mutually agree to pay them out and let them go immediately.

6.    Remember, just as with a performance issue, staff members are well within their rights to lodge a personal grievance if they are not happy, whether you believe you have done everything correctly on not.

There are many cases in business where the owner or manager may use a redundancy process to get rid of an underperforming staff member. There may well be a legitimate reason for this, but this is an area to tread carefully.

If you are making a person's position redundant simply to avoid a lengthier performance management process, it is likely the person will see this for what it is. Their legal representative (which they will probably engage) will also see it for what it is. The staff member could then claim you have **Unfairly Dismissed** them, and you may face reinstatement of the staff member or face a hefty compensation package.

Again, seek advice.

## Are you within the 90-day trial period?

You may well follow very thorough recruitment processes, but it still does not mean you will always get it right. 90-day trial periods exist for this reason. Use them.

If a new employee is not working out, be respectful but move them on. It is so important you include this clause in the IEA. **It is also critical new staff sign the IEA before the person does any work for you**. If they were working casually or even carried out a few hours work before signing the IEA, it could void this clause.

If you decide to remove someone under the 90-day trial, you don't need to provide detailed reasons. Doing so may cause unwanted complications.

If you are using the 90-day trial as a lazy option instead of following a good recruitment process, keep in mind it does not come for free. For one, it wastes time, impacts the person and you still must pay out their notice period, which could be several weeks' pay.

## Is the person a casual employee?

Casual employees have similar rights to any other employee and can lodge personal grievances. The major difference is you don't offer the employee guaranteed rosters. **If they are working a defined roster, they are not a casual.** They are more likely to be permanent part-time.

It is very common for small businesses to say they have casual employees, yet the law sees them as permanent part-time employees. Getting this wrong could prove very costly if you end the person's employment believing they are casual when they are not.

Casual employees do not get annual or sick leave and have a higher hourly rate to compensate for this (typically 8%). Each time you offer them a shift, they are effectively being re-employed. If you are unhappy with them or have no more work, then you are not obliged to offer them further shifts.

However, if you make commitments to them for shifts and then cancel them without agreement or end their work mid-shift, you may be in breach of the IEA, which opens you up to challenges.

## What action can a dismissed or redundant staff member take?

Any staff member has a right to lodge a **personal grievance** against you. This may be while you still employ the person, and they could lodge the grievance for many reasons. These may have nothing to do with a dismissal situation.

If you receive a formal grievance following a redundancy or a dismissal, consider it carefully and, you guessed it, seek advice. How you respond will vary depending on the grievance and what the employee is seeking.

If you cannot resolve this directly with them, it is likely they will instigate a formal **mediation** process, typically held by the Ministry of Business, Innovation and Employment or equivalent government agency. This gives both parties the opportunity to have their respective positions heard and, hopefully, a mutual settlement agreed.

Mediation is a negotiation. The onus will be on the other party to indicate what they want to resolve the matter with you. It could be a reinstatement of their position or a cash settlement. You will need to be clear what the cost of meeting their needs is versus countering with an offer you can live with.

Reinstatement is usually one of the worst scenarios for you. If you are in mediation, it's likely your relationship with the staff member is now severely damaged.

You could hold your position and refuse to meet the other party's requests. You risk the process going to the next stages, namely the **Employment Relations Authority** and then the **Employment Court**.

Compensation claims can get into the tens of thousands of dollars, so taking this step is not one to be done lightly.

If the matter proceeds to the Employment Relations Authority, the person may pursue partial or full reinstatement, *"compensation for lost wages"* as well as compensation for *"humiliation, loss of dignity and injury to feelings"*. The successful party may also claim compensation for legal costs.

When the Employment Relations Authority makes its decision, it is legally binding. If either party is dissatisfied with the determination, they can apply to the Employment Court - and further legal appeals could also occur.

The stronger your case, the better you treated the person, and the better your process, the lower will be your risk. This is the time you will be very glad you sought that advice, acted professionally and in good faith, had sound employment documents in place, and documented everything during the dispute.

It is likely the person lodging the grievance will have legal support. This support person may have limited legal knowledge, or they could be a qualified lawyer. New Zealand does not require qualified lawyers to represent people through the employment process. This ensures the process is more accessible and cost effective for anyone to use, not just those that can afford a lawyer.

It is possible the person's legal representative will be on a **no-win-no-pay arrangement,** in which case they will fight you for every dollar.

The longer the process progresses, the more costly it will become to all parties, including the staff member. If your legal advice is telling you your position is strong and the amount being pursued is significant, it may be worth the risk of allowing them to continue beyond mediation.

> If you are pursuing legal action on principle, be careful. It may be worth cutting your losses and mediating an outcome, even if you feel wronged. Remember, you have a business to run.

## _These processes can be soul destroying_

It is very difficult not to come away from these processes without being cynical and losing faith in people. The staff member may have been damaging your business, effecting other staff, and had to go. You are likely to feel, and justifiably so, that after you followed all the correct processes, with an employee who was totally out of line that you still had to pay.

This is, sadly, the reality when things go wrong. It hurts. It will make you angry, frustrated and feeling like you never want to employ a person again.

While this is understandable, you must come to grips with this. The good people you still have are too important. The ongoing success of your business is too important.

Chalk it up to experience. Learn from it, but you must work on ways to move on from it.

# CHAPTER 13

## LEADERSHIP

## "KNOW YOURSELF, ACCEPT YOURSELF, FORGET YOURSELF"

Very often, the owners of a small business apportion the difficulties they face to the staff they employ or oversee. Managing and leading staff is difficult, and it is not for everyone. Unfortunately, often the biggest issue for a small business owner is not the staff, but the owner's leadership style. The staff may not be the problem - it may be the owner.

## Our management and leadership skills

If your staff are unhappy or leaving, before blaming them, you do need to look at yourself. This may be a tough pill to swallow, but such self-awareness could be a major contributor to your success as a leader and business owner. The humility to accept feedback, including self-feedback, accepting our limitations as people and leaders, and then doing something about it, is at the heart of leadership.

> *"People will join a business, but they will leave their boss."* - ***Unknown***

As a manager and business owner, you need to create a work environment that is not based on fear. If you instil fear or punish people for making mistakes, your staff will only do the bare minimum to get through the day. They will also avoid doing anything more for the business than they must - and many will simply leave.

We can be guilty of over-complicating the management and leadership of staff. You need to be yourself, show interest in your staff, care for them, set standards and adhere to them, and communicate often. People fill in the gaps when there is a lack of information, and it's usually filled with unproductive or incorrect information.

Explain to people what you want them to do, but more importantly, why you need it done. They may not agree, but at least they know why.

*"People will do almost any WHAT if you give them a good WHY."* - **Friedrich Nietzsche**

# Know yourself; accept yourself; forget yourself

Consider this statement about what makes a good leader: *"Know yourself; accept yourself; forget yourself."* Leadership is about being self-aware and accepting what you do well and not so well. You then need to accept your limitations and play to your strengths. And finally, and most importantly, you need to park your immediate self-interests and do what is best for the business.

Leadership is about being selfless. If you put your staff and the business before your own needs, it will build loyalty and you will receive rewards in many other ways from your staff.

Sadly, there are too many cases of business failures where the self-interest of the leaders or owners destroyed the business.

That self interest may range from businesspeople who cared little about their staff, or took significant funds out of the business for personal use. The worst examples are those like the failed finance company directors who were jailed for fraud in the fallout from the Global Financial Crisis.

Leading a successful business requires humility and self-awareness, and often means you must put your own immediate interests to one side for the benefit of the business. Most business owners and leaders do this. Unfortunately, many don't, and the effects of such self-interest are usually not good for anyone - including the business owner or leader.

## New Zealand finance company collapses.
## A story of self-interest and poor management.

The losses in the USA which occurred during the Global Financial Crisis (GFC), including the failures of Bear Stearns, in March 2008, Lehman Brothers in September 2008, and others are now the basis of folklore. The combined losses drifted into trillions of dollars.

The GFC also saw a significant upheaval in New Zealand's finance sector.

Between 2006 and 2010, 49 finance companies collapsed in New Zealand, costing investors over $8 billion. The government stepped in to bail out many of these companies. The highest profile failures included Hanover Finance, Bridgecorp and South Canterbury Finance.

The customers of these finance companies were individuals and small businesses who wanted more flexibility or more credit than banks were prepared to offer.

In the decade of rapid growth in New Zealand's property sector up to 2007, finance company lending expanded rapidly. These second tier lenders filled the gap of higher-risk lending that the banks wouldn't provide, deeming it too risky.

This competition eventually saw banks drifting more into the property sector and taking on higher-risk lending. This lead to the finance companies having to take on even greater risks to maintain their position in the market and to compete.

Finance companies were less diligent in understanding the risks faced by those they lent to or their capacity to repay. While irresponsible to both their own businesses and their customers, it was considered acceptable.

Many of these finance companies did not adequately disclose the level of risk, and some deliberately sought to reduce the perceived risk difference between themselves and the banks. When the GFC hit, these risks were realised, and most New Zealand finance companies collapsed.

The Serious Fraud Office pursued the leaders of 15 of these finance companies, including Bridgecorp and Hanover Finance. Around 20 directors faced jail time or home detention for their roles in these failures. Bridgecorp's director and majority shareholder, Rod Petricevic, was jailed for over six years. He was deemed to have shown no concern for his investors, used company resources for personal use, was untrustworthy and unethical.

A parliamentary investigation found a range of reasons for the finance industry's demise [1]. The findings included criminal misconduct, poor governance and management, poor communication with investors, and weak supervision. They also questioned the ability of the leaders of these businesses to understand the risks their businesses faced. And finally, the report questioned the values of some of these leaders who showed greater self-interest than interest in their customers, their staff, or their own business.

# The Johari Window

The Johari Window represents the concept of self-knowledge. It is illustrated below.

The American psychologists Joseph Luft and Harrington Ingham created the **Johari Window** in 1955. (The name is a combination of the two men's first names.) You could also call it the Johari House, with four rooms. It represents a simple perspective on self-knowledge. Ask yourself a few questions about which "*rooms*" you have never been in or the "*rooms*" that others have never been in and how that might be affecting you and your business

How blind are you of the things others see of you when you are working in your business? What might you be hiding from others that you know may be affecting your business? How might you learn about your unknown self for the benefit of your business?

| KNOWN TO SELF | NOT KNOWN TO SELF |
|---|---|
| **OPEN** | **BLIND** |
| THINGS WE KNOW ABOUT OURSELVES AND OTHERS KNOW ABOUT US | THINGS OTHERS KNOW ABOUT US THAT WE DON'T KNOW |
| HIDDEN SELF | UNKNOWN SELF |
| **HIDDEN** | **UNKNOWN** |
| THINGS WE KNOW ABOUT OURSELVES THAT OTHERS DON'T KNOW | THINGS NEITHER WE NOR OTHERS KNOW ABOUT US |

Self-knowledge is a lifetime journey. As we age and life exposes us to fresh challenges, we learn more about ourselves. Self-knowledge is a powerful tool that all too many people disregard because it's difficult, uncomfortable, or inconvenient to devote time to. The more you can come to grips with this, the more you will enjoy working in your business. You will also be more efficient and have a greater chance of achieving your version of success.

## Consider your 'circle of competence"

The one thing I cannot advise you on in this book, as it relates to your business, is the training and skills you bring to your business. No matter what business you are in, you will bring education, training, certificates and life skills to that business that are likely to be unique. Hopefully, the business you are in allows you to maximise the benefit of these skills.

These skills are usually what is the easiest step in being self-aware, the easiest thing for you to measure and explain to others. How good an electrician, plumber, builder, mechanic, arborist, florist, accountant, architect, engineer are you?

If you're looking to branch out into other businesses or buy a new business, be cautious about venturing too far outside your **circle of competence**. Avoid making investments or buying into industries or markets you know nothing about. They may well have a reputation for producing sound financial returns, but if you lack the required skills, you are less likely to achieve the success you seek. You may become heavily reliant on others who have those skills. If they leave, they may leave you stranded.

There may also be other competencies the business needs that you don't have and need to bring in. The most common of these is bookkeeping. In building your self-awareness, test what competencies you have, whether they are a point of difference for you as well as testing the competencies your business needs that you don't have.

> *"Learn from the mistakes of others. You can't live long enough to make them all yourself."* - **Eleanor Roosevelt.** Former First Lady.

# How can you better understand your personality?

The American Psychological Association defines personality as:

> ***Personality refers to the enduring characteristics and behaviour that comprise a person's unique adjustment to life, including major traits, interests, drives, values, self-concept, abilities, and emotional patterns*** [2]

Competence is a part of our skill set that is relatively easy to quantify.

It is far more difficult to understand who we are and how we tick. These are often, incorrectly, called our soft skills. Failing to understand who we are when running our business can be damaging.

Our personality forms part of who we are from the earliest stages of our lives. Understanding this will help us succeed in business.

Your personality is the sum of all your thoughts, feelings, temperaments, emotions and behaviours that make you unique. Personality arises from within you and remains consistent throughout your life.

> "*There is much to be gained by appreciating our differences, and much to be lost by ignoring them or condemning them. But the first step toward seeing others as distinct from yourself is to become acquainted with our own traits of character.*" - **David Keirsey**, Please Understand Me II. [3]

# Emotional Intelligence (EQ)

The concept of emotional intelligence rose to dominance in 1995 following **Daniel Goleman**'s book *"Emotional Intelligence"*. [4] While Goleman was not the first to use the term as we now know it, his book brought the concepts into mainstream conversations.

Goleman argued that our view of intelligence, as defined by the **Intelligence Quotient,** or **IQ**, was too narrow and that our emotions play a far greater role in thought and decision-making than was being acknowledged.

Goleman identified the five "*domains*" of EQ as:

1. Knowing your emotions.

2. Managing your own emotions.

3. Motivating yourself.

4. Recognising and understanding other people's emotions.

5. Managing relationships.

At the core of emotional intelligence is empathy, or the ability to recognise the emotions and feelings in other people. It's unlikely people will volunteer this information. Those with empathy or strong emotional intelligence are more intuitive to this and better able to engage with these people.

In most personality tests, like **Myers Briggs Type Indicator** (MBTI), **eDiSC**, **Keirsey Temperament Sorter**, there are no good or bad answers. They simply recognise your preferences and help you better understand yourself. You need to be careful on how much credence you place on these tests. While they are useful tools, they will only provide a small insight into who you are.

With EQ testing, we would hope to get results that show we have high levels of emotional intelligence, or greater empathy. Unfortunately, emotional intelligence does not come easily to all of us.

By coming to grips with your level of EQ, you are in a better position to improve on it or at least be more cognisant of the effects you may have on others if your EQ is lower than you would like.

# Hone your management and leadership skills

When you finally reach the time to employ people or have been doing it for years, you can either approach it with dread or take it on with a positive mindset. Being a solo can be lonely. It's exciting to share your successes with someone else and uplifting to have someone beside you if you make mistakes. It gives you the chance to build the leadership and management skills you probably have always had but never needed to use.

Here are a few tips for being a better small business leader:

- Remember that your employees are a whole person who have a life outside work. Be prepared to engage with the whole person and learn about them.

- Remember, *"Know yourself; accept yourself; forget yourself."* Spend some time learning more about yourself and confide in those you love and/or trust to help you on this journey.

- Be prepared to delegate responsibilities to your staff. They may require your guidance, mentoring and oversight, depending on the staff's experience. You don't want to set them up to fail.

- You cannot lead others if you don't know yourself and you can't lead yourself. Having clarity on your strengths and weaknesses, your personality, your emotional intelligence will make you a better leader. You won't be expected to know everything. Remember that you, like every leader, are human.

- Stand by your staff and they will back you. They will make mistakes. Human error is normal.

- When mistakes happen, your first thought should never be to find who did it and to apportion blame. If your staff fear retribution for making a mistake, they won't do anything for fear of getting something wrong. They will also hide mistakes and they may direct blame elsewhere - and no one learns anything. The key is they own their mistakes, they do something about the mistake, and they learn from them.

- Communicate often with your staff. Err on the side of entrusting them with more information than less.

  *"Trust but verify,"* and

  *"Surround yourself with the best people you can find, delegate authority, and don't interfere as long as the policy you've decided upon is being carried out."* - **Ronald Reagan**, former US President.

# CHAPTER 14

# BUSINESS RISKS - AND LUCK

Running any business of any size in any industry involves risk. We could face events that are out of our control and could be seen as bad luck or good luck. Risk and luck are an integral part of small business

## What is risk?

The Oxford dictionary defines "*risk*" as:

> *A situation involving exposure to danger. The possibility that something unpleasant or unwelcome will happen.*

The reason risk exists is that we cannot predict the future. While our pre-frontal cortex allows us to develop possible future scenarios and play out possibilities before we embark on a path, this will never provide the certainty we might seek.

Accompanying this uncertainty in business is the consequences of different futures eventuating. If things go according to plan, that is great - our view of the future came to pass. However, other outcomes, more positive or much worse than expected, could also eventuate.

> We can't predict the future. We can consider future scenarios. We can then assess how likely these scenarios are and the consequences if they occur.

I will discuss Pumpkin Patch's liquidation after its failed moves into the USA and the UK. I've already discussed the impact on the finance sector following the Global Financial Crisis. In New Zealand, one of our biggest industries, dairy, is impacted by two things over which it has almost no control - the weather and world milk prices.

Your small business faces significant risks from a wide variety of factors you have little control over. You need to pause and consider the risks that could seriously hurt you.

> No one, even those using the most sophisticated risk management process, can predict the future. We will be wrong most of the time and when we are right it might well have been luck.

You can, however, consider credible events that could seriously damage or end your business, and do what you can to reduce or manage those risks.

Sticking our heads in the sand and hoping everything will work out is not an effective risk management strategy - unfortunately it is a little too common, especially in small business.

## Risk - the "What if...?" events you should consider

Larger companies go to extensive lengths to document and manage their risks, especially at board level. You won't need to go to the same lengths as these organisations to manage your risks, as these processes can be overwhelming and unnecessarily complicated. However, understanding the principles of risk management could be very helpful to even the smallest business, even if you don't document them in detail.

Asking a simple two-word question *"What if...?"* explains the key principle of what risk management is all about.

Basically, *what are the worst-case scenarios you could think of that could really hurt your business? What would happen if they occurred? Could they cripple or destroy your business? Could they affect you, your family, or your personal assets?*

Typical risks that you may consider include:

- Losing a major client.

- Poorly managed growth.

- Losing a major contract.

- Loss of key staff.

- Health of the owners.

- Changes in external market conditions, especially the property market.

- A large client fails to pay.

- Disputes between shareholders or partners.

- Marriage break-ups.

- A serious health and safety incident.

- Cancellation of your lease.

# Business involves taking risks

Business involves risk. It involves making decisions without knowing what will happen. If you don't take measured, calculated risks, you will go nowhere. The key is to quantify those risks as best you can and, where possible, put controls in place to manage or minimise those risks.

> *"If no one ever took risks, Michelangelo would have painted the Sistine floor."* - **Neil Simon**

How might you do this? What processes do businesses follow to quantify and manage risks? Let's go through the most common process businesses follow.

# Formalising your risk processes

Identifying and managing risks is one of the key responsibilities of any board of directors and has become accepted best practice on the boards of New Zealand businesses - assuming those boards follow best practice.

Many large organisations follow the standard ISO31000 to develop their risk management process.

While this standard would be an overkill for any small business, it is what I follow in outlining the principles of risk management. You should consider where, if at all, you might use some of these processes to guide you.

## Risk categories

Risks will typically fall into a few categories, such as financial risk, health and safety risk, legal risks and risks to your reputation.

Under each of these headings, consider what events will seriously damage your business, like those examples listed above.

### 1    Likelihood of the event occurring

After listing all those *"What if...?"* events that concern you most, decide what the likelihood that these events will occur. If it is extremely unlikely to occur, you would rank it as **Rare**. This might be something that a business would never expect to occur in the business' lifetime.

At the other extreme, consider those events that have already occurred or you are very confident are going to occur soon if you did nothing. You would rank this with a likelihood of **Definite**.

In between these two extremes would be the rankings: **Unlikely**, **Possible** and **Likely**.

There are different definitions of what each of these five likelihoods mean, depending where you find them. Maybe that the event could happen in the next one, two or three years. Don't get too hung up on this. Just make an approximate call on where the likelihood sits on the spectrum from Definite to Rare. In fact, the biggest error businesses make is to overcomplicate the risk management process.

## 2     *Consequence if the event occurs*

Now consider the consequence should the event occur.

Say, for example, your largest client deliveries only 5% of your sales. If you lose them, the consequence may only be **Minor**. If, however, they are your only client, losing them could end your business, so the consequence is **Catastrophic**.

In between these extremes, the consequence could vary, depending how you rank them. In this example, a customer with 15% of your sales might be a **Moderate** consequence, 40% **Major** and 75% **Severe**.

As with the likelihood, don't get too hung up on a completely accurate assessment of exactly how to measure the consequence. Just rank it where it feels about right between Catastrophic and Minor.

## *Risk Matrix*

This now presents you with the information you can enter into a five-by-five matrix to quantify your risks.

If the event's likelihood and consequence combined place it in the dark shaded area in the top right-hand corner, then you need to do something. If these events did occur, they will really hurt you.

These are the events you need to focus on. You need to consider what you can do to reduce these risks. *Are you able to reduce the likelihood the event will occur? Can you reduce the consequence if the event occurs? What controls can you put in place to manage these risks?*

If we use the customer example above, the best way to reduce the risk is to diversify the business and chase different customers. You could also negotiate more formal agreements with existing customers to agree on guaranteed terms.

A risk matrix chart with CONSEQUENCE on the vertical axis (from bottom to top: MINOR, MODERATE, MAJOR, SEVERE, CATASTROPHIC) and LIKELIHOOD on the horizontal axis (from left to right: RARE, UNLIKELY, POSSIBLE, LIKELY, DEFINITE).

## *Even the basics are better than nothing*

Even if you don't formally sit down and document risks, assess their likelihood, consider their consequence, create a table using the above method, and then document the controls you will put in place, at least consider the principles.

Even if you ask the following questions and jot down the answers, you have gone a very long way to identifying your risks and managing them.

1. What events could occur that would seriously damage your business, even shut it down?

2. Which of these events are most likely to occur?

3. What could you put in place to prevent these events from occurring?

4. If you have no control over the event occurring and can't prevent it, what can you put in place to reduce the impact of that event?

> No one can predict the future with certainty. When people get it right, they are lauded as having great foresight. If they get it wrong, they are treated as a footnote in history and forgotten.

# What part does luck play in business?

Risk and luck are intertwined concepts.

There is truth to the cliches that *"you make your own luck"* and *"the harder you work the luckier you get"*. However, every business will face events that are totally out of their control, whether the event is a blessing or bad luck.

> *"I'd rather have a lucky general than a smart general. They win battles."* - **Dwight D. Eisenhower**

> *"Eighty percent of success is showing up."* - **Woody Allen**

The Oxford dictionary defines *"luck"* as:

> **Success or failure apparently brought by chance rather than through one's own actions.**

An even more thought-provoking definition of luck is from Michael Mauboussin's book, *"The Success Equation"*. [1]

> *"Luck is a chance occurrence that affects a person or a group (e.g., a sports team or a company). Luck can be good or bad. Furthermore, if it is reasonable to assume that another outcome was possible, then a certain amount of luck is involved. In this sense, luck*

*is out of one's control and unpredictable. Luck is a residual: it's what is left over after you've subtracted skill from an outcome."* - **Michael Mauboussin**

## *Right place, right time and luck*

Malcolm Gladwell, in his book *"Outliers"*, [2] challenged the rags-to-riches stories of people like Bill Gates, Steve Jobs and the oil and steel magnates like John D. Rockefeller. He argued that when they were born, the specific family circumstances they were born into, and the environment they grew up in, were something over which they had no control, but which directly contributed to the success they became famous for.

Gladwell argued that the lore of success too often dwells on an individual's personal qualities, focusing on how grit and talent paved the way to the top.

There is no question these businesspeople grasped the opportunities they had and used their skills, passion, and dedication to turn that luck into the success they sought. However, luck played a part in their success, which needs to be considered.

Around half of the top 12 richest men in US history were all born within the 10-year period from 1830 to 1840. Yes, when I say *"men"*, it is not from a terrible choice of words. Being born a woman in that era was bad luck if you wanted to succeed in business. Women never had the same opportunities men did.[3]

These richest men were well placed to be at their peak at the time of the Industrial Revolution, with the growth in the railways and when the oil boom hit the USA. Had they been born in the period that saw them peak coming into World War I, the Great Depression and World War II, perhaps we may never have heard of names like J. P. Morgan, John D. Rockefeller and Andrew Carnegie.

## *We are not always in control*

Experience, skill and knowledge will always play a significant part in setting the best future path for your business. However, if past successes are assumed to be entirely of your own making, are accompanied by misguided overconfidence, or even arrogance, you could form your own **halo effect** -

you could start to believe you are infallible. This may not end well the next time, if there was an element of luck in those past successes.

We can all be guilty of assuming we were clever when we look back on an event that went well in our business, knowing what we now know. Likewise, we often chastise ourselves for getting things wrong, again, with the luxury of hindsight, when it might have just involved some bad luck.

## _Many CEOs are kidding themselves - they are just lucky_

Daniel Kahneman challenged the notion that the leaders of large organisations have the level of control over their businesses that they think they do. He believes it is an illusion that if these leaders have understood the past, it somehow assumes they can manage future events. He believes these illusions are comforting but are just that - illusions.

Kahneman challenged the level of control senior executives had in the success of their large organisations. He challenged the extent to which business leaders and their management practices influenced the outcomes of their business. His research showed that they certainly have an influence, but the effects are much smaller than a reading of the business press, leadership books and magazines would have us believe. He found that there is only a very loose correlation between a company's success and the CEO who leads it.

As Kahneman so eloquently puts it:

> _"It is difficult to imagine people lining up at airport bookstores to buy a book that enthusiastically describes the practices of business leaders who, on average, do somewhat better than chance. Consumers have a hunger for a clear message about the determinants of success and failure in business, and they need stories that offer a sense of understanding, however illusory. There is a fine line between enlightened business leaders who get it right all the time and those who had an element of luck on their side."_ - **Daniel Kahneman** [4]

As a small business owner, you will have a far greater influence over your business than a CEO has over a large corporate. Even so, always keep some perspective about good or bad events and what aspect of these could

---

be attributed to you and what aspect could be attributed to factors over which you had no control.

> We can't ignore that luck may have played a part in a success. Being in the right place, at the right time.

## Hindsight is 20/20

This is where **hindsight bias** can trap us. We can look back on past events with absolute clarity. There is no uncertainty anymore as the event has happened, and we can analyse the event with total clarity. Hindsight is a great thing.

A decision or prediction looks much more obvious after it has occurred than before it happened when the outcome was a complete unknown. When things go well, we want to praise those who delivered this, and when things go wrong, find someone to blame. We do this with the benefit of hindsight. A healthy dose of luck, good or bad, could have been involved.

We want to feel like someone was in control when success occurred. We want to believe that when bad things happen, there is someone we can hold to account. This is especially the case with our political and business leaders.

However, with every business success or failure that has occurred we need to remember that there were just as many business owners who were just as smart, with just as good an idea, who worked just as hard, and followed all the same principles, yet did not share in the same success as another business.

## Luck does run out - skill does not

While I have discussed the role luck plays, it would be an insult to look at a business that has exceeded all expectations and simply say *"They were lucky"*.

In examining a business' success, we need to focus on the things that were truly controllable, that could be replicated and be realistic about the aspects that may have been luck or out of anyone's control.

We can never replace skill, experience, hard work, and good decisions. Just be careful not to apportion all successes solely to that skill or failures to a lack of skill. Keep some perspective. You should stop and ask, *"Hey, was there an element of luck in that?"* If the answer is *"Yes"*, ask what happens if the luck runs out next time around.

> *"To be successful, you have to be out there; you have to hit the ground running. And if you have a good team around you - and more than a fair share of luck - you might make something happen."* - **Sir Richard Branson,** in his autobiography, Losing My Virginity.[5]

---

## Solid Energy's luck ran out

Solid Energy was New Zealand's largest producer and exporter of coal.

In 2000, what was left of this business was owned by the government. They were keen to carve it up and sell if off as they believed it was a business with no future. However, Don Elder, a Rhodes Scholar with international experience, became CEO and saw a very different future for the business.

From its early years under Elder until around 2012, the business went from strength-to-strength delivering significant profits and returns to its shareholders, the New Zealand government.

---

As Solid Energy's success depended heavily on selling coal into the lucrative export market, the company took a particular interest in determining where world coal prices were heading.

After decades of stable and flat prices, Solid Energy predicted a significant increase in coal prices, which occurred in 2008, followed soon after by a collapse.

Their prediction delivered a significant windfall for the company and elevated Don Elder to a status that allowed him direct access to the highest levels of government and business in the country.

Sadly, for the company, it also entrenched a level of self-belief that if they got it right this time, they would always get it right.

In a paper in 2009, Don Elder stated he could not see any scenario in the following decade other than a continued upward trend in energy and coal prices. Many around him, including the government and business analysts, challenged this view. Solid Energy treated such challenges with contempt considering their research and expertise to be beyond challenge.

On the back of such confidence, and Don Elder's appetite for growth and status, the company borrowed significant amounts of money to pursue higher risk developments like underground gas mining, lignite production, and biomass production.

Sadly, for Solid Energy, they did not look upon past predictions and success as having an element of luck, luck that if it were to run out, would destroy the business.

In 2012, there was a downturn in coal prices because of several factors that occurred and conspired against the worldwide coal industry. While this downtown was relatively small, it lasted for some time and with Solid Energy's level of indebtedness, they could not recover from what they saw as "*bad luck*".

They owed the banks and creditors over $400 million, and they were forced into liquidation. The banks had lent this money on the belief that if Solid Energy failed, the government would cover the debt. The government stated on many occasions they would not do this. They were true to their word and the company collapsed.

Over 1000 people, including Don Elder, unnecessarily lost their jobs, a government-owned business disappeared and the creditors, including the banks, lost hundreds of millions.

# Insurances - a control to manage risks

Insurances are an important risk management strategy. They are an effective way to manage those *"What if..."* scenarios. There are a wide range of insurances to cover the risks in your business. You need to assess how real those risks are, and the costs to insure against them.

If you are looking for insurance options for you or for your business, find a good **insurance broker**. If you are not sure where to look, ask other people in your business network. People who have been in business for many years are likely to have had a broker who has been with them throughout their business journey.

An insurance broker can be a huge help. They will present all the options for insurance and shop around for the best deals. As you grow and take on more risks, they will become another key advisor.

The following questions will guide you on the insurances you might need.

- What if you get seriously ill and can't work?

- What if a key staff member cannot work for a significant period of time?

- What if you are prosecuted for breaching a law?

- What if your advice leads to a problem, and a client decides to pursue you?

- What if an event occurs, like theft, fire, or natural disaster, that stops you from running your business?

- What happens if your computer systems are hacked, and you lose all your data or it's released to the public?

Insurance exists for these and other business scenarios.

Just a note. You can't ensure against the fines you may receive if you breach of the **Health and Safety Act**. You may be able to insure against the legal costs to defend yourself and possibly any compensations the victim may claim against you.

Insurers may also offer you legal support if you are being pursued. It is in your insurers' interest to defend you. If you lose, they may need to pay.

It is really important if an issue arises that may be covered by insurance that you talk to your broker who will talk to your insurers. If they aren't told and things get too advanced, that may not help in your defence and may undermine your claim.

If your business is a little larger and you have experienced staff, they may take the lead if you were ill and cannot work in the business.

If you are in a partnership or have other shareholders, you will need to build clauses into the agreements covering the possibility that one of you can no longer work or, worse still, a shareholder dies.

This could include the appropriate insurance to cover these tragic scenarios.

## *You can insure your business against most scenarios – at a price*

There is a saying that you can get insurance to cover almost anything – if you are prepared to pay for it. While this may not be completely true, there are a huge variety of insurances you could put in place for your business.

Getting all the business insurance options that are available is not cheap. Insurances can be a significant overhead for a business.

This is where you need to consider your risks. If you can put things in place, you are confident reduce a risk to an acceptable level, you may not need insurance. There may be many risks you can't manage and you have to get insurance.

Putting all these insurances in place will add up to significant costs. As with any risk, you will need to assess the risk of not putting these insurances in place, versus the cost of doing so. Typically, as a business grows, the need to consider these options also grows.

Remember, insurance is simply a means to manage your risk. The hope is you never need to call on it. However, if the risk eventuates, and you have done nothing to protect yourself, you could be in very serious trouble.

## *There are many types of insurance*

There is a very long list of events you can insure you and your business against. This list is not complete and I am also not suggesting you need to insure against these events. However, if there are risks you've identified above and they really worry you, there may be a way to insure against them.

### 1    Trauma insurance

This covers an individual should they become permanently disabled and unable to work.

### 2    Life insurance

If you should die, life insurance may provide an immediate source of funds to allow your surviving personal partner to continue operating the business and support the family.

### 3    Income protection insurance

This provides the holder with a source of income should they fall seriously ill and become unable to work in their normal role. These may have a finite period to give you time to return to work.

### 4    Loan and mortgage protection insurance

This insurance provides financial support to cover loan repayments if circumstances, typically health issues, prevent you servicing mortgage repayments. This insurance may not come with the business insurance package but may more align with life or other health insurance considerations.

### 5    Professional indemnity insurance

If your small business offers designs or advice to other people, professional indemnity protects you. If someone was unhappy with that design or advice, they might pursue you. Engineers and architects usually pay large amounts for this insurance, as their mistakes could lead to serious consequences, (e.g., a building collapse).

## 6 Public liability insurance

Public liability insurance protects you against claims if you were to damage someone else's property.

If you are at someone else's business and caused damage, depending on the situation, that damage could cost the other party significant amounts of money. Say, for example, you drove into a critical piece of equipment on a factory site and stopped production. This is why the amounts covered for public liability are so high. Typically, you may need to be covered for many millions of dollars, even if you are a very small business.

If you are a small business that works for larger businesses, it is common that they will check to see you have adequate insurance cover or they may not engage with you. They will typically request evidence that you have a minimum amount of liability insurance. This might $1million or $10 million.

## 7 Vehicle insurance

This is one type of insurance you are likely to be familiar with because of your own private vehicle. It can often be the insurance that costs the most in premiums, especially if you have a few vehicles in the business and if you have made claims.

## 8 Loss or damage of assets

Think about this like contents insurance for your home. If, because of an event your equipment, inventory, or other assets are damaged or stolen, you can claim.

## 9 Building loss or damage

If you own the building you are in, you'd need it insured. Some landlords will pass some or all of the insurances on to the tenant.

## 10    Business interruption

If an event occurred, and you could no longer run your business normally, you may incur losses in sales or costs to set your business up somewhere else. An example might be a fire in the location you work forcing you to relocate to temporary premises.

## 11    Marine and freight insurance

If you have goods freighted to your premises, you ship your products to others, or you import or export goods, you need to be clear where ownership for the goods shifts and who carries the risk if the goods are damaged or lost in transit.

Some freight companies within New Zealand will cover the damage to goods if it was clear it was their fault. They may not if the damage was due to the way you packed it.

Typically, overseas shipping companies won't insure what they carry on their vessels even if the loss or damage is their fault. It will be up to you to insure it if it's loss or damage is a significant risk.

## 12    Cyber protection insurance

In the last decade, there has been an increase in cyber-attacks on businesses. This can result in the loss of critical business information or stop the business operating it the online information is critical to operations. It might also result in sensitive personal information being made public meaning a breach of privacy laws.

While insurance can protect against the financial damage of a cyber-attack, it may be far wiser to implement IT practices that protect your systems and data from such attacks.

## 13    Fraud insurance

You can protect yourself against an employee or other party carrying out fraud on your business. Sadly, many businesses have had trusted employees stealing from the business.

## 14    Key personnel insurance

This insures the business should key members (such as you, the owner) fall seriously ill.

## 15    Directors' and officers' insurance

This insurance protects directors and those in the senior decision-making roles in a business form personal losses if someone were to make a claim against them personally. If you are the owner and director of your small business, it is an important insurance to have.

If you are a director for another business, it is especially important. Many business insurance packages will include this without a significant increase in premiums.

## 16    Revenue protection insurance

This provides you with cover should you suffer any injury or illness and are unable to work. This benefit can pay for any business expenses like staff wages, buildings or utilities.

# Wills and Powers of Attorney

You may never want to think about it, especially if you are young, but what happens to the business if you die or are mentally unable to make decisions?

If you are the sole director and shareholder in the business and the income from this business supports the family, what happens then?

Your partner may not be legally permitted to take over the business and keep it going, even if they have the skills. Unless you have clearly defined what happens in this scenario, your partner and family may have no ability to sell the business or sell assets or do anything with the business except let it sit and whither. This will be happening at a time when people dear to you are also coping with significant grief and sadness.

When you start to build up assets and especially if you have business interests, you need to have a **Will** in place and **Powers of Attorney** (POA). While getting the **Public Trustee** to set these up will be much cheaper, it might be worth paying the extra to use a lawyer who can also give you broader legal advice on all aspects of your business.

# CHAPTER 15

# FINDING MONEY TO FUND YOUR BUSINESS

From time to time, you will pursue goals that require access to external funds. If your goal is growth, you are unlikely to achieve it without external funding. You may also have large swings in outgoing and incoming cash from month-to-month and need extra money to manage this. Whatever the reason, it is unlikely you will go through your business' life without using someone else's money.

You may be nervous about seeking external funds, as it involves risks. The key is not to avoid the risk but to assess it; consider the scenarios (good and bad) and make the decision that meets your business' needs at a risk level you can tolerate.

## Borrowing money - debt

There are a number of places you can go to borrow money for your business. These are the most common.

### *Using your own savings*

As a small business owner, it's likely you will have put some of your own savings into your business. You may also have stopped paying yourself much of a salary, compared to the salary you could earn if you worked in someone else's business. This is no different to lending your business money. You want to get it back and even get a return on it, just like any other investor. Unfortunately, this is far from guaranteed. But you may have no choice.

Your business will hopefully reach a point where you can reclaim that money and start paying yourself something like a decent salary. You should think of this money as a loan rather than a donation. You also need to consider the business as a separate entity to you, even if you are a sole proprietor.

If the amount you have lent your business is large, and you have many creditors, you might consider setting up a formal **loan agreement** and **security agreement** for this money. This will require a lawyer's input, so it may not be cheap. However, if your business gets into trouble, and you owe a lot of other people money, at least you can regain the money you lent the business ahead of them.

You are probably going to run out of personal cash to keep injecting money into the business. Even if you do have the cash, you should stop putting your own savings into the business and start accessing funds from other sources.

## *Borrowing from friends and family*

After a small business owner uses their own money, they may then turn to the *"Three Fs"* for funding: **family, friends and fools**. While this may seem like a harsh thing to say, it holds merit, but still might be a legitimate option.

It is possible this money will come without the same interest charges or restrictions that a bank or other third party may place on you.

But beware.

Borrowing from family or friends could create its own unique issues for you. Some family members or friends may believe that lending you money gives them the right to meddle in the affairs of your business. You may have only wanted their money, but ended up with an uninvited partner. This could damage your relationship or your business.

Businesses and close relationships, especially relationships based on love, are not always a good mix. While the family member or friend may have complete trust in you as a person, things may turn rather nasty if you strike problems and can't pay that person back.

You can certainly make this work if you and the family member are completely open about the arrangement from the start and if you try to keep the business and personal relationships separate. The more you can discuss how you will handle all the following potential scenarios, the better.

- What if the family member wants or needs the money back early?

- What if you can't meet their repayment requirements?

- Where do they appear on the list of priorities to be repaid if your business fails?

- What if the family member fears losing their money and wants you to run the business differently?

I am not a believer in informal business relationships, especially with money. I would recommend documenting the basis of the lending, interest rates (if any), repayment expectations and where this money ranks in terms or repayments should the business get in strife. These are the same loan and security documents mentioned when you lend your own money to the business.

## Borrowing from banks

Banks are likely to be your next port of call for money.

Borrowing from a bank is probably something you have already done for your house, car, and credit cards. Banks are in the business of lending you money. They will usually do the best they can to achieve this for you. However, they are also in the business of getting their money back. They will expect you will do this, irrespective of the impact getting it back may have on you or your business.

While banks want you to succeed, they can't advise you. Most banks will monitor the behaviour of everyone to whom they lend. They will assess how you are meeting your loan commitments. If they see a pattern of unacceptable behaviour, they may step in, which is definitely not what you would want to happen.

If you are ever struggling to meet the bank's requirements for the loan(s) you have, talk to them. Often, they will work with you to make repayment more workable.

All banks have internal boundaries and guidelines to lend money to small businesses. It will depend on the risk appetite of each bank, but typically they will be more comfortable with either some level of security over the business' assets or some form of **personal guarantee** to give them greater confidence they will receive their money back.

Usually, a personal guarantee will have to be backed by a physical asset. This may be something that you or your business owns, including your home.

I spoke about the protection a limited liability company can give you if your business gets into trouble. Basically, if your business fails, you are likely to be forced to turn all the company's assets into cash (liquidation). If there isn't enough money from this to pay everyone you owe, these people will have to go without. Typically, no one should be able to touch anything you own in this situation. However, the minute you give a personal guarantee for an asset, this protection may be at risk.

You may seek lending that is not backed by assets. This is **unsecured lending**. Some banks simply won't do this and would rather turn you away than take the risk. Others may do it, but they will want to know a great deal about your business before they will even consider it. If they do, it will come at a much higher rate of interest and with other requirements, such as reporting regularly on how you are going.

I'm sorry to say that small business owners are not who the banks like lending to without some security. In their eyes, you are statistically more likely to fail, won't borrow as much as the big guys, and are likely to be more work for them, relative to the money you borrow.

Keep in mind that Kiwi banks are not always acting by their own rules. Very often it is the laws of the government of the day, the Reserve Bank of New Zealand, and, for the big New Zealand banks, their parent companies based in Australia.

The fact you may have been with a particular bank for many years, even decades, means nothing. Don't be offended if the bank says *"no"* after years of loyalty. All that matters to the bank is your ability to meet your debt obligations at that point in time, and the specific circumstances of the lending you are chasing. Even if you owned a business in the past, and paid off all your debts, and then seek money for a new venture, it is only this new venture the bank will care about. The bank may not even give you a credit card for the new venture because that new entity has no trading history.

> Just because the bank lends you money does not mean what you are doing will work. The banks can't give advice. Whether the decision requiring the funds is a good or bad idea remains with you.

## Types of bank borrowing for small business

There are many types of bank lending you can pursue. The key is getting the correct loan for the specific need. The following are the most common lending options.

### 1    Credit cards

I'm sure you know a great deal already about this form of bank borrowing. You may have been able to negotiate a higher limit on your business credit card than you could on your personal credit card.

Your business should have a credit card linked to a bank account that is solely for business purchases and held in your business' name. Use your personal credit card for personal use and business credit card for your business purchases. Don't mix the two.

Your credit card and bank account should be linked to your accounting software so you can link your spending to the correct cost code so you can accurately track costs.

Choose as low a limit as you can manage and make sure you pay the credit card off before it's due. Interest rates can be horrendous.

### 2    Bank overdraft

I mentioned earlier that your business might need additional cash to fund the day-to-day operations. While your credit card can help a little, it might not have a high enough limit for your needs and the interest rates it attracts may be much greater than an overdraft.

If your business has built up good cash reserves, you may decide not to seek any money from the bank for the day-to-day cash you need.

Overdrafts can have high interest rates and you need to be disciplined in paying them back so you don't exceed any limits, or they could incur even higher charges. The more you ask for, the more it could cost you, so manage your overdraft to as low a level as you can. Also, shop around for the best deal.

## 3    Asset financing

Banks will also offer funding for assets like vehicles and machinery, and they will secure the loan against the machinery. They are still likely to want to see all the financials for the business before approving the loan. It is not wise to use your own cash to buy assets unless you have a really strong cash position. It could leave you short of money to cover all the normal monthly cash requirements.

You may find you can get great loan deals from the company you are buying the vehicle or equipment from. They may not be concerned about the rest of your business' numbers, so there may be fewer hoops to jump through than a bank to get the loan.

Second tier or non-bank lenders may be more inclined to lend than a bank and not ask for as much information about the entire business as a bank would. However, keep in mind they may be taking on more risk, so could charge higher interest rates and require shorter repayment periods than the bank.

This is definitely one form of lending you should shop around for and not just call on your existing bank to finance the asset.

---

### Solid Energy, Pumpkin Patch and too much debt

Borrowing beyond one's means has been a contributing factor to the failure of many businesses.

Solid Energy had operated for most of its life, debt free. In 2012, the company pursued a significant growth strategy. To do this, they borrowed over $200 million from five banks in New Zealand and abroad.

---

Solid Energy's growth projects were high cost, required a long-term injection of funds with a high risk they would not deliver any revenue. The primary source of funding to service this debt was a few coal mines that relied heavily on the assumption that world coal prices would remain high.

When the coal prices dropped, Solid Energy could not service the debt and collapsed.

Pumpkin Patch had also operated for most of its life debt free. Even though it raised about $60 million when it listed on the stock exchange, it borrowed an additional $80 million to fund its overseas growth strategy. The only way they could service this debt was through healthy sales across the globe. Instead, their new UK and USA shops underperformed. These stores were closed and eventually the entire business failed.[1]

# Non-bank, or second tier lenders

The Global Financial Crisis wiped out the second tier lending market in New Zealand. In earlier chapters, we discussed how over 45 finance companies collapsed. Examples included Hanover Finance, Bridgecorp, and the largest of all was South Canterbury Finance. Only a few survived, including UDC Finance, who were not lending into the property market.

New players have started re-entering the market.

Non-bank lenders cannot take deposits from customers, so have to source their money from other institutions so they can lend to you.

The second tier lenders are not bound by the same restrictions as the banks, so are more likely to lend. However, because they are taking more risk than a bank, you will usually pay higher interest rates and be required to pay the money back quicker. This can put more pressure on your cash flow.

# External equity investment

Equity funding is far less common for small businesses in New Zealand. However, it is still a very important form of funding. It is most often the choice of small business start-ups and businesses with higher growth potential.

Equity is the part of the business that you and any other shareholders own. By seeking equity funding, essentially you are looking for someone else to take a share in the ownership of your business. A person who takes a share in your business will not receive interest repayments (unlike a bank where they provide you with debt). Also, the investor will not seek personal guarantees. They, like you, are prepared to take on risk, back the business and make their money from its success. They will rank last of those who will be repaid should the business fail.

People who want to take some ownership of a small business face bigger risks than the bank that lends you money. They will look to make a lot more money than they would by simply keeping their money in another investment. Therefore, good investors look for those businesses that have potential to grow and bring a healthy return on the initial investment.

People may also want to invest in your business for reasons other than growth. For instance, someone who sees themselves as a successor or someone with a desire to be more deeply involved because they believe in what you are doing.

Most investors will want some level of direct involvement in the business, considering the risks they are taking. This could be good or bad, depending on how the investor might contribute. They may not only contribute money. They may bring expertise you don't have.

By bringing in external investors, it's unlikely you can expect the same freedom and control as when you were on your own. That's why you need to be extremely careful about who you decide to bring into your business.

There may be some investors who do not want to play an active part in the day-to-day running of the business. They will, however, still want to know what you are doing and are unlikely to let you do anything that may put their investment at risk.

The more funders you have, the more shareholders you will have, and, therefore, the more people with a vested interest in the business.

## *Venture capital*

High wealth investors, either directly or through venture capital funds, often invest their cash into small businesses with significant growth potential. As this is equity funding and not a loan, the investor is purchasing shares in the business. If the business experiences the predicted growth, these investors could achieve a significant gain on their investment. These investors are looking for the unicorn - that rare startup that goes from someone's garage to becoming a multi-million-dollar business, like Navman, Xero or VEND.

The owners who seek venture capital are comfortable to give up a percentage of their shares to attract more money to grow the business, increase its value, and therefore increase the value of all the shares. The original owners may well even give up the controlling interest in the business to attract a larger amount of equity. This is likely to mean the new investors, and shareholders, will want representation on the board.

The way the business, and therefore the shares, are valued differs from the way a traditional business is valued. It will be based on a perception of the future growth potential rather than on past performance.

While some start-ups will attract investors very early in their life, more astute investors will want to see some level of performance to inform them of what may happen in the future.

Many start-ups have to **bootstrap** their initial growth. That means the owners fund the initial start-up themselves and only grow as fast as the revenue they earn allows. Kiwi start-ups are well known for being very prudent in the initial stages of the business' life by not spending what they don't have. This is not typically through choice but more because of the limited options available in New Zealand to find this type of funding.

Some investors can be spellbound by an entrepreneur's idea. Typically, the entrepreneur is extremely passionate about their idea, is very driven, and can put forward very compelling arguments - because they believe in their business. This can convince an investor to stump up the cash. The entrepreneur sees the confidence shown in their business by this investor as validation that their idea will work. Sadly, the people that really count, potential customers, may not agree. Before anyone realises it, the business has grown, but it is struggling to deliver on expectations as the customers don't feel the same way as the owners and investors.

> Remember, investors don't validate start-up ideas. Customers do.

The successful start-ups have usually succeeded through significant hard work up front. They will have engaged with customers, demonstrated the demand exists and achieved solid initial sales. They usually test the market with **Minimum Viable Products** (MVP). [2] This means the business does not pursue perfection in the product before going to market. They test the market as early as they can, as long as the product works, impresses potential customers, and does not damage the brand.

The business then pursues more funding, based on proven performance, not solely on the promise of what might be.

In some economic environments, cash may not be as readily available, and investors become less keen to spend. If you are desperate and struggling, you may take money from anyone - throwing your values out the window.

The best investors may not just be the people with the most money. They may be the people who bring more than just cash. Their industry connections may be invaluable for you. They may be based in another market you cannot otherwise access, like overseas. Their skills and industry credibility may attract other investors. Even if money is more readily available, no one is going to hand it to you. You will have to knock on many doors for a very long time, and get many *"NOs"* before you get a *"YES"*

Your idea could be amazing, customers want it, and you have proven sales. If the venture capital investors can't see that translating into exponential growth, they are unlikely to invest. In the last decade, software and technology start-ups have attracted the most investments. They have a much greater chance of seeing significant growth compared to many other businesses.

For example, **VEND,** a point-of-sale SaaS was started in 2010 by **Vaughan Rowsell,** and sold to the US business Lightspeed in 2021 for around $500 million. Keep in mind Vaughan Rowsell and those who joined him at VEND worked unbelievably hard, in often extremely stressful situations, to achieve this success.

Start-ups seeking capital must knock on a high number of doors, offering a compelling argument why someone should invest before they finally invest. Most start-ups never get the funding they need and disappear before we even hear about them.

## Angel investors

Angel investment is a variation on the venture capital raising. These are higher wealth individuals looking to place money in businesses with the potential for significant growth. They may place their funds with venture capital funds or invest more directly. There are angel investor associations and investor networks within New Zealand who bring these people together with companies seeking funding.

They may not put in enormous sums (say, $50,000 to $250,000), but they could well be investing in many small businesses to diversify their risk.

> Don't expect an angel investor to give their money over easily. You need to have a very good story, a plan for your business, and a plan for how you intend using their money.

The same risks exist in choosing to approach and work with an angel investor as any other type of funding. Don't get dazzled by the money or their credentials. If the person does not fit your business, your values or your goals, remain cautious. Ensure you can work with that person and do your homework on them as much as they do on you.

## Equity-based crowdfunding

Since the inception of the **Financial Markets Conduct Act 2013**, organisations can now raise equity through crowd funding websites. These sites attract people to pledge amounts to buy a share in the business. These could be very small amounts.

Prior to this legislation, offering shares was tightly regulated. A share offer was usually associated with an **Initial Public Offering (IPO)** to list on the share market. The business was required to meet stringent disclosure requirements, including a *"product disclosure statement"*. This Act now allows a lower standard if the amount being raised is under $2 million in any 12-month period. This provides another source of funding to small businesses that did not previously exist.

You cannot sell existing shares using equity crowd funding. Only new shares can be issued.

Low-growth businesses, and businesses in their very early stages of development that have not yet generated any revenue, are usually not candidates for this funding option. Going out on your own as a builder, plumber, electrician, or opening a small retail outlet, are not the businesses that will attract interest from investors.

While the extent of information is not as in-depth as other share offers, the equity crowd funding providers make it clear to investors, who could be from all walks of life, that the investments are risky. Once shares are purchased, there is no guarantee they can be sold when the buyer wants.

New Zealand crowdfunding sites include the **Snowball Effect** and **Pledge**. They provide a lot of information, including current offers and the businesses that have successfully raised funds in the past.

Keep in mind, going through a crowdfunding campaign will result in several new shareholders in your business. The campaign will raise funds, but may water down your control, depending on what percentage of shares you sell. If your percentage falls below 75%, you will lose the ability to make **special resolutions** without referring to the other shareholders. It may also add complications should you want to sell the business in the future or if you want to bring in larger investors.

# How high growth start-ups are valued

I will cover the process of valuing a traditional business in later chapters. This is the process that will be followed for most businesses that are valued and sold in New Zealand. This is based on the historical financial performance of the business, typically in the last three financial years.

For high growth businesses, who are seeking large injections of equity, the valuation is quite different. It will be a prediction of future revenue that will determine the business value. The performance to date will show what the future growth might be. The better the past performance, even if it hasn't translated into significant revenue, the greater will be the investors' confidence.

Investors also look at other factors, including the capability and passion of the owners, and the **cost-per-employee**, to test how frugal and efficient the business is. They are also likely to look at how much cash the business is spending to gauge how quickly it will use the money invested before needing further funding.

However, no matter what factors an investor considers, the valuation is a prediction of the future, something no one can do with complete confidence. Therefore, these investments are higher risk.

If the start-up business grows and matches, or exceeds, projections, this will strengthen the appeal for further investments at later stages. The investor will gain confidence the business will become profitable and deliver them a return. Alternatively, the investor is hoping a larger business will step in and buy the business even before they become profitable.

If they do not meet expectations, investors get nervous and may not invest more. Often these start-ups cannot survive off the revenue they generate - in short, they are not yet profitable. They will spend a lot of money developing the business. Without additional injections of funds, the business could struggle, and this could happen rather quickly. The business may have to downsize to save costs. There is every chance the business simply can't survive.

## The Tracksuit story

Tracksuit provides its customers with a simple and much lower cost method to track the health of their brand. In short, they state they can answer marketers' key question, "*Is what we're doing working?*"

Traditional advertising agencies would charge vast sums and deliver weighty reports to answer this question. Tracksuit offers a SaaS system that delivers this and much more at a fraction of the cost.

Venture capital investors are particularly attracted to SaaS start-ups. Strong SaaS businesses, over the last 10 to 15 years have offered higher margins, and high rates of growth. SaaS systems are based on subscriptions which are typically locked in for a year, and if the system offers what is says, people will continue to subscribe. This gives investors greater confidence in future performance.

# Tracksuit

This was very much the case with Tracksuit.

The owners, Connor Archbold and Matt Herbert, started the business in 2021 as a joint venture between two other businesses. It followed a genuine belief that helping businesses understand their brand could be done so much better than they had traditionally seen.

In their first few years, Tracksuit operated with a small team being funded solely from initial subscriptions. They offered healthy discounts to initial subscribers if they paid ahead of the service being delivered. These customers were being asked to place faith in Tracksuit that they would deliver - which they did.

What made Tracksuit appealing, apart from the capability of the two owners and the small team, was the innovative nature of their offering, the self-funded subscription revenue they had already delivered, and the tight controls they had over their spending.

They acquired new customers without a significant level of cost. Many of the customers they had attracted were high value, high profile, and expressed strong satisfaction with what Tracksuit were delivering.

This put the business in a strong position to seek investors. This is where the work really started. Connor and Matt spoke to every venture capitalist who was prepared to hear what they were doing.

In their first funding round, in February 2023, they were valued at a multiplier significantly higher than would be the case for a traditional business. This multiplier is tightly guarded in these deals. The business seeking the funds will set as high a multiplier as the market will accept and that they can defend. If initial investors agree to this multiplier, further investors may have greater comfort and join the funding at that value.

After the first investment round, the business was valued at over $40 million. Tracksuit then offered many of their key staff shares through an Employee Shareholder Ownership Plan or ESOP scheme.

They went out for a further funding round in February 2024.

They spent many weeks on phones and talking to as many investors and other people as they could, in New Zealand, Australia and particularly in the USA. They spoke of their purpose, their values, their goals and the Tracksuit offering over-and-over.

The popular view that people like Matt and Connor could walk into a "*Dragons' Den*", do a pitch to a panel and then walk out with money could not be further from the truth. Businesses like Tracksuit, who secure such funding, have a proven track record, even if it is only over a short period. They absolutely believe in what they are doing, and they work bloody hard to get investment.

The multiplier that was agreed on in the second round of funding had increased even further than the first round, as well as the business achieving a much higher revenue. These combined to deliver a business value of $152 million, and they were able to attract more investors who together invested $22 million.

The investors who were convinced of the business' potential included Icehouse Ventures in Auckland, Blackbird Venture Capital, and US based investors Altos Ventures and Footwork Venture Capital. They also attracted investments from higher wealth US and Australian-based individuals.

They did not just chase anyone who was prepared to offer money. They were looking for people who could bring knowledge into the business, who could open doors around the globe, and who could introduce them to new potential customers and markets.

The early signs for this Kiwi business are very good. Maintaining this success, as for any growing business, will require significant work as they aim to grow into a business with over 150 staff in multiple countries. Time will tell if Tracksuit becomes one of New Zealand's next unicorns.

# Other sources of funding

## Family or friends

We already spoke about turning to family or friends for a loan. There may also be an approach where a family member or friend could buy into your business. The advantage of this is that you know each other before proceeding. They may also be more inclined to invest than would an external investor if significant growth was not your goal.

However, unlike the case of lending, the family or friend may want to be involved in the business because they part-own it. This may be what you want and even expect.

It's even more important that you consider the effects of this arrangement on your relationship before you enter it. What may start out as an exciting, shared adventure could end in a serious break-up of the relationship - and the business.

## Asset finance

Those businesses selling assets, like the major car sales or heavy machinery sales businesses, will often offer finance at competitive rates. Non-bank lenders may offer a range of lending options, including asset finance. Some non-bank lenders, like **UDC**, **Speirs**, or **MTF Finance** specialise in lending to fund assets.

These lenders tend not to look at the total business to lend money, as a bank will do, but focus on the specifics of the asset. The asset is the security. If you default, they will repossess the asset, but are likely to leave the rest of the business alone. They usually charge higher interest rates and may require payment over shorter periods, which can put greater pressure on cash reserves.

## Invoice or debtor financing

This is another source of funding to help with cash for the day-to-day running of your business. If your business is paying money to suppliers but your customers don't pay you until many weeks later, invoice financing may be an option to consider. It does not apply to businesses paid in cash or at the point of sale (POS). Unlike an overdraft, the providers of the invoice financing don't want security over any of your assets. They are relying on getting their money from your customers.

Small companies with rapid growth can also use invoice financing, as they may struggle to keep on top of their payment processes, including making sure they have cash coming through the door when they need it.

Typically, the invoice financing company will pay you a large percentage of your outstanding invoices the moment you send them out to your customers. This is typically around 80%. You have cash straight away to continue your business and don't have to stress about waiting for your customers to pay the bill.

When the customer pays the invoice, the invoice finance company gives you the outstanding money, less their fees. These fees vary and can be higher than an overdraft rate.

You may hear it described differently in different places. **Debtor financing**, **invoice financing** and **receivables financing** are all essentially the same thing.

Different companies have variations on what they offer. Some manage all your invoices with all your customers, and some are prepared to assist with individual invoices. Some will manage your entire payment process, while others leave you to manage all the interactions with your customers and just handle the money part. Others may only provide the finance for specific customers, such as government businesses or larger corporate businesses.

Like any funding option, you need to ensure you fully understand it. Invoice financing does not increase the amount of cash you have access to; it just ensures you get the cash you are owed straight away.

It can prove more expensive than an overdraft, but should not put personal assets at risk. Many invoice financing companies may offer a more hands-on level of support for your business than would a bank. If you use the invoice financing company to manage all your invoices, it can take a major load off you.

However, it may be costly, as well as putting someone between you and your customers. Also, if you get attached to the invoice financing company, it might make it difficult to return this process to your business at a later date.

## Non-equity crowdfunding

We already discussed equity-based crowd funding, where investors are seeking a shareholding in the business. There are also crowdfunding options where investors provide small amounts of money with no expectation of share ownership. People invest because they believe in what you are doing and donate money. The business could also offer access to new products for a significant discount or before they are available to the market.

Crowdfunding sites also allow people to put up an idea on the website and request funding from anyone who may be interested in the idea. Typically, a certain amount of money is requested with a target listed. If the target is reached, you get the funding, as well as wider exposure from the process.

Many businesses seeking crowdfunding donations have a strong social or environmental purpose to attract people with similar values.

The money you can expect to raise will vary widely but is usually much smaller than equity crowd funding.

## Funding options to cover unpaid taxes

When a business is struggling to meet their tax obligations, options exist to repay tax without using other sources of funding. Discuss your options with your accountant, who should know what tax repayment options exist.

Instead of paying the IRD directly on the required date, you can pay into a **tax pool** managed by an intermediary approved by the IRD. They then manage the payment of taxes as they fall due on behalf of you and all the businesses who have paid into the pool. Some businesses overpay their tax when they have the funds or overestimate tax payments required. Likewise, others under pay if they have a shortfall in cash. The pool allows those who can't pay to meet their IRD requirements.

If you are late paying the IRD, you will face penalty interest. The interest you pay for tax pooling is usually lower.

Other funders allow you to cover short-term cash problems by borrowing against provisional tax that you have already paid, such as

**GoTaxi.co.nz.** You pay less interest than an overdraft, but these are typically for very short-term cash shortages, like a few months.

Some circumstances exist where you may be able to borrow money against taxes you have already paid into the pool to fill short-term holes in your cash flow.

# CHAPTER 16

## GROWING YOUR BUSINESS

One of the great opportunities for starting small in business is your ability to grow. When I talk about growth here, I don't mean a steady increase in the profit in the business through improvements in efficiencies. I mean it is developing new products, new locations, bigger market share or orders of magnitude increases in sales. While I fully understand it is not for everyone, I certainly love to see small businesses growing into a medium to large business - and beyond.

Growth, like any business venture, needs to be thought through. Uncontrolled growth can be just as dangerous as a major decline in your business. Both can end in tears. The risk is that you over-commit and do not consider the worst-case scenarios. Significant growth comes with increased risks.

Your small business may not set out to grow when you start, but you may see a growing demand for your products or services. You see great potential and want to realise this. This is exciting, but it can also be scary.

Critical questions to ask yourself are:

- Do I want this growth?

- Have I the drive and commitment to see it through?

- Does it fit with my goals?

- Does it align with my core purpose?

- Can I achieve it without compromising my core values?

Your goals in starting the business may not have included the stress and workload that significant growth can bring. If it doesn't meet your goals, values and purpose, don't feel you must grow just because you can.

If you decide growth is what you want to pursue, it's exciting so let's discuss the things you need to consider.

# Growth plan

During a period of growth, you could feel you are slightly out of control, managing continual change. While planning may seem like a lost cause because of the pace of the change, there is still a need to put plans in place, no matter how often you need to review them.

> "*In preparing for battle, I have always found that plans are useless, but planning is indispensable.*".
> - **Dwight D. Eisenhower,** former US General, who lead the D-Day invasion,

This plan needs to be very clear on reminding you of your purpose, your values, what you will and won't do, and your goals.

You will need to plan on when you may need additional funds, staff, or inventory. The timing of actions like these could make or break your growth.

The planning process may also help you develop the discipline to stop before making decisions that you may have otherwise made on the run and later regret.

Some examples of what could happen if you do not plan.

## 1.  Sales don't meet targets.

If you foresee a significant growth in sales, you may choose to invest in staff, stock and office space to match this growth. If sales do not meet expectations, you could face significant fixed costs without the associated revenue. Unwinding this may take more time than you think while you are bleeding cash.

## 2.  You fail to meet customer expectations.

If you commit to a significant increase in sales and offer a level of product and service quality, the risk is you cannot deliver to those standards. Customers will be very dissatisfied, and your brand could suffer irreparable damage.

### 3.   Suppliers can't meet your requirements

Delivery of your products to customers will depend on the speed and volume that your suppliers can deliver to you. If they cannot do this and you carry insufficient stock, you may not be able to fill customer orders resulting in angry customers.

### 4.   Unable to attract staff

Sustaining your growth may require employing more staff. Finding the right people and then employing them takes time. Under pressure, you may take shortcuts which results in employing the wrong people. Rather than spending your time on growth, you end up spending on managing messy human resource issues

### 5.   You have insufficient cash

You may have the customers in place and are achieving a growth in sales. Your suppliers are meeting your orders, but you have not established the level of cash to pay for the supplies you need. Gaining bank approval for an additional overdraft will take time and you may be late paying suppliers. They may stop supplying you until you pay what you owe and then you can't meet customer orders.

While all these examples may turn you off growth, they shouldn't. They, like any other risk, are simply those things you need to factor into your growth plans. All these risks can be managed. You just need to consider them and plan for them.

# Scenario planning

Scenario planning, like strategy, had its birth in the military. It is a technique that considers history and past trends that led to the current situation the business finds itself and the world it operates in. Rather than predicting a single future, scenario planning assumes that all predictions of the future are, to some extent, wrong. Instead of considering one likely future, it considers several credible future scenarios. This will typically include a best- and worst-case scenario, as well as the most likely scenario based on what you currently know.

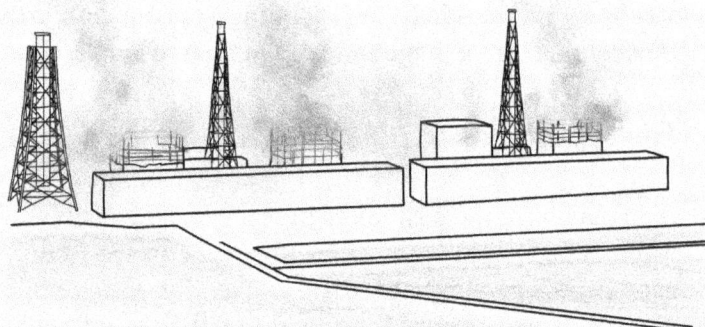

## The Fukushima nuclear plant and failing to consider the worst-case scenario

The world is full of too many examples of businesses that failed to consider scenarios with catastrophic consequences. The Fukushima nuclear plant, owned by the Tokyo Electric Power Company, is one extreme example.

This power plant is on the east coast of Japan, about 300 kms north of Tokyo. When it was built in the 1970s and after many subsequent modifications, worst-case scenarios were factored into the design, including earthquakes and tsunamis that were common in Japan. Reviews were also done after the Chernobyl disaster in 1986. The Japanese were confident all was well as their technology was far superior to the flawed Russian designs, and it had already survived severe earthquake events.

A seven-metre-high sea wall plus an additional three-metre-high land wall were felt to be more than adequate to deal with any tsunami.

In March 2011 a huge earthquake hit off the east coast of Honshu, the main Japanese island. It was later determined to be over 9 on the Richter scale, the largest in Japanese history.

While the Fukushima power station was struck heavily by the earthquake, it survived almost unscathed.

Little did they know that the earthquake had generated a tsunami beyond anything anyone had contemplated.

Less than 30 minutes after the quake was recorded, waves exceeding 14 metres hit the site, overtopping the barriers, flooding the entire facility, and shutting down all electrical supplies, including to the reactor cooling.

This occurred before the reactors could be safely shutdown. This risked a full nuclear meltdown on three reactors, and explosions that would have been worse than the Chernobyl disaster.

The site manager ignored the orders of senior executives, who failed to fully understand the extent of the risks, and flooded the reactors with sea water. While this destroyed the reactors, it prevented a catastrophe.

The actions of the site manager and his staff, who remained facing risks to their own lives, saved the plant. They were called the "Fukushima 50" and are now part of Japanese folklore.

The best- and worst-case scenarios are where you need to consider the things that could go very well or badly, and what you might do if that happens.

Solid Energy never considered a scenario of a protracted fall in coal prices. South Canterbury Finance and all the other New Zealand finance companies never considered a scenario of a deep fall in property prices that became the Global Financial Crisis. Pumpkin Patch did not consider the consequence of below expectation sales in the USA and UK, and I could continue listing example after example.

The issue is not about looking at the worst-case scenario, and then allowing it to scare you off doing anything. Scenario planning is about considering the worst-case, what signs you might see if such a scenario was coming to pass, in part or in full, and then what you will do to mitigate or manage the issues as they arise. Most importantly, if that scenario comes to pass, what is the consequence? It's unlikely to be a catastrophic nuclear fallout like Fukushima, but it could still be catastrophic for you.

If you feel you can deal with and survive such worst-case scenarios, then everything is upside from there and you should proceed with greater confidence.

> If you feel you can manage and survive the worst-case scenario then it's all upside from there and you can continue growing with great confidence.

# Funding for growth

There are many examples of businesses that have grown from nothing to substantial organisations in New Zealand predominantly funded from the revenue the business generated. This is definitely a lower risk option but requires patience and control as spending must remain within the business' means. Spending can't outpace the growth in sales.

Typically, most businesses seeking significant growth will need to call on external funding to achieve their goals. This will typically require money from several sources and at different stages. Money from the owners of the business, bank lending and money from third parties prepared to back the business, namely investors.

I covered the specifics of these in the previous chapter. Debt is the most straightforward. You need to convince the bank you have the assets to secure loans and the cash flow to fund it. You might have a good relationship with your business banker, but they must convince their credit department, who doesn't care about you or your great idea. They want to lend money, but they want to be sure they will get it back, with interest.

As you continue to growth there is likely to be a point where the bank becomes uncomfortable lending you more if their exposure is increasing and the equity in the business is low. They may not lend further until you attract other equity funding.

Investors will not open their purse or wallet to hand you money easily. While you may see huge potential and a great opportunity in what you are doing, and you may be very genuine in pushing your case, others may only see risks - with you, the owner, being the greatest risk. Are you able to show that you have the skills, the passion, and the commitment to deliver the growth you are asking others to fund?

Equity investors may have little interest in investing in your business if they can't see significant growth. The type of investor you may look for is one who wants a direct involvement in the business' operations. These people may have a lower expectation of growth than does a venture capitalist.

## Staffing to support growth

If you are growing rapidly, you cannot do it alone. You will need more people involved. While you may achieve growth using external parties, or short-term skills, it is likely you will need to take on more full-time people within your business. Read the chapter on employing staff.

In times of high growth, businesses can cut corners in their recruitment processes and take on people that prove to be a major headache. Be very careful. If you rush the process and get the wrong people, you could find your time is being diverted away from growing your business to dealing with poor performance, behavioural issues or worse.

## Systems for growth

It's possible the pace of your growth will outstrip the capability of the systems you are using. You need to factor in systems development to support the growth. Re-look at the chapter on systems and processes. When choosing systems, keep in mind their ability to grow as you grow. If you increase your customers, your projects, jobs, and the number of staff but your systems are not up to the challenge, you could end up with a mess.

## Buying other businesses to grow

Buying another business is a straightforward way to build immediate growth. If you want to grow into a new location, a new market segment, to grow upstream or downstream on the supply chain, then this may be the perfect way to do it. Check out the chapter on buying a business.

You need to let people know you are in the market for such sales. As most will happen confidentially, if you are not well connected in the business sales market, you may miss opportunities. Get in front of the brokers in the location or business segment where you are keen to buy and make sure they know your criteria. Be ready to act if an opportunity presents itself.

Think hard about how you will fund the purchase. Buying a business as a going concern will come at a price. It may include significant amounts of goodwill. If that is the case, will you risk destroying that goodwill by changing trading names and branding to match your existing business?

Consider carefully how you want to run the business after the purchase. Will you keep the original and new businesses at arm's length? Will you set it up as a separate company? How will you manage the new business without compromising the existing business and vice versa?

## Growth through joining or working with other businesses

You could look to other like-minded businesses or people that you might be prepared to align with to grow through the shared capabilities of both parties. You could achieve this through an informal relationship or through more formal legal arrangements.

The typical ways this could occur include:

- Two businesses agreeing to merge into a new, single, bigger business.

- Two or more businesses joining in a joint venture for a specific project, setting it up as a new company, with a 50/50 share ownership.

- Agreeing to work together through a formal or informal alliance or contractual relationship.

As with any coming-together of partners, shareholders, companies or individuals, the success will depend heavily on whether the parties get on, if there is an alignment of the parties on their purpose, core values and goals.

Before starting on this journey, be sure you are very clear about what happens if things don't go according to plan. While there are examples where success has been achieved between two aligned parties, based on a handshake, this is rare. It is far more advisable to formalise the relationship with binding agreements.

Hopefully, things go well, and you never have to use the documents.

# Growth by franchising your business

If you have been in your business for some time, if it is running efficiently and you believe you have a genuine opportunity to expand the business, you could look at **franchising** the business.

The previous discussions on being a franchisee will inform you of the advantages and disadvantages of being the franchisor. It is definitely a way of growing your business and sharing that risk with others.

The franchisee is the owner of the new franchised business, not you. They have to fund it themselves, run it, employ staff, and manage the growth rather than you.

Just as your risks are reduced, so too are the potential rewards, as you can only expect a small percentage of their sales revenue.

Selection of the right franchisee is also important.

If they do not believe in your business, its products, processes and what you are trying to achieve, you could find yourself in a battle from day one. If they have limited skills, you could spend a lot of time helping them and even preventing a disaster if they get things really wrong.

You will also need to ensure your existing business can look after itself while you chase the new franchise arrangements. They could be all-consuming for a period.

# Can my business be franchised?

Not every business is suitable for franchising. These are a few of the key characteristics that need to exist if you want to grow your business through franchising.

- Will there be a demand for your product or service in different geographical locations or is the success of your business determined by your current location?

- Is your business profitable? If your growth is purely off the back of external funding and not yet profitable, it is unlikely another owner will want to take on the risk.

- Can other people pick up the skills quickly so they can run the business without your involvement? If your business is heavily reliant on you, or requires specialised skills that are difficult to get, franchising is unlikely to work.

- Are your systems and processes mature, proven, and easy to use? If you do not have excellent processes and systems and they are in a poor state, you will need to get these sorted before considering franchising.

- Can potential franchisees afford to buy a business like yours? If your business has been built up over an extended period, has significant plant, equipment or stock to operate, it may be very difficult to replicate quickly and be unaffordable.

- Has your business been operating for long enough to give franchisees confidence about the future?

- If the business has not been around for long but has the potential to be franchised, can you develop a pilot business with a like-minded franchisee who is keen to be involved from the start? [1,2]

The businesses that have proven most successful using a franchise model are those that comprise many small units operating in a market without a dominant chain or big player. Fragmented markets without stiff competition from large established businesses are more likely to offer franchise opportunities.

# Really understand your numbers, especially your breakeven.

If you are growing rapidly, you will probably take on additional debt. You will employ more staff, and increase your costs (e.g., additional premises, more vehicles). Your time is likely to be spent on the growth, and the details about cash flow may drift down the priority list. Even if you are very keen to be all over this, the pace of the change may make it very difficult to assess exactly where you are.

---

> When things are moving fast, the financial numbers can become a blur. You could be in trouble and not even know it.

---

It's so important you are all over this, or if you don't have the time, someone in your business is all over it.

If your continued growth relies on increased sales, what sales must you achieve to breakeven each month? Are you generating the cash flow to service additional debt? If sales don't meet expectations, do you have the cash on hand or bank facilities (e.g., an overdraft) to carry this until sales pick up? And what do you do, and in what order do you do it, if sales don't eventuate and you can see the cash running out?

---

### Death of a Kiwi icon -Pumpkin Patch and the risk of growing

Sally Synnott started Pumpkin Patch in 1990 as a provider of children's wear, through mail order catalogues. She opened her first retail store in Auckland followed by a retail store in Australia in 1997.

Pumpkin Patch was listed on the New Zealand stock exchange on 9 June 2004 and raised over $100 million. However, over $60 million of this was used to purchase shares from existing shareholders, leaving limited cash to fund a planned expansion overseas.

---

Following the listing, Pumpkin Patch borrowed from the ANZ bank to support their planned growth. Pumpkin Patch had no debt in 2005, but by 2008 it exceeded $80 million.[3] With this amount of debt, good sales in these new markets were essential.

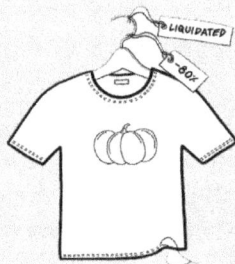

Pumpkin Patch opened stores in Asia, the Arab countries, the USA, the United Kingdom, Ireland, Russia, China, Singapore, Malaysia, Indonesia, South Africa, Pakistan, and South America. At its peak, it had over 230 stores in 21 countries and over 2000 employees. It had its peak sales of over $400 million in 2009 and was the Kiwi exporter of the year in 2010.

If any business has weaknesses in their internal systems and processes prior to its growth, they are likely to be magnified and prove costlier as it grows. Pumpkin Patch underestimated the impact their ambitious growth plans were going to have on their internal operations. Its internal systems and processes were adequate for a small retailer in Australia and New Zealand but were never sophisticated enough to manage the international business they were becoming and at the pace they were growing.

The troubles for Pumpkin Patch first started to appear in the USA and the UK. The expansion into these countries was rapid and almost totally funded by debt

Unlike their competitors, Pumpkin Patch were not vertically integrated, relying on a few suppliers who did not always deliver. To cover their inefficient systems and these supply problems, the business held additional stock, which did not move quickly and would go out of fashion. They were then forced to sell this stock well below normal price. Customers would wait for discount sales rather than buying at full price, devaluing the brand and reducing revenue.

Pumpkin Patch's time to create new designs and get them into stores was slow by industry standards, so they could not keep pace with changing customer needs.

As larger vertically integrated outlets entered the market, like Cotton On, Zara and H&M, the problems deepened for Pumpkin Patch

All these issues contributed to sales falling well below target, especially in the USA and the UK. Eventually the company had no choice but to close their US and UK stores in 2012 and exit these markets. This exercise cost the business almost $100 million, most of which was funded by debt.

Pumpkin Patch did not ignore these issues, bringing in external expertise to look for options in 2014. They took aggressive action, selling stock and assets, reducing costs and changing management. Sadly, with this much debt, high fixed costs, and falling sales, they could never act fast enough, and the end was inevitable.

The company's directors resolved to put the company into voluntary administration in October 2016. The company owed the ANZ around $60 million.

The receivers tried to find a buyer for Pumpkin Patch, but this was unsuccessful. They later sold Pumpkin Patch's name and other intellectual property for about $2 million to an online retailer - a tragic fall from the $400 million high.

Pumpkin Patch Limited was delisted from the New Zealand stock exchange in June 2017,

The failure of Pumpkin Patch saw the closure of all its 230 stores and the loss of well over 1400 jobs.

# Your role - Can you run a bigger business — really?

It's likely your role in your rapidly growing business will need to change. As you grow, you simply can't do everything like you may have done when the business was smaller. You will need to become much more disciplined on what role you must play in the growth process and what you can delegate. You may find you have to do far more *"leading"* and a lot less *"doing"*.

If your motivation and passion is taking your idea and the development of the business, the growth process, seeking funding, selling your dream, and all the exciting stuff that goes with growth, be very wary if you are really the right person to run this growing business. Running a larger business requires different skills.

Remember, this business may well be your baby. How do you let go and entrust your staff to run all or parts of it? Are you comfortable putting processes, procedures, and rules in place to ensure the day-to-day stuff happens? What about the administration, paying and chasing bills, the management of staff, the inevitable staff issues that will come, the customer complaints that may come in, ordering stock and so on and so on?

Far too many start-up entrepreneurs believe the approach and skills they used to grow the business are the same skills required to run the business. Sadly, the self-confidence to sell the business' story, the single-minded passion for that business, and the ego one needs to take an idea and make it a viable business may not be attributes that sit too well with the staff you bring on. Just read the case of the collapsed finance companies. Most of these were start-ups, driven by entrepreneurs with big egos focused on growth, self-interest, rather than running stable, long-term businesses with great cultures.

Think seriously if running a larger business is for you. If you are certain, it is, test this with those you trust. Far too many entrepreneurs feel they can *"do it all"* when they can't, and the growth rapidly unwinds as new staff can't find the exit door quick enough. The successful start-up entrepreneurs accepted they would not enjoy or would not be any good at running a business and brought in managers and/or sold the business and moved on to the next opportunity.

# CHAPTER 17

# EXPORTING AND DOING BUSINESS OVERSEAS

While New Zealand might be a large country in terms of its geographical size, it has a small economy and is on the other side of the planet. We have one of the most remote capitals on earth. Therefore, many Kiwi businesses look offshore for additional opportunities.

Our economy relies heavily on what we sell overseas. Dairy is our biggest exporter, bringing in over $25 billion. This is over 25% of our total exports.[1] Meat is next, followed by timber, fruit and nuts, and finally beverages, including wine. But what we export is diverse and small businesses are active exporters.[2]

## Some export statistics

In New Zealand, 23% [3] of small businesses are directly engaged in exporting. When one considers there are over 560,000 businesses in New Zealand, [4] this is a serious number who are operating successfully in overseas markets – over 120,000. However, when we consider that 95% of businesses in NZ are small, there is still a huge potential for more of us to venture into overseas markets.

There are a wide range of ways New Zealand businesses engage in overseas markets. We not only put products on ships and send them offshore. We offer skills and knowledge through a range of service-based businesses.

Many of our larger exporters rely entirely on overseas markets to survive. There are also businesses who do almost all their business locally but dabble on the margins in other countries.

Our top ten export countries, which make up about 75% of all our exports, are China, USA, Australia, Singapore, South Korea, Japan,

United Kingdom, Taiwan, Malaysia, and Hong Kong. Other countries that pop in and out of the top ten include Thailand, Indonesia and India.

While most of what New Zealand exports is to these countries, we export to over 230 countries. [5,6]

You should not be afraid to look for markets offshore if you genuinely believe what you offer could be sold there. There are thousands of Kiwi businesses of all shapes and sizes doing it. As with any strategic business decision, it will involve risk. The more you understand those risks, the better.

# Export basics are business basics

Whether you are selling in your local town, across New Zealand, or considering selling overseas, you still need to remember the basics of business. This is not a time to park your purpose or values. If anything, it is a time to work even harder to maintain them. Be clear on what your goals are before entering new markets. You need to know your customer, your point-of-difference and how to reach these new customers. While the principles are the same when dealing in another country, the market, the customer and their needs could be very different.

If you must employ staff, they are still people and the business' culture, and your leadership is just as important. The challenge now is you are operating in a different recruitment market, operating under different laws and with different cultures. Do your homework.

You still need excellent systems and processes, no matter where you operate.

You need to understand where you are likely to have the greatest demand for your products and services. No point launching into a new market if no one there has any interest in what you are selling.

It's likely you will also need more money than you think. It is possible to start and run a business with almost no money in New Zealand, at least initially. This is not the case when you go offshore.

Knowing your market will extend into all the detailed business and marketing considerations we have, and will discuss in this book.

How do you handle language barriers? What regulations exist in these countries that differ from New Zealand? Do you need to consider differences in the industry jargon from New Zealand to the country you are working in? How will your marketing processes differ on your website and social media pages? The advertising channels that work well in New Zealand may be very different in another country.

## What makes it great here makes it difficult there

I provided a lot of statistics in the earlier chapters to show how good it is doing business in New Zealand. It is one of the easiest places on the planet to start and run a business. Unfortunately, this means everywhere else will be more difficult. You really need to do your homework and understand where you are going and what challenges you might face.

While the principle of being honest in business activities and doing the right thing will mean you are meeting most laws in New Zealand, this may not apply equally in other countries. New Zealand is one of the least corrupt and most transparent countries in the world. You may well be entering countries where this is not the case. Again, do your homework and seek good, local advice.

You may want to engage local experts or businesses who will represent and support you in the country you are entering. Many Kiwi businesses who already have a presence in these countries may make connections for you.

Nothing beats understanding another country more than walking its streets and engaging with the locals. If you have lived and operated in New Zealand, what you take for granted as *"normal"* may be very different in another country. If you have travelled a lot but never done business, you will appreciate the subtle, and not so subtle, differences in countries and cultures. This makes traveling and doing business overseas so rewarding. However, it is also what adds additional risks to business.

*"Get a plane ticket and get there to talk to people who might be customers or partners. It makes things infinitely easier to get some locals on your side to start with.... Don't let uncertainty or the mysteriousness of foreign markets scare you. The world really is a small place in that it's super-easy to get around, and it's BIG at the same time.* **Vaughan Rowsell**. Founder of VEND Software [7]

Go to any of the many expos, trade shows and conferences that relate to the industry you are in and the markets you want to sell to. It's not only about the displays you'll see and the presentations you will hear, but the people you bump into. There are cases where New Zealand agencies are present at such events. Piggy-back off these agencies at these events if you can. They could make introductions or help you in other ways.

# Export examples

Nearly all the Kiwi businesses I've discussed throughout this book have ventured into overseas markets. Most did so with very limited prior experience exporting or operating in other countries. The story of how all of them achieved this is very similar. They did a lot of research. They got on a plane; they talked to lots of people; they worked hard, and they took small steps.

- From First Table's humble beginnings, it now has its offering in 2000 restaurants in New Zealand, Australia and the UK. This is an example where it's not a product being put on a ship and sent offshore. It is an online offering to help restaurants around the world.

- Connor Archbold and Matt Herbert of Tracksuit started the business in New Zealand in 2021. By 2024, they had offices in London, Sydney, and the West Coast of the USA. They also attracted large USA companies like Footwork Venture Capital and Altos Ventures Management of California to invest in their business. Their London office has also grown, building a new start-up venture serving the UK. They achieved this through many hours on the phone telling their story over-and-over. They went to these places in person and talked to anyone who was prepared to listen.

- Geoff and Bev of Shoof International had no overseas experience when they attended the Warwick Royal Show in England in 1979. Unlike the businesses of today, they had limited information available to research what was happening overseas. The internet was over a decade away. They took a chance, jumped on a plane and the rest is history. When they sold their business in 2023, they were operating in four countries and exporting around the world.

- A small three person, Hamilton based consultancy called **Thermal Chemistry**, offers advice on industrial steam, water and metallurgy into the geothermal, electricity, energy, and industrial sectors. They have done this in New Zealand, the USA, Japan, India, Oman, Saudi Arabia, Egypt, Algeria, Tunisia, South Africa, Canada, Australia, Turkey, Vietnam, Philippines, and Europe. They are also asked to speak at conferences around the world (I know this because my wife is one of those three people).

- Seequent was named Export Innovator of the Year at the New Zealand Innovation Awards in 2017. Its exports were not physical products, but software.

- Sadly, there are examples where Kiwi businesses ventured offshore, grew rapidly, and got things very wrong. Pumpkin Patch is one such example.

> There are so many Kiwi small businesses who have successfully ventured offshore. It just shows that if they can do it, so can you.

# Where to turn for help

New Zealand wants (and needs) businesses to export to build a robust economy. While we export a lot, small businesses in this country have a potential to export far more. We have great small businesses producing some amazing products and delivering innovative services that we can offer the world.

While support for small business in New Zealand is pretty much non-existent in almost all areas we operate, the support you can get to export is more extensive. The product or service you are looking to offer overseas will be diverse, so only you can decide who amongst these agencies is best placed to help. Don't be shy. Running a small business can be tough and lonely, with very few places to turn for help. If you want to export, chase these agencies to get whatever help they offer. They want you to succeed and they want to help.

Here are some people you could turn to.

- **New Zealand Trade and Enterprise (NZTE):** The NZTE has some excellent resources where you could start your research. They have market guides, market research reports, articles, templates, case studies and much more. They run online courses, and you can contact them for specific advice. This is what the NZTE are there to do. They want to grow exports from New Zealand, so contact them.

- **The New Zealand Story.** The New Zealand Story is a government initiative to build New Zealand's brand overseas. The New Zealand tourism industry uses the *"100% Pure"* brand, but New Zealand business is far more than that and most overseas people know very little about this country. If you are an exporter, you can get their permission to use the New Zealand Fern logo, which is protected across the planet. They have some amazing video and imagery you can use.

- **New Zealand Foreign Affairs and Trade (MFAT).** MFAT offer advice on what's happening in what countries, and where they recommend you should and shouldn't travel. MFAT also offer great market reports targeted at Kiwi exporters. They have a major part to play in establishing international free trade agreements that can make your efforts to access other markets that much easier.

- **Ministry of Primary Industries (MPI):** MPI can assist if you want to export food products into other countries. This includes providing export certificates to vouch for the product. An export certificate provides the country your business is exporting to confirmation from the New Zealand Government that your product meets certain standards and requirements.

- **Chambers of Commerce**. There are Chambers of Commerce within New Zealand that can issue you with **Certificates of Origin** (CO). These are an essential component of international trade. They confirm that the goods in a particular shipment have been sourced, produced, manufactured or processed in a particular country, in our case New Zealand.

  The Chambers will also be involved when delegations come to your area or if there are delegations leaving New Zealand on trade tours.

  The Chamber is a world-wide body and may make introductions through other Chambers in the country of interest.

- **Freight Forwarders**. If you are putting products on a ship to send offshore, get a good freight forwarder, as we discussed in the chapters on importing.

- There are **many websites** that provide examples of businesses that have ventured offshore. Most are small businesses. Read their stories. Reach out to these people. The small business community wants to share the lessons they have learned.[8,9]

Finally, ask around. There are bound to be businesses in your networks who have done business overseas. Your lawyer, accountant, or other advisors may have some experience or know those who have.

Join your local Chamber of Commerce and other industry associations who can put you in touch with those who are exporting into the regions you are considering.

Perhaps it's time for that well-earned holiday to travel to somewhere you feel you could do some business. You can enjoy some time away from the day-to-day and gain insight into other countries, cultures and people to see if you can expand your business – and have a holiday at the same time.

# CHAPTER 18

# HEALTH AND SAFETY AND THE HUMAN ELEMENT

If you own any type of business in New Zealand, you cannot ignore the health and safety of everyone in your business and the health and safety of those external to your business that you may affect. The extent that it affects your business will depend on your risks. If you are an arborist, scaffolder, painter, electrician, machinery operator, construction business, your safety risks will be greater than the owner of a small retail store in a shopping centre. No matter what your small business does, you must pause and consider what you need to do to keep everyone you interact with safe and well.

## The New Zealand health and safety landscape after Pike River

New Zealand's workplace health and safety record has not been one to be proud of.

While in recent years the numbers are improving, as detailed in the table below, far too many Kiwis go to work and don't come home to their families at the end of their workday. [1,2]

☞ While the laws are tougher now, the focus of health and safety has never changed – it is about caring for people.

| YEAR | ACC WORKPLACE CLAIMS | WORKPLACE FATALITIES |
|------|---------------------|---------------------|
| 2015 | 197,013 | 59 |
| 2016 | 200,805 | 74 |
| 2017 | 205,048 | 80 |
| 2018 | 211,495 | 62 |
| 2019 | 210,146 | 110 |
| 2020 | 189,828 | 69 |
| 2021 | 196,851 | 64 |
| 2022 | 194,850 | 59 |
| 2023 | 195,396 | 37 |

Sadly, it took the tragic death of 29 men in the Pike River mine explosion in 2010 to see New Zealand change its approach to health and safety in the workplace.

This tragedy saw the government replace the **Health and Safety in Employment Act of 1992** with the **Health and Safety at Work Act of 2015**. It also saw the birth of the new regulator, **WorkSafe**.

# It's about people, not compliance

If your starting point for implementing good health and safety practices is solely to comply with the law, then you have already missed the point. This implies you are pursuing a safe work environment out of fear – the fear of being punished for failing to comply. If this is your motivation, it's very likely it will be your staff's motivation. They will stay safe simply to obey the rules and avoid punishment for breaking those rules.

When human beings act out of fear, they deliver the lowest level of performance. They deliver the minimum that is needed so they are not punished. They hide mistakes, in this case near misses and incidents, and will probably only comply when someone in authority is watching them.

As the owner of a small business, you need to focus on ensuring no one at your workplace is seriously injured, either physically or psychologically. If you work closely with your staff on the ways you could seriously injure someone, and do everything you can to prevent this from happening, then you are on the right track.

> If you are only putting practices in place to satisfy a regulator and doing it because you have to, then you have failed even before you start.

# Behaviours are not the problem

The greatest contributor to accidents and injuries at work is human behaviour. Behaviours more than any other factor will determine how safe your workplace is. But keep in mind the following quote:

> *"Behaviours are not the problem; behaviours are expressions of the problem."* **Clive Lloyd**. Psychologist, safety specialist, and author. [3]

This quote reinforces our earlier discussion on values when developing the strategy for the business. Behaviours are what you see. They reflect the underlying values of the environment the people are working in. If you are unhappy with the health and safety behaviours you are seeing, think carefully before punishing these behaviours. The reason people are behaving in this way is simply a reflection of deeper issues. So, step back, pause, and dig deeper.

Blame and punishment for unsafe practices are likely to backfire. People are more likely to push issues underground for fear of what will happen. Your staff won't report incidents if they fear being reprimanded. Continually pointing out faults in what people are doing will see them disengage.

If you put a disproportionate value on job completion, speed to get work done, workmanship, costs, or any other priority, but overlook substandard health and safety practices, then you should not be surprised to see poor health and safety practices.

If you reward people for not being injured, you are encouraging people to hide injuries. You can't address problems you know nothing about. Likewise, if you punish poor behaviours without understanding why those behaviours exist, then people will focus more on avoiding punishment than on acting safely.

Work with your staff on creating practical, workable methods that keep them safe rather than criticising or punishing them for carrying out poor practices.

If you force safety practices on your staff that are unworkable or make no sense, then people will simply ignore them or work around them.

People don't deliberately injure themselves. They are human, so they make mistakes. Hopefully, no mistake will kill or seriously injure anyone. What you need to focus on is ensuring if one of your people makes a mistake, it delivers a good learning experience rather than a death or serious injury.

## The Health and Safety Triangle

There are many models and diagrams to simplify the factors that, if implemented, will deliver better health and safety performance in a business. If you find something that works for you, great. The **Health and Safety Triangle** is one I have seen and used for many years that helps guide me when things become overwhelming.

Basically, if you want a safe workplace, it requires a combination of your culture and values, represented in the behaviours you see, good equipment, tools and engineered solutions and finally your processes and systems. You need a combination of all three to get it right.

## 1. *Human behaviours*

We have already highlighted this. Getting this right will contribute most to a safe and healthy workplace. Sadly, it is by far the most difficult to implement, especially if you and your staff have traditionally placed an unhealthy focus on getting the job done or looked cynically at implementing new health and safety practices.

## 2. *Engineering*

If your team have suitable tools and equipment, well-maintained plant and if you can engineer out any safety risks, it will help with efficient work practices and better health and safety. Yes, it costs money, but, as we discuss below, implementing sound practical safety solutions may also improve the business.

If the cash is really tight and you simply can't buy that better gear or engineer the solution you want, at least look for the most practical way to deal with it, until you have the money to do it properly. Even with tight budgets, there is usually a solution to reduce risks and keep equipment in reasonable working order.

## 3. *Systems and procedures*

If you are actively working on building a culture that drives the right behaviours and you have engineered out the risks you can practically remove, then the last step is using documents and a system that informs everyone and contributes to a safer workplace. Toolbox meetings, PPE, Job Safety Analyses (JSAs), Safe Work Method Statements (SWMS), risk assessments, incident reporting are all examples of what makes up a system.

Remember, if your staff do not use the system, it's pointless. Developing a system is one challenge. Making sure everyone is following the system in carrying out their work is an even greater challenge

Your business may be purely office based. You may have heard the old cliché that *"our only risk is paper cuts"*. While a business like this need not incorporate the same safety systems and procedures that businesses in high-risk environments require, they still face risks. One is the risk of effecting an employee's mental health. Excessive stress, a toxic work environment, bullying or harassment, including racial or sexual harassment, can be immensely harmful. Therefore, you still need to develop systems to protect your staff from this type of harm.

# The hierarchy of controls

The above triangle reflects the need to take a wholistic approach to safety. It's about people, engineering and it's about systems and processes. Another way of putting it is the widely used **hierarchy of controls.** When reviewing any work practice that involves health and safety risk, consider the following order to remove, reduce, or manage the risk.

## 1.　Elimination.

Can you avoid carrying out the task all together so you remove the risk?

## 2. Substitution.

If you have to carry out the task, can you substitute something to reduce the risk? For example, replace toxic solvents on a job with non-toxic alternatives.

## 3. Engineering controls.

If the task has to occur, can you implement engineering modifications to isolate the risk and reduce the chance of harm? For example, fencing off and installing guards on rotating machinery.

## 4. Administrative controls.

If none of the above can remove the risk completely, look at the procedures, risk assessment, or other practices people should follow.

## 5. Personal protective equipment (PPE).

This is the last resort if you cannot implement any of the above. You might include the use of PPE on the job.

When you run your businesses, you face many risks. It's the nature of business. Safety is just another of those risks. Actions like the list above are simply to reduce the risk and manage it as best you can.

# Being safe may also be good for business

Far too often, small businesses look upon safety as a burden to their business. Basically, *"if I put all these safety requirements in place, I'll go broke"*.

Yes, implementing safety processes and finding engineering solutions to unsafe equipment can be costly. But as a small business, you need to consider the benefits a safe work environment can mean.

---

If the safety processes you implement have the support of your staff, and they feel they are being implemented to protect them from harm, then it's also likely it will improve the efficiency of the job.

There are so many examples of this.

- Using scaffolding when working at heights helps get the job done quicker and safer.

- Correct guarding on machinery will mean people can work faster without fear of injury.

- Correct training and certifications on hire equipment means your staff will use it correctly, and safely with fewer mistakes.

- A tidy, well laid out workshop allows faster work and ease of finding tools, as well as removing trip and slip hazards.

Larger organisations who are considering engaging your small business may require evidence of your health and safety record and your systems. Often you will need to achieve pre-qualification with a third party before you can work for them or even access their sites. More and more large organisations will reject a small business, and refuse working with them if their practices are unsafe.

If you are prepared to invest in safety, to gain the standards these businesses require, it could allow you to access jobs your competitors can't. It will provide your business with an important point of difference.

Therefore, good safety practices, and a strong safety culture, may be expensive to implement but will not only be good for your staff, but could also be good for business.

## Start by knowing your risks

The best place to assess where you need to focus your efforts is to determine your highest health and safety risks. Start with the task that, if things go wrong, could lead to a death or serious injury.

Consider the serious incidents that have occurred in other similar businesses to inform you. I've listed some cases below where prosecutions have occurred, which may help.

Consider how the risk changes if a staff member is feeling stressed or tired or is inexperienced. It will increase the likelihood of mistakes.

I've duplicated the risk matrix from previous chapters here, as it is very effective for identifying health and safety risks.

The worst health and safety **Consequence** your business could face is a death, which is **Catastrophic**. A serious, disabling injury would be a **Major** consequence. You would rank minor injuries as lower consequences.

Then assess what the likelihood of these incidents. If the incident has occurred before, it is **Likely** or **Definite** that it will occur again. At the other extreme is an incident which would be **Unlikely** or **Rare.**

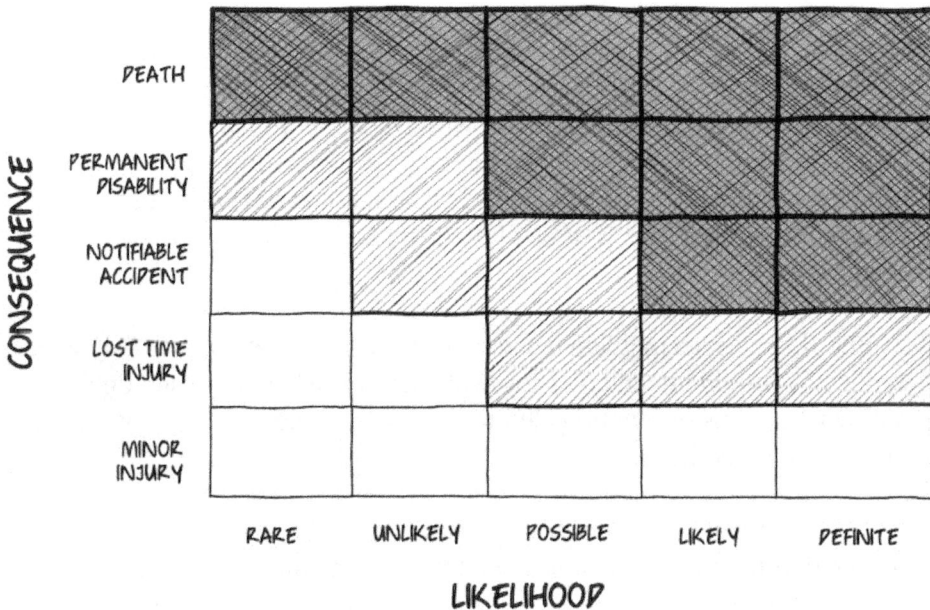

While you should never be satisfied with any injuries, your priority is the tasks that expose your staff to risks in the shaded areas.

Your next priority is to use the **hierarchy of controls** discussed above to reduce the risk to more acceptable levels.

Record all this information and track the status of your higher risks.

This is called your **health and safety risk register** and is a key part of any health and safety system.

## ...and now you need to ensure you are compliant - health and safety systems

I do not want to lull you into a false sense of security that if you build a culture and implement the suggestions above that you have, by default, met all your legal obligations. Clearly, that is not the case. The message I am sending is you need to shift your thinking, so the priority for making your workplace safe is to ensure the wellbeing of everyone. It should NOT simply be to comply with the rules, and to keep you out of trouble.

Unfortunately, many businesses who want to comply hire a third-party health and safety expert to provide documents covering all the areas to achieve compliance. The problem then is the business only uses part of the system, if they use it at all. Often the staff do not even know these systems exist.

Should a serious incident occur, and WorkSafe investigates, they won't care what you documented. They will focus on what happened on the job and what actions or inactions led to the incident, not what you wrote in a document stored in the office.

If you intend implementing a health and safety system, don't even bother if you will not make it practical and something that your staff will use to do their work. It needs to work for your business, your staff, and genuinely make them safer. If not, you won't be fooling anyone.

If the systems and processes are practical and followed by staff, the hope is an incident won't occur. If, after all this, an incident does still occur, hopefully it won't be as serious. If an investigation occurs, you will have a more defendable position.

## *How do I get the right health and safety system for me?*

There is a huge amount of online information available to assist you in understanding what you need to do to meet your health and safety requirements. The regulator, WorkSafe, is an excellent place to start, but there are many others.

My warning about getting a system set up for the sake of it does not mean you should be afraid to use third party experts. There are many high calibre, practical providers out there who will meet your business' needs. You just need to shop around. There are also some excellent online tools. As with any system you choose, ask around and do some research.

The ISO standard most referenced to develop health and safety systems in New Zealand is **ISO45001**.

The key is making it very clear to the provider that whatever they provide, it MUST be fit for purpose for YOUR business and needs to be implemented so that it is being used by all. Challenge them on how they intend delivering this before hiring anyone.

> *"Having a written process but not following it is the same as having nothing at all,"*, **Dr Catherine Gardner**, WorkSafe (about a death at Affco's Meatworks in Wairoa in 2020).

It may be possible for you to develop the system yourself. If you intend doing this, do your research. It is a complicated area requiring expertise. If you can't afford a third party, this may be your only option. It is much better to do the best you can than to assume it is all too hard and do nothing.

# What should your health and safety system include?

The following references are some of the key points from the standard ISO45001. This is what you would typically find in a health and safety system.

### 1.   Health and safety policy.

This is a one-page document developed by you, the owner, and posted in your business stating what your philosophy and expectations are around health and safety. It is a high-level document.

### 2.   Identification of risks.

If you have developed a **risk register**, as detailed in this chapter, you should have met this requirement.

### 3.   Reporting of incidents.

Processes need to be provided to all staff that encourage them to report safety incidents and near misses. Where appropriate, they need to be investigated and issues addressed. More serious incidents may need to be notified to WorkSafe.

### 4.   Competences.

You need to ensure all staff have the qualifications, or tickets they need to carry out their roles. You should develop a training program that ensures all these details are recorded and are all up to date.

### 5.   Emergency preparedness and response.

You need to identify emergencies that may occur in your business and determine what should then be done. For example, evacuating the site because of a fire.

### 6. *Health surveillance.*

If employees are exposed to excessive noise, dust, or other potential health risks, you need to determine the level of exposure. The correct controls need to be put in place to protect your staff and manage the risk. As a minimum, this would be personal protective equipment. You also need to consider if hearing and lung testing are required.

### 7. *Hazardous substances.*

If you use any hazardous substances, you will need to identify all of them, have **safety data sheets** outlining their risks and what you need to do if exposure occurs. You also need to ensure they are stored correctly.

### 8. *Contractors.*

If you use contractors in your business, you will need to ensure their health and safety practices meet your requirements, as you can't offload all your responsibilities to them.

### 9. *Consultation, communication and reporting.*

You need to have options for staff to communicate health and safety issues with you and with each other. This could include health and safety meetings, or toolbox meetings. You may also need a staff health and safety representative if your business has grown.

## If you get it wrong — the consequences might be severe

Sadly, while I hope your focus on safety is solely driven by the wellbeing of your staff and not the law, it would be naïve to ignore the legal risks. They are significant. Health and safety is the risk that is most likely to get a business owner in legal trouble, more than any other.

Should a serious health and safety incident occur, it could destroy your business and put you personally in the sights of investigators. It is also something you cannot get insurance cover for. If you are prosecuted, you might get some help with legal costs but not the fines. Many excellent businesses have disappeared after a serious injury or fatality, with the business owner suffering significant financial damage.

If an employee is seriously injured or killed in your business, it is likely you will never recover emotionally from it. While our staff will always present challenges, most of us in small business care a great deal about them. Many times, they become close friends and are like family. Seeing someone you care about hurt or killed because of your actions or inactions is incomprehensible.

Even if you feel there was little you could have done and you show genuine, deep remorse for a serious accident, the law doesn't care. They will probably come down hard and it is possible there will be legal and financial consequences. One need only spend a few minutes looking through WorkSafe's prosecutions, like the samples below, to realise what the impacts might be.

While there are few prosecutions for mental health related injuries, Australian regulators and Australian courts have set a precedent with prosecutions. It is only a matter of time before prosecutions will follow in New Zealand. [5,6] Besides, if you are not pursued under the Health and Safety Act, you could still be pursued under the Employment Relations Act or Human Rights Act through a personal grievance if you don't consider the psychological wellbeing of your people.

I fully understand how the cases below might cause you to fear the worst and act to protect yourself. If you start with your staff's wellbeing in mind, and you then do everything reasonable to protect them, including the points covered in the safety triangle above, the hope is this situation will not eventuate. If a serious incident does occur, you will be significantly better placed to come out the other side.

The cases detailed below show businesses that failed to build a safe culture, ignored engineering solutions and, in many cases, had no systems at all, or had systems that no one followed.

# Prosecution examples

The following are but a small sample of how businesses and the owners and directors were punished where their employees were seriously injured or killed:

- In 2019, a young apprentice at Aimex, a marine and engineering business near Nelson, suffered a serious brain injury after exposure to toxic fumes while cleaning an engine room. Aimex was prosecuted and during its investigations, WorkSafe was informed that a similar incident had happened to another employee the week prior. This was refuted by Aimex. However, an internal whistle-blower later informed WorkSafe that the management of Aimex had destroyed and/or hid documents relating to the previous incident. WorkSafe informed the Police of the cover-up, who prosecuted the individuals involved and they were jailed.

- Ron and Natalie Salter built Salters Cartage from a single truck to a fleet of vehicles. In 2014 Jamey Lee Bowring, 24 was welding atop a tank at the yard in Wiri, South Auckland, when it exploded, killing him. It was believed he did not know the tank contained a flammable mix of fumes. The company was prosecuted, fined over $400,000, and Ron Salter escaped a prison term, being put on home detention. Worse still, in a first for New Zealand, the police are pursuing over $11 million from the company, equating to earnings they have made since the death as *"the proceeds of crime"* - that crime being the death of Jamey Bowring. In Oct 2024, Salter agreed to settle the case for $4 million. [7]

- In November 2021 Create and Construct Limited of Auckland asked two of their crew to work on a roof before the edge protection had arrived on site. One of the two workers fell three metres from the roof, breaking a collarbone and hand. The company was prosecuted in 2023, and fined $300,000, although this was reduced because of a guilty plea, past good character, and the remedial steps they had later taken.

  Unfortunately, there are many similar examples of prosecutions for breaches of working at heights. It is an all-to-common cause of death and injuries.

- In 2018, a bus owned and operated by Ruapehu Alpine Lifts crashed while descending from the ski field, killing an eleven-year-old passenger. The company was deemed to have had insufficient safe work practises and training for those driving their buses over several years. They were fined $500,000, but by the time they were prosecuted, they had gone into liquidation

- Bays Boating Limited, a retail boat seller based in Motueka, was redeveloping its site. Before bringing a business on site to demolish a building, it engaged an asbestos removal company to remove the asbestos in the roof. This business warned Bays Boating that asbestos also existed in the walls. This was not removed, but the building was still demolished without the demolition company being made aware of this. The subsequent demolition also left a contaminated area on the site, exposing all those nearby, including customers, to a potential risk. Bays Boating Limited were prosecuted and fined $108,000.

- One of the highest profile and most tragic prosecutions under the new Health and Safety Act followed the death of 22 people when the Whakaari White Island volcano erupted in 2019. While it is an extreme example, it highlights that even with the best intentions, if people are seriously injured or killed because of a business' activities, they will be punished. All the businesses, and many observing the case, felt the tragedy was, to an extent, beyond their control - an act of God. The law saw it very differently. The five businesses who were ultimately prosecuted, including the family whose company owned the island, were made to pay fines, and reparations of approximately $13 million. Even after imposing such heavy fines, the judge stated:

  > "*There is no way to measure the emotional harm survivors and affected families have endured and will continue to endure. Reparation in a case like this can be no more than a token recognition of that harm.*" **Judge E.M. Thomas.** District Court Auckland 26-28 Feb 2024. WorkSafe v Whakaari Management Limited et. al.

# CHAPTER 19

## THE LAW AND YOUR SMALL BUSINESS

No matter what business you are in, there will be laws and regulations you have to meet. Many are obvious, some are not so. Ignorance of the law is never an excuse, nor will the small size of your business be an excuse.

It would be an impossible task to detail all the laws and regulations that would apply to small businesses, considering the variety of industries that exist within New Zealand.

The laws will vary for different industries, towns, and councils. If your business sells or operates in another country, then this further complicates the laws you must consider.

However, I will cover many of the most common laws that apply to every business in New Zealand.

## Start by doing the right and honest thing

While you must know and abide by the law, there are a few basics that, if you follow, will help you get through your business life without knowing the laws in fine detail.

If you always act with honesty, truthfulness, authenticity and ethics, you will meet many of your legal requirements. When you deliver what you say you will deliver, that too is a big plus. When you lie or deliberately deceive, cut corners, or knowingly hide mistakes, you will be in trouble under many laws.

If you deliberately avoid paying others what you owe them, including the IRD, it won't end well. If you don't take care of your staff, treat them respectfully, pay them what they are owed, keep them safe, keep their information private, then there will be laws you are likely breaking.

So, the first step in meeting your legal obligations is doing the right thing.

# The laws that impact every business

The following list is a large sample of the legislations that will probably apply to all small businesses, no matter the industry. The extent that they apply to you is an assessment you need to make.

As you can image, the list of laws that apply to businesses in New Zealand is very long. These are some of the most important acts. [1]

## *Employing and caring for staff*

- Health and Safety at Work Act 2015.

- Hazardous Substances and New Organisms Act 1996.

- Employment Relations Act 2000.

- Holidays Act 2003.

- Human Rights Act 1993.

## Dealing with your customers and competitors

- Consumer Guarantees Act 1993.

- Fair Trading Act 1986.

- Privacy Act 1993.

- Personal Property Securities Act 1999.

- Insolvent transactions under the Companies Act 1993.

- Commerce Act 1986.

- Unsolicited Electronic Messages Act 2007.

## Managing land and resources

- Resource Management Act 1991.

- Building Act 2004.

- Property Law Act 2007.

## Dealing with tax and financials

- Income Tax Act 2007.

- Financial Transactions Reporting Act 1996.

- Credit Contracts and Consumer Finance Act 2003.

- Anti-Money Laundering and Countering Financing of Terrorism Act 2009.

# Let's elaborate a little more

Let's elaborate in a little more detail some of the most relevant of these.

## *Health and Safety at Work Act*

We've discussed this already. If you haven't read this chapter, go back and read it, as this legislation applies to every small business owner, including you. Of all the legislation you face, this is perhaps what could expose you to the greatest risks.

## *Employment Relations and Holidays Acts*

While the consequences of not meeting this piece of legislation may not be as severe as health and safety laws, they are significant. As it is integral to how you manage your staff, it has its own chapter. Make sure you read this.

## *Human Rights Act*

Just as an employee can pursue you for a breach of the Employment Relations Act via the Employment Relations Tribunal, they could also pursue a grievance for a breach of the Human Rights Act. They could pursue you through the Human Rights Review Tribunal. Claims could be because of discrimination, sexual harassment, racial harassment or religious discrimination.

## *Privacy Act*

You need to be cautious about what information you collect about staff and customers and how you store and use that information. You can't hand over personal information without a person's permission. This includes an email address, residential address , credit card details, medical information and more.

If customers use credit cards to buy from you, ensure you destroy this information immediately. This includes when a customer provides their credit card details to purchase from you over the phone.

E-commerce sites will typically use third party payment systems, like **Stripe**. If you are keeping credit card information, there are very important requirements you must meet. Unless this is absolutely necessary, it's best not to keep this information.

The Human Rights Review Tribunal also hears any claims made for a breach of an employee, customer or other party's privacy. A breach could include sharing medical information, personal photos, contact details, and emails without the person's permission.

## Consumer Guarantees Act

If you sell products or provide services for personal or household use, then this will apply to your business. [2]

A consumer means a person who buys your product or service for personal, domestic, or household use. It excludes commercial business relationships.

If you sell products, you need to ensure:

- they are fit for purpose and not knowingly faulty.

- they match the description given.

- they align with any samples or demonstrations given.

- you sell them at the agreed price,

- you sell them at a reasonable price even if you didn't agree a price with the customer.

- you can sell the products legally within New Zealand (e.g. imports meet New Zealand regulations).

If you are a provider of services, like a tradesperson, accountant, or architect, you would need to ensure you provide the service:

- with a reasonable level of skill and care.

- that is fit for purpose.

- that you and the customer agreed on.

- at the agreed price and agreed timeframe.

- for a reasonable price if you had not previously agreed to the price.

- in a reasonable time, if you and your customer had not agreed on a timeframe beforehand.

---

## The bathroom heater that could kill - Serene

Serene Industries Limited, a Christchurch based business, was importing small, elegant wall mounted bathroom heaters out of Hong Kong. The company was registered in New Zealand in 2018 and traded under the name "*Serene Living*". They were selling the heaters though most electrical wholesalers, white good retailers and the large hardware chains throughout New Zealand. Sales were very good.

One of New Zealand's major white goods retailers proudly promoted the brand with:

> "*Serene Living is a brand committed to producing superior quality, efficient, and reliable heating and home products...Serene has taken the industry by storm with its new brand, Serene Living.*"

---

Justin Sollitt, a registered Kiwi electrician, had been invited to establish the Australian division of *"Serene Industries Ltd"* in 2015, well before Serene Industries Limited was even registered in New Zealand.

Serene had purchased the heating products from the highly regarded company SKOPE that Sollitt knew well. However, soon after he took on the business, complaints started being made and investigations by Australia's safety regulator followed.

The heaters' internal wiring and insulations did not comply with Australia and New Zealand's electrical safety standards, posing a serious risk of starting fires.

Sollitt got out of the Australian business. He then went to great lengths to warn New Zealand regulators of the risks. This included writing to the Minister of Workplace Relations and Safety in 2019. He had little success.

Serene was still manufacturing and distributing non-compliant heaters throughout New Zealand after Sollitt's warnings.

The exact numbers of heaters sold in New Zealand since 2018 are not known but it would in the hundreds of thousands.

It wasn't long before accidents started happening.

At least 15 fires involving Serene appliances were recorded in New Zealand. A Queenstown hotelier had the heaters installed in most of his units. It was only through luck he was in one of the rooms when a heater caught fire.

It was not until April 2024, well over five years after Sollitt had warned regulators, they issued a prohibition notice and started recalling the non-compliant heaters.

Sadly, even as late as August 2024, the heaters were still being mentioned on some major hardware suppliers, white goods sellers, and plumbing outlets' websites. [3,4,5,6.]

## Fair Trading Act

The Fair Trading Act encourages fair business practices. It prohibits misleading and deceptive conduct, false representations, and unfair practices. This could include.

- Misleading promotions of a product.

- Not meeting a warranty or a safety requirement for a product that was clearly stated.

- Advertisements like *"was $200, now $100"* when the price was always $100.

- Not disclosing hidden costs.

- Accepting payment for a product you can't provide.

- Using threats or undue pressure to complete a sale.

## Commerce Act

The Commerce Act aims to encourage competition within New Zealand for the benefit of consumers. The Commerce Act is overseen and enforced by the Commerce Commission. [7]

Any agreement or arrangement between you and another business that substantially lessens competition could be illegal under the Commerce Act. These agreements could be a written contract or an informal understanding. It may still be illegal even if it wasn't deliberate or if the arrangement was agreed but not implemented.

A **cartel** is a form of price fixing, which would be illegal under this act.

A cartel is where two or more businesses agree not to compete. This conduct can take many forms, including price fixing, sharing markets, rigging bids or restricting the output of goods and services.

If a competitor approaches you to see if you can both set your prices to the same level and customers have few other options, you are likely to be in breach of this Act. Another example is if a supplier forces you to sell your products at a certain price if you are to stock their products and takes actions against you if you decide to sell at a lower price. They can recommend prices but cannot force you to sell for any particular price.

Don't think because you are small that the Commerce Commission or other aggrieved parties, like a competitor, won't bother pursuing you. Anyone can lodge a complaint with the Commerce Commission if they feel you are in breach of this act. If the Commerce Commission investigates you, this alone is a huge issue because of the time and legal cost involved in responding to them. If they decide to pursue a prosecution against you and succeed, the penalties are severe.

## Resource Management Act (RMA), Building Act, and Council rules

If you own, bought or renovated a property or are in the building or construction industry, you will have had plenty of experience dealing with council regulations and consents.

These can be tedious, bureaucratic and difficult. As a result, far too many people take the risk and avoid complying with them without understanding the risks.

If you decide to carry out new operations at your business, you need to ensure they don't breach any RMA, council or other local laws, otherwise you could invest time and effort only to have the councils step in. As a minimum, you may not have the appropriate code of compliance on the activity, so you may not be able to sell the property. You could also face significant fines.

There are many examples where businesses have found themselves on the wrong side of a regional or district council. These are typical examples of where this has happened.

- Opening a business in an area not zoned for that purpose.

- Increasing heavy vehicle movements into the business from a public road or highway that affects traffic.

- Discharging something off the site like wastewater.

- Adding activities that generate noise or smells from the business.

- Taking water from a local water source.

- Changing an existing building or adding additional buildings on the site.

- Burning waste products on the site

If you have a **home-based business,** you need to be careful if it grows and affects the neighbourhood.

Running your small business from home is not only common but also a low-cost way to do business and allows you to be at home. This was very acceptable through the COVID-19 pandemic. However, be careful, because if neighbours complain and your home is not in an area zoned for business, the council may get involved. They might force you to move your business activities with little or no notice.

## *Credit Contracts and Consumer Finance Act 2003*

This is unlikely to apply to your business as it typically applies to those who lend money, like the banks and second tier lenders. How it will affect your business is what the lenders are required to get from you to approve loans. The legislation aims to protect individuals and businesses from irresponsible lending practices, such as offering a loan to someone who cannot repay it.

The government of the day may loosen or tighten what the legislation defines as *"responsible lending"*. This could make it easier or more difficult to get a loan approved. For example, the government may require lenders to request a lot more details on a lender's spending behaviour and personal budgets before they will approve a loan.

# Some other legal areas for small businesses to understand

I have already mentioned the variety of legal contracts and agreements you need to put in place for buying or selling a business, purchasing a franchise, or setting up a partnership, as well as documents required when employing staff.

I will now cover a few specific areas of the law that may apply to your small business.

## *Leases*

If you operate from home or own the building or land you run your business from, then you don't need a lease. However, very often small business owners will need to find a location and rent the property to carry out their business.

When signing a lease with a landlord, never accept non-standard lease agreements. The **Auckland Law Society** provides the most widely used lease conditions. Landlords, tenants and lawyers are familiar with these.

Unless you have worked extensively with these documents, seek a legal opinion before making changes or accepting changes to these standard contracts.

These are a few things to consider before deciding on a property and signing that lease:

- Does the property need to be changed so you can operate? If so, who's paying for it?

- How long is the lease for? Are their review periods and if there are, when are they?

- Do the review periods only allow lease rate changes, or could the landlord ask you to vacate?

- What is the consequence for your business if the landlord asks you to leave? If it could kill the business, pursue a longer lease.

- Likewise, what if you have a long-term lease but want to leave early?

- If you sell the business or vacate the property before the lease period expires, and another party takes over the lease, consider if you will still have to hold the personal guarantees. The new buyer might refuse to sign the personal guarantees, so the landlord may refuse to release you from these, even though you are no longer on the property.

- If the landlord increases the lease, are you able to get an independent market assessment? If not, how do you know the increases are at market rates and fair?

- Make sure you understand who pays rates, utility charges and other outgoings.

- Clarify who insures what. Is it your responsibility or the landlords?

Don't be surprised if the landlord does not jump to address every issue you have, even if it is their responsibility. You may need to persist and continue chasing them to get things done. If it's a minor issue, you may have to sort it yourself so it gets done and you can get on with business.

## Business legal structures

You will need to decide what legal structure your business should have.

The three most common structures small businesses are likely to take are a sole trader, a partnership, or a limited liability company.

### 1. Sole trader (Sole proprietor)

Becoming a sole trader is the simplest of all structures and is typically what a person, on their own, starts out as. The business and the person are the same in the eyes of the law and the IRD. There is no formal or legal process required to become a sole trader.

If you have no intention of growing, at least in the immediate future, and have no intention of hiring other people, there is no real advantage in setting up a company for your business. A company does add additional costs, tax complications and more administration.

As the sole trader, you are entitled to all the profits. You are also liable for all business taxes. Effectively, you pay tax through your personal tax return.

The primary advantage of a sole proprietorship is that it is very easy to start, is subject to relatively few regulations, is fully autonomous regarding the owner's business decisions, and is easy to discontinue. On the flip side, you are personally liable for any debt, and your liability is unlimited.

This is one of the major disadvantages of a sole proprietorship. As a sole trader, you are personally liable for all business related obligations. If your business defaulted on a loan or failed to pay a supplier, for instance, those parties could pursue you and your personal possessions to get their money.

As you grow, take on more risks and employ people, remaining a sole trader becomes difficult. It's a great way to get started, but if you intend growing you should think about becoming a limited liability company.

Sole proprietorships are also harder to fund and sell if that becomes your goal. People outside the business will see no distinction between you and the business. As a sole trader, you might find you have simply set yourself up in a low-paying job rather than a business if you don't adequately separate yourself from the business.

## 2.   Limited liability company (LLC)

Limited liability companies are the most common business structure in New Zealand. While there is a procedure to set up a limited liability company in New Zealand, it is very simple. You can get an accountant or lawyer to help you, or you can do it yourself through the **Companies Office.**

If you are setting up the limited liability company alone, you would be the shareholder and the director. As the shareholder, you are the owner of the company. As director, you are the person legally accountable for the running of the company.

A limited liability company is a separate legal entity from you. This is the distinction between a *"business"* and a *"company"*. All entities of any legal structure carrying out business activities are a *"business"*. However, when I refer to a *"company"*, I am only referring to a *"business"* that is a limited liability company registered with the Companies Office.

Once you are registered with the Companies Office, you will need to keep your records site up to date on the Companies Office. For example, adding or removing directors, changing your address, or a change in your accountant needs to be recorded. You need to file an **annual return** every year that ensures all this information is up to date.

If you are unsure what you need to do, spend some time on the Companies Office website or speak with your accountant.

The IRD also taxes the company separately from you. You must get your accountant to complete a set of accounts for both your company and for you. The tax rate for a company is 28%. It will be different for you.

A limited liability company can have multiple shareholders and directors. Shareholders can be other companies or a trust.

The term *"limited liability"* is a very important consideration. If the business gets into trouble, it is critical to understand what exposure the business has to losses and what personal liability you have for them.

A limited liability company provides ways to limit the risks to the company and not to you. As you take on debt in your business, sign personal guarantees, buy goods on credit get some advice especially if you do not understand your risks.

You might need to look at putting your assets into a family trust and set up another trust to be the company's majority shareholder. This will provide a complete separation between you and the company.

Seek good legal advice on all this.

## 3.   LLCs and shareholder agreements

If you have other parties that you want to be shareholders in your company, other than a spouse, it's important to develop a shareholder's agreement. (If it's a spouse, laws relating to your marriage will apply if the relationship breaks down that effect the business).

The preparation of a shareholder agreement is a straightforward process through your lawyer. What is not straightforward is ensuring you and the other shareholder(s) are completely open about your expectations of the relationship. You all need to discuss your motivations before signing the agreement and make sure the agreement reflects what you decide.

Typical issues you will need to discuss and clarify include:

- How will you handle a situation where one shareholder wants to sell their shares?

- What happens if you want to bring additional shareholders into the business?

- How do you value the business and the shares in these situations?

- What happens if one party wants to take a very different direction in the business to the other party or parties?

- Who has what decision-making powers?

- If there are two shareholders with equal shares, what happens when they can't agree?

## 4. Partnerships

If there are two people wanting to start a business, a limited liability company is an option, with all parties becoming shareholders. However, a partnership is also an option. The partnership is not a separate legal entity. Assets and responsibilities are shared between the partners and the relationship is defined in a partnership agreement.

These are common in service-based businesses like accountancies, consultancies, and legal firms.

No matter the agreements or structure you choose with someone else, the most critical thing is you and your partner, or partners, trust each other, have shared values, and get on with each other, otherwise you could face problems.

Each partner normally contributes finances, property, skill or labour, although a person may contribute nothing and still have the rights of a partner. There can be different partnerships that may alter the level of their involvement, liabilities, and tax.

Before discussing the legal aspects of the relationship, you need to discuss candidly the personal aspects of the partnership. Having a partner or partners for the wrong reasons could end in disaster. You all need to voice the issues you consider important before you face them.

What happens if one partner wants to leave? What happens if one partner believes the other is not pulling their weight? How do you manage a dispute?

Have the debate before you start the partnership, not when you hit your first business speed bump.

These discussions may be far more effective if you use an independent third party experienced in partnerships. They will pose questions to you and your partner(s) that you may not consider or are simply reluctant to address.

These discussions can be even more difficult if you have a personal relationship with the partners in the business. That might be your husband, wife, friend or other family member.

It is important to get a well-documented partnership agreement prepared by a lawyer experienced in this type of commercial work.

## 5. Societies

A society is a legal entity that needs to be registered on the Companies Office. They are very common for sporting clubs or local community groups. A society has 10 or more members, has a committee to oversee the running of the society under a constitution. Being a separate legal entity, it protects the individuals in the society.

## 6. Charities

If the purpose of your business is charitable, it can offer tax advantages. This is covered by the **Charities Act 2005** and overseen by **Charities Services**. If the purpose of your company or trust meets any of the following criteria, it is worth investigating it further:

- The relief of poverty.

- The advancement of education.

- The advancement of religion.

- Anything else that benefits the community.

If your business provides a public benefit and is not aimed at creating private financial profit, then research if you are a charitable business.

## 7. Social enterprise

A social enterprise is not a legal entity. It is just a term that defines what the purpose of the business is, namely that it aims to benefit other people, society or the environment. It may meet the requirements to be called a **charity**. There are also funders within New Zealand whose sole purpose is to fund social enterprises.

## 8. Trusts

There are different trusts that may apply to your business activities. This is a specialist legal area, but most lawyers are well versed in what is required. The following are the most common trusts you will come across.

> **Family trusts** are a mechanism that separates you from your business activities to protect your personal assets, such as your home. The family trust is not you. It is another entity where you, and typically, your children, are beneficiaries of the trust. If your business takes on more risks, like personal guarantees, general security agreements, loans, or credit, it is advisable to ring-fence your personal assets so no one can target them through the business.

> **Trading trusts** are trusts that trade or carry out business activities. It could be a family trust. The business of the trust is undertaken by a trustee. A trust board could be set up to oversee the trust's activities. The board can be incorporated, meaning it takes on its own legal status and is registered with the Companies Office. This means the board takes on the risk rather than individual trustees on the board.

> **Charitable trusts** are a trust whose purpose is charitable, as we discussed above. If a board of trustees oversees the charitable trust, it is recommended, like a trading trust, to incorporate the board.

> The Charities Services defines the level of detail required for reporting of a charitable trust. The bigger the trust, the greater the level of reporting required.

# Taking on the big guys - and protecting your business

Just as a customer, competitor or member of the public can report you for potential breaches of the law, or poor practices, so too can you report others. If others have done the wrong thing by you and hurt your business, you do not have to take it. There are several organisations you can turn to if you feel you have been treated unfairly, or you have seen unethical, even illegal, activities, especially where they affect your small business.

Here are a few bodies that can assist. You can find more by searching online under *"Ombudsman"* in New Zealand. There is a lot more information about what they can and can't help you with and usually list cases they have pursued on each of their websites.

## 1. Banking Ombudsmen

The Banking Ombudsmen is an independent service overseeing the banking sector. You can lodge a complaint if you feel your bank has not acted appropriately or followed industry policies or procedures. You can find information on what the Ombudsmen can and can't do on their website. They are always open to discuss the merits of a complaint and whether they can help before you proceed.

## 2. Advertising Standards Authority

The Advertising Standards Authority is an industry based organisation, supported by advertisers, advertising agencies and media organisations and is self-regulated. Their aim is to ensure advertising is presented truthfully and is socially responsible. If you see any advertising that you believe is irresponsible, deceptive or dishonest, you can lodge a complaint

## 3. Real Estate Authority

The Real Estate Authority is a government body who promotes a high standard of service and professionalism in the real estate industry. It helps protect buyers and sellers of property. This also includes business brokers who are involved in the buying and selling of businesses.

## 4. Commerce Commission

The Commerce Commission enforces competition, fair trading and consumer credit contract laws and has regulatory responsibilities in the electricity lines, gas pipelines, telecommunications, dairy and airport sectors. The Commission considers complaints about several laws, including the Commerce Act, Credit Contracts and Consumer Finance Act, and the Fair Trading Act.

## 5. Consumer Protection

Consumer Protection is part of the Ministry of Business Innovation and Employment (MBIE) and handles complaints on products and services that do not meet expectations. These may be in breach of the Consumer Guarantees Act, or Fair Trading Act,

## 6. Motor Vehicle Disputes Tribunal

The Motor Vehicle Disputes Tribunal investigates complaints about purchases of vehicles from registered traders.

## 7. Building Performance

Building Performance is a part of the MBIE. It provides policy and technical advice on New Zealand's building system, rules and standards, and implements building legislation and regulations to meet New Zealand's current and future needs. If you are unable to resolve building issues with your provider, you can lodge a complaint with them.

## 8. Disputes Tribunal

The Disputes Tribunal is quicker, cheaper, and less formal than the courts. You can use the Tribunal to settle small claims up to $30,000. You represent yourself, as there are no lawyers or judges involved.

Most of these agencies will first encourage you to take up the matter directly with the other party and make efforts to resolve it yourself. They may not jump to attention and charge in to address your concern without challenging that you have done all else to resolve the matter first.

Even if you receive no compensation or a resolution to your satisfaction, lodging the complaint brings the other party to the regulators attention. The party who has done the wrong thing by you is aware they need to pick up their performance.

Always balance the cost and effort to take on the fight and what outcome you want. Long-winded battles on principle alone may simply take your focus away from what's really important. They will also cost you time, money and cause stress, even if you are morally or legally in the right.

# Personal guarantees

If you have asked your bank for money, asked a supplier to offer you credit, signed a lease, a franchise agreement or other agreement, it is very likely you have signed a personal guarantee. This means that should your business not repay the loan or pay the supplier, or you breach a lease or other agreement, you are guaranteeing you will pay these people back.

This shifts the risk away from your company and on to you.

As your business grows and you borrow money, sign agreements and contracts, and are offered credit, it is unlikely that you can avoid personal guarantees. They are a common part of business.

You could decide not to sign, so you do not take on the risk. However, it's likely you won't get the loan, the supplier won't offer you credit, and the landlord may either refuse you the property or force you to put some other guarantee in place–like a bank guarantee, which you probably won't get.

Therefore, it is very unlikely you can run a growing business without having to sign a personal guarantee at some stage.

Even though you may have no choice, take the time to get some advice if these documents are new to you.

Personal guarantees increase your risk significantly, but you can put things in place to reduce these risks. Consider this like you would insurance. The hope is it never happens, and you can pay everybody you owe money. However, if your business gets into trouble or is liquidated, you don't want it to affect your personal assets.

One of the best protections is to put your personal assets into a **family trust**. A family trust will take time for your lawyers to set up and can be costly. Consider this well before your business grows and you are required to borrow money or sign personal guarantees.

Likewise, if you are offering customers credit, or asking other parties to sign contracts before you will do business with them, consider asking them to sign a personal guarantee. Get a lawyer to help draft your terms of trade. These are the standard conditions someone must fulfil for you to offer them credit.

## Securities and the PPSR

If you have borrowed money to buy an asset, like a vehicle, it is likely the lender will have a security over that asset. If you can't repay the loan, the lender can take the asset off you. Typically, when this occurs, the lender will register that security on the **Personal Property Security Register (PPSR)**. This is attached to your company details on the Companies Office website.

Your bank could also register a security over your entire business. This is a **General Security Agreement (GSA),** meaning if you borrowed money from the bank and fail to pay, the bank can engage a **Receiver** to come into the business. They can sell what they need, like equipment and motor vehicles, to recover their money before any other party can make a claim.

If you have signed a supplier's terms of trade when they offer you credit, not only will you have a personal guarantee, but the supplier may also lodge a security over what they sell you or over your business. If you don't pay them, they have a right to take back what they sold you and the security means they will rank above other creditors should your business fail. When you come to close the account with them, say in the case you sell the business, and you still owe them money, they may not lift that security from the PPSR, and it could affect the sale.

You can find out what securities are lodged against you by logging into the Companies Office website, searching for your company and then paying a small fee to access this information.

You too can register a security on the PPSR against a customer who you have offered credit. If you don't register your legal claim on the PPSR, a liquidator could sell the products to pay other creditors who have lodged a security as they will rank ahead of you.

You can register the security yourself by following the instructions on the Companies Office website or ask your lawyer to do it for you to ensure it is registered correctly

## _Securities for when you lend your own business money_

Another important situation where you should consider lodging a security is if you use your own money to fund your business. Remember, if you have a limited liability company, in the eyes of the law, it is separate from you, even if you are the only shareholder, director, and employee.

You might fund the purchase of your business, in part or in full. You might use your own money to build up spare cash or to fund assets instead of borrowing from the bank.

In these situations, you can prepare a loan agreement which sets out the terms of how you will be paid back, but more importantly, you can lodge a security against your own company. What this means is you will rank above anyone else should your business fail, and you are forced into liquidation.

If the amounts you are lending are small, it may not be worth it, as these could be quickly gobbled up in legal fees developing the documents. However, if the amounts are becoming significant, and you really need to get that money back at some stage, it is worth pursuing this option.

# Intellectual property (IP)

In starting a new business or developing new products or services, you may need to consider what unique value they may have and whether you need to protect this value. For many of the largest businesses in the world, it is these **intangible assets** that hold the greatest value, and they defend them vigorously.

For most small businesses in New Zealand, the cost and complexity of the process usually means they take the risk and trade with no formal registrations or protections. In most cases, this is not a problem.

Like many other topics we've discussed, only you can weigh up the risk of not doing this versus the cost of doing it. If you put a high value on your brand, and if someone copied or used it without your permission, and these actions caused serious issues for your business, then I'd look at formally protecting your.

## What is intellectual property?

Nothing about intellectual property (IP) is simple. Even finding a consistent, simple definition is no easy task. The **World Intellectual Property Organisation (WIPO)** defines it as:

> *Intellectual property refers to creations of the mind, such as inventions; literary and artistic works; designs; and symbols, names, and images used in commerce.*

The process of protecting your unique creations may not be simple and can be expensive. The more you want to protect, and the more countries and regions you want protection in, the more the process will cost you.

The most common types of that you are likely to come across are:

- Copyright.

- Website domains and company names.

- Patents and designs.

- Trademarks.

This is a specialised legal area. If you decide to formally protect your intellectual property, you should use specialist legal support to do a full search and to apply for the protection. You can do a lot of initial investigation before spending and money. Places to start your search include the **New Zealand Intellectual Property Office** (www .iponz.govt.nz) or simply doing detailed web searches to see what currently exists.

I do not intend explaining all the processes you need to follow to protect your IP. This is quite detailed and complex. However, there are some key things you should consider and there are also some simple low-cost actions you can take to protect your IP.

## *Copyright*

Copyright protects your creative ideas that are expressed in forms such as songs, artwork, drawings, paintings, writing, sculptures, films, software, architecture, websites, graphics, and video games. Copyright does not protect the idea, only the way these ideas are expressed. In short, you must translate the idea into something real.

In almost every country, your work has automatic copyright protection without you having to take any formal action to protect it. Once it is in a tangible form, it is protected. This protection lasts while you are alive and typically many decades after your death.

You should add the symbol © with your company name on all documents you want to protect. While your rights are already protected, many people still choose to reinforce this by adding the statement "*All rights reserved*" even though they don't need to. It makes someone think twice before copying your material.

There is no formal process in New Zealand to register copyright as it is automatic.

# _Trademarks_

Trademarks are those names, distinctive words, phrases, graphic designs, slogans or logos that distinguish your products and services from anyone else's.

Your brand represents everything about you. Your logos, product names and company identifiers are a key part of your brand. As such, you need to ensure they are distinctive from any competitors, and you need to consider if there is value in legally protecting them.

Unlike copyright, trademarks are not automatically protected.

You need to establish what value you will gain from protecting your logo, your brand name, or your trading name. Many businesses have operated for many years, with distinctive logos that were never registered as a trademark. Even this presence in the marketplace affords you an amount of automatic protection. However, registration guarantees it and even the largest, wealthy businesses cannot conflict with a registered trademark, no matter their efforts to do so.

Your choice to register may also depend on your long-term goals. If you are considering growth and want to use your distinctive brand as part of your strategy, consider registration.

Be very cautious about choosing business names, logos, or other material that conflicts with anything business that already exists, especially if that business has registered a trademark. It will not be good for your business if, after months of operation, hard work, and costs to then receive a letter from an IP lawyer saying your image or words conflict with another company who will act if you don't remove it.

As a minimum, search the trademark office website and do as wide an online search as you can before choosing your branding material. Things get far more complicated if you intend trading overseas. An experienced IP lawyer will do a more thorough search. If an issue comes up, they can advise what the risks might be.

If you have something you want to protect, as a minimum you can use the _"TM"_ symbol. This shows to the world that you are claiming ownership of it. You could do this from the time your trademark is released into the market while you are going through the registration process.

If you decide to register, be careful to register variations of your logo, different colours, shading, and variations in shapes. The registration doesn't automatically protect variations, even if those variations are self-evident. If you want to protect variations to the main trademark, you will need to register all of them.

You will also need to consider the classification applicable to your product or service. There are around 45 classes that are internationally recognised that the NZ IP Office use. Class 1 to 34 covers goods while Class 35 to 45 cover services. These are a few examples:

- **Class 1**: includes chemicals used in industry, science and photography,

- **Class 4**: includes industrial oils, greases, and lubricants.

- **Class 8**: includes hand tools and hand operated implements; cutlery.

- **Class 15**: musical instruments.

- **Class 25**: clothing, footwear, headgear.

- **Class 35**: advertising, retail and business.

- **Class 43**: services for providing food and drink; temporary accommodation.

As the above indicates, registering a trademark is not simple if there are any possible conflicts with another business' trademarks. It can also be very expensive and time consuming.

## Website domains and company names

Your online presence will show a lot about you and your brand. Your choice of keywords, domain names, and company details will also assist you being found in online searches.

---

Consider the role your domain *www.<your company name>.com* and your registered company names *<Your Company Name> Ltd.* plays in your IP.

Ideally, you'd like a company name that is the same as the name you trade under. This is not always possible. You may also sell a range of different products or services with different brand names, but through one company. The company name is far less critical than your trading name, which is what the world sees. You will often see in the fine print the statement, *"John Smith Limited, trading as Smith's Biscuits"*.

If you have or intend to build a website, you will need to choose a unique domain name.

The perfect outcome is to have a company name, trading name and website domain that are all the same. For example, *"Smiths Biscuits Ltd"* trading as *"Smiths Biscuits"* with a web address of *www.smithsbiscuits.co.nz*.

Once you have done this, no other company can register this name. However, it remains possible that the company name you chose breaches another party's trademark and they may have a right to challenge you.

In short, before settling on a unique domain name, company name, logo or slogan, it is worth searching to see if you could be at odds with an existing company's trademarks.

Secure domain names as soon as you have settled on them, even if you don't intend to build a website. It is relatively cheap, and you have it for future use.

## *Patents and designs*

A patent is a legal right granted to the patent owner, giving them the exclusive rights, for a limited period, to use and develop an invention. Not all *"inventions"* are patentable. They need to be novel and useful in an industry. The invention cannot already be known and in use when the patent application is being made.

Securing a patent is perhaps the most complicated IP registration and you will need help with it.

It is very important that you do not disclose an invention you wish to patent. Once it is in the public domain, been described or used, you may lose the right to patent it. Even if this were not the case, you may face the risk of the idea being taken before you can register it. Therefore, it is critical that your invention remains confidential until you have protections in place.

There are different types of patents. They typically fall into three categories: Utility Patents, Design Patents, and Patents of a New Plant Species.

- **Utility patents** cover new products, processes, equipment or machinery of some kind.

- **Design patents** are to cover a unique and novel appearance or ornamental design of a product. For example, a drink manufacturer may design a unique glass bottle for their drink that identifies their product over the bottles of their competitors.

- **Plant patents** relate to unique plant varieties.

The substance and term of patents vary from country to country, so you will need to consider this. You should, as a minimum, do a preliminary search to see if your invention has already been patented. You will need to seek the expertise of others to do a more thorough search.

---

## Katie Perry vs. Katy Perry – David vs. Goliath

Katheryn Hudson was born in 1984 but changed her name to Katy Perry in 2002 and soon after became a household name with major hits from 2008. The Katy Perry brand became a worldwide phenomenon. This included tours across the planet, including in Australia. As occurs with all touring entertainers, merchandising was a major part of the offer to fans.

Katie Taylor started selling a range of her own designer clothing in Australia from 2007 under her birth name of Katie Perry. Having her own designer clothes brand was a dream she had since the age of 11. She was also determined to have all her clothes made locally, in Australia, a goal she had maintained from the day she began trading.[8,9]

---

She registered the Katie Perry brand name in 2008. It was registered under Class 25, "*mainly clothing, footwear, and headwear for human beings*".

Katie Taylor felt that Katy Perry, the singer, was infringing on her local trademark registration, so took legal action against her in 2019.

The singer's legal team argued she had been operating internationally before the designer had registered the trademark and already had an international reputation in music and entertainment, less so than clothing. They approached Taylor to see if she would allow both brands to operate in Australia, as they were sure the two businesses could do this without confusion to consumers. Taylor refused.

The singer's team then pursued having the designer's trademark cancelled.

In April 2023, the courts agreed with the designer and ruled she had sole rights to the trademark. They dismissed the pop star's bid to cancel the Katie Perry trademark.

Taylor expressed her relief about the decision.

> "*Earlier today the Federal Court of Australia published its decision in which I won the biggest battle of my business career, the '*David and Goliath case*" - my legal action against the singer, Katy Perry, and her companies, for infringing my Katie Perry trade mark in Australia – which I've held since 29th September 2008.*"[10]

The pop star's team was dissatisfied with this outcome and appealed the decision.

On 22 November 2024, three judges overturned the original decision ruling that Katy Perry, the singer, can use her stage name to sell merchandise in Australia, despite the designer's claim over the trademark.

The court agreed with the singer's legal argument that she had been using the stage name five years before Taylor began selling clothes and was entitled to use the name in Australia. They also stated that Taylor had registered the trademark after realising Katy Perry's reputation. They alleged Taylor had, at times, aligned herself with the singer.

The court stated:

> *"This case is an unfortunate one in the sense that two enterprising women in different countries each adopted their name as a trademark at a time that each was unaware of the existence of the other,"*

The courts expressed little sympathy for Taylor after hearing the singer had offered her the option to coexist. The judges ruled that Taylor's own trademark license would now need to be cancelled as the possibility of returning to peaceful co-existence had gone.

In this particularly David and Goliath battle, there was no happy ending for the small guy.

Taylor was clearly disappointed with the decision

> *"This case proves a trademark isn't worth the paper it's printed on. My fashion label has been a dream of mine since I was 11 years old and now that dream that I have worked so hard for, since 2006, has been taken away."* [11,12]

This case showed how complicated intellectual property law can be. Taylor's efforts to protect her brand were well founded. However, taking on a person with the resources at Katy Perry's disposal was very risky, especially when the singer offered Taylor a deal that, in hindsight, she should have accepted.

There was always the risk that a legal battle like this could be protracted and expensive, and the result could always go either way.

In this particularly David and Goliath battle, there was no happy ending for the small guy.

# CHAPTER 20

# THE FINANCIAL BASICS and your FINANCIAL STATEMENTS

No matter what type of business you run, it has to generate money to survive. While making a profit may not be the business' core purpose, if you don't make enough money, your business will not survive.

It is really important you have an understanding of the financial statements that make up your business and what the numbers mean.

## Profit, "the bottom line" — or maybe not?

*"The bottom line"* is an often overstated phrase about what is most critical in a business.

The Oxford English Dictionary defines the general term *"the bottom line"* as:

**The fundamental and most important factor.**

In a business' financial statements, the bottom line is usually considered to be the final dollar number that pops out of the business after all the money comes in and you have paid all the bills. Most typically, this is called your **profit**.

If you consider both the financial and the general meanings of this phrase, it implies that the profit is the most important factor in your business and, as such, should be where you focus all your attention.

I put a slightly different slant on the meaning of *"the bottom line"* in your business:

> The *bottom line* comes by paying attention to everything above that line.

Don't get me wrong. If you're a commercial business, you are there to make money, and the more money you can make, the better. However, don't get blinded by an unhealthy focus on that line. Don't forget that what pops out at the bottom of your financial statements is determined by everything else you do above the line - it's everything you do in your business that will determine what your bottom line is.

If you have paid attention to all the previous chapters, the bottom line should look after itself.

Many small business owners dislike bookkeeping. Unless you are a closet accountant, I am quite sure you didn't get into your small business to look at the financials all day long.

However, whether you like it or not, you must understand the accounts to a reasonable level and you can't hand it all over to someone else and hope for the best. Sadly, tracking financial performance is often done poorly in many small businesses.

I have come across many business owners who feel intimidated by the financials and sit with their accountant, fearful to ask what may seem like a dumb question.

> *"There are naive questions, tedious questions, ill-phrased questions, questions put after inadequate self-criticism. But every question is a cry to understand the world. There is no such thing as a dumb question."* - **Carl Sagan**, author and scientist.

Remember, if you don't ask questions, you won't understand. If you don't understand your business, who else can you expect to understand it?

> ☞ If you don't understand your numbers, please ask - and ask again until you do.

The next few chapters aim to give you enough information to understand the financial aspects of your business. It will not teach you how to prepare your annual accounts. You don't need to be an accountant to understand and use the financial information about your business.

You need to know enough to keep track of how you're going, extract the information you need when you need it and, most importantly, use that financial information to make the best decisions you can.

Your financial reports are a view of the past. They tell you if all the things you did (or didn't do) produced the financial results you wanted. That said, they have future applications. By tracking the past, you can make decisions to produce a better result in the future.

To help you understand the financials, I will walk you through the basics. You may well have a strong understanding of your financials already, but I always believe the occasional refresher is not a bad thing.

## Cash versus accrual accounting

There are two ways to develop your financial statements - using **cash accounting** or **accrual accounting**. You don't need to decide which to use. You should instead discuss this with your accountant, although accrual accounting is by far the most common.

- In **cash accounting**, you only record transactions in your profit and loss statement when the money comes into or out of the business as cash.

- In **accrual accounting,** you record transactions as they occur, even though you have not received cash from a sale or paid cash for a purchase.

In the long run, the two methods will line up. However, they differ on when the money is recorded as coming in and going out of the business.

## *Why use accrual accounting?*

The method that would seem simplest and most obvious is cash accounting, yet it's rarely used in business. In the end, aren't you only interested when the cash arrives or leaves the business?

While that's correct, if you pay on credit and offer credit to customers, your sales and purchases will not line up each month and will make your financial accounts confusing.

When you use accrual accounting, your profit and loss statement records all your sales and all your expenditures at the time you make the sale or receive the goods, even if money is yet to pass hands.

Cash accounting cannot account correctly for inventory.

The two methods may also produce different tax results, so your accountant will need to advise you on the choice for tax purposes.

When I go through all the following discussions, I assume you will be using accrual accounting, as it is overwhelmingly the most common method.

# The non-negotiable financial "rules"

Let's start with a few key concepts that every small business should consider.

## 1. Don't do it all yourself

Get an experienced bookkeeper or accountant to prepare your financial reports and advise you on taxation. As mentioned, this is to help you but not let you off the hook.

A bookkeeper will cost you money. An accountant will cost you more. Getting your financials wrong, including taxation, could destroy your business. Even if you're one of those owners who loves doing it, and is good at it, it's always preferable to have a second set of eyes.

## 2. Separate business and personal money

No matter which company structure you choose, you need to define the lines between you and the business. If you blur these lines, you can find yourself in a mess as time goes on.

Small businesses, especially sole proprietors, frequently blur the lines between business finances and personal finances. You need to be disciplined in separating the two.

Record all movements of money between you and the business. This separation also goes to the heart of separating the business risks from your personal risks.

## 3. Keep good records

When you spend money on the business, keep your receipts. This does not mean storing every receipt in a box to go through later. Take a photo and save it. Record what the purchases were and where you spent that money. Use the business debit or credit card for business purchases. Make sure you link your spending to the correct code in your accounts. The amounts may be small, but the discipline is critical, and every dollar counts.

## 4. _Put systems and processes in place that work for you_

Consider the accounting system you will use. We discussed some options in earlier chapters and how to choose the best one for you. Make sure you set these systems up correctly, that you connect them to the correct bank account, that cost codes accurately reflect your business, and that you **reconcile all transactions** regularly.

Reconciliations are where you allocate every expense that comes into your bank account against the correct cost code. If you are new to this, ask for help.

## 5. _Pay the taxman - PLEASE_

Tax is an unattractive topic for any business, but the price of getting it wrong can be huge. Sadly, I know business owners that are no longer in business purely because they let their taxes get out of control.

This is such a critical part of your small business that I will devote a chapter to it. For now, understand your tax obligations from day one, and if you are unsure what they are, talk to your accountant. Your accountant may claim to offer many other services, but if they can't give you good tax advice, and ensure you get no tax surprises, they aren't doing their job.

> Your accountant may claim they can offer you a lot of services. If they can't offer you good tax advice and ensure no tax surprises, get another accountant

## 6. *Chase every dollar owed to you - vigorously.*

I don't think I need to tell you how hard you must work to make money. When you provide your customers with a product or service, you deserve to be paid.

You may get paid for your products or services on the spot, like a retail shop or coffee truck. You may send your customer an invoice and expect to get paid sometime later. If so, you are offering them interest-free credit. When they don't pay you on time, chase them vigorously. If they have a bad month that's one thing. If they do it all the time, they are showing you no respect, so don't be afraid to end the relationship – you deserve better.

## 7. *Pay your bills on time*

You want your customers to pay you on time, so you too should pay your suppliers on time. You really don't want to get a reputation for being a bad or late payer. At best, it will affect your reputation. They could refuse to supply you anymore. Worse still, the suppliers could report you to credit agencies, limiting your ability to access loans or could take more formal action.

If you have a strong relationship with your suppliers, and pay them on time, they are more likely to lend you a little slack if you do genuinely face a shortage of cash.

## 8. *Cash really is king*

Customers have asked me many times what is the one thing they should do to manage their finances. While I say there are many more than just one, if you had to choose, look at the cash sitting in your bank account every day and know what's going to come out and what is supposed to be coming in. If the money in the bank is disappearing faster than you can top it up, it's pretty obvious where things will ultimately end for you.

Like tax, the management of cash is so critical I will devote a chapter to it.

# The profit and loss statement

Let's look at the first financial statement - the **profit and loss statement**, or the P&L. It is sometimes also called a **Statement of Financial Performance** or the **income statement** as it reflects the income you have made, the costs you have had to pay and then what is left over.

If what's left over is positive, you have a profit. If you have a negative number left over, you have a loss. The profit and loss statement shows you what money you have made and spent over a defined period, typically a year or a month.

## A basic profit and loss statement

No matter how big or small a business is, the profit and loss statement will include the same components.

REVENUE

— COST OF SALES

= GROSS PROFIT

— EXPENSES

= EBITDA

— INTEREST

— DEPRECIATION

— TAXATION

= NET PROFIT AFTER TAX

where EBITDA is **Earnings Before Interest Tax and Depreciation**.

Here are some definitions of what you'll see in your profit and loss statement.

## Revenue

The total of all money made from sales in your business before you pay any bills is your revenue. You may decide to separate out the sales by product or region or in a way that allows you to understand what parts of your business are delivering what sales. The way you set up the coding in your accounting system will define how you split this out.

## Cost of sales

The costs that you can directly attribute to the revenue you have earned are your **cost of sales**. These could include the raw materials you use to manufacture a product. It could be the products you buy off your supplier that you on-sell to your customers. These are sometimes called the **cost of goods sold.**

If the amount you sell increases, your cost of sales will increase. Likewise, if the amount you sell decreases, your cost of sales should also decrease. Therefore, these are **variable costs**.

Your cost of sales gets more complicated if you hold stock (inventory).

If you purchase raw materials or components to manufacture a product, you would code these as **purchases** in your cost of sales. If you take raw materials or components out of stock to manufacture a product then this is a change in stock. This is typically detailed as the **opening stock** at the start of a period, less the **closing stock** at the end of that period.

The following formula applies to the movement in stock and appears in your cost of sales.

COST OF SALES = OPENING STOCK − CLOSING STOCK + PURCHASES

If your business does not sell products, but provides a service, you could call these costs your **cost of services.** If your service relies entirely on your time, your cost of services are the hours you bill to a client, or your **billable hours.** This applies to service-based businesses like architects, accountants and consultancies.

Trade-based businesses will also have trade staff who would bill their time for a repair or installation job. Therefore, include these individuals' wages or salaries in the cost of sales

> If you run a trade-based business the wages of trade staff that you would book to jobs are a cost of sale. Don't include these in your expenses.

It is more common your profit and loss statement will include these wages and salaries in the expenses, because you must pay your permanent employees no matter where you allocate their time. However, if you employed the staff member to do billable work, then you should include their wages or salary in the cost of sales.

Unfortunately, no employee can ever bill 100% of their time to a client's job. They will spend time in meetings, doing administrative tasks, on sick or annual leave, training, travel and also unproductive time. Even though this is the case, it is still important that the staff you employed to deliver billable hours are grouped and included in the cost of sales.

You can more accurately understand the efficiency of your staff's time if they record the hours they spend and where they spend their time, whether to a client's work or on administrative tasks. This is done through **time sheeting.**

I will discuss the impact of **idle time** on your business when we discuss margins and %GP, as it is often the biggest contributor to declining margins in a business.

On occasions, some business owners will include **direct costs** in their cost of sales. These are costs you might normally code into expenses, but vary as your sales increase or decrease. An example of this could be diesel, which you may use more of when you are a lot busier and selling more.

I prefer to keep the cost of sales purely as those costs that you can directly link to the production of a product or where you can directly charge labour hours to a client's job. If you cannot directly link a cost to the sale of a product or service, then leave it as an expense, NOT a cost of sales. The reason for this is the importance that needs to be placed on the margins you make (measured by the %GP) which we discuss shortly. This really should only include genuine variable costs.

> Including the wrong information in your cost of sales can distort the real value of your %GP and provide an inaccurate picture of your financial performance.

## Gross Profit

If you subtract revenue from the cost of sales, you are left with the **Gross Profit.** (This is also called **Gross Margin**). This is where the financial battle for small businesses is won or lost. Most small businesses usually have few expenses and most of these expenses can't be reduced to any great extent. However, sales and the costs to produce those sales, and therefore the Gross Profit, can be influenced significantly by the actions of the business owner. Gross Profit is fundamental to the financial success, or failure, of a small business.

## Expenses

These are the costs that must be paid no matter what the business is producing. They are also called **fixed costs**. As your business becomes more complex or grows, it will attract more fixed costs. Typical fixed costs in a small business include:

- Computer expenses.

- Travel.

- Entertainment (e.g., coffee with customers).

- Training courses.

- Printing and stationery.

- Wages for your bookkeeper.

- Rent on your office.

- Advertising.

- Credit card fees.

- Insurances.

## *EBITDA*

This is an abbreviation for **Earnings Before Interest, Taxation Depreciation and Amortisation**. This is where small businesses should focus. Firstly, managing the Gross Profit and then on keeping fixed costs under control.

The value of a business is calculated based on the EBITDA. It is also usually the figure used to determine performance (at risk) payments, assuming you are offering key staff this.

### *Interest*

This is the interest the business is paying on loans or any borrowings. Interest is included as an expense and is tax deductible. Keep in mind, this excludes repayment of the principle on loans. Principle repayments do not appear anywhere on a profit and loss statement. They will appear on your cash flow statement.

> The principle repayments on loans do not appear in your profit and loss statement. Your profits need to be enough to service these loan repayments.

---

# Depreciation

Most of the assets you purchased for your business will age. When they age, they will also reduce in value. If you sold an asset some years after its purchase, it is likely you will receive far less for it than what you paid for it. It would seem only fair for this to be considered in your financial statements. This is **depreciation**.

Your accountant will have defined rules guiding how fast you are allowed to depreciate your assets. These rules are set by the IRD. For example, a computer will depreciate much faster than a motor vehicle.

There are also different rules set by the IRD on the method you can use to calculate the depreciation. Should you depreciate the asset faster at the start of its life or the same each year? The first is called the **diminishing value method** and the second the **straight-line method.**

After you have calculated the depreciation, the value of the asset will be less (which is reflected in your balance sheet). The amount the asset depreciates is considered an expense and is included in your profit and loss statement. It will reduce your profit and consequently your tax.

The key point to remember with depreciation is that no money passes hands. It is purely an accounting calculation, but it does affect your profit, how much tax you pay, and the value of your assets.

The value of each asset as it is depreciated each year may not reflect what it is worth if you wanted to sell it. The depreciated value of the asset in your financial statements is its **book value**. What someone is prepared to pay for it may be very different. This is the **market value.**

# Amortisation

This is a similar concept to depreciation, but it is applied to intangible assets. This includes intellectual property like trademarks and patents. It is unlikely you will need to worry about this, and it is rare to see it in a small business' profit and loss statement.

## Taxation

In New Zealand, the company tax rate is 28%. It excludes GST which I will discuss separately. I cover taxation in more detail in later chapters. As taxation is calculated on past performance, and then paid in instalments in the future, it does not always appear on the profit and loss statement. It will be included in the cash flow statement. I will discuss taxation and cash flows a little later.

## Net Profit After Tax (NPAT)

Well, you've reached it - the bottom line. The word *"net"* is included as it indicates the profit is net of everything that has already been considered.

# Increasing revenue by setting your prices correctly

I briefly touched on the principles of pricing when we discussed the Four Ps of Marketing. So, what price will you charge for your product or service?

## Research your competitors

While you should not become assessed with any competitor, you need to know what they are doing and especially what they are charging. If they are cheaper than you are, you will need to assess if you can drop and match their pricing. If not, you need to consider if you can offer something else to justify the higher prices.

It may not always be easy to establish a competitor's prices, as most businesses will protect this information, but here are some ways to establish this.

- If you miss out on a job, ask why. If it was price, ask how far out you were. Most businesses will tell you as they want all their suppliers to be pushing prices down.

- If you are in a retail business, it will be much easier to access prices. Many will list them on their website. Take a walk into their store and check out the pricing. If your competitor knows who you are, ask someone you know to do this for you.

- Suppliers should be able to offer you their recommended price tiers for wholesale, trade and retail customers. Competitors who also buy off them will probably use their prices as a guide.

- The more you ask around, the more information you will pick up.

Ultimately, you may never get all this information, so just focus on your own costs and what the best prices you can offer that ensure you will meet your gross profit target.

## Wholesale, trade, and retail price structures

If your business is in the **wholesale or distribution business**, there is more to think about. It can be especially tricky if you offer all three pricing options depending on the business you are selling to.

### Let's use an example

Suppose you are a small business buying a line of consumer gardening products directly out of China.

You may not be doing enormous volumes, but the price is very good, and you can buy enough to justify supplying retail shops rather than only selling direct to customers. This means you are a wholesaler. However, you still decide to build an e-commerce site and sell directly to everyone. This means you are also a retailer.

But how will your retail shops feel if they find out you are selling around them in the same region and effectively undercutting them because you can charge less?

Is it possible to be a retailer and a wholesaler at the same time?

There are a few options to deal with this common scenario, including how you price.

- Don't sell to retail customers in a region where you have a retailer you supply. Just direct customers to their shop and promote your retailers on your e-commerce site.

- Let all your retailers know your **Recommended Retail Price (RRP)** and sell at this price to all retail customers. If you do this, the customer should be indifferent whether they buy from your retailer's shop or from you online. The retail shop is also well within their rights to sell at a discount to the RRP or any price they choose (NB: Review the clauses in the legal section on anti-competitive pricing. You can't force a customer to sell at a specific price).

- If your retailer also sells your products to a trade customer who then uses the product in the provision of a service, they can offer a discount to the trade customer who can also make some money when they sell the product on.

This would mean you have three price tiers**, wholesale, trade** and **retail**.

## What to do when all you are selling is your time – service businesses?

You may run a small business that only offers a service to your customers. This is where people are paying for your skill and expertise rather than buying your products. You may not use any materials to provide that service.

Here, the biggest cost of providing the service is your time, and the time of your staff.

What price do you put on your time?

There are a few things you need to consider and things you must track in running a service-based business.

- How much can you charge for each hour you provide? What does the market allow?

- How many hours can you work in a week and how many hours do you want to work?

- How much time must you set aside to run the business and carry out activities you can't charge the customer for?

- How many hours do you feel you can bill to customers in any week?

## An example.

Suppose you run a small business where the only person in the business is you, and you only offer a service.

- You work a normal 40-hour week and have four weeks leave each year. Therefore, the maximum hours you will work in any year is 40 x 48 = 1920 hours/year.

- You charge $100/hour for your time, as that is a little below what your competitors charge, but you feel it is a fair hourly rate. This means the most you could make in a year is $192,000 (1920 hours x $100/hour).

- However, you spend one day a week (8 hours) doing administration, writing proposals and bookkeeping.

- You spend another day each week (8 hours) marketing the business, chasing potential customers and networking. You could certainly use more customers.

- Therefore, there are only 24 hours each week you can charge customers. The most revenue you can make is $115,200 (24hours/week x 48 weeks x$100/hour).

- Your fixed costs are, say, $40,000 a year (running a car, computers, and so on).

- This means the very best you can expect in the year, before tax is $115,200 - $40,000 = $75,200

The difficulty with a service-based business is you can only work so many hours, charge so much for those hours and, therefore, the revenue you can make is limited. It is also common for the work coming in to be up-and-down from week-to-week. You can bill out more one week than the next.

In this example, if you are unhappy with the $75,200 you will need to charge more hours out per week (your billable hours), work more hours each week, take fewer holidays, or charge more per hour, or a combination of all these things.

## *Other options than just quoting hours*

Some options service-based businesses can choose to pursue, other than working more hours, include:

- Look at ways to turn the business' services into products that the owner can sell without requiring their time. (e.g., if it's your knowledge you are selling, put it into booklets and sell them online, or to other businesses).

- Employ more people and ensure they bill out more hours to customers.

- Look at ways to offer the service to larger numbers of people (e.g., group training or workshops). You can offer the service at a lower price per person but attract a higher hourly rate.

- Offer packages where you can discuss the value of the output of your work, not the hours you intend working. You can then sell the overall value of the outcome of your service to the client rather than debating hourly rates.

An hourly rate only measures the time you put in. It does not measure the value the customer gets from your time.

You will always have limited time. You can only work so many hours in a week and rarely can you charge for all those hours. As a result, you can probably work out the maximum income you will ever make using a model based solely on hourly rates.

## *You are selling your skills and knowledge – not your time*

Customers will often compare your hourly rate with other people, even in unrelated businesses based solely on a dollar-per-hour.

For example, a customer could ask the following question about three services they receive:

> *"Why does my accountant charge $200/hour, my tradesperson $90/hour, but my lawyer $400/hour?"*

If this customer had a burst water pipe, $90/hour is amazing value. If someone was suing this same individual, suddenly $400/hour seems superb value.

If you offer a service, there is a risk a customer will think it is only your time you are selling. You only offer the service because of your training, qualifications, and years of experience. An hourly rate does not reflect this.

If your service is offering advice, such advice can seem obvious after you have provided it to a client. Sadly, clients may not realise you make it sound obvious only because you spent many years of study, research and experience to build up that knowledge.

---

> It is your skill, expertise and experience and the value that you bring that your customer is paying for.

---

Try to price the value you add, not just the hours you put in. It may take time for you to understand your market and test its boundaries. You will also find different customers will have very different views of the value you add, even if they all receive the same service from you. There is a point where you simply need to hold your ground and say *"no"* to those who undervalue what you offer.

# How do you pay yourself?

There are several options that you can choose from to pay yourself. In the end, there is not much point working in your business if you can't pay yourself anything.

In the early days of the business, there is every chance you are making very little, and cannot deliver enough revenue to pay you anything. With time, this will hopefully change, and you can start earning an income from your business. There are a few options on how you can take money out of the business.

## *Sole trader*

If you are a sole trader, you and your business are the same thing in the eyes of the law and the IRD. Here, you can pay yourself as you see fit. However, you will need to get your accountant to complete your personal tax return at the end of the year. The 28% tax rate, which applies to companies, will not apply to you. Your tax rate will be determined by your personal tax rate, based on the money you have made from all sources.

---

### *A solo success story- and keeping healthy*

When Jenny Tulloch, in her HR role, had to make many people redundant, and choose who these people would be, she knew it was time to get out of the large power company she was working in. The environment was at odds with her values, and she was on the verge of complete burnout. The money was good, but her mental health was more important. Jenny's passion was exercise, fitness and health, and something she wanted to pursue.

---

She enrolled in a course in the exercise industry. While the part-time study gave her a little more knowledge, increased her confidence, and probably resulted in some external recognition, it was not essential to her plans. Jenny felt, like most small business owners, that it would be experience, not education, that would bring her success. It was now time to just start.

Pulse Personal Training was born in 2006.

Jenny was under no illusions about how difficult achieving success would be as a personal trainer (PT). The typical lifespan of a PT was two years. But Jenny was passionate about giving it a go and, had it failed, was prepared to go back to working for an employer to pay the mortgage.

Jenny's first clients were friends and associates. She joined a women's networking group. She placed some adverts in some local newspapers and walked the streets doing paper drops.

Her networking soon paid off. An opportunity to do group activities with the senior population came up, which she grabbed. It would thereafter remain a part of her business.

Jenny found many people in the exercise industry, as well as general businesspeople, were quick to give her advice on what a successful fitness business had to be. "*You have to pick a niche*". "*You have to grow*" "*You have to take on staff*" "*You have to do weight, BMI and body measurements to gauge client performance*". Advice from bigger, longer standing businesses was compelling. Jenny almost felt she had to take this advice, being so inexperienced. But she held her ground and remained determined to run the business she wanted and believed in.

Jenny would train the young, the old, male or female, fit or unfit. She loved one-on-one or small groups and found this suited her personality more, and gave her more job satisfaction than focusing solely on group work.

Her core values were authenticity, honesty, and respect. She applied these values when training all her clients, and she asked for it in return. Jenny was always on time, was prompt with her communication, and took pride in her reliability. These little things were important.

She cared about her clients, and respected her clients as people. Such care meant challenging them about their lifestyle, their diets, or their exercise routines.

Most took on the advice, knowing it was being given from a place of care, intending to help them achieve their goals – no matter how uncomfortable.

She ran a cash business, and her clients almost always paid her on time. Jenny would not offer further classes to anyone who didn't pay. While she set up a limited liability company, she felt remaining a sole trader may have achieved the same outcomes.

Word of mouth spread and over time, Jenny did not need to advertise. She found that word-of-mouth brought in the best clients, as they knew what was on offer and what they could expect. Jenny now has a waiting list. The pressure to employ grew, and several times it was seriously considered, although she never wanted to run a large business. In every case that she took on staff, it didn't last long. Staff did not approach clients or did not have the work ethic she did. Success for Jenny was remaining as a solo PT, and she saw no reason to shift from this.

Jenny has continued her journey for 18 years, and she has no intention of giving it away anytime soon. People who remain active well into their 70s inspire her – a goal she is confident she too can achieve, and possibly even working to this age in some manner.

Jenny knows she will never be a millionaire as a PT, but she has fulfilled a dream and has achieved success. Her story shows that business success can be achieved by remaining small, like the other 70% of solo businesses in New Zealand. Hard work, excellent customer service, putting customers before her personal life, particularly in the early stages of her business, has definitely paid off and been the cornerstone of her success.

## *Wages*

If you own a company, and you work regularly in the business, it might be simpler to set yourself up as an employee. This assumes you are making sufficient revenue to fund a regular wage. In the early years of a business, this may not be the case.

Your payroll system will need to be set up to pay the IRD your PAYE, KiwiSaver and student loan (if applicable). You, just like any employee, will need to complete all the appropriate IRD forms to allow this process to occur. You should have a personal bank account so you can transfer your wage from the company's bank account into your personal bank account at every pay period.

If you are a PAYE employee, you would code your wage as a cost of sale, if you are billing your time to customers, otherwise as an expense. In either case, your wages will reduce your profit, which will reduce your taxes.

Normally, if you were an employee, you should have a job description and IEA. However, if you are the only employee, and also the shareholder and director, you can't really sack yourself, so such documents won't achieve much. It might be different if you were working in your own company, and it grew to a size where you had independent directors and other shareholders. While unlikely, they could sack you from your own company, so in this case, you'd want these documents. A job description may also help clarify your role within the business and with other employees, so all roles are clear.

## *Drawings*

If the revenue your company will make each month is uncertain, especially if the business is still finding its feet, you may struggle to pay yourself a regular wage. You might have to see what money is available each month and take it from whatever is available. These are called **drawings**.

You can take drawings in several ways.

You could transfer money from the company bank account to your own bank account or you could buy personal items using the company credit card. You could also pay personal expenses (like your home electricity bill, or your home mortgage) with direct debits out of your company's bank account.

This all sounds simple, but if you don't code all these transactions correctly, and don't keep track of what you are spending, you will see your cash draining away and you may not understand where it has gone.

You may also find you have more administration to determine what spending was for the business and what was personal. If you don't track and code what is personal, it will remain as a business expense. This means you may not be paying the correct tax, which the IRD will frown on. This is an all too common occurrence in small business, so most accountants chase this when they do your end-of-year accounts. If you did not track your drawings throughout the year, your accountant will have more work completing your end-of-year accounts and you will face a larger bill.

Sadly, many small business owners take regular drawings, don't track them, and then wonder where the money has gone. If you feel you don't have the discipline to track all your drawings, a fixed monthly drawings, or a wage is probably the way to go. Transfer this money into your personal bank account and only use your business credit card for legitimate business expenses.

## Dividends

If your business had an exceptional year and, after the accountant has sorted out your tax, you may decide to pay yourself a **dividend** from the **Net Profit after Tax.** You should only consider this a nice bonus at the end of the year and something you can't rely on.

Rather than paying yourself a dividend you may decide to use this money t9 fund additional business activities, like extra marketing, or buying new equipment.

The other issue with dividends is you may well have made a profit, but there may be no cash in the company bank account to pay a dividend when you finally calculate it. I will explain why this happens when we discuss cash flow in later chapters

# Let's look deeper at what the profit and loss is telling you

Now that you have a better understanding of what the terms in your profit and loss statement mean, it is now time to make sense of the numbers, so you know what they are telling you about your business.

## % Gross Profit – The Golden Ratio

In the business world, you will have heard the business gurus talking about financial ratios, many of which you may or may not understand.

**Price-Earnings Ratio, Debt-to-Equity ratio. Liquidity Ratios. Interest Cover Ratio,** and I could go on. If you have not heard of these and don't know what they are about, don't worry. You don't need to know.

However, the following is one ratio that is critical in every business and is fundamental to the financial success of a small business. This is a ratio you must understand.

It is the **% Gross Profit (%GP)** or the **% Gross Margin**. I call this **The Golden Ratio.**

$$\frac{\text{SALES} - \text{COS}}{\text{SALES}} \times 100\% = \%GP$$

When you sell a product or a service, you need to make money on every sale. This is the margin, or % margin, on the individual sale. It does not consider your overheads or fixed costs, just your revenue from the sales and the costs you incurred to make those sales.

If you total every sale that you've made, the total margin on these sales is the **Gross Margin.**

Often you will see the term **Gross Profit** used. Don't worry too much about the terminology, as they mean the same thing. **Gross Margin = Gross Profit** or as many abbreviate it **GP** or **%GP.**

However, I will use the word **margin** a lot when I'm discussing pricing decisions.

You want this margin to be as high as possible. Typically, values are between 25 and 50%, although they will vary between industries.

If you see growth in revenue but a decline in your % Gross Margin, you need to consider whether the growth is worth pursuing. It may be growth with a disproportionate increase in your costs.

The temptation when small businesses grow is to offer discounts, or special offers to get more sales. It gets harder to track what all your staff are doing and the time they are billing to jobs. This will start reducing the %GP. Sometimes, if the sales volumes are high, this may be OK, as the increased sales compensate for the reduced margins.

> Be very cautious following a growth strategy that sees a slow decline in your %GP

I will discuss how to calculate your **breakeven** a little later in the book. This will show you how critical the effect %GP has on whether you are making money or not.

## *Know your margins on each product*

This is also a useful exercise to do on each product rather than just the entire business.

Some products will cost less to make and sell for a higher price. Others may not. You need to be sure the products with a higher margin are not paying for the products with poor or no margin. If you are selling low margin items in high volumes, that's OK. The greater revenue from the larger volume makes up for the smaller margins.

However, if you are not selling a lot and achieving low margins, it's worth asking yourself why you are persisting with that product.

## *Billable hours – Variable labour must be included in %GP*

We discussed the challenges for businesses that only sell their time. There are also many businesses, particularly in trades, construction, food and beverage, where the job or sale requires both the input of materials and labour. The way these businesses consider the time they spend is critical to the understanding of the %GP.

As I have discussed above, many small businesses will only ever include the wages and salaries they pay their staff in the expenses, even if those staff members time should be billed to a customer.

This would, on the surface, make sense. You must pay your permanent employees whether or not the sales are occurring. Based on the definitions, you would consider this a fixed cost.

Typically, when a business uses subcontractors, you would include their time in the cost of sales as you only hire subcontractors when there are jobs to do. When they finish or you are quiet, you send them away. This is correct as they are a variable cost.

When you calculate your %GP and exclude your permanent labour, it will look very healthy. However, this is not correct. Always include the hours of those you employed to work on customer's jobs as a cost of sale so you include them in the %GP.

These employees are there to work for a paying customer and their labour is a genuine input to completing the sale. Without this labour, you cannot deliver the product or service. However, unlike a subcontractor, you can't send a permanent staff member away when it's quiet. You still must pay them. They will also have meetings, training and wasted or idle time, or the work may simply not be there and you put them on other administrative duties

Inefficient use of labour is one of the most common reasons small businesses see a decline in the %GP. This is why it is critical to track where an employee's time is being used.

If the %GP is falling, you need to have the data at hand to establish if it's because of the inefficiency of your labour. This is why many legal firms force employees to log their time every fifteen minutes. It is why many consultancy businesses request all staff to complete timesheets religiously. Some business won't pay their tradespeople until they complete their time sheets for entry into the payroll system.

Whatever the technique you use, you must track where your billable staff are spending their time. It could make or break your business

You should include any labour that is clearly administrative, such as the bookkeeper or office manager, in expenses. You cannot allocate their time to clients, so they are a fixed cost.

# Margin vs. Markup — Be very careful!!

One of the mistakes small businesspeople make is how to set their sales prices based on the cost of sales. Remember, the most critical indicator of business profitability is the margin. **Some people confuse margin with markup.** This can be an extremely costly mistake.

To show you the implications of confusing mark-up and margin, we'll do an example.

Let's say you need your gross margin for the business to be **30%** because you are confident you will do well at this margin. Therefore, you want your sales price to deliver a 30% margin over the cost price. Your product costs **$100** to buy. Typically, many people apply the following formula to determine the sales price:

$$\$100 \times 1.3 = \$130$$

You apply this principle across the entire business with all your products and assume the gross profit you will generate for the entire business will be 30%.

Unfortunately, this is not correct, but is sadly common and can be a very costly mistake.

To show this, let's use the **Gross Profit calculation** (The Golden Ratio) from above on our example.

You used the above equation of ($100 x 1.3) to set your sale price for this product at  $130. The cost price, or cost of sales, is $100, so the %Gross Profit will be:

$$\frac{\$130 - \$100}{\$130} \times 100\% = 23\%$$

23% is a material difference to the desired 30%

Multiplying the cost price by a percentage, ($100 x 1.3), is a **mark-up**, and this is not correct. In short, don't use mark-up to set your prices. It should only ever be about margins.

The way to ensure you apply the correct margin to a cost price is algebra. In our example you have a cost price of $100 and want a 30% margin. Using some simple algebra on our Golden Ratio calculation, this is how to set your sales price:

$$\frac{(\text{SALES PRICE} - \$100)}{\text{SALES PRICE}} \times 100\% = 30\%$$

Rearranging this formula results in a sales price of:

$$\text{SALES PRICE} = \frac{\$100}{(1 - 0.3)} = \$142.85$$

This is significantly different from **$130**.

If you can only charge $130 to remain competitive, then you are only making a 23% margin. If you need 30% gross margin to cover expenses and debt repayments, then you are in trouble, and you may not even know why.

Therefore, the way to calculate the sales price when you know your margin and you know your cost of the product, or the cost of sale, is:

$$\text{SALES PRICE} = \frac{\text{COST OF SALES}}{(1 - \%GP)}$$

☞ Don't ever use mark-up to set your prices. Use margin. Make sure you know the difference, as getting this wrong will cost you.

# Breakeven analysis and percent Gross Profit

If your sales fall, there will be a point where you will only be making enough to cover your expenses (fixed costs) and be making enough profit to pay your loans and drawings with nothing left. This is your **breakeven sales.**

As your sales fall, so too will your cost of sales. What will hopefully remain constant is the % Gross Profit.

What is critical is to understand what sales, or revenue, you must make every month as a minimum to ensure you are covering all your costs and breaking even. If you can make more than that, it's money in your back pocket. Less than that and you will be going backwards.

The standard breakeven analysis is usually only based on the profit and loss statement. It calculates what sales you need to make so that you just make a profit.

Unfortunately, the profit and loss statement does not include money you need to pay off any loans, dividends, drawings, or funds for new or replacement assets. These come from your balance sheet or your cash flow statement. Therefore, you will have to make a profit that is above zero, so you have enough left to cover these items.

The way to do this is to produce a modified profit and loss statement that also includes loans, drawings, asset purchases and an estimate of tax. It will look something like this.

If you are breaking even each month, *"What's left"* **will be zero.**

REVENUE
‐ COST OF SALES

= GROSS PROFIT
‐ EXPENSES

= EBITDA
‐ TAX

= NPAT
‐ DRAWINGS
‐ LOAN REPAYMENTS
‐ ASSET PURCHASES

= "WHAT'S LEFT"

## *Let's do a breakeven example*

The following are some assumptions for this example business.

- There are no plans to buy any assets in the months ahead.

- The monthly loan repayment is $500 per month.

- Drawings are $550 per month.

- The business expenses are $1,000 per month, and

- The business has delivered a Gross Margin (%Gross Profit) of 25% each month.

Keep in mind the business needs to keep aside around 28% of the profits for tax.

There are a couple of ways you can deal with tax in a breakeven calculation. The simplest is to exclude it, considering a lot of non-cash items that aren't in the breakeven calculation, like depreciation, will reduce tax.

However, any breakeven calculation is an estimate, and I'd prefer to assume the worst, and that means you have to pay provisional tax which reduces *"What's Left"*. Therefore, I always make a rough estimate of tax.

Let's round tax up to 30% to make the math's simpler, and it never hurts to leave a little extra aside for tax.

> You must work backwards from the bottom and work your way up the profit (or loss) until you determine your breakeven sales figure.

We can now start at the bottom and enter the numbers we know in the following steps.

1. To achieve breakeven, that is *"What's Left"* = $0.00, the **NPAT** must be $500 (loans) + $550 (drawings) = $1050/month.

2. We now need to estimate the profit ***before*** tax, by making a rough estimate of tax at 30% and adding it to the NPAT. This means the business needs to deliver $1050/(1-0.3) or a before tax profit of approximately $1500.

3. If we add the monthly expenses of $1000 to this, then the Gross Profit would need to be $2,500.

4. This is now where the %GP becomes critical. Keep in mind that the COS will vary as the sales vary based on the %GP.

We now refer back, yet again, to The Golden Ratio.

$$\frac{SALES - COS}{SALES} \times 100\% = \%GP$$

and also, from our profit and loss statement we have the formula.

$$SALES - COS = GROSS\ PROFIT\ (\$)$$

So, substituting this into The Golden Ratio gives.

$$\frac{GROSS\ PROFIT\ (\$)}{SALES} = \%GP$$

Or rearranging.

$$SALES = \frac{GROSS\ PROFIT\ (\$)}{\%GP}$$

Therefore, in our example, where the %GP is 25%

BREAKEVEN MONTHLY SALES

= $2,500/0.25

= $10,000

Let's plug all these numbers in to show what a **monthly breakeven profit and loss statement** would be for this example.

|   | | |
|---|---|---|
| | REVENUE | $10,000 |
| | COST OF SALES | $7,500 |
| = | GROSS PROFIT | $2,500 |
| − | EXPENSES | $1,000 |
| = | EBITDA | $1,500 |
| − | TAX | $450 |
| = | NPAT | $1,050 |
| − | DRAWINGS | $550 |
| − | LOAN REPAYMENTS | $500 |
| − | ASSET PURCHASES | $0 |
| = | "WHAT'S LEFT" | $0 |

You can see that *"What's left"* is $0.00, so you must make at least $10,000 in sales every month to survive.

# The impact of improving your percent GP on breakeven

The breakeven process is also a great way to show just how critical the margin, or %GP, is to your business.

Let's run the same example but assume you have **improved your %GP by just 1%** with everything else remaining the same.

You still need to make a Gross Profit of $2,500, because none of your costs have changed. But the breakeven sales are now:

$$\frac{\$2,500}{0.26} = \$9,615$$

This means you now only need to make $9,615 to breakeven. If you could still make $10,000, but at 26%, you would have $385 left in your bank account each month.

If you could improve your %GP to 30%, this means your breakeven sales would be

$$\frac{\$2,500}{0.30} = \$8,333$$

This would mean, if you could still meet the $10,000 sales target, you would have $1,666 left every month or $20,000 per year.

If you look through the above profit and loss statement, there is almost no other way to achieve such a significant improvement in the bottom line. You might trim a few dollars off your expenses, but even if you have no expenses, which will never occur, you could only save $1000. You can't reduce your loans and yes, you could reduce what you pay yourself, but you have to make a living.

Look back at the section on **margin vs. markup** just above. If you consider the difference, just a 1% difference in margin has on your overall financial performance, image how much damage this simple mistake that resulted in a 23% margin compared to the desired 30% margin would have. **The minor details around margins are so critical.**

> The best way to improve your profitability is to focus your attention on increasing sales without increasing your fixed costs and improving your percentage gross profit.

## How else can you improve the bottom line — and 1+1+1 ≠ 3?

By completing the above calculations, you can analyse how financially healthy your small business is. Your financial accounts reflect what has happened in the past. If you are unhappy with the results, you need to understand what has contributed to them so you can change the business to achieve the financial results you seek.

All the above analyses will allow you to ask, and more importantly, answer the following questions:

1. How much am I selling and is it producing sufficient revenue?

2. How well do I understand what it costs to produce each of my products and services – my cost of sales?

3. Am I producing a good margin on each product or service and, therefore, for the entire business?

4. Are my fixed costs reasonable or are they eating into my earnings?

5. How can I lift my revenue and reduce my variable and fixed costs without compromising the service to my customers, my core purpose, and values?

To show you how even minor changes in your revenue and costs can have on your business, carry out the following simple calculation that I call the **1 + 1 + 1 ≠ 3 test:**

- Increase your annual revenue by 1%.

- Reduce the related cost of sales by 1%.

- Reduce your expenses by 1%.

I am very sure the increase in your earnings is much greater than 3%. My guess is it is probably closer to 25%. Imagine the benefits you would see if you could increase revenue by 10 or 20%, especially if you can do it without increasing your cost of sales or expenses by the same percentages.

# Developing a budget

We discussed the importance of developing a budget as part of your strategic planning. Typically, this is an estimate of the profit and loss for the year, calculated monthly. When you are doing this, keep in mind your breakeven calculations, as these will help you determine your minimum monthly sales targets.

Typically, budgeting is on a financial year basis. In New Zealand, that is normally from April to March.

The starting point to develop your budget is to take the figures from the past 12 months. Now look at what costs you know have changed or will change over the next 12 months. E.g., your lease is going up.

If you are a start-up and you have no history, you will need to determine what costs you have to run the business in the first year as your starting point.

Consider any major expenditure you might need, like new vehicles, extra staff or other assets you need to buy.

Don't worry about too much accuracy. You are predicting the future, and no one can do that accurately.

Whatever budget you develop you will be wrong, just hopefully not too wrong. You are predicting the future.

You will need to adjust the budget as the year progresses.

You can use the budget to run a few scenarios to see what impact they have on the business. For example, say you have a 5% increase or decrease in sales, or your suppliers increase their costs by 5%.

Re-run the breakeven calculation over your budget for the year to establish what your minimum sales need to be to survive.

Hopefully, you will do better than breakeven.

# CHAPTER 21

## THE BALANCE SHEET

The balance sheet provides details of what the business owns and what it owes to others, at a specific point in time.

The profit and loss statement includes the income and costs over an entire period, like a tax year, financial year or over a month.

The balance sheet is a snapshot in time. It is a financial statement that small businesses don't need to look at often, and typically don't, but is a critical indicator of the health of a business.

A good analogy for your profit and loss statement versus your balance sheet is an apple tree. The apples represent the profit, and the roots represent the balance sheet. Like the roots of a tree, you may not see the impact of a weakening balance sheet straight away.

Your debt may be high and increasing and your cash may be diminishing. Your liabilities may grow and could even exceed your assets, so you have no equity (this is a sign of insolvency).

The apples may keep coming for a while, but the root system may be weaker. The weak roots will eventually whither, and the apples will stop coming – maybe forever.

## It must balance

Let's go through a few key concepts of the balance sheet.

The three basic parts of any balance sheet are your assets, liabilities, and equity.

- **Assets** - what the business OWNS.

- **Liabilities** - what the business OWES.

- **Equity** - what remains that belongs to the owners of the business.

The balance sheet is so called because the following formula must balance every time:

$$ASSETS = LIABILITIES + EQUITY$$

A simple way to explain the balance sheet is the purchase of a home. You buy a house that costs $800,000. You contribute $200,000 of your own money and borrow $600,000 from the bank. The value of the asset is $800,000. The liability, your debt, is $600,000 and the equity, the part of the house you own, is $200,000.

Therefore, it balances:

$$\$800,000 \ (ASSETS) = \$600,000 \ (LIABILITIES) +$$
$$\$200,000 \ (EQUITY)$$

A typical balance sheet is further broken down into different categories of assets, liabilities, and equity

Let's explore what all the typical elements of a small business' balance sheet mean.

# The Typical Balance Sheet

## ASSETS

### CURRENT ASSETS

BANK ACCOUNT

ACCOUNTS RECEIVABLE

STOCK ON HAND

WORK IN PROGRESS

### NON-CURRENT ASSETS

PLANT EQUIPMENT VEHICLES

GOODWILL

INTELLECTUAL PROPERTY

## LIABILITIES

### CURRENT LIABILITIES

ACCOUNTS PAYABLE

OVERDRAFT

### NON-CURRENT LIABILITIES

LONG-TERM LOANS

LOANS FROM SHAREHOLDERS

SHAREHOLDERS CURRENT ACCOUNT

## EQUITY

SHARE CAPITAL

RETAINED EARNINGS

DIVIDENDS

CURRENT YEARS EARNINGS

# Assets

## *Current assets*

These are assets that are expected to convert into cash within one year in the normal course of business. They include cash, accounts receivable, and inventory.

### 1.  Cash in your bank account

As money comes and goes into and out of the business, your bank account will fluctuate. Some small businesses run more than one bank account. This might be money you set aside to pay taxes with another account for the day-to-day running of the business.

You will often hear the term **liquidity** used to describe assets. The more liquid an asset, the easy it is to turn into cash. It is much harder to sell a building quickly and turn it into cash than to use the cash already in the bank. The most liquid asset is cash in the bank. As you work your way through your balance sheet, the assets become less liquid.

### 2.  Inventory (or stock on hand)

Inventory, or stock, includes materials you purchase and store for later use. You may also produce extra goods that you have not yet sold. When you take an item from stock and sell it, the inventory in your balance sheet is reduced, the sales it generates are added to revenue, and the cost of the product is added to the cost of sales.

### 3.  Accounts receivable

If you sell your goods and services and offer customers credit, you are providing them with the product or service, but not being paid for some time later. This is a critical part of cash flow management that I cover shortly.

As this is money owed to the business, it is an asset.

If you believe you will never receive some of this money, it will become a **bad debt**. You would remove it from the accounts receivable and add it as an expense in your profit and loss statement.

## 4.    Work in progress (WIP)

Through the year, some companies who are manufacturing goods or involved in longer running projects, like a builder constructing a home, will have **work in progress (WIP)**. WIP is the cost of all the unfinished goods, like the labour and raw materials. Typically, these products or projects will be completed within the year. As such, they are a current asset.

It is preferable to have as small a WIP as possible, because it is notoriously difficult to calculate accurately, and the sooner it can deliver a final sale, the better. Unfortunately, in many cases, especially in the building industry, WIP can drag over several months, so it is unavoidable. WIP needs to be calculated as best as possible. Ignoring it misrepresents the state of the business.

## Non-current assets

The business' long-term assets, those that will last beyond one year, are your non-current assets.

## 1.    Plant, equipment and motor vehicles

In New Zealand, any asset you purchased that is greater than $1000 and will last more than a year is a non-current asset. You can include assets less than $1000 in your expenses, in the profit and loss statement.

Keep in mind this value has been changing. The IRD increased it as part of the relief to small businesses during the COVID-19 pandemic and then dropped it again.

As the value of the asset depreciates each year, this needs to be taken off the value of the asset. Some balance sheets will highlight the depreciation as a separate line item against each asset.

## 2.   Goodwill.

If you purchased your business as a going concern, the valuation is likely to have included goodwill. I will discuss this when explaining the process of buying or selling a business. This is an intangible asset, as you can't touch it like a vehicle or stock. It is a non-current asset, as it will last for the life of the business.

If you have never had your business formally valued, goodwill may not appear in the balance sheet.

You need to be cautious about putting any real value on goodwill when looking at the balance sheet. Banks and other parties will not consider it as a true asset. Its value will vary continually as your profitability changes. Only formal valuations can calculate it. Such valuations are of little benefit unless you want to sell the business.

## 3.   Intellectual Property (IP)

While most small businesses will have copyright, or trademarks as part of their business, they are difficult to value and businesses rarely include them in the balance sheet. However, cases may occur where a business has purchased IP or produced IP and had it valued. If so, it will appear as a non-current asset and is an intangible asset.

# Liabilities

## Current liabilities

These are the business' debts and other obligations that are due to be paid within one year. They include any short-term debt, overdrafts and accounts payable.

## 1.   Accounts payable

If you buy goods and services with credit, you will have received them but are yet to pay for them. Just as accounts receivable need to be tracked closely for managing cash flow, so are your payables. You need to pay your suppliers on time. If cash is tight, talk to them. If you get a reputation as a slow or bad payer, suppliers may stop offering you credit or not sell to you until you have paid.

Many suppliers will do credit checks on you before they let you set up an account. If you have a reputation as a slow or bad payer, they may not let you open an account.

As this is money owed by the business to someone else, it is a **liability**.

## 2.   Overdraft

This is a lending facility a bank offers that allows you to take more money out of your account than you put in, meaning it can become overdrawn. There will be limits on how overdrawn it can become.

If you need an overdraft facility, talk to your bank. The bank will require details of your business accounts and the process could take time.

An overdraft is especially helpful for a business that has monthly swings in cash in the bank. However, most overdrafts are not secured against assets, so pose a greater risk to the bank. Therefore, you will pay higher interest rates compared with other loans.

You should avoid being overdrawn as much as possible. If the overdraft works well and your business is doing OK, you should return to a positive cash position as quickly as possible. If you are in overdraft all the time or, worse still, hitting your overdraft limit regularly, you need to be careful. It means there may be bigger issues facing the business.

You can ask to increase the overdraft limit, but this might just be digging yourself a bigger hole if you don't understand why you are in that situation.

## 3.   Working capital

This doesn't appear in any accounts but is a term very often used in business, so I will define it here. Working capital is the cash the business has access to for its day-to-day operations. The calculation for working capital is shown below

$$\text{WORKING CAPITAL} = \text{CURRENT ASSETS}$$
$$- \text{CURRENT LIABILITIES}$$

The more cash you have access to, the better will be your working capital. However, it's not very common for small businesses to have spare cash in the bank. More often, we never seem to have enough.

How much working capital should you be aiming for?

There are several rules of thumb, although each business is different.

Ideally, you would like to have enough cash on hand to cover a month's worth of fixed costs. These include your expenses, loan repayments, and wages.

You also need to ensure you have cash set aside to cover GST and other taxes. Some businesses set up a separate tax account and allocate about 15% of all their sales into that account each month to ensure the money is there come tax time.

Another ratio I will introduce that you could use to assess if you have enough working capital is the **current ratio.**

$$\text{CURRENT RATIO} = \frac{\text{CURRENT ASSETS}}{\text{CURRENT LIABILITIES}}$$

The current ratio gives an indication of the level of cash (liquidity) available in a business. This also tells a business what working capital is available.

If your **current ratio is *"1" (or less)*** it means there is no working capital and your cash situation isn't good. Many small businesses may battle to achieve a current ratio of "1" when times are tight.

The following would be a reasonable current ratio to strive for which I will use in later chapters.

# CURRENT RATIO = 1.5

Some businesses will want a better ratio than this, say *"1.75"* or even *"2.00"*.

## Non-current liabilities

These are your business' debts and other obligations that are due to be paid beyond one year. They can include long-term loans from the bank or from you, the business owner.

### 1.   Long-term loans

If you have borrowed money to buy assets, like plant, equipment or motor vehicles, repayment of these is likely to extend beyond one year, so they are non-current liabilities.

### 2.   Loans from shareholders

You, like many small business owners, may need to put your own money into the business to get it started. The business may also need you to put more of your own money in the business if it hits tighter times. You can achieve this by setting up a formal loan arrangement that the business needs to repay.

The risk for you is that if the business gets into trouble, you may never see your money because it may go to all your creditors. Therefore, it is important, if you put larger amounts of your own money into the business, that you not only formalise this lending with a loan agreement but also consider putting a security agreement in place and registering it on the PPSR. This means you will rank above anyone else if your business gets into trouble. At least you will get your own money back before others do.

### 3. Shareholder current account – It is confusing!

The concept of the **shareholder current account** is one of the more confusing financial aspects of your company's balance sheet. If you are a sole trader, there are no shareholders, as the business is you, so there is no shareholder current account. However, if you are a company, in the eyes of the law and the IRD, you and the company are different entities, so the company's money is not the same as your money.

I will explain the shareholder current account in more detail in the chapters on cash flow and tax. For now, to explain the balance sheet, the shareholder current account is a record of what money the company owes its shareholders. Therefore, it is a liability.

# Equity

After you remove what your business owes (liabilities) away from what the business owns (assets), what you have left in your balance sheet is the owner's equity. Otherwise put, equity is what the business owner's own. Another way to look at equity is the amount left if you sold all the assets for the values listed in the balance sheet and paid off all your debts.

These are the typical items you will find under equity in your balance sheet.

## Share capital

Typically, this is the amount of money you pay to buy a nominal number of shares when you first set up your company. It is a small amount, typically $1/share and 100 shares, so $100.

## Current year's earnings

The current year's earnings are the business' profits at any point in time during the year. If the profits change, the current year's earnings on the balance sheet will change.

At the end of the financial year, you or your accountant will calculate the after-tax profits and those go into the calculation of your **retained earnings**.

## Dividends paid

The directors of the company will decide what the dividend should be. This may well just be you making that decision if you are the sole director. You should not pay dividends if your company has not been profitable and you should only issue dividends if the company is solvent. Your company is solvent if you can pay your bills when they fall due and your company's assets exceed its liabilities.

Your accountant is best placed to advise on dividend payments if you are new to this process.

## Retained earnings

At the end of the financial year, after you calculate your profits and calculate your tax, what is left is the **Net Profit After Tax** (NPAT). If this is healthy, you can pay the shareholders (including you) a dividend. After you have paid dividends, what you are left with is **retained earnings**. This money belongs to your company.

RETAINED EARNINGS =  LAST YEAR'S RETAINED EARNINGS

+ NET INCOME (LOSS) FROM THIS YEAR

– DIVIDENDS

You record retained earnings in the balance sheet in the final year's accounts. This value does not change as the year progresses.

While the retained earnings may be healthy, it does not mean that cash is available for you to use in your business. The cash collected through the year from sales may differ from what the final income says exists at year's end.

Remember, any cash you used to buy assets, like stock or other equipment, or that you used to pay off loans, does not appear in the NPAT. So, the NPAT could look very healthy, which means the retained earnings look good, but you may have no money in the bank.

Therefore, retained earnings may not reflect what cash you have in the bank.

# Why look at the information on your balance sheet?

It's more common for small business owners to keep their eye on the profit and loss statement than on the balance sheet.

The profit and loss statement reflects the amount of money coming in and out of the business. Small business owners often leave the balance sheet until the end of the year or leave it for their accountant or bank to worry about.

While the profit and loss statement is the critical financial report to monitor closely, it's important to understand your balance sheet and to monitor it. It contains information you won't find elsewhere. Here are a few key things to consider.

- The balance sheet shows the underlying strength of your business, and this is what will carry you through the years. The hope is you are building up the assets in your business, especially cash. It is hopeful you are reducing the money you owe other people. This then results in you increasing the money you, the owner, have in the business, which is your equity.

- The balance sheet is a snapshot in time. It will change daily as cash moves in and out of your business and as your profit changes. The longer you wait between your reviews of your balance sheet, the bigger the changes that will have occurred.

- The balance sheet will show you a summary of your debtors (who owes you money) and your creditors (who you owe money to). You need to analyse these reports regularly. Very often your accounting system (e.g., Xero) will have their own reports detailing your accounts receivable and payable.

- The balance sheet is the only place you can go to see how much cash you can get your hands on in a hurry. This is the **liquidity**. Cash is the most "*liquid*" asset. A house or your property is not liquid.

• You could be profitable but you could be slipping in and out of solvency without even knowing it. You are solvent when your assets exceed your liabilities.

Any lender (especially the banks) will gauge the health of your business and their appetite to lend you money, not only on profitability but also on the health of your balance sheet.

Therefore, keep a close eye on your profit and loss statement but also on your balance sheet. The more you look, the more you will become comfortable, and the less time it will take each time you look.

# How the profit and loss and balance sheets interact — examples

There are long-standing accounting principles that define how transactions are recorded in your financial statements. These have been around a very long time so that no matter where you are, when you read a set of financial accounts, they follow the same accepted principles.

Such accounting practices can be traced back thousands of years to the cradle of civilisation in Mesopotamia Egyptians and Babylonians. [1]

**Double entry accounting** is a fundamental principle of accounting and it has been around since the 14th century when it was believed created by an Italian Franciscan Friar, Luca Pacioli [2]. The Medici family used double entry accounting extensively. They dominated the banking landscape in the 15th and 16th centuries in Florence, Italy. They funded some of the greatest art works in history, most notably by Michelangelo.

*"Every debit has its credit – every amount that is charged to on account must be placed to the credit of another".* **Luca Pacioli circa 1494** [3]

The **Generally Accepted Accounting Principles (GAAP)** are one of the most widely accepted standards and have been used around the world, including in New Zealand, for almost 100 years.

We have already discussed the basics of a balance sheet. Assets must always equal liabilities plus equity. They must balance. If you carry out a transaction that affects one part of your balance sheet, you have to make adjustments to another part of the balance sheet.

Likewise, adjustments in the balance sheet may affect your profit and loss statement and changes in the profit and loss statement can affect the balance sheet.

The best way to show you these interactions is to walk through some common transactions you will do when running your business. If you use an accounting system, it will carry out these transactions automatically so you don't have to worry about doing any of these. However, it never hurts to understand them as it will help you understand how your financial decisions impact your financial reports and your business.

I will start with a really simple profit and loss statement and a simple balance sheet so you can see how each example affects these.

# *Starting balance sheet - Example*

I've highlighted the connection between the profit and the current year's earnings. As the profit changes, it changes the current year's earnings. The retained earnings were the profit at the end of the previous financial year, in this case $200.

In this simple example, this business starts out with no loans and no assets, so the current assets and current liabilities are zero.

As each transaction occurs, I will walk through how the financial statements change.

## BALANCE SHEET

CURRENT ASSETS

| | |
|---|---|
| CASH | = $200 |
| INVENTORY | = $100 |
| ACCOUNTS RECEIVABLE | = $50 |
| TOTAL | = $350 |

NON-CURRENT ASSETS

———

CURRENT LIABILITIES

| | |
|---|---|
| ACCOUNTS PAYABLE | = $50 |

NON-CURRENT LIABILITIES

———

EQUITY

| | |
|---|---|
| CURRENT YEARS EARNINGS = | $100 |
| RETAINED EARNINGS | = $200 |
| TOTAL | =$300 |

## PROFIT & LOSS

| | |
|---|---|
| SALES | = $600 |
| COS | = $300 |
| GP | = $300 |
| EXPENSES | = $200 |
| PROFIT | = $100 |

ASSETS = LIABILITIES + EQUITY

$350 = $50 + $300

## Example 1 – Buying a new vehicle

You buy a vehicle for $1000, but you borrow the money to fund this.

- The new vehicle is a non-current asset (it will last more than one year).

- You did not use any of your own money to buy it, so the cash in the bank remains the same.

- You borrowed the $1000 from the bank, which appears as a non-current liability.

## BALANCE SHEET

CURRENT ASSETS

| | |
|---|---|
| CASH | = $200 |
| INVENTORY | = $100 |
| ACCOUNTS RECEIVABLE | = $50 |
| TOTAL | = $350 |

NON-CURRENT ASSETS

| | |
|---|---|
| VEHICLE | = $1000 |

CURRENT LIABILITIES

| | |
|---|---|
| ACCOUNTS PAYABLE | = $50 |

NON-CURRENT LIABILITIES

| | |
|---|---|
| LOAN ON VEHICLE | = $1000 |

## EQUITY

| | |
|---|---|
| CURRENT YEARS EARNINGS | = $100 |
| RETAINED EARNINGS | = $200 |
| TOTAL | = $300 |

## PROFIT & LOSS

| | | |
|---|---|---|
| SALES | = | $600 |
| COS | = | $300 |
| GP | = | $300 |
| EXPENSES | = | $200 |
| PROFIT | = | $100 |

ASSETS = LIABILITIES + EQUITY

$1350 = $1050 + $300

## Example 2 – Using inventory to make a sale

You now take a $50 stock item out of the warehouse and sell it for $100.

- The inventory in your current assets in the balance sheet will decrease by the value of the product ($50).

- The item is sold for $100, so the $50 is added to your COS on the profit and loss, and the $100 is added to sales.

- The profit increases by the margin between the cost of the product and the sales price, $100 - $50 = $50.

- The sale increases the cash in the bank by $100.

- The profit goes up by $50, so your current year's earnings go up.

### BALANCE SHEET

CURRENT ASSETS

CASH      =      $200 + $100 = $300

INVENTORY = $100 - $50 = $50

ACCOUNTS RECEIVABLE      = $50

TOTAL      = $400

NON-CURRENT ASSETS

VEHICLE      = $1000

CURRENT LIABILITIES

ACCOUNTS PAYABLE      = $50

NON-CURRENT LIABILITIES

LOAN ON VEHICLE      = $1000

EQUITY

CURRENT YEARS EARNINGS = $150

RETAINED EARNINGS      = $200

TOTAL      = $350

### PROFIT & LOSS

SALES = $600 + $100 = $700

COS      = $300 + $50 = $350

GP      = $350

EXPENSES      = $200

PROFIT      = $150

ASSETS = LIABILITIES + EQUITY

$1400 = $1050 + $350

## Example 3 – Depreciation in the value of the new vehicle

The accountant applies depreciation to the vehicle you purchased.

- The depreciation is shown as an **accumulated depreciation** (of -$100) in your non-current assets. This reduces the value of your assets in the balance sheet.

- The depreciation is tax deductible and appears as an expense in your profit and loss.

- Your profit reduces so your current year's earnings reduce.

## BALANCE SHEET

CURRENT ASSETS

| | |
|---|---|
| CASH | = $300 |
| INVENTORY | = $50 |
| ACCOUNTS RECEIVABLE | = $50 |
| TOTAL | = $400 |

NON-CURRENT ASSETS

| | |
|---|---|
| VEHICLE | = $1000 |
| ACCUMULATED DEPRECIATION = | -$100 |
| TOTAL | = $900 |

CURRENT LIABILITIES

| | |
|---|---|
| ACCOUNTS PAYABLE | = $50 |

NON-CURRENT LIABILITIES

| | |
|---|---|
| LOAN ON VEHICLE | = $1000 |

EQUITY

| | |
|---|---|
| CURRENT YEARS EARNINGS | = $50 |
| RETAINED EARNINGS | = $200 |
| TOTAL | = $250 |

## PROFIT & LOSS

| | |
|---|---|
| SALES | = $700 |
| COS | = $350 |
| GP | = $350 |
| EXPENSES | = $200 |
| DEPRECIATION | = $100 |
| PROFIT | = $50 |

ASSETS = LIABILITIES + EQUITY

$1300 = $1050 + $250

## Example 4 – Selling the vehicle for more than its book value

Someone offers you $1100 for the vehicle, so you decide to sell it and pay off the loan.

- The vehicle, accumulated depreciation, and the original purchase price are removed from non-current assets.

- The loan is paid off, so it is removed from non-current liabilities.

- After the loan was paid off you are left with $100 cash from the sale, that will go into your bank account (current asset).

- You sold the car for $200 above the book value ($1100-$900). This is a profit that you reflect in your profit and loss statement. This $200 is called **depreciation recovery income.**

### BALANCE SHEET

($1100-$1000)
(SALES PRICE) (LOAN)

CURRENT ASSETS

CASH = $300 + $100 = $400

INVENTORY = $50

ACCOUNTS RECEIVABLE = $50

TOTAL = $500

NON-CURRENT ASSETS

~~VEHICLE~~ = ~~$1000~~

~~ACCUMULATED DEPRECIATION~~ = ~~$100~~

~~TOTAL~~ (BOOK VALUE WHEN SOLD) ➤ = ~~$900~~

CURRENT LIABILITIES

ACCOUNTS PAYABLE = $50

NON-CURRENT LIABILITIES

~~LOAN ON VEHICLE~~ = ~~$1000~~

### EQUITY

CURRENT YEARS EARNINGS = $250

RETAINED EARNINGS = $200

TOTAL = $450

### PROFIT & LOSS

($1100-$900)
(SALES PRICE) (BOOK VALUE)

SALES = $700 + $200 = $900

COS = $350

GP = $550

EXPENSES = $200

DEPRECIATION = $100

PROFIT = $250

ASSETS = LIABILITIES + EQUITY

$500 = $50 + $450

---

# Example 5 – Writing off damaged stock

You carry out a stocktake and $30 worth of stock is damaged and can't be sold, so you have to dispose of it.

- Your inventory in the current assets is reduced by $30.

- This appears as a cost of sale in the profit and loss.

- As no sale occurs, there is no change in the sales and your profit reduces by $30.

- This reduces the current year's earnings in equity.

## BALANCE SHEET

CURRENT ASSETS

| | |
|---|---|
| CASH | = $400 |
| INVENTORY = $50 - ($30) | = $20 |
| ACCOUNTS RECEIVABLE | = $50 |
| TOTAL | = $470 |

NON-CURRENT ASSETS

CURRENT LIABILITIES

| | |
|---|---|
| ACCOUNTS PAYABLE | = $50 |

NON-CURRENT LIABILITIES

## EQUITY

| | |
|---|---|
| CURRENT YEARS EARNINGS | = ($220) |
| RETAINED EARNINGS | = $200 |
| TOTAL | = $420 |

## PROFIT & LOSS

| | | |
|---|---|---|
| SALES | | = $900 |
| COS | = $350 + ($30) | = $380 |
| GP | | = $520 |
| EXPENSES | | = $200 |
| DEPRECIATION | | = $100 |
| PROFIT | | = ($220) |

ASSETS = LIABILITIES + EQUITY

$470 = $50 + $420

# Example 6 – A customer does not pay what they owe you

A customer fails to pay a $50 invoice even though you completed the work.

- This was in the accounts receivable but is has to be removed as you won't receive this money.

- This is listed as a **bad debt** in the expenses in the profit and loss statement.

- This reduces the profit by $50 which reduces the current year's earnings by the same amount.

| BALANCE SHEET | | PROFIT & LOSS | |
|---|---|---|---|
| **CURRENT ASSETS** | | SALES | = $900 |
| CASH | = $400 | COS | = $380 |
| INVENTORY | = $20 | | |
| ACCOUNTS RECEIVABLE = $50-$50 | = $0 | GP | = $520 |
| | | EXPENSES | = $200 |
| TOTAL | = $420 | DEPRECIATION | = $100 |
| **NON-CURRENT ASSETS** | | BAD DEBT | = $50 |
| ——— | | | |
| **CURRENT LIABILITIES** | | | |
| ACCOUNTS PAYABLE | = $50 | PROFIT | = $170 |
| **NON-CURRENT LIABILITIES** | | | |
| ——— | | | |
| **EQUITY** | | | |
| CURRENT YEARS EARNINGS | = $170 | ASSETS = LIABILITIES + EQUITY | |
| RETAINED EARNINGS | = $200 | $420 = $50 + $370 | |
| TOTAL | = $370 | | |

A good financial accounting system, like Xero or MYOB, will automatically manage all these transactions and your accountant will fix any mistakes come tax time. It is still important to understand that every action in your accounts creates an equal or opposite change.

The better you track and code all these transactions through the year, the more accurate will be your financial statements and the easier will be the job for your accountant at the end of the financial year.

# CHAPTER 22

# TAXATION — THERE IS NOTHING MORE CERTAIN

There is absolute certainty that you will pay taxes when you run your small business, assuming you make a profit. It's very important you get this right, so I will devote this chapter to taxation.

## Death and taxes

While there are many others who have used the term *"death and taxes"*, this is one of the earliest records of its use.

> *"Our new Constitution is now established and has an appearance that promises permanency; but in this world, **nothing can be said to be certain, except death and taxes.**"*—**Benjamin Franklin**, in a letter to Jean-Baptiste Le Roy, 1789

We all know taxation is inevitable and we all know we must pay it. However, sadly, it is the most likely reason a small business will be forced into liquidation, usually instigated by the **Inland Revenue Department (IRD)**. It is also an all-too-common reason for people being charged with fraud when they deliberately avoid paying the taxes they owe, and hoping they will get away with it.

I do not intend to give you detailed tax advice in this book. Get your accountant to do that for you.. However, there are some key principals and considerations I will discuss.

Tax rates have been increased and decreased many times since Kiwis first paid income tax in 1896. GST was introduced in 1986. Tax has been and will continue to be a political football. For all of us in small business, this means little. We have no say in the tax rules and even if they make no sense, we still must pay them.

# Don't let the tail wag the dog

If you are paying little or no tax, your business is in bad shape or you are breaking the law. If you are paying lots of tax, your business must be making money.

So, let's start our discussion on taxation with the goal that you want to pay lots of tax, because it will mean you are making heaps of money. You shouldn't focus too much effort on running the business to reduce tax. This means the tail-is-wagging-the-dog. Your main focus should always be on delivering your business goals. Taxation is a secondary focus and usually one for your accountant to deal with.

The biggest challenge with paying tax is having the cash available to pay what you owe when you owe it. I will discuss how to manage cash flow in later chapters.

# The IRD - We may not like them, but we need them

Most business owners and most taxpayers often hold the IRD in very low regard.

Taxation can be complicated and the IRD may not be that easy to deal with. No one enjoys seeing large chunks of their earnings disappearing into government hands, especially when we were not expecting it.

The country's ability to function relies on the efficient collection of taxation. So, whether we like them or not, we need an effective IRD.

*"Taxes are the price we pay for a civilised society."* - **Oliver Wendell Holmes Jr** former Massachusetts Supreme Court Justice

# What is the IRD all about?

Of the total annual revenue of approximately $153 billion raised by the New Zealand government (in 2024), over $111 billion or over 70% comes from taxation. [1]

The country would cease to function without an effective tax department to collect taxation.

The **Tax Administration Act of 1994** describes the role of the IRD to be:

> *Use their best endeavours to protect the integrity of the tax system.*
>
> *... the integrity of the tax system includes—*
>
> *(a)    taxpayer perceptions of that integrity; and*
>
> *(b)    the rights of taxpayers to have their liability determined fairly, impartially, and according to law; and*
>
> *(c)    the rights of taxpayers to have their individual affairs kept confidential and treated with no greater or lesser favour than the tax affairs of other taxpayers; and*
>
> *(d)    the responsibilities of taxpayers to comply with the law; and*
>
> *(e)    the responsibilities of those administering the law to maintain the confidentiality of the affairs of taxpayers; and*
>
> *(f)    the responsibilities of those administering the law to do so fairly, impartially, and according to law.*

# The IRD – They are expected to chase every cent

The IRD's statutory responsibility is to collect as much tax revenue as it legally can. The legislation states:

---

*"It is the duty of the Commissioner to collect, over time the highest net revenue that is practicable within the law".*

Therefore, we should not be surprised when the IRD chases every cent it can from those who owe them taxes.

## New Zealand's unpaid tax burden

While the IRD collects a lot of tax every year, we also owe them a large amount in unpaid taxes. In June 2024 the tax debt from all kiwi companies was $4.8 billion. This was an increase from $2.5 billion in June 2021. [2]

## TOTAL COMPANY TAX DEBT

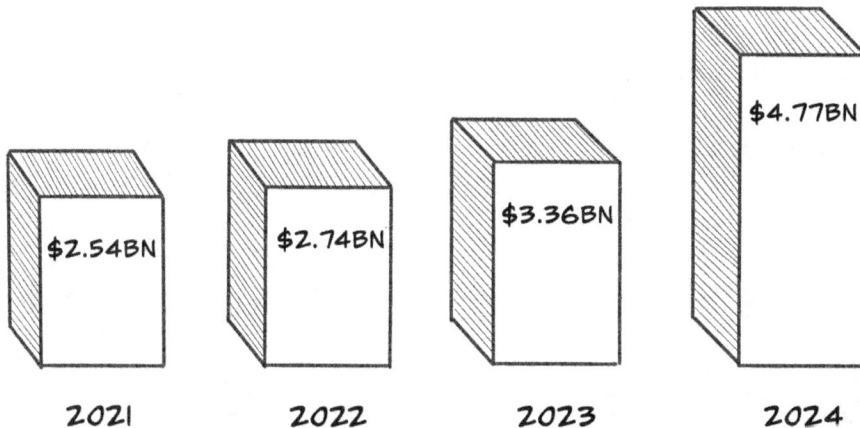

$2.54BN — 2021
$2.74BN — 2022
$3.36BN — 2023
$4.77BN — 2024

During the COVID-19 pandemic, the Government had little interest in going heavy-handed on small businesses who, through no fault of their own, where struggling to survive, let alone pay their taxes. During this period, under pressure from the Government, the IRD were less diligent in pursuing unpaid taxes. This led to an increase in overdue taxation, as the statistics above highlight.

While all business owners could empathise with this decision, the risk now is that the tax will eventually need to be repaid, or the country will be left short of billions.

The banking sector also gets nervous lending into an economy where excessive taxation is owed. At a national level, growing tax debt makes lenders nervous.

# Setting up a myIR account with the IRD

When you have set up your business, you will need to get an IRD number if you do not already have one. If you're a sole trader, you can use your personal IRD number. If you're in business as a company or partnership, you'll need a new IRD number. You can use this number for your GST as well.

The IRD website will help with this or talk to your accountant.

Once you have an IRD number, set up a **myIR** account with the IRD. This means you can track all your tax information. You can also file your tax returns, make payments to the IRD, communicate with the IRD, and find details of when you need to file and pay your taxes.

While I would recommend gaining the advice and input of your accountant, it is worth having a level of understanding of what you need to pay and when. The myIR will assist with this.

# The different taxes you could pay — the basics

The New Zealand tax laws are complex, and I won't advise you on tax. This is where you must rely on your accountant. I just want to cover the basics.

As a small business, you will have a selection of taxes you will need to pay. You need to know when they are due, how they are determined, and how you pay them.

Nothing is simple with taxation, but hopefully the following explanations will give you a good starting point.

## Pay as you earn tax (PAYE)

If you pay yourself and your staff wages, you will need a payroll system that establishes the tax rate that relates to each person. You are paying the employee's income tax as they earn it, rather than them having to do this themselves. When you pay them their wages, you will need to pay the IRD the PAYE on their behalf.

If you were to withhold paying PAYE and keep it within the business, the IRD sees this as stealing your staff's money. The IRD looks very dimly on businesses who have unpaid PAYE tax. They put a greater focus on unpaid PAYE and will be more aggressive in pursuing businesses with unpaid PAYE than other taxes.

## Goods and Services Tax (GST)

In 1986, New Zealand implemented a broad Goods and Services Tax (GST) of 10%. Since then, it increased to 12.5%, and in 2010 to its current level of 15%. While high, it is still lower than the OECD average, which is between 19 to 20%, with Denmark's rate being 25% [3]

If you are GST registered, you must pay GST on what you sell and can claim GST on what you buy. GST may not apply to all expenses in the business. For example, GST does not apply to wages, bank interest, bank charges and KiwiSaver payments.

If you earn $60,000 or more in the year, you must register for GST. This figure may well change over the years, so make sure you know what it is at the time you are applying.

Some small business owners, typically sole traders, who have been earning less than the $60,000 will avoid doing additional work to ensure they don't pass the GST threshold. This is so they don't have to register and, therefore, pass on an additional 15% to their customers. [4].

You need to calculate your GST and pay it to the IRD every two months (paying six-monthly is also an option). The challenge this poses for almost every business is managing the cash flow.

I cover how your GST is calculated in the Appendices. Your accounting system will help with this and, if you are unsure, your accountant can check everything is in order.

The IRD sets the date to pay your GST based, typically, on the GST from the previous two months. Sometimes it may be from earlier months. For example, the GST from October and November must be paid by early January.

The gap between when you calculate your GST and the date when you need to pay it can cause real cash flow issues, especially if you haven't set the money aside. In the example of the January payment, this may be your quietest month of the year, so you may have no cash available. However, October and November, which are Spring months, and leading into Christmas, could be your highest earning months and therefore the months generating you largest GST bill.

> Some businesses set up a separate bank account and set aside at least 15% of their sales each month to ensure they don't spend their GST. The money is there at tax-time.

If the IRD is paying your business back GST regularly, which often happens in the early stages of a business' life, it's pretty obvious that it's a situation that can't last. This means the business is spending more than it is making.

## Provisional tax

Income tax and provisional tax are the same thing. For your company, it's the tax you pay on the profits you've made each year. Instead of paying this tax based on a calculation of your profits during the year, or in one lump sum at the end of the year, it's usually paid in instalments over the year.

You or your accountant can estimate these instalments.

Typically, the way you have to calculate this is to take your taxable income from the previous year, add 5% and then divide it by the number of instalments. There are different methods to calculate and pay your provisional tax. Talk to your accountant.

Therefore, not only do the IRD assume the year you are in will be as good as the previous year, but they also want you to assume it will be **5% better**. You might well be in a growth cycle, where this is a fair assumption. However, you could also be having a terrible year compared to the previous year but are being forced to pay even more tax.

Sadly, the tax system is in the IRD's favour, not yours. The only upside is if you end up paying too much, you will get a refund. Cold comfort if the tax you paid through the year prevented your business from spending that money on something else.

While a little unfair, it is still important you pay the instalments and avoid paying too little. If you underpay, you could get a more serious shock at the end of the year when the IRD hits you with a more significant tax bill than you expected. This may well be when you don't have the cash available. This is where you really need your accountant working for you – you don't want any big tax surprises.

## Terminal tax

If you paid too much provisional tax through the year, you will get a refund. However, if you did not pay enough in your provisional tax instalments, what's left to be paid at the end of the year is called **terminal tax.** This is normally due in February following the end of the tax year (or you might get more time if your accountant organises payment).

## Resident Withholding Tax (RWT)

If you earn interest on the money in your bank accounts, the bank must withhold the tax on this interest. This is called **Resident Withholding Tax (RWT).** The bank must then pay the IRD directly on your behalf before they pay you the interest.

This works a lot like your PAYE.

With PAYE, when the company pays an employee's wage into their bank account, the company has already taken out the tax they owe, withheld it from the employee, and paid it directly to the IRD. Therefore, the employee doesn't have to worry about it. The same happens with income from investments. It is "*withheld*" before going to the IRD.

## Fringe Benefit Tax (FBT)

This is one form of taxation you should not have to pay if you are managing things within the business. It most commonly becomes an issue if you offer yourself or staff benefits beyond their normal pay. A very common situation is using work vehicles for personal use.

The other is if you take more money out of the business than the business owes you. This is called an **overdrawn shareholder current account.** The IRD sees this as an interest free loan to you and, therefore, a benefit the company is offering you that needs to be taxed.

## Personal tax

As a sole trader, you will combine your business and personal activities together, and the IRD will calculate your tax as if you are one entity.

If you are a shareholder in a company, you may pay yourself drawings, dividends and possibly a **shareholder's salary** that the accountant will calculate at year's end.

We discussed the importance of keeping your business and personal spending separate. This also applies to tax.

Tax returns will be required for your business and for you personally as a shareholder. Your accountant will establish the company's profit and then decide how much of that to distribute to you. This is the minimise the tax both you and the company pay.

You may also have been paying yourself a wage or salary as a PAYE employee, which will combine to determine your total income and, therefore, your total personal tax.

## Dividends, Dividend Withholding Tax (DWT) and imputation credits.

If there are profits left after your accountant has calculated your tax, as the shareholder, you may decide to pay yourself extra. These are **dividends**. If there are multiple shareholders, you will need to share the dividend in proportion to the percentage of shares owned by each person.

You might decide to leave the money in the business for future growth. These are **retained earnings.** Retained earnings are recorded as equity in your balance sheet in the end-of-year financial accounts.

If you pay yourself dividends, you will take the money out AFTER you paid the company tax at 28%. When you receive dividends, you should not pay that tax again. What you should pay in tax is the difference between your personal tax rate and the 28%. The IRD sets a tax rate of 33% for anyone receiving dividends, so what you owe in tax is 33% less the 28%, **or 5%.**

When you transfer the dividend from the company to you, just like PAYE and RWT, you must withhold that 5% tax and pay this directly to the IRD. This is called **dividend withholding tax** (DWT).

After deducting company tax, you don't want to pay additional tax on the dividends you have received. Your accountant will keep track of the money that has already been taxed at 28%, so if you receive dividends, you won't have to pay tax again. These are the **imputation credits.** Your accountant will record these in an **imputation credit account** in your financial accounts. This needs to be kept because these credits could have occurred from dividends you received many years ago.

Even though your dividends have been taxed at 28%, your personal tax rate will differ from this.

When your accountant does your company's tax return, they will also need to do your personal tax return. They will include all your sources of income, including the dividends, to decide if you have paid too little tax or if you will get a refund.

As mentioned, this is a really confusing and messy process, and one best left to your accountant. However, a basic understanding is still important.

## *Shareholder salary and the shareholder current account*

When your accountant completes your tax accounts at the end of the financial year, they will look at how best to minimise the tax you will pay.

If the company has achieved a healthy pre-tax profit, the accountant may allocate this to you as a shareholder's salary. They will add this into your company's expenses, which reduces the profit the company will pay. You will then have to record this shareholder salary as a personal income. The accountant will only do this if your personal tax rate is less than the company tax rate.

If there is no cash in the company's bank account to cover your shareholder's salary and dividends, then the company owes you money. This is all recorded in your **shareholder current account**.

The shareholder current account is a record of what the company owes a shareholder. If there is more than one shareholder, each shareholder will have a separate shareholder current account. If it is your shareholder current account it's a record of your money, not the company's money.

If you take money out of the business as drawings, you are taking it from the shareholder current account, as it is your money to take. If you take more out than your company owes you, this results in an **overdrawn shareholder current account**. This is like your company offering you an interest free loan. You will need to pay Fringe Benefit Tax on this so you should avoid overdrawing the shareholder current account.

Small business owners who don't keep track of the drawings they are taking from the business can end up with an overdrawn current account without even knowing it.

# When you don't pay the IRD — penalties and interest

The IRD will charge you extra if you are late filing your tax returns. They will also charge you interest if you have not paid all the tax you owe.[5] The penalties you will pay for filing late and the interest on late payments vary for the different taxes. While the IRD explains all the background behind interest and penalty payments, I would not devote time to understanding what these are. Use that time to make sure you know what you owe, when it is due, and ensure you pay it so you avoid any penalties.

If you are struggling to pay the tax you owe, talk to your accountant about options, or talk directly to the IRD. There are payment plans you can pursue.

If you are facing interest and penalties, it means you owe the IRD money. This means you are simply adding more pressure on yourself, as the tax bill will quickly get worse.

You may qualify for a late payment grace period if you've paid all your taxes on time for the previous few years. The IRD are also more accommodating if you have made a mistake, and you own up before they find it.

If you know your returns or payments will be late, contact the IRD before the due date. They may work with you to reduce the penalties.

If the IRD agrees you can pay off the tax you owe in installments, you need to deliver on what you agreed. The IRD won't be so accommodating if you do not meet these installments.

# "Cashies" and dodging your taxes

There is a good old Kiwi tradition of doing a job for a mate, getting paid in cash, and putting those dollars in your back pocket. Our mate gets their job done, we get paid, we don't have to bother with taxes, so all is good. This is the good-old "cashie".

*"It's only illegal if you get caught."* - **Unknown**

Many small businesspeople have asked me if this is OK, as if they are seeking justification for what they know is wrong. Many seem shocked when I say that it's very simple. Cashies are tax fraud.

While none of us have too much sympathy for the IRD, they are collecting taxes for all of us, so you are not just stealing from the IRD. You are stealing from other Kiwi taxpayers.

If you use your business' money for personal reasons and claim it as a business expense, you are committing fraud. If you take cash on a sale and put it in your pocket rather than through your business, you are committing fraud.

☞    Justify it any way you want but fraud is fraud

Cashies are part of the hidden economy in New Zealand, which costs all of us millions, possibly billions, every year. The IRD are not mugs. They know it is happening and they are looking out for it.

While the IRD are always on the lookout, it may be a tipoff that catches you out. A competitor, an observer, or even the person you did the cashie for may report you to the IRD.

> *"Each year across all sectors, we get nearly 7,000 anonymous tip-offs about cash jobs. That shows a level of concern by New Zealanders and their belief that paying the correct amount of tax is the right thing to do."* **Richard Philp**, Inland Revenue spokesperson. [6]

Sadly, I am confident that many small business will believe I am over-reacting and will continue doing this, and there is every chance no one will be the wiser.

However, it is very simple. If you do this deliberately you do it at your peril. If someone decides to report you or you get caught and prosecuted by the IRD, no one will have any sympathy.

> Let's stop the crazy desire to achieve a petty, short-term gain by avoiding paying tax and focus on running a good business - and paying the tax you owe.

Not only is it illegal, but unrecorded cash work will also affect you in other ways. It is income that is not recorded, so the bank won't see it if you want to get a loan. If you decide to sell your business, this cash will not appear in your financial statements and will reduce the true value of your business.

## Those who tried to cheat the IRD - and lost

There are far too many stories of businesses, or individuals, who tried to avoid paying their taxes, and the IRD pursued them. All the following examples show people who deliberately did not pay the IRD what they owed. The IRD warned these offenders before they stepped in. If you make mistakes, even if you are late and can't pay, you are likely to get support from the IRD, as long as you are honest and upfront. If you ignore the problem or, worse still, try to deceive the IRD, they will pursue you, and the punishments are severe.

These are a small sample of court cases listed on the IRD website. [7]

- Elizabeth Julian Tangikau, a mother of six, was sentenced to two years and three months' jail in 2024. Tangikau ran a café in Highbrook, Auckland. Over the course of six years, she evaded her income tax and GST obligations by filing 75 false tax returns that significantly understated her business income and claimed excessive expenditure. Tangikau also misappropriated payroll taxes (PAYE).. Rather than paying the IRD the PAYE she deducted from her employees, she kept the amounts for herself. The IRD tried repeatedly to help Tangikau, ensuring she had access to the resources to comply with her obligations. She did not.

- Scott McCormick of Christchurch imported alcohol drinks to the New Zealand hospitality industry. Analysis of his businesses bank accounts showed no evidence of income from sales and no evidence of business expenditure in the account. It was all cash withdrawals, transfers or payments to himself, his family members, or associated entities. McCormick prepared and filed 49 false GST returns, hiding what he was earning. He received an 11-month jail term.

- Christopher David Win, a Christchurch builder, was sentenced to 12 months home detention for evading GST and income tax plus making PAYE deductions for staff but not paying them to the IRD. He employed eight workers and deducted PAYE from their wages and filed PAYE returns, but he didn't pay the deducted amounts to the IRD. Both the IRD and his accountant contacted him, reminding him of his obligations. When he failed to act, the IRD took legal action.

- Mohammed Naseeb and Rehana Ali were sentenced to three years' jail in July 2024. These were for multiple charges, including personal income tax and GST evasion, and failures to account for PAYE for their housing construction company *Supreme Constructions Civil and Drainage Works Ltd*. The offending occurred over a six-year period between 2010 and 2015 and amounted to $800,000. The judge described it as very deliberate offending where income was under-reported through filing false tax returns.

- A Papatoetoe painter, Ke Kia Lam of *Paintplas Ltd* was sentenced to six months community detention and ordered to pay $150,000 for tax evasion. In 2017 and 2019, Lam filed false personal tax returns, which didn't include his self-employed income.

- A South Auckland man, Samuel Aki, was sentenced to home detention after taking money meant to help businesses suffering during the COVID pandemic. Between May 2020 and May 2022, he dishonestly applied for six Small Business Cash Flow loans, four Resurgence Support Payments and two Small Business Cash Flow top-ups when he knew he wasn't entitled to any of them.

- Hugh James Bevan Lloyd was sentenced to 6 months' home detention and was banned from being the director of a company for 5 years. He was charged with aiding *Scanlan IT Staff Ltd* to take PAYE and other deductions from their employee wages, but not paying those deductions to the IRD.

...and there are many, many more examples.

# The cash of last resort and the tax spiral

Often, taxation does not have to be paid immediately. When the cash gets really tight, you may be tempted to prioritise your spending on what is most immediate, and use the money set aside for tax. This might include paying the wages bill, paying the bank the principal on loans, and paying your most important suppliers. If the GST or your next provisional tax payment isn't due for some time, you may use the available cash to deal with these more pressing issues.

When the tax falls due, the cash may not be available, and you still have payroll due, banks to pay and suppliers to pay – and you still need to pay yourself something to live.

If you can't get on a payment plan with overdue tax quickly, it will trigger penalties and interest, further increasing the tax bill.

Therefore, the cash problem could escalate quickly.

> If you fail to pay your tax on time, you will incur interest and penalties. This will compound the problem. It will add to other cash pressures which, if not managed, could spiral out of control.

I will discuss techniques to manage your cash flow in later chapters.

# Dealing with end-of-year (EOY) accounts

No small business owner, except perhaps a small business tax accountant, got into business to complete their annual tax returns. Usually, by the time you receive your completed EOY accounts, the events occurred so far ago they have no practical benefit to the business. However, you need them to determine the tax you owe or that the IRD owes you.

Banks will need a completed set of accounts if you want to borrow from them. These accounts are also necessary should you want to get a valuation of your business done, to finalise dividends, and, if you are a charity, to meet the Charities Commission's auditing requirements.

The best way to make this process as painless as possible is to keep really good records throughout the year. If you don't keep good records, you will face a far more painful and expensive time at EOY. It's also not good for decision making as the year progresses if the information in your financial system lacks accuracy and detail.

The best way to achieve this is to use your financial management system well and remain disciplined throughout the year. This will include:

- Code your expenses correctly.

- Keep your reconciliations up to date

- Attach invoices, statements and receipts to each transaction in your accounting system as you reconcile through the year.

- Chase what others owe you (a topic I have covered already and we will discuss at length in the chapters on cash flow).

- Keep good track of your stock. If your system does not allow active tracking of your stock, do more regular stocktakes with a thorough stocktake at the EOY.

- Talk to your accountant early. EOY is their busiest time, and you need to get in early.

# Paying taxes means you're making money

None of us like paying tax. Some businesses, perversely, feel satisfied if they don't have to pay much tax. All this means is they made little or no profit.

If you are paying lots of tax, then your business is making a healthy profit. Therefore, your goal should be to pay as much tax as you can. Clearly, you do not want to pay a single cent more than you are legally required to pay – the reason a good tax accountant is so important. What is most critical is that you ensure the cash is available when the tax falls due.

You also need your accountant to ensure there are no surprises about what tax you owe. If you have had a bumper result a year or two go, you may get a horrible surprise that you owe more provisional or terminal tax this year when you may be quieter and short of cash.

# ...and it's not your money anyway

Whether we like it or not we are the short-term custodians of the IRD's money.

When you pay your staff, you must take the PAYE from their wages and pass it on to the IRD. That money does not belong to you or your business.

When you sell your products or services, 15% of that money, the GST, is the IRD's. This will be offset by the 15% GST on the goods and services you must buy to run your businesses. The difference is simply the money you hang on to for a short period before handing it over to its rightful owner - the IRD.

Hopefully after all this you make a profit. 28% of that profit is not yours either and, at some point, the IRD will be after it as provisional tax. So, you also need to set that money aside.

# It's simple, really — it's just not easy

It would seem immensely obvious and an extremely simple concept to grasp - you must pay tax.

The tax system is immensely complex, and the IRD are not always the most pleasant bunch to deal with. However, there are many people who spend their careers helping people get it right - most often accountants - so there is little sympathy out there for those of us who get it wrong.

Why, then, is failing to pay taxes so common?

Is it laziness, is it poor organisation, denial, that we make mistakes or is it cash difficulties?

We know we must do it. We know what happens if we don't, but too many of us don't do it or can't do it and end up in real trouble.

# CHAPTER 23

# CASH IS NOT JUST KING — IT MIGHT BE THE ONLY THING

The quote *"Winning is not everything–it is the only thing"* has been used by many people in professional sports. **Red Sanders**, who had one of the most successful records as a US College Football coach, first used the phrase in the 1930s.

While there are so many things you need to consider to succeed at small business, or simply survive, it is the management of cash that will see a business thrive or collapse - and the distance between success and failure can be small.

It is very common for business owners to look at the profit and loss statement, look at retained earnings and the shareholder's current account, and see healthy numbers. However, when you look at the money in the bank, there is nothing there, which poses the often asked question, *"Where did the money go?"*

What this shows is the significant difference at any point in time between cash and profit. In the end, the cash is what will make or break you. Understanding the difference is really important.

# Where does the cash go in your small business?

Let's follow the flow of cash as it comes into your business and track it until we find what is left in your bank account at the end of a month's trading. Remember, this is your business' bank account, not your personal bank account.

The journey of each dollar is illustrated in the drawing below

While these concepts are very similar to the profit and loss statement, there are important differences that I will go through now.

## *The cash coming into the business - Sales*

Firstly, your cash will come into the business in different ways. A retail shop will get the vast majority via an EFTPOS machine directly into their bank account, which typically appears at the end of each day. This is the best method of getting cash into a business.

It may also arrive as physical cash. While less common these days, plenty of people still want to pay this way. While many people think businesses should be happy to see cash, it is a lot of work. You do need to put it through your business – we discussed the dangers of *"cashies"* in the chapter on tax. Customers may think we'll pocket the cash and give them a discount – don't do it. You must also track this cash, so the numbers add up. You need to get the cash to a bank to deposit it. There is also the fear that having cash sitting in the business leaves you open to theft. Basically, EFTPOS facilities are far more appealing so where you can avoid physical cash.

Many small businesses will not receive cash when they complete a sale. They will invoice their customers and receive the cash some time later. Therefore, the cash arriving this month will be the cash the business earned from previous month's sales.

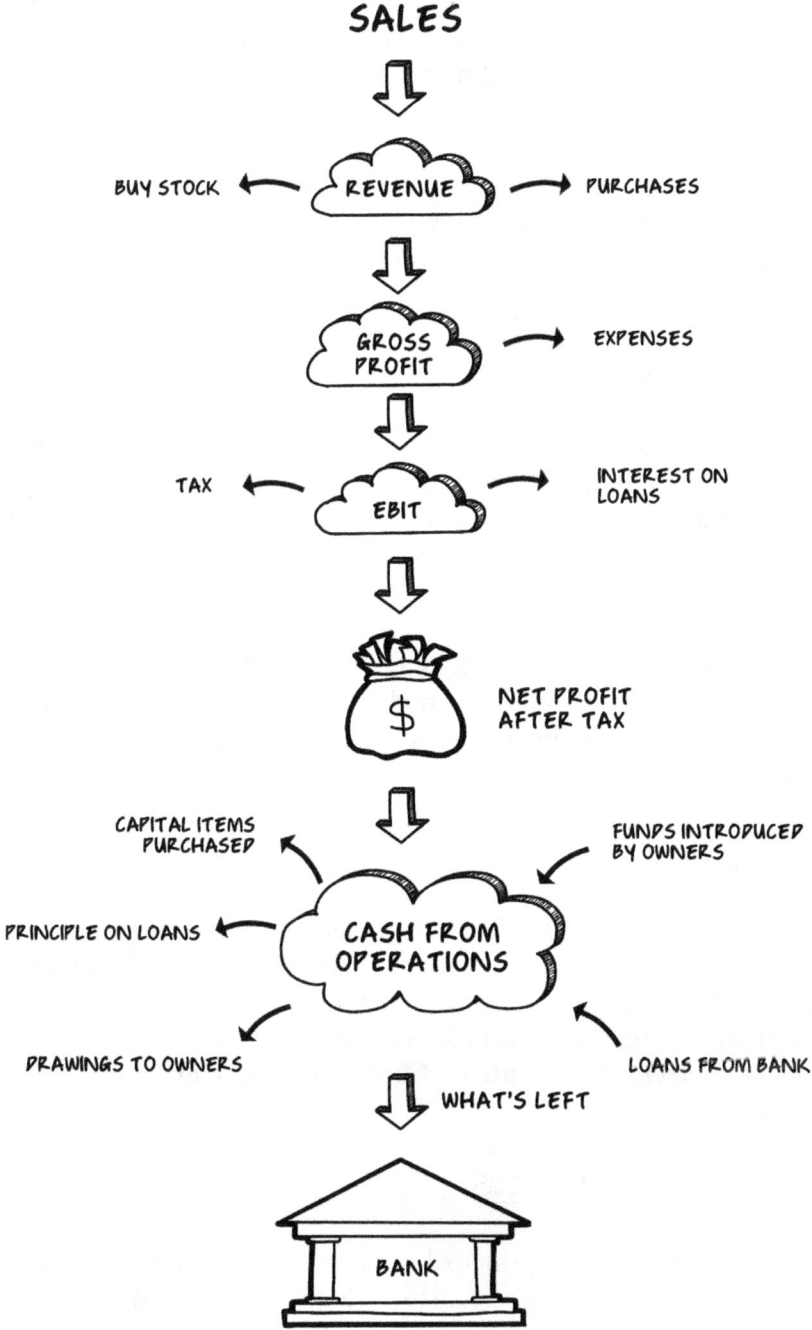

**SALES**

⬇

BUY STOCK ← **REVENUE** → PURCHASES

⬇

**GROSS PROFIT** → EXPENSES

⬇

TAX ← **EBIT** → INTEREST ON LOANS

⬇

$ **NET PROFIT AFTER TAX**

⬇

CAPITAL ITEMS PURCHASED ↖        FUNDS INTRODUCED BY OWNERS ↙

PRINCIPLE ON LOANS ← **CASH FROM OPERATIONS**

DRAWINGS TO OWNERS ↙        LOANS FROM BANK ↗

⬇ WHAT'S LEFT

**BANK**

## Purchasing goods and inventory

The purchase of goods to support the sales will come from suppliers and will typically be paid as per their payment terms, typically on the 20$^{th}$ of the following month. The money you are paying this month is likely to be for goods you received last month.

If you are buying these goods to build up stock, you would code these into your balance sheet. They won't appear in your profit and loss statement, but the cash will leave the business. So the profit may look good, but the cash will be disappearing in the inventory sitting in your warehouse.

## Wages and salaries

Wages and salaries are normally the biggest cost for your small business, even if you only have a few staff. This goes out weekly, two weekly or monthly, depending on when you pay staff. If you are a service-based business, paying wages and salaries will be the most significant cash flow out of the business.

The amount going out in wages and salaries may vary in some of the longer months of the year. For example, if you pay every two weeks, there are usually a couple of months where you have to pay staff three times in the one month.

## Expenses

Your expenses are your fixed costs, and you will need to pay them no matter what your sales are like. Some will come out routinely each month, like rent. Other expenses will vary each month, like electricity and gas. Others may be larger one offs in the same month each your, like insurance, accountants fees, or **Accident Compensation Corporation** (ACC) payments.

## Loan repayments

Any repayment of the principal on loans will not appear in the profit and loss statement. The interest on those loans will be in your expenses in the profit and loss statement, but not the principal on the loan. This is a balance sheet item. Typically, repayments are monthly.

## Assets that you can't expense

You can expense any asset you buy that costs less than $1000, like tools. However, assets more than $1000 are capital, and you need to add these to your balance sheet and then depreciate them. Therefore, they won't appear on in the profit and loss statement. Keep in mind that the IRD sets this $1000 amount, and it has changed over the years.

## Money to and from shareholders

If you take any money out of the business as drawings, for personal reasons, it will not appear in the profit and loss statement. Likewise, if you provide money to the business from your personal funds, this will increase the business' bank account, drain your own bank account, but it won't appear in the profit and loss.

## Goods and Services Tax (GST)

When you work your way down the cash flow cycle, the cash coming into the bank account will include GST. The money going out will also include GST. The difference between the GST on your sales, (which is what you owe to the IRD) and the GST on all your purchases and expenses, (which is the GST the IRD owes you) will be what you have to set aside when the GST is due.

The profit and loss statement may be reported including GST or could be recorded excluding GST.

## Provisional and terminal taxes

Provisional tax is an estimate of what tax you will pay this year, but is calculated based on last year's results. This can be a real cash flow challenge as the current year could be going very differently than previous years.

Provisional tax can catch out a startup business after its first year. If you make a net profit in your first year, you'll need to pay tax on this.

Making regular voluntary payments or putting money aside during your first year can ease your cash flow for your second year. Sadly, many start-up businesses are too busy reinvesting the money they are making in their first year to keep it aside for tax.

As provisional tax is a best guess, so you may pay more or less tax than you should have through the year. This is what **terminal tax** is about. It makes up for any shortfalls. You need to pay this once a year, and its timing could be distant from the year it relates to.

If you have over-estimated your provisional tax, you will be taking too much cash out of your business. This could put undue pressure on your cash reserves through the year. This may mean you are unable to commit to business initiatives you would have pursued if the cash was available. It's nice getting a tax refund at the end of the year that you weren't expecting but it may be too late.

All this uncertainty and variability makes provisional and terminal tax a significant cash challenge for a small business.

## Shareholder current account — "so where's my money?"

In the chapter on tax, we discussed how your accountant may allocate you a shareholder's salary to manage the tax you and your company pay. You may also have paid yourself a dividend.

After you calculated the tax you owe and you paid yourself a dividend, the money remaining is your **retained earnings.**

It would be nice to see the cash associated with your shareholder salary and your dividends arrive in your personal bank account. It would also be great to see the cash associated with the retained earnings sitting in the company's bank account to kick off the next financial year.

Sadly, you may have no cash in your business' bank account to pay for this. You may even have a large overdraft.

**So where did this cash go?**

You have likely already spent this cash long ago on drawings for yourself, paying off company debts, buying plant or equipment and increasing stock that you haven't yet sold. This is the spending that is recorded AFTER your Net Profit After Tax in the profit and loss statement. So you may have achieved a healthy profit, but there is no cash to show for it.

If there is no cash in the bank account to cover your shareholder's salary and dividends then the company owes you money. This is all recorded in your shareholder current account.

The shareholder current account is a record of what the company owes a shareholder. If there is more than one shareholder, each will have a shareholder current account.

If you transfer money into the company from your personal funds to help the business, this is called **funds introduced**. It will be added to the shareholder current account. You should hope to be paid back at some stage.

If you take money out of the business as drawings, you are taking it from the shareholder current account, as it is your money to take.

As the shareholder current account represents money owed by the company to someone else, in this case you, as a shareholder, you would code this as a liability on the balance sheet.

What happens if you take out too much money from the shareholder current account and this account goes negative? This is called an **overdrawn shareholder current account** and creates several problems for you and your company.

- It is an interest free loan from the company to the shareholder, which is considered a fringe benefit. You will have to pay Fringe Benefit Tax (FBT).

- If you have drained the shareholder current account, it's a pretty good sign you are taking more money out of the business than it can afford. This could start compromising the running of your business.

- If you don't have the cash to run your business because you've taken too much out for personal use, you will need to pay it back. If you don't have the money, you may then have to use your overdraft to run the business, which is at high interest rates.

- The worst-case is if your company gets into financial distress and the company owes creditors, like the IRD, money. If these creditors force you into liquidation, the liquidator will chase you to pay back the money owed to the shareholder current account. If you don't have it, they could bankrupt you and seize your personal assets.

If your shareholder current account is overdrawn, it means you, the shareholder, owe your company money. This means the shareholder current account will switch from a liability to an asset in your balance sheet.

# The difference between profit and cash — let's summarise

If you are struggling to get your head around the difference between cash and profit, let's summarise. What could be contributing to the big difference between cash and profit?

Here are a few major factors to look at.

- You record a sale in your profit and loss statement when you send an invoice to a customer. However, you may not get paid for several weeks. Therefore, you record the invoices in the profit and loss statement, but the cash may not arrive in the bank for some time.

- You record costs when you receive an invoice from a supplier. You may not pay suppliers for some time.

- You will pay GST in instalments, typically every two months. You pay the GST after the sale or the purchase occurred. Therefore, it will be at least two months later.

- You will pay your provisional tax in instalments throughout the year. It is an estimate, so may not reflect exactly what you should pay, as it is based on prior years' performance. If it is wrong, you pay terminal tax to make up the difference. These all happen well after you made the profit.

- The principle you pay on loans comes from cash in the bank account, but you won't record this is in the profit and loss statement. If you are carrying a lot of debt, you could be making a healthy profit, but it will be disappearing in debt repayments.

- If you buy assets of more than $1000, the money will leave the bank account but does now appear in the profit and loss statement.

- If you take money out for personal use, you will record it as drawings. Therefore, you will not record this in your profit and loss statement, but it will reduce your cash.

- Construction and building companies may be paid on milestones on large projects, but have money withheld until everything is completed. These are known as **retentions**. The construction or building company may not receive this money for some time, but will have incurred the costs.

- Your work-in-progress (WIP) may not be correct. You may have spent far more than you have recorded and your cash may be worse than you thought.

# Chase every dollar

Let's discuss a few very important considerations to give you the best chance of getting every dollar owed to you.

## *Include your payment terms with every transaction*

You need to develop a document that outlines your **terms of trade.**

If you offer credit, avoid providing that customer anything until they have agreed to the terms of trade and signed them.

Include some of the key terms from your terms of trade on each invoice. These could include your payment terms.

If your customer pays by EFTPOS or with cash, you will not normally need the terms of trade. However, there may be other terms that apply in this case. These could include whether you will charge fees if a customer uses **PayWave**, or if you have return policies. Make sure you display these where the payment is going to happen, so there is no debate later.

Typically, your payment terms might include the following.

- Within how many days you require payment after the customer receives your invoice?

- What penalty charges will you impose if they are late?

- What checks do you intend carrying out before offering them credit (For example, calling their suppliers)?

- What might you do if they refuse to pay (for example, use debt collection and charge them)?

You may feel uncomfortable asking customers to sign such a document. Most times, you won't need to enforce it. However, most people in business are very aware of the issues around being paid and your request won't surprise them. Most expect it and will like the certainty it brings.

If a customer refuses to sign your terms of trade, you need to ask why. You may keep them as a customer, but you should not offer them credit terms. They would need to pay before you sell them anything or do work for them.

If you are unsure what to include in such a document, there are templates available online. Otherwise seek help from an experienced person (such as debt collection business or a lawyer) to draw up your payment terms. You will only need to do this once, as you can use them for every transaction thereafter.

## Chase the people who owe you money

It is critically important you put a process in place that allows you to record exactly when money is due. All accounting systems will have **accounts receivable** and **accounts payable** reports. Keep a continual eye on these reports.

> Make sure your accounts receivable and accounts payable are accurate and monitor them regularly.

Develop a process you will follow every month to ensure you are paid every dollar owed to you. Consider using the following steps:

1. Send a polite email the day after the payment is due as a reminder. This process is normally automated in most accounting systems and it may send out multiple reminders before what is owed is paid.

2. If you hear nothing within several days, call them. Most customers will have a legitimate reason and will usually chase it.

3. As the days pass, if no payment occurs, increase the communication and strengthen the tone of the correspondence.

4. It is often beneficial to get your bookkeeper to do the initial approaches. If they can't make progress, they can then escalate to you.

5. If the customer is struggling to pay, discuss payment plans as some money is better than nothing. If the customer agrees to a payment plan, make sure they adhere to it.

6.   If the customer refuses to pay or after an extended period, you have heard nothing, you can engage a debt collector who will also post the business' name on credit watch sites. Keep in mind, if the amounts owed are small, a debt collector may not be interested.

If a customer has been a good payer, but strikes cash flow issues, you might work on more flexible repayment processes. Whatever the circumstances, stay on top of this. If you have good payment terms and the situation deteriorates, you will be in a much better position to take more formal action to get your money.

You may really hate the processes of chasing bad payers. Don't worry, most people hate it. Just remember, it is your money, and your business needs it to survive and thrive.

## The risks of using your suppliers to manage cash flow

A strategy that some businesses will use to manage cash shortfalls is to delay paying suppliers as long as possible. These suppliers are unlikely to charge interest, and if your business were to fail, they are unsecured creditors, so would be unlikely to get their money.

If you use an overdraft or secured funding to manage cash shortfalls, you will face higher interest rates and they may involve a security or personal guarantee which places more risk on the business.

Some large organisations may place extended payment terms on smaller business. **Fonterra** was such an example requiring 60-day payment terms. Small business, desperate for Fonterra's business, took the risk. Fonterra came under significant public and political pressure and changed this to a more standard 20th of the month terms, but only for small businesses.[1]

Other large businesses will ask for 60-day payment terms or charge, a fee (2.5% in the case of a large New Zealand electrical wholesaler), if you want 20th of the month terms.

> *"If I'm struggling, my suppliers need to play their part."* **An anonymous business owner.**

The owner of a medium-sized building business with many subcontractors used the strategy of paying suppliers late as a normal course of business. It was the view of this particular business owner that he was offering these subcontractors a continued flow of work and they needed to play their part in helping him manage cash flow. He did this rather than using bank cash facilities.

While this is a strategy used by some businesses, it comes with its own risks.

Diligent creditors will be chasing their money and will only tolerate late payment for so long. They are likely to be far less patient if there is no communication with creditors who are late to pay.

Larger suppliers will eventually put credit stops on poor payers.

Word will get out there about who are and aren't the good payers. The list of people you can use to give credit checks for when you open new accounts will decrease.

If a creditor has personal guarantees or a security in place, they could enforce these through their lawyers, if they have made reasonable steps to get payment from you.

I've already discussed the risks of delaying payments to the IRD to manage cash flow.

All creditors have different appetites for late payments by their debtors. At one extreme, suppliers may be patient, especially if you work with them and have had a good relationship with them. At the other extreme are suppliers who will have no hesitation in acting swiftly and forcefully, especially those who have been burnt by bad payers in the past.

At a moral level, large businesses can destroy small businesses if they refuse to pay on time.

This strategy can also be extremely stressful for those in your team who have to manage it. Businesses who have not been paid can and should be persistent in their pursuit of payments. The longer this drags on, the more aggressive they will become. It may be your bookkeeper or accounts person who will face this aggression, not you.

I have never supported this strategy to manage cash flow.

If you can pay your suppliers, do so on the date they are due to be paid. If you are in genuine difficulty, talk to them early and set up a payment scheme.

> Using suppliers as a way to manage your cash flow comes with its own significant risks. It is not a sound strategy.

# A few other ideas to manage cash

These are a few additional tips that may help ensure you get paid:

- Look at how you could get paid in part or in full before doing any work. This could include a 50% deposit to fund any materials you have to buy for a job.

- Reduce your payment terms so customers pay you weekly rather than monthly.

- Don't be afraid to check a company's creditworthiness, especially if the job involves sizable sums, or they are strangers to you. Debt collection businesses can provide these services at a small cost.

- If you have any unease about a business, only allow them to pay on same-day terms, by credit card or a bank transfer, and before you provide the customer with the product or service.

- Check if your bank has more automated and mobile ways to pay. EFTPOS machines are the most common, but other cheaper tools exist.

- Talk to the bank about ways to restructure your loans to see if better interest rates are possible, if you can go onto interest only arrangements, or extend the repayment term to reduce the monthly loan repayment amounts.

- Free up cash from existing assets by refinancing them.

- If you have a fleet of vehicles, fleet leasing businesses may purchase some (or all) of your vehicles and lease them back to you. This injects cash and takes the pressure off the management of your vehicles.

- Sell slow moving inventory. If you do this as a special offer with associated marketing, it may also create more interest in the business.

- Sell plant and equipment that is not being utilised any more. You may not get what you want for it, but if cash is tight it is better that cash is sitting in your bank account than in equipment that is not working for your business.

# The risk of using your cash to buy plant and equipment

If you need to buy larger assets, you may be tempted to dip into your bank account to pay for them. Asking the bank for funds takes time. They will want a security over the asset, and possibly the business as well, and you will pay interest on the loan. It would seem simpler just to spend your own money, if the bank account can cope with it.

The danger with this is that taking a sizeable sum of money out of your bank account may cause a much bigger hole in your cash in later weeks than you might think.

The variability of your cash flow, especially if you don't have accurate cash flow forecasts (and don't worry, few businesses do), could mean that at the time of deciding to use your own cash, things may look healthy. But a few unexpected costs later, a GST bill, and a slower month could see things worsen quickly.

Keep in mind that every dollar you spend out of the bank account has fallen out at the bottom of your cash flow. Consider our discussion on breakeven and %Gross Profit in earlier chapters. To deliver that dollar at the bottom of the profit and loss could require you to make four or five dollars in sales, depending on your % Gross Profit.

## *Let's do an example – buying a vehicle with your own cash*

Let's use an example to show you how hard it is to pull back a big cash outlay.

|   | | |
|---|---|---|
|   | REVENUE | $15,000 |
| − | COST OF SALES | $11,250 |
| = | GROSS PROFIT | $3,750 |
| − | EXPENSES | $1,000 |
| = | PROFIT BEFORE TAX | $2,750 |
| − | TAX | $825 |
| = | NPAT | $1,925 |
| − | DRAWINGS | $550 |
| − | LOAN REPAYMENTS | $500 |
| − | ASSET PURCHASES | $0 |
| = | "WHAT'S LEFT" | $875 |

We'll use the breakeven scenario from the past chapters. I will assume the business is performing better than breakeven, leaving $875 at the end of each month.

We discussed **working capital** in earlier chapters. This is the money you want on hand every month to pay the bills. It will go up and down from month-to-month. However, ideally, you want enough working capital to cover, say, two months of the cash that is leaving the business.

In our example, this will be:

WORKING CAPITAL = 2 X (EXPENSES + DRAWINGS + LOAN REPAYMENTS)

= 2 X ($1,000 + $550 + $500)

= $4,100

Let's say you have $30,000 in the bank. You are in good shape because this is well above your working capital target of $4,100.

You need to buy a new vehicle for $25,000. This will leave you with $5,000 in the bank.

The bank is charging high interest rates and requires repayments over five years, equating to $550/month. This means you would end up paying about $40,000 for the vehicle if you borrowed the money. You hate borrowing money as the bank has you on the hook. You'll also pay a lot more for the vehicle in the long run.

The bank also wants a security over both the vehicle and the business.

***Therefore, you decide to use the cash in the bank to buy the vehicle.***

***Was this the correct decision?***

Your financials show that, while you are making a pre-tax profit every month of $2,750, only $875 cash is falling out of the bottom of your business each month. Assuming you can sustain this sales target, it will take you nearly three years to get back to where you were before buying the vehicle ($30,000/$875 = 35 months).

The other problem is you now have very little money in the bank account for anything else. While what is left after buying the vehicle, namely $5000, meets your working capital target of $4,100, you have very little room for errors.

If you have any bad months directly after purchasing the vehicle, it may cause your bank account to go into overdraft. You only need to be hit with other unexpected expenses, customers who don't pay on time, your GST or other tax falls due, and you are in a bigger hole. Not only is the interest rate very high for your overdraft, it could take many weeks to get the bank's approval if you don't have an overdraft in place or you look like hitting your overdraft limit.

If you can't get the overdraft, you may have to put more of your own funds in the business, stop paying yourself the $550 drawings per month, or delay paying suppliers.

Suddenly you went from a very comfortable situation, with a business that was exceeding breakeven, had lots of working capital, was profitable, with a good %GP. You are now in a more stressful situation you can't control, and it could take many months to recover.

If you had taken out the loan, yes, the bank has a security over the vehicle, and possibly the business, and you'll also pay a lot more in the long run. However, you would still have had a healthy amount of working capital, you could have covered the repayments, and still be above breakeven, if only slightly.

> Don't be afraid to use debt, especially on assets, if you can meet the repayments. Using working capital to buy assets could leave you without cash to run the business.

# Cash flow forecasting - it's not simple but is very powerful

If you are always battling to keep on top of cash flow, consider developing a cash flow forecast.

This differs from the budget I talked about in other chapters because a cash flow forecast focuses entirely on the money coming in and out of the bank. This includes all the cash items on the profit and loss statement, like sales, purchases, and expenses. It also includes all the cash movements that do not appear on the profit and loss, like loans, drawings, GST, provisional and terminal taxes.

Budgeting usually ignores GST payments. Estimating what the GST will be and when it needs to be paid is a critical part of cash flow forecasting. This is one of the more difficult aspects of developing an accurate cash flow forecast and makes a cash flow forecast more complicated.

> Calculating your GST and when you pay it is a difficult aspect of cash flow forecasting but is important to the accuracy of the forecast.

Another key aspect of an accurate cash flow forecast is the timing. To create a good cash flow forecast, you need to consider when the money is coming in and out of the bank account – and this could vary significantly.

As a result, the cash flow forecast is far more complicated to develop than a typical budget based on a profit and loss, but it is an immensely powerful tool.

A spreadsheet is the best tool to use. The best place to start is to take the cash flow report from your accounting software for the previous year.

If you can't get this from your accounting software, the next best thing is the profit and loss from the previous year. To be of any use, the cash flow forecast needs to be at least monthly and done over a full tax year.

You need to consider the following:

- You will need to estimate the sales. You could start with the previous year's results if you have no feel for the year ahead or use your breakeven sales.

- Consider the seasonality of your sales. For example, most Kiwi businesses are slower over Christmas.

- Assuming you know your %GP, you can calculate the COS and gross profit from the sales estimate.

- If you believe your stock level will be reasonably consistent throughout the year (what comes in, goes out) then your COS already includes this. However, if you have a plan to increase stock over the year, this will affect your cash flow.

- If you purchase stock in large orders, that take time to sell, include these in the forecast as an increase in stock in the months you believe you will make the purchase.

- When doing the cash flow forecast, do it as GST inclusive as you will need to calculate the GST and account for that when you are due to pay the IRD. (I show you how to calculate GST in **Appendix 2**).

- You will need to include when GST payments are due. This is typically every two months. The payment schedule is provided by the IRD.

- The GST you owe will be based on the sales for the two previous months.

- The GST the IRD owes you will be based on the purchases and all your expenses for the previous two months. Remember, some expenses will exclude GST (e.g., wages).

- Your provisional tax payments are also due every two months. If you are unsure what these might be, ask your accountant to estimate these and add them to the forecast.

- Your terminal tax is due annually (usually around April). If you, or your accountant, know what this is likely to be, put it in the forecast in that month.

- Include loan principal repayments. If you know what they already are, add them to the forecast. If you are looking to borrow and are yet to be given the loan repayment details, go to any of the bank's websites and use their loan calculators to determine the repayment requirements.

- For more accuracy, don't spread expenses out over the year. Determine when larger bills are due, like ACC, insurances, accountancy fees, and include them in the correct months.

- If you pay wages weekly or every two weeks, some months will have an extra pay period.

- Start the forecast with the actual money in the bank, then add your monthly forecast and trend this over the year.

- Compare your estimate of the bank account with what is in the bank each month. Do this at the conclusion of each month. If there is a big difference between the forecast bank balance and the actual bank balance, dig deeper to understand.

I have included a sample cash flow forecast in **Appendix 2** for a four-month period. This also includes how to calculate the amount of GST you owe and the amount the IRD owes you.

Forecasts are very powerful, but they are a prediction of the future that will be wrong. No-one can predict the future with certainty. Update your forecasts with actual results.

To do a detailed cash flow forecast is no simple task. Even if you walk through this process and jot down some estimates of what is happening in each month, and which months are likely to be tightest, it will be a big help.

# CHAPTER 24

## WHAT'S YOUR BUSINESS WORTH?

While you may have no intention of selling your small business or buying another business, it is still important to understand how to establish the value of your business. The factors that increase its market value are also the factors that will improve your business even if you have no intention of selling it.

The processes to value a small business are often misunderstood and I've seen many examples where this has led to heartache.

There are various methods of valuing small businesses, but none is an exact science. Often, the greatest skill in valuing a business is research and curiosity, rather than analytical skills. The greater your knowledge of the type of business and market you want to buy or sell in, the better.

I always recommend you use experts to value your business. Only use those who are active in the sale and purchase of businesses. This will also offer you an independent and objective result, free of emotional attachment.

Even if you use third parties to do a formal valuation, you should still understand the process for valuing a business yourself.

## Valuation methods — Historical Earnings Method

The Historical Earnings Method is the most commonly used method to value a small business where it's the intention to keep the business going after the sale. This is called selling the business as a **going concern**.

There are variations on this valuation method where a business needs to be liquidated or where an existing shareholder wants to buy (or sell) part of the business.

The **Historical Earnings Method** looks at how profitable the business has been over the previous years. While this does not guarantee the business will continue to be as profitable in the future, it provides a great insight into the business.

This method relies heavily on the accuracy of the historical financial reports. You should only use those accounts that were prepared by an accountant and those that have been used for tax purposes. Proceed cautiously with the valuation if the financials are abbreviated, out of date, or in a poor state.

## Future maintainable earnings (FME)

To value the business, you need to review past results to establish what you feel the future earnings are likely to be. This is called **future maintainable earnings (FME)**.

You will need to establish the profitability over the previous years of operation. You need a few year's results to assess performance.

While more recent years usually reflect the most relevant earnings, you need to be careful. If the business' latest year was extremely good and much better than previous years, you need to understand why. If this is a one off, look closely at the prior years as they may better represent the real earnings.

If a business is on a significant growth path, looking back will undervalue the business. If the business is in a declining market, the past results will over value the business.

How many years you look back may depend on the business. It is most common that you would use at least the last three years. However, if profitability has been volatile, you may need to look back further. The last few years in the industry the business is in may have been very strong. It might be worth looking at a few years prior to this to see how the business coped when things weren't so good.

You should look closely at what makes up the profit, as it may hide factors that will affect the new owner's profitability

The key thing you are trying to establish is what money will the business generate for the owner. Some call this the **seller's discretionary earnings (SDE)**

Once you have done all the adjustments, some of which I will cover below, the figure to focus on is the **EBITDA**. This separates out any lending, taxation, and interest issues from the business. These are the sellers' concern to sort out, not the buyer.

Normally, you would exclude depreciation in the calculation of FME because it is not a cash amount. There are situations where you may need to include depreciation, especially if the business is reliant on a large asset fleet that is depreciating.

Depreciation is a way of measuring the reduction in the value of plant and equipment that you will need to replace. Very often, the calculation of depreciation bears no resemblance to the actual value of the asset. For example, some vehicles hold their value very well and if you sold them, you'd get far more than the depreciated (or book) value.

However, sometimes, the depreciation matches the actual decline in the value of an asset. If a buyer needs to replace all these assets soon after buying the business, the depreciation is a good reflection of the decline in value. Therefore, you may leave depreciation in the calculation of FME because it will reduce the FME, reduce the purchase price of the business, and set aside extra cash you will need to replace plant and equipment.

Some other adjustments you may need to consider:

1    **Other activities not done at market rates**

There may be other items in the financials that do not reflect the market rate that a new owner may have to pay. For example, the business may be housed in a building that belongs to the current owner's family, so the owner is paying little or no rent. The building is not part of the sale. If you were the new owner, you are likely to pay full rent.

## 2.    One-off revenues or costs

There may be events in the past financials that were one-offs and are unlikely to occur again. These could be both in revenue and in costs. You should remove these or they may distort the valuation.

## 3.    Inconsistency in the financial results over each year

You may find that the financial results have differed over the years. This could be a consistent climb or decline in performance or volatility from year-to-year. You will need to dig more deeply to understand what this means. If the earnings have grown or reduced over the years, you will need to find out if this is likely to continue.

## *Taking into account the owner's wages or salary*

One of the more confusing aspects of a small business valuation is how to consider the owner's wages or salaries. In a large organisation, the manager or CEO will be paid a salary which will normally be based on market research. If they are not paid at a reasonable market rate, the person would leave.

In a small business, an owner may pay themselves next to nothing or could pay themselves far more than any business like theirs would pay. Some small business owners pay themselves a wage and others may take drawings. Some pay family members a wage even when they do almost nothing in the business.

When valuing a business, the first step is to take all these payments out and then ask *"if I had to employ someone to do the job of the owner, what would I pay them?"* This should be the number that goes into the valuation.

## *"One proprietor" and EBPITD*

One change those carrying out a valuation, particularly brokers, often do for a small business, is to add the owner's salary back onto the EBITDA. This increases the FME and increases the value of the business.

The rationale behind this is an owner of a small business usually works within the business and not only makes money from the profit from the business, but they also make money from the salary they earn. A new owner will benefit from both. The owner can work in the business and make that money.

However, they could put more value on their free time and employ someone in that role and forgo that wage. In either case, it adds to the seller's discretionary earnings.

This adjustment to the EBITDA is called the **Earnings Before one Proprietor's income, Interest, Tax, and Depreciation**, or **EBPITD**.

While this is a very popular method, it could be over inflating the value of the business. It is cleaner to make an estimate of what the owner should pay themselves as a wage, based on a market assessment for the role, and include that in expenses which will then form part of the FME.

# Considerations other than profitability

The EBITDA, or EBPITD, will be the figure upon which you would value the small business. This is the most significant contributor to the business' value.

However, there are other non-financial factors you need to consider that highlight how risky the purchase will be and these will influence the price.

## *Transferability*

An important factor that you need to consider in the sale of a small business is how transferable it is. A small business is often heavily reliant on the owner. This reliance might be so great it removes any chance of a sale, no matter how strong the profitability has been. If the existing owner leaves, there may be no business.

Those owners who can make the business more independent of themselves are the ones most able to increase the business' value and generate a sale.

## Will the transfer be unencumbered?

If the business has assets that are tied to securities, this makes the sale far less attractive. A business sale usually assumes the business has no securities hanging over it from creditors, including bank debt, or any security over assets. An unencumbered asset is much easier to sell or transfer than one with an encumbrance.

## What are the prospects for the business?

Some buyers of a small business will look for a business they can purchase at a lower price and then increase its value beyond what the current owner could manage. Basically, purchase the business at a discount, then step in and realise its true potential.

Buying a business at a discounted price might be possible if the existing business was not managed well, or the current owner was forced to sell below the market price for personal reasons.

How the buyer and seller see the future potential of the business and how the buyer and seller perceive the business is being managed may differ. This will affect each party's view of its value.

If the current owner believes future sales will be much greater than the past financial performance shows, they may seek a higher price before selling. The buyer will need to consider this when negotiating the ultimate price. Is the future potential real and worth paying a premium, especially if someone new is managing it?

The buyer might say that they are not prepared to pay a premium because the only way the business can truly realise its value in the future is if it is in the hands of new management. That being the case, why should they pay more for this?

# The future, the risks, and The Multiplier

If you have established your FME, and are confident you can defend this, you can ask yourself some further important questions in determining the value of the business:

- How far into the future should you consider?

- How many years ahead do you expect these earnings to continue?

- Will earnings grow, decrease or stay about the same?

- How soon would a buyer want to pay back the money invested in the business from future earnings produced by this business?

- What are similar businesses selling for?

- In comparing two similar businesses for sale, which one is riskier, and how does that affect the value?

- How do you relate the future maintainable earnings to the final value of the business?

The number by which you multiply the FME is called **The Multiplier**.

The Multiplier is a rule of thumb and involves judgment, and a knowledge of what businesses in the current market are selling for. The Multiplier also considers how risky the business is. If it is more risky, the business may not be able to make the same FME for as many years, so a buyer would not pay as much for the business.

Another perspective to consider is how quickly would you like to pay off any money you lent to buy the business? The riskier the business, the quicker you'd like the business to pay off that debt. This is an assessment of the risk. The greater the risk, the smaller The Multiplier, and the lower the sale price of the business.

Some choose the more elaborate term for The Multiplier called the **Capitalisation Rate**, which is simply the inverse of The Multiplier.

## The Multiplier and the Capitalisation Rate

The **Capitalisation Rate** shows the percentage return coming from the business that you would expect to earn in a year to recover the money you spent on the business. This assumes you paid cash for the business (rather than paying off a loan).

If you had money to invest and put it in a term deposit, it is a low-risk investment, so you expect a low interest rate. Say about 5%.

If you invested in shares, you face a higher risk, so expect a higher return. This might be around 15%. Both these options don't require any effort on your part after you've invested the money.

If you buy a small, privately owned business, you face significantly higher risks. The content of this book is testament to this. Therefore, you'd expect a much higher return on your money.

$$\text{CAPITALISATION RATE} = \frac{1}{\text{THE MULTIPLIER}}$$

For example:

1. If **The Multiplier is 1.5**, the Capitalisation Rate is 66%, which is very high. This indicates the buyer needs to pay back 66% of what they paid for the business in the first year because the business is risky and future income is uncertain. The business is more risky, so the value of the business is lower.

2. If **The Multiplier is 3.0**, the Capitalisation Rate is 33% which is lower. This indicates the buyer is happy to only pay off 33% of their original purchase price for the business in the first year. This is because they have more confidence the business will continue delivering a return over a longer period. The business is less risky, so a buyer will expect to pay more.

## What effects The Multiplier / Capitalisation Rate?

The factors to consider in determining The Multiplier include:

- There may be conventions for your type of business.

---

- Research the trade press for businesses that are on the market or make enquiries with other similar companies that have been through a sale process.

- The lower the perceived risk, the higher The Multiplier.

- Inconsistent revenue over previous years increases the uncertainty and the risk so reduces The Multiplier.

- The economic situation and the supply and demand for businesses will affect The Multiplier.

## *An example....*

Here is an example to give you an idea of how The Multiplier works.

Let's say there are two very similar businesses on the market for sale, **Business A** and **Business B**:

1. **Business A** is a small construction and building business. It has been around for many years. Its future maintainable earnings are $200,000. The business has several future projects locked in and a good pipeline of leads. The business has mature systems and processes, including for work management, finance and safety. It has a couple of long-term skilled employees who can operate independently of the owner. The plant and equipment in the business are worth $300,000.

2. **Business B** is a similar construction company operating in the same market for almost as long, with the same future maintainable earnings of $200,000. However, Business B relies heavily on the owner. He is *"old school"*, putting little down in the way of repeatable processes or documentation, relying on his experience and knowledge. He has a couple of loyal staff, but they operate only under his direction. The key customers deal only with the owner. The plant and equipment in the business are worth $250,000.

The value of Business A is likely to be higher than Business B. Business A is more likely to maintain the same profitability after the existing owner has gone. Therefore, The Multiplier you would use to value Business A will be slightly higher than Business B.

If the future maintainable earnings are $200,000 for both businesses, what might they be worth? What value do you multiply the $200,000 by to determine their value?

We cannot determine this accurately from the information I have provided. We do not know what businesses like this have sold for in the recent past, but we'll make an estimate.

To complete our simple example, let's make an *"educated guess"* at what their values might be. Let's say the industry standard Multiplier, based on recent sales, is 2 to 3.

**Business A**: The Multiplier is determined to be around 2.5, making it worth around 2.5 x $200,000 = $500,000.

**Business B**: The Multiplier is around 2.3, making it worth 2.3 x $200,000 = $460,000

There is a high level of estimation in this process. The experts operating in the market will determine the value much better than my *"educated guess"*. However, it is still an estimate.

It is also common for a valuation to provide a range. For Business A, the range might be, say, 2.3 to 2.6 and for Business B it might be 2.0 to 2.5. This gives the seller an indication of where they might start negotiations and where they might withdraw from discussions and not sell at all.

The most important valuation is not from an expert, but the value the buyer and seller agree upon. In the end, this is the only thing that will decide the value of the business.

## The goodwill in each business

We discussed **goodwill** in the chapter on the balance sheet.

The higher the goodwill relative to the value of the **tangible assets**, the greater the risk to the buyer. This may also effect the value of the business. You can turn plant and equipment into cash if your business gets into trouble. You cannot turn goodwill into cash.

In our simple example, the goodwill is calculated as the sale price less the value of the plant and equipment:

- For **Business A**, goodwill = $500,000 - $300,000 = $200,000

- For **Business B**, goodwill = $460,000 - $250,000 = $210,000

## *Everyone has a method - and an opinion*

While there is a significant amount of literature on valuation methods, it remains a subjective process. Calculating earnings over the previous few years is a relatively simple and well understood process. This is where the mathematics stops, and the opinions start.

A seller will try to justify ways to push the price up by reducing the risk and increasing The Multiplier. The buyer will want to do the opposite. The bank will be more comfortable lending when the business has assets to secure against (lower goodwill) and good cash flows. They may not want to lend at all unless the buyer has other assets to secure against (e.g., their personal properties).

If the business is being sold in a very uncertain economic environment with high interest rates, buyers will not be prepared to pay as much. Likewise, if the economy is doing well, funders are keen to lend.

If there are not a lot of businesses for sale in the market, buyers will have to pay more. Supply and demand will also have an impact on a business' value.

# Another valuation method — the Asset Based Method

The **Asset Based Method** involves adjusting each asset and the liability on the balance sheet to reflect the fair market value of all the assets in the business. This does not use the depreciated or **book value of assets** in the balance sheet, but what they would likely sell for. Once this has been done, the value of the assets is reduced by the value of the liabilities to give a net asset value. This is common if the business is not being sold as a **going concern.** The proceeds of the sale will fund clearing all the debts.

If you were the buyer of this business, you would not be concerned with the liabilities. You might agree on a market rate for the assets and pay the owner for these. It might also come with intangible assets, like websites and customer lists. You may then run the business as a going concern, but leave the repayment of liabilities to the original owner.

This method could also be used if the value of the assets in the business is greater than the value determined by the **Historical Earnings Method.** Basically, this means the business has high-valued assets, but the business is not generating enough profit from those assets. A buyer may take over the underperforming business and make it profitable. If this were the case, the buyer may offer the seller a price based solely on the market value of the assets and nothing for goodwill.

This is a very useful method to be used with the Historical Earnings Method. It shows the lowest price a seller would be prepared to sell the business for.

# ...and if a large corporate wants to buy you?

There may be circumstances where a large corporation or private equity fund has a desire to buy smaller businesses as part of a larger strategy. For example, a large overseas corporation may want to gain a position in New Zealand, so they aggressively seek suitable businesses to buy to achieve that.

In these cases, the larger company may be prepared to pay a premium for the business, well beyond what the Historical Earnings Method determines the value to be.

In this case, it would be unwise to produce an information memorandum with a value on the business calculated using traditional methods. It would be best to leave the buyer to present the offer if they are motivated to buy. They may put a value on the business that fits in with a bigger strategy that you may not be aware of or cannot measure. You may have a business that is far more valuable to them than you realise.

They are sure to do their own detailed due diligence but may calculate the value using their own internal cost-benefit analysis.

If you are the owner of such a business this could be an exceptional outcome.

Sadly, these situations are not very common.

# Valuing shares in a small business

At some stage, you may wish to bring other people into the business as shareholders or increase the ownership of existing shareholders. No matter the reason, you would need to know what the shares are worth.

This is a simple process for a business listed on the stock exchange where the market decides the value of the shares. The share value is publicly available. This is not so simple for a privately owned, small business.

For a small business, it starts with the value of the entire business, as we calculated using the Historical Earnings Method. However, because the person is buying into the business, they need to take on their share of the debt that exists, and they should also benefit from any other assets that were not considered in the Historical Earnings Method.

# Plant, equipment and inventory are excluded.

A mistake many small business owners make in valuations is adding inventory, plant and equipment to the value they calculated using the Historical Earnings Method.

If we consider our examples above, it would mean that Business A would be worth $500,000 **plus** the plant and equipment of $300,000, making the value $800,000. If there was also inventory, you would, incorrectly, add that as well.

This is not correct, although many valuations do this. You would not have achieved the $500,000 value if it wasn't for the inventory and the plant and equipment.

Another way to consider this is by asking *"if I had no inventory and I sold all my plant and equipment would I still achieve the same profit?"*. Clearly the answer is *"no"*. Therefore, when you calculate the future maintainable earnings, you are already including those assets that directly contributed to you achieving that profit.

> The calculation of a small business' value and share value includes inventory, plant and equipment. Without this the business would not have achieved the profit. You DON'T add these onto the business value.

You don't add inventory, plant and equipment on to the business value, and you don't add it into the calculation of share value.

## Seller's discretionary earnings (SDEs)

A key principle to keep in mind when valuing a small business and, therefore, the shares in a small business are earnings to the shareholders that are considered discretionary. These would be earnings shareholders could take out of the business that would have no impact on the running of the business.

A very successful business will be generating a lot of extra cash and assets so will have a lot of discretionary earnings available to the shareholders. If this is the case, the business and its shares are more valuable.

With a sale as a going concern, this is often called the **seller's discretionary earnings (SDE).**

Therefore, when valuing shares, you need to determine the value of the business, then consider surplus assets in the business less the liabilities the shareholders have to manage.

## *Surplus assets – how to calculate*

When determining what is discretionary and available to pass onto the shareholders, you can't include the cash that is required to run the business, namely the **working capital**. You also can't include any cash needed to pay outstanding taxes. You need this money to run the business, so **it is not discretionary money** you, as a shareholder, can take out of the business without it effecting the business.

To establish the shareholder value, you will need to calculate what the working capital should be, as it is not a surplus asset.

### Option 1

If you know what your working capital needs to be, and you have set it aside in a bank account, it makes this calculation simpler. You may also have an amount set aside for tax, which is clearly not discretionary as it belongs to the IRD and it is sitting in the bank waiting to be paid. If you know what these are, use the following calculation (remembering surplus assets do not include plant, equipment and inventory).

```
SURPLUS ASSETS =  TOTAL ASSETS
                    - PLANT AND EQUIPMENT
                    - INVENTORY
                    - WORKING CAPITAL
                    - GST & TAX ALLOWANCE
```

## Option 2

If you don't know what your working capital should be, and you don't set aside money for taxes you can use the **current ratio** assumption that I discussed in previous chapters. It is a good rule-of-thumb for determining how much working capital is enough to run the business. I've repeated this below.

```
CURRENT RATIO = 1.5
```

If the business has a current ratio that is "*1.5*" or less than the business has no surplus cash, so you don't need to consider this in the share valuation.

```
SURPLUS ASSETS =  TOTAL ASSETS
                    - PLANT AND EQUIPMENT
                    - INVENTORY
```

If it is more than "*1.5*" then there is surplus cash which will be included in the share valuation. This means the surplus asset calculation will be the following:

```
SURPLUS ASSETS =  TOTAL ASSETS
                    - PLANT AND EQUIPMENT
                    - INVENTORY
                    - (CURRENT ASSETS - 1.5 X CURRENT LIABILITIES)
```

There may be very different opinions within the business about how much cash you need to set aside to run the business. People with a greater risk appetite will be happy to run with very little. Some may even run with an overdraft, that is, no cash. Others may want to keep as much cash as possible in the business. The person selling the shares is likely to have a different view to the person buying the shares.

Therefore, calculating surplus assets can be subjective. If you have prepared a **shareholders agreement** ahead of time, include the key assumptions on how you will calculate share value to ensure there are no arguments when you are buying or selling shares in the business at a later date.

## *Total share value*

Now we can calculate what the value is of all the shares:

$$\text{TOTAL SHARE VALUE} = \text{BUSINESS VALUE}$$
$$+ \text{SURPLUS ASSETS}$$
$$- \text{NON-CURRENT LIABILITIES}$$

The **business value** is calculated using the Historical Earnings Method. We have already considered current assets and current liabilities in the surplus assets calculation, so we only need to consider the non-current liabilities – what the company owes other people over the long-term.

If you have the number of shares listed for your company in the Companies Office (typically 100 shares), then the **price per share** will be:

$$\text{PRICE PER SHARE} = \frac{\text{TOTAL SHARE VALUE}}{\text{NUMBER OF SHARES}}$$

# An example....let's use "Business A"

I will use the example of **Business A** from above to calculate the share value. We need to look at Business A's balance sheet, which will include some of the information we've already discussed.

The owner isn't sure what working capital is required and doesn't know what money should be set aside for tax, so is happy to use the current ratio estimate.

## Business A's balance sheet at the time of the share valuation

Let's take a look at what Business A's balance sheet might look like

### ASSETS

#### CURRENT ASSETS

| | | |
|---|---|---|
| BANK ACCOUNT | = | $60,000 |
| ACCOUNTS RECEIVABLE | = | $40,000 |

#### NON-CURRENT ASSETS

| | | |
|---|---|---|
| PLANT AND EQUIPMENT | = | $300,000 |

### LIABILITIES

#### CURRENT LIABILITIES

| | | |
|---|---|---|
| ACCOUNTS PAYABLE | = | $30,000 |

#### NON-CURRENT LIABILITIES

| | | |
|---|---|---|
| LONG-TERM LOANS | = | $100,000 |
| SHAREHOLDERS CURRENT ACCOUNT | = | $80,000 |

### EQUITY

| | | |
|---|---|---|
| RETAINED EARNINGS | = | $110,000 |
| CURRENT YEARS EARNINGS | = | $80,000 |

Taking this information we can calculate the surplus assets.

```
SURPLUS ASSETS =   TOTAL ASSETS                           = $400,000
                     - PLANT AND EQUIPMENT                 = $300,000
                     - INVENTORY                           =      $0
                     - (CURRENT ASSETS - 1.5 X CURRENT     = $55,000
                        LIABILITIES)
                                                          _____
                                                           $45,000
```

This means the total share value can now be calculated.

```
TOTAL SHARE VALUE =   BUSINESS VALUE                    = $500,000
                      + SURPLUS ASSETS                  = $45,000
                      - NON-CURRENT LIABILITIES = $180,000
                                                        _____
                                                        = $365,000
```

If someone was to buy all the shares in the company and continue running the company as is, they would pay $365,000 The change in shareholding would be detailed on the Companies Office and the new shareholder would have to manage the existing debt and cash.

If the owner of Business A only wanted to sell half the shares, the new shareholder would pay 50% x $365,000 or $182,500

If the current owner of Business A was to sell the business as a **going concern**, the buyer would take over the business, but any debts or cash remain with the original owner. In this example, the buyer would pay $500,000. They would typically set up a whole new company.

# Valuing shares is an imperfect process - be reasonable

As with all valuations methods, including the process to value shares, the answers can be very subjective. Even two experts could look at the same business with the same financial reports and come up with two different results – and arguments could go on for months.

The key in valuing shares is that an accepted method is used, like what I've described here and, most importantly, that those involved in the valuation are reasonable.

Ultimately, the person selling the shares and the person buying the shares need to discuss this, and hopefully agree on a value they can both live with. If they can't, the share sale won't happen

> Share valuations in a small business are subjective. Before you complete the shareholders agreement you need to agree on the assumptions you will use to value shares.

# Why not just use the equity value from the balance sheet to value shares?

The question you might justifiably ask is *"Why don't we just use the equity figure on the balance sheet to calculate the share value"*.

This would seem logical, considering that is what the shareholders own. That is, why wouldn't you just use the following?

## EQUITY = TOTAL ASSETS - TOTAL LIABILITIES

The first reason is **goodwill**. This can add significant value to a business but may not appear in a balance sheet. If it does, it may be old and incorrect. The only way to calculate this is using the Historical Earnings Method outlined above to determine the business value.

Also, equity includes other factors like **retained earnings** and **share capital**. Retained earnings were locked in from the last financial year and may no longer be relevant. Share capital is the money you paid to buy the shares way back when you set up the company. This is also no longer relevant.

# CHAPTER 25

# BUSINESS SUCCESSION -

# I WANT TO BACK OUT

In the early stages of your small business, you will want to stay heavily involved in the business. In fact, you probably have little choice. As time passes, your motivation to deal with the day-to-day activities may decrease. You may find the sacrifices you are making in your personal life are too great and you want to regain your life.

Some long-standing businesses, especially family-owned businesses, might want to hand the business to another family member, such as an adult child. An owner may wish to back out of the day-to-day running of the business and take up a less hands-on role.

The other less fortunate reason that may force you to back out of the business is your health, which may give you little choice and, sadly, can happen with little notice.

You may also be exhausted, have lost your energy and motivation, and feel that if you keep going, you will burn out. This is not a feeling to take lightly. Burn-out is a pre-cursor to more significant mental disorders like depression or anxiety, both of which can cripple you and therefore your business.

Sadly, when small business owners reach the point of exhaustion and just want out, they may have few options. You want to think and plan for succession well ahead, so you never reach this point.

Around 70,000 businesses cease to exist each year. [1] Considering there are only about 2,000 liquidations per year, most businesses cease to exist because the owners chose to bring them to an end.[2]

> All options to depart your business take time. You need to plan it well ahead of time

Whatever the reason, if you want to get out of the business in the best mental and financial shape possible, you need to plan well ahead, as it could take a significant amount of time to be ready for whatever form of exit you choose.

# Delegating to or hiring a successor

The first option that will allow you to be less involved in the business is to either develop an internal person to take the load off you or to employ another person who can do this. If this proves successful, it may take so much load off you that you regain your motivation to stay in the business longer. If you get the wrong person, you may have no choice but to return to the business and have a bigger mess to clean up than what you left.

Selection of this successor, whether internal or external, could be the most important hiring decision you will ever make.

***Does anyone within your small business have the skills and desire to take over from you?***

If the answer to this question is *"no"*, then you have more work ahead of you. You either have to look externally or look to see if someone, with support, could develop into this over time.

If the answer to the question is *"yes"*, then here are a few additional questions you need to ask:

- Does your successor share your passion for the business?

- Does your successor have similar values to yours?

- Do you and your successor have similar views on where you want the business to head?

- Can you define what skills your successor will need to take over from you?

- Are you prepared to guide and mentor this person so they can build up these skills?

- Do you know how long this process might take?

- Are you clear on what role you and your successor will take when you withdraw?

- Are you prepared to let your successor act independently of you? Will they have the freedom to decide?

- Are you clear on what your personal financial position will be in your new role? Can the business afford to still pay you as well as your successor?

Even if the existing person does not meet all these criteria, they may still be the only choice as a successor. You may simply need to mentor them so they are better placed when they take over.

If you have no one internally who could take over, you may need to recruit externally. This gives you the opportunity to look for a more experienced person. You still need to consider the points above and allow them time to find their feet before you back out. Finding the right external person is no easy task. It could be the most critical employment decision you may ever face.

## Developing the right systems and processes

Irrespective of your desire to be less involved, every business should have appropriate processes and systems to run their business. Far too many small businesses attempt to run their business relying on the owner's memory, paper-based processes or inadequate computer processes.

There is no reason for a business of any size to be without systems and processes appropriate for their business and their budget. There is a large choice in the market.

This becomes an even greater imperative if you want to be less involved in the business. If you develop your systems well, people will use them. If staff leave your business, it's much easier for new staff to pick up their new roles quickly.

Even if you have a very capable successor in mind, they will be in no position to take over if everything is in your head or strewn across a disorganised set of illegible pieces of paper, or in documents hidden away on your computer.

Because of the time it can take to set up such systems, you can't wake up one day, wanting to back out and expect this to happen quickly. If these systems and processes are not already part of the business, you need time to implement them.

## Part sale or shared ownership

You may wish to sell only a part of your business and are looking for someone to buy into it. This will be a more difficult task for a small business than a larger business. Interest may come if your small business shows potential for significant growth. People who are already close to you (family, friends, employees, or a close colleague) may express interest for reasons other than growth.

The reasons a part-sale might be appealing to you are to:

- provide additional funds that you would otherwise not have access to.

- bring different skills to the business.

- increase the long-term commitment a person will have for the business if they are a part-owner.

- keep critical staff by giving them a level of ownership.

- help share the workload and risk.

You do, however, need to be very mindful of the risks:

- With joint ownership comes joint decision-making and control. What if you can't agree?

- If there is an existing personal relationship with the potential partner, then it may change. It may put undue pressure on that relationship (e.g., family members or friends taking ownership).

- The excitement of getting another person involved can soon sour when you get to know each other in the stressful environment of business ownership. This is particularly the case if your values are not aligned.

- It may be more difficult for an owner to get out of the business because the remaining party can't afford to buy them out.

- If you want to sell the business at a later date, the new owner could block the sale.

- If the part-sale involves ownership for an employee, it can get very difficult if the employee's performance drops and requires disciplinary action.

A critical consideration before proceeding with a shared ownership arrangement is developing a **shareholder's agreement**. This needs to consider a wide range of scenarios, good or bad, that may arise in the future. You need to consider the risks listed above in this agreement. It is much better to reach an impasse on an issue before the part-sale goes ahead rather than after it is complete.

## ESOPs — A small piece of the action

You may have recognised individuals in your business who have become critical to your success and their loss could prove painful. While you hope they want to stay because they love the environment, want to work for you, and feel well compensated, you may need more to keep them.

The first key thing is to understand what motivates these people. It may be money, but could well be other things. If your business is experiencing really solid growth, the employee may feel they are working really hard just to make you wealthier, which is not a great motivator.

Having a share in the business may motivate them. You can achieve this through selling or gifting the employee shares or providing an **Employee Shareholder Ownership Plan** or **ESOP**.

With ESOPs, you are giving employees a small share in the company at no up-front cost. If they leave the business before a certain time, typically a few years, they lose the shares. If they leave after this time, the company buys the shares from the employee at an agreed market rate. The number of shares is usually small and does not give the employee any voting rights.

The ESOP may offer **share options** that an employee can only access after they have been in the business a certain period. This means they don't have any shares, just the option to gain them after a certain period of time or if they meet certain conditions.

ESOPs are attractive where a business is growing. This means the value of the shares will increase over time, which is a greater motivator for people to stay.

While an ESOP aims to keep key employees, that won't matter if the work environment is poor. People are always likely to put more value on the culture, how you treat them, and the value they get out of their role than they will from a few shares.

An ESOP can be a complicated document and it would need to be developed by a lawyer expert in this area.

# You must withdraw from the business quickly

Another possibility is that you must leave the business because of ill health or other unfortunate personal reason.

If you have not prepared for this situation, you could face serious financial pressures and it could mean the end of your business. This will only add to the significant trauma that you are probably already facing.

Even if the business can survive without you, can you survive without the income your business delivers to you? This might disappear in part or in full if you cannot work in your business.

This is where your insurances can play a critical part in lessening the burden if you have to exit rapidly. I covered this topic earlier in the book. If you have no insurances to cover this situation, re-visit this chapter.

If you are at the stage where you are not as prepared as you would like, but you simply have to get out as soon as possible, you ideally want this to occur with the least financial burden you can.

Consider the following before closing those doors:

- Call on your team, or others outside your business who can step in and help. If you are going through some difficult times, people will help.

- Talk to your bank if you owe them money. They will want to be re-paid no matter your situation. They may re-look at things and restructure your lending.

- Try to get all those who owe you money to pay as quickly as possible. Chase this hard as it's your money and you need it more urgently than ever.

- Do all you can to pay those you owe money to. If you shut your doors still owing people money, it's likely they will chase you.

- If suppliers are holding securities over anything, they will not release these securities until you have paid them everything. (Refer to the chapters on the PPSR and personal guarantees).

- If you have assets to sell, like plant and equipment, make sure the price you pursue covers any outstanding debt on the asset. Hopefully, you can sell for more than that and get some extra cash.

- You will need to give staff notice under their employment agreements and you will need to pay them outstanding holiday pay and any other money you owe.

- If you owe the IRD any money, they will not allow you to close your company. If the amounts are significant, talk to them or get your accountant to talk to them.

- If you have any long-term leases, the landlord may not let you leave until there is a new tenant. Make sure you know what the lease says. See what the landlord is prepared to do. If they aren't willing to help, you could still be responsible after closing the business.

- Set aside money for lawyers and accountants. You will need them to help with the closure process, and these bills can mount up quickly.

You can see, even when you want to get out quickly, it will take time.

I can't reinforce how critical it is to plan ahead.

> Plan the exit from your business from the first day you start it. If you haven't done that, start planning now.

# CHAPTER 26
## SELLING YOUR BUSINESS

In the previous chapter, we discussed ways to reduce your involvement in your business or to get out completely. One of the best exist strategies is to sell your business as a **going concern**. A new owner buys the business and continues running it in essentially the same way that you were.

Your reasons to sell may be the same as your reasons to back out of your business. It is likely that any small business that survives for long enough will go through some form of sale process. Some business owners sell for the right reasons, but some sell at the wrong time for the wrong reasons.

## Be cautious about selling just because you want out

I have advised and supported business owners that have emotionally *"hit a wall"*. They have been through very tough times, lost the desire to go on in the business and want out. This is not a good mindset or time from which to be considering a sale. Instead, it's an important moment to seek a calm external voice. A sale may not be a good option as it might leave you in a worse situation emotionally and financially.

The sale of a small business can also take a significant amount of time to complete and a lot of time and energy. Therefore, it is really important to look at your longer-term goals well before you consider a sale.

If you have a desire to sell, you can't afford to wait until you are completely burnt out and over it. It's likely the business is already suffering if your passion has gone. It is not a good idea to enter a sale process if you are already at rock bottom. Things are only likely to get worse.

If a sale is part of your longer-term plans, I would recommend giving yourself at least a year from the moment you decide *"that's it, I'm definitely ready to sell"* until you hand the keys to a new owner.

If you definitely want to sell, go back and look at how you value a traditional small business. This will give you a sense of what the business is worth. If it falls short of your expectations, you need to decide if you are happy to sell below expectations or hang onto the business and attempt to increase its value.

Hopefully, this chapter will help you make that final decision, and then assist in how to complete a successful sale process.

# Why some businesses may not sell

The reality is many small businesses go on the market and either don't sell or take a significant time period to be sold.

There is a range of reasons for this:

- Past profitability is not great.

- The future for the business or the industry sector is not strong.

- The business is overvalued (the owner expects too much).

- The business is too risky.

- The owner is the business. If he or she leaves, there is no business.

- There is a lack of effective systems or processes.

- The business is unique, or complicated.

- No-one will lend money to the buyers for this business.

- There is a lack of interested buyers.

- The owner has not packaged or marketed the business for a sale.

- There may be messy legal, property, or security issues attached to aspects of the business.

# How do you make your small business more sellable?

If the longer-term plan for your business is a sale, you need to understand what will help make it more sellable. What will make your business more sellable is also likely to make it far more appealing to keep. You may need to start this process a long time out from a sale, as none of this happens quickly. However, you will benefit from doing all these actions whether you decide to sell or keep the business.

## *Make it more profitable*

If you need to achieve a better sale price for the business, the best way to do this is to make it more profitable. Clearly, if this had been easy, you would have done it already. Keep in mind the way you value a business. If, for example, **The Multiplier** is 2, you will increase the sale price by $2.00 for every extra $1.00 you can add to your EBITDA.

Business buyers are also looking to buy your business as a going concern. They are looking for cash flow, mature systems, and a business with a future.

If your business has strong potential, but you have failed to realise that potential in terms of profitability, then you can't expect a buyer to pay more. The buyer will be the party who has to realise that potential and may not pay extra for it. It may, however, make the business more sellable.

If you genuinely believe you have much greater potential to increase profits and want a better sale price, but are struggling to realise this potential, it may be time to round up some expertise to see what is possible if you were to keep the business. If you can realise this profitability, you may decide to delay the sale for a year or two.

## Make it transferable.

The business must survive without you. How transferable is your business?

If you are the business, and you leave, then no-one is likely to want to buy it. Before you consider selling your business, you need to ensure that you can sell it. This is something that could take several years to achieve. Therefore, strategies like a business sale need to be considered well ahead of time.

The best way to make the business more independent of you is to delegate activities to your staff. If you don't have staff to delegate to, then the business is you and it won't sell.

The more developed your systems and processes, the better the chance of another person being able to pick up and run the business without you being there. If everything is in your head, it may be time to write it down, load it into a suitable system, and pass it on to others.

If you make the business more profitable, if you can also offload things to others, and your systems are in good condition, it's good for your business and good for you – and perhaps you may decide to hang on to it for longer rather than selling.

## Provide vendor finance

A buyer might accept the price for the business but may struggle to access sufficient funding to buy it. The buyer may not have the personal funds and their bank may be reluctant to lend for different reasons. This may become more common as younger buyers struggle to access bank funding because they have no assets to borrow against.

In this situation, you, as the seller, may be prepared to receive payment for the business over time after you complete the sale. This could be for the full sale price or just the gap between what the buyer can afford and what you will accept. This is called **vender financing,** where the vender is you, the seller.

This poses far more risk for you. You need to ensure you document the repayment process well, with a loan agreement, including interest requirements, and a security agreement. Even with these documents, the risk of the buyer failing to repay you remains high. This risk will be worse if the business has significant goodwill.

This is not uncommon, but you must ensure you understand the risks, get very good legal advice, and don't compromise on the legal documents that must form part of the sale.

## Increasing asset value and its effect on business value

Will improving the assets in the business, upgrading assets or purchasing new assets improve the potential sale price?

If you apply the Historical Valuation Method, then the answer will be *"no"*. Unless these assets improve profitability, it is unlikely to increase the value of the business. It may make the business more attractive to a buyer and make it more sellable. It may reduce the risk and improve The Multiplier. However, if you are looking to sell in the immediate future, you should be very careful spending too much on your assets unless it is critical to the day-to-day running of the business. You may get nothing for it.

## To use a broker or not?

Just as it is common to use a real estate agent to sell your house, it is common to use a broker to help sell your business. There are a few good reasons to use a broker.

- They know the market as they are buying and selling all the time.

- They know how to value businesses and have all recent sales data.

- They will filter out frivolous enquiries and only present you with genuine buyers.

- They must deliver. If they don't sell the business, they don't get paid.

- The **Real Estate Authority (REA)** regulates and oversees the activities of business brokers, so there is someone you can turn to if they do not act appropriately.

- They usually have a database of potential buyers.

- They may help produce all the legal documents and save some legal fees.

- They will maintain confidentiality.

- They will do all this so you can forget about the sale process and focus on running the business until the sale is complete.

There are also some downsides to engaging a broker to sell the business:

- They are expensive. They will take around 8% of your sale price when they complete the sale.

- Some also ask for funding to market the business upfront.

- They may not appear to do very much considering how much you have to pay them.

- They are less likely to sell lower valued businesses as there is not enough in it for them.

- They will push for a sale even if you are uncomfortable as they want to be paid.

- Even though you are paying the broker, they may favour the buyer's position if it secures the sale.

- They sit in between you and the buyer. You cannot always gauge what the buyer is thinking, as you rely on the broker to pass this on.

If you know potential buyers for your business, you can avoid the need for a broker. This could save you time and a lot of money and it may be a more productive handover.

No matter whether you pursue a purchase through a broker or directly with a seller, don't do it alone, especially if it is the first time you have done it.

If you don't have a buyer and decide to sell the business yourself, these are some things to consider:

- You will need to get the business valued. You can pay a broker to do this, even if they won't be selling it, or you could get your accountant to do it, assuming they know how (some do, most don't).

- You will need to produce the Information Memorandum, get a confidentiality agreement and sale and purchase agreement drawn up.

- You will need to advertise the business. This is a little tricky when you only want potential buyers to know, but you don't want anyone else to know. **TradeMe** is an option and there are other business sale websites like **NZ BizBuySell**. You will need to use cryptic language in the advert that creates interest, but doesn't give away who you are.

- Send blind emails to people who you think might be interested. You can just direct them to the TradeMe advertisement and not give away who the email is from.

- You will have to sort through potential buyers and coordinate all the interactions.

All this is very achievable, but there are some things to be cautious of.

The above actions take a lot of work, and you have to keep running your business while the sale process is progressing. During this time, no one can know it's for sale.

A broker can help mediate the sale process, which is more difficult for you to achieve when you are so invested. An advisor or your accountant could also assist with this.

You may feel confident, but the buyer may not understand what they are doing and could make the process particularly difficult. Even though the broker is engaged by you, they can guide a buyer through the process.

# Sale and purchase agreement

This is the key legal document that will cover all matters around the sale of the business. It is common that brokers will want a potential buyer to sign a **conditional sale and purchase agreement** BEFORE they can begin due diligence. This means the buyer and the seller have agreed on a sale price, and the key terms, before the potential buyer gets complete access to all the seller's commercially sensitive information.

It is the responsibility of the seller to produce the conditional sale and purchase agreement, and present it to the buyer. The potential buyer can then review this and counter with their offer. If you receive a counteroffer that is below your expectations, you can counter again, or you can simply reject the buyer's offer and walk away. If you are using a broker, they will facilitate this back-and-forth.

This is where you need to be clear on the not-negotiable terms of your offer. The broker may put pressure on you to accept the buyer's terms. They may even use tactics like reducing their commission to get you to accept the offer. Remember, the broker wants a deal to happen or they don't get paid. We discussed negotiation techniques, including the term **BATNA** in earlier chapters. Read this before entering the negotiation.

If you are comfortable with the offer, then the due diligence period can begin.

If, during the due diligence process, the potential buyer decides they do not wish to proceed, they can withdraw for any reason they wish.

In New Zealand, the **Auckland Law Society** has produced a standard sale and purchase agreement that is not too dissimilar to that used in the sale of a property. I would be wary of using any agreement that differs too far from this. Both your lawyer and the buyer's lawyer will be very familiar with this document.

If the buyer returns the agreement with additional clauses and edits, you can accept them to progress the process, but make sure your lawyer is happy with these before you accept them. There needs to be an obvious reason to venture away from the standard contract.

While the above is typical of most business sales, particularly those lead by a broker, the process you and a potential buyer follow is entirely up to you. Just keep in mind a few key principles.

- You don't want *"tyre-kickers"* looking through all your sensitive information. You only want to deal with serious buyers.

- Get the buyer to give an indication of the price they are willing to pay before you give them access to your business. Too often, in private sales, the buyer will show great interest in your business until they have to commit to a price.

- Be very clear on your walk-away terms.

- Confidentiality is critical. If someone leaks that your business is for sale, and then the sale falls through, it could be very damaging especially if you decide to keep the business.

## Typical clauses in a sale and purchase agreement

The standard clauses that will be in the sale and purchase agreement that you need to understand include:

- Purchase price, value of assets, stock, and goodwill.

- The length of the due diligence period, the settlement date, and the handover date.

- What is and isn't included in the sale (e.g., a list of assets and equipment).

- Restraints of trade, preventing you from competing with the buyer after the sale.

- Inventory levels expected at handover, and what you will owe the buyer if you don't meet this inventory level.

- Warranties and guarantees about what is being sold.

- Confidentiality.

- Finance conditions.

- Expectations of the support you will offer after the sale.

- Consequences if either party defaults.

Most sale and purchase agreements will have additional points listed at the back of the document. For example, clarify what information is being provided about employees, and what might happen with staff.

# Inventory — manage it carefully when selling

When you put your business on the market, potential buyers will want to know the inventory that they will have when they take over. No buyer will want to start their new business only to find they have to spend large amounts rebuilding the stock.

At the time you put the business on the market, you will need to show what the value of your inventory is. The buyer will assume this is the amount of inventory required to produce the profit detailed in the sales documents, and what is needed for the business to continue generating the future maintainable earnings. Therefore, this will be what their offer price will be based on.

The buyer will normally want to do a stocktake with you at the time of handover and before the final settlement. This is a very common expectation in standard sale and purchase agreements. Therefore, it will be difficult to hide the inventory levels from a diligent buyer.

If you go to market with a much higher level of inventory than you would normally hold, you will be obliged to ensure that level of inventory exists at the time of handover. If falls below this level, you will be required to pay the buyer the difference. This will come out of the sale price. Therefore, you will have increased your stock for no good reason and lost money on the sale.

If the inventory level is below what you need to operate normally, a buyer may question this during due diligence. If the level of inventory is above what you listed in the sale and purchase agreement at the time of handover, the buyer could decide they don't want that extra inventory. You may have to sell it or take it with you.

This might seem an irrational action by a buyer. Why reject inventory they could sell and make money from? Unfortunately, the buyer may decide there are product lines you stock that they have no interest in selling when they takeover. If your inventory is above what's in the sale and purchase agreement at the time of handover, you may give the buyer an excuse to offload stock they don't want.

The simple message is to reduce your inventory down to as low a level as you can before going to market, but no lower than what you need to run the business normally. From there, your goal is the keep your stock as close as possible to the figure in the sale and purchase agreement.

## Restraints of trade

All standard sale and purchase agreements will list restraints of trade that will apply to you after you sell the business. This is because the new owner will not want you to sell the business, then start a similar business, take any of your loyal staff or your customers. This is all part of the goodwill they paid for and if they don't apply these restraints, it could destroy this goodwill.

Typically, restraints of trade will prevent you from starting any business that is like what you are selling for a specified time, and within a specified distance from the business you are selling. This would typically be two years and 100km, or more. The restraint of trade should not prevent you getting another job. You just can't start another business.

Therefore, it is critical you have planned what you intend doing after the sale, as you won't be able to duplicate the business you've sold.

# Staff considerations in a sale

When you sell your business, you are effectively making your staff redundant. This is a process you need to consider, as it can be very unsettling for your staff and there are obligations you have to meet. You, like most small business owners selling their business, will also want to ensure the new owner looks after your staff.

Managing the confidentiality of the sale, caring for staff, and meeting your legal obligations can be a difficult balancing act and it requires careful consideration.

It is really important to manage who knows the business is for sale. If your staff hears about it before you complete the deal, it could create significant uncertainty. They may leave before they've understood what the buyer's intentions are. This may affect the sale, or if the sale falls through, or you decide not to sell, you may have lost key employees.

Some buyers may want to meet key staff before they make the final decision. You are not obligated to do this.

If you have well prepared Individual Employment Agreements, it should contain an **Employment Protection Provision.** If you have not included this in your agreements, you still have to meet this as it's a legal requirement.

While you don't want anyone to know about the sale until it's unconditional, including your staff, this would be a breach of your obligations under this provision of the Employment Relations Act. As your staff are losing their jobs because of redundancy, you need to follow a similar process to that discussed in the chapter on employing staff.

You need to inform them of the potential sale with sufficient time for them to comment and provide feedback.

If you were restructuring in the normal course of your business, the feedback staff provide may genuinely shift your thinking on the details of the restructure. With a sale, it would be unlikely that the staff would come back with anything that would change your mind on a sale. Unfortunately, this doesn't matter as you are required to consult.

Many businesses who are selling may choose to take the risk and not inform their staff until the deal goes unconditional. This is common and is also understandable as there is always a chance the sale may not go ahead. However, it exposes you to the risk of employees taking action against you. How significant this risk is will depend on how well you know your staff.

> You are legally obliged to tell your staff their jobs will be redundant even before the sale goes unconditional.

If the sale becomes unconditional, you need to inform your staff, in writing, that their jobs are redundant. The period between when the deal goes unconditional until when you hand the business to the buyer must be no shorter than the notice period in your employee's IEAs. Typically, the buyer will want at least four weeks to organise everything, which should normally cover most notice periods.

You cannot force the buyer to employ your staff and the buyer cannot force your staff to take up employment with them. That is entirely up to both parties. However, under the Employment Protection Provisions, you need to ensure the buyer presents the options available to your staff as soon as possible. These may or may not be the same conditions that they are currently working under.

The variation to this situation is for **Vulnerable Employees.** The most typical example of this is cleaners, but there are others. These are typically employees in industries where restructuring is frequent, where they have their conditions undermined, leaving them with little bargaining power.

A new employer may have no choice but to employ this class of employee if they want the job with the new owner. This may also be the case if the Vulnerable Employees are contracted to the business rather them employed.

The other key consideration is how you will handle the staff's outstanding entitlements. This would include annual leave. Do you transfer these to the buyer, or do you pay them out completely, and leave the buyer to start with new conditions from scratch? The buyer and your staff may want to see the conditions transferred, as your staff may not want to lose these conditions and have to start again.

## The handover processes

We discussed, in the chapter on buying a business, what a buyer needs to consider between when the deal goes unconditional and the handover. Read through this if you are selling as it will guide you on what you, as a seller, will need to consider.

There are tasks that will be specific to you as the seller in this period.

- The buyer may want a lot of your time. You will need to support them, but be careful, it's not at the expense of running the business. Even though the deal is unconditional, it is still your business.

- You need to pass on all the material agreed under the sale and purchase agreement to the buyer.

- You need to pay off as many suppliers as you can so you can get any securities listed in the PPSR cleared. A supplier won't release a security if you still owe them money.

- Talk to your bank, if you haven't already, about how you can pay off any debts from the proceeds of the sale and clear securities.

- Talk to your lawyer and accountant to assess any actions you need to conclude.

- If you have contracts in place for things like your EFTPOS machine, you might have to pay off these contracts after the sale if the buyer does not want to take them over. Discuss this with your provider and the buyer.

- You will need to ensure the buyer has changed over all vehicles into their name.

- You may be required, under the sale and purchase agreement, to introduce the buyer to customers and suppliers.

- You and the buyer may send out a joint notice about the business transfer. If this doesn't happen, send your own communication.

- You will need to assist the buyer to change over utilities (e.g., electricity).

- Make sure the buyer communicates the change in bank accounts. There is every chance after you have sold the business that customers will not have changed bank accounts and will pay you rather than the new owner. You will need to transfer this money to the buyer.

- Set aside time to do a full stocktake as close to handover as possible. You will need to prepare material to help the buyer and ensure a smooth stocktake can be done.

- The lease and other contracts need to be transferred to the buyer. Your lawyers will need to sort this before settlement.

- The deal is not complete until you have the money in your bank account. Your lawyer will take the lead on this.

Most buyers will not want to take over your limited liability company. If they did, they risk having historical risks associated with that entity remaining with them. Typically, a buyer will set up a new limited liability company. This is also beneficial for you as it gives you plenty of time to settle all outstanding matters related to your company in your own time, after you have completed the handover.

# CHAPTER 27

## HELP!!

## MY BUSINESS IS IN TROUBLE

All those who set out on their small business journey did so with hope of success, however they defined success. While we all know that setting out on this journey involves risks, none of us expect to fail, otherwise we would never have done it. Those who become overcome with such fear invariably never take the step.

Unfortunately, things do not always go according to plan. For many reasons, businesses get into trouble. This can be just the normal cycle of tough months that all of us have experienced at some stage but have come back from. Sadly, some businesses don't recover and get into more serious trouble.

If you do face troubles, what are the warnings? What can you do? If things get more serious and recovery looks very unlikely, what are your options?

# Failure in numbers

The failure of small businesses is an all-too-common occurrence. Most businesses that startup in any year are small businesses. Unfortunately, they are also the most likely to disappear if not in the first year, certainly within five years.[1]

This is a situation that has been occurring over many years, as the trend shows.

## BUSINESS SURVIVAL RATES IN NEW ZEALAND

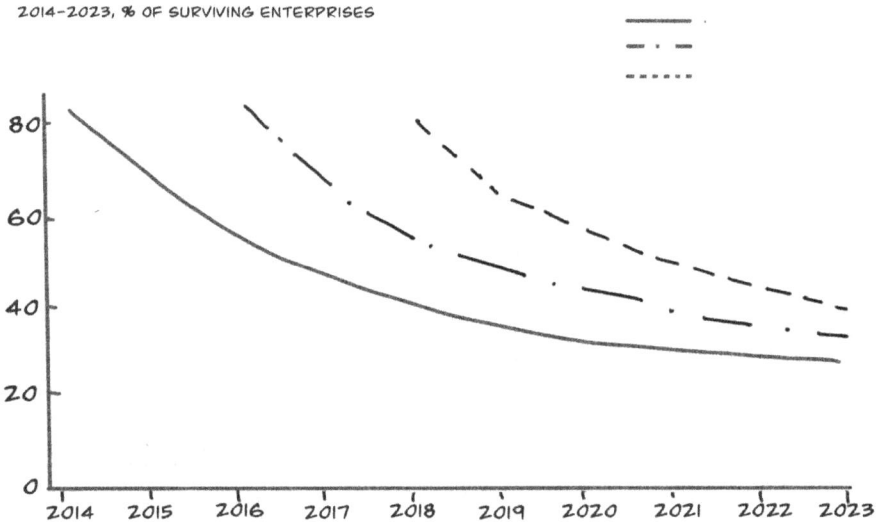

2014-2023, % OF SURVIVING ENTERPRISES

Statistics New Zealand tracks the number of businesses that start in any year (**births**), and the number of businesses that cease to exist in any year (**deaths**). For example, in 2023, a little over 70,000 businesses came into existence, but about 64,000 disappeared, and this is not a recent trend. The number of businesses that start and close varies, but the trend has been similar over many years. There are almost as many starting as are disappearing. In 2010, at the height of the Global Financial Crisis, a little over 49,000 businesses started, but over 55,000 disappeared. In short, lots of us start businesses in New Zealand, but just as many of us get out of business as well.

Sadly, the statistics have consistently shown over many years that when we start small businesses, most of them won't last that long.

Of the businesses that started around 2013, only 40% remained five years later in 2018, but only a further 10% had disappeared five years later in 2023. Therefore, the good news is that most businesses that reached the five-year mark continue as the failure trend flattens off thereafter.

In short, if you make the five-year mark odds are you'll be around a lot longer.[2]

# Are you in trouble?

The first and most critical thing is identifying that you are actually in trouble as early as possible. If you identify there are serious problems and consider it early, there are many things you can do to save the business and hopefully reverse the situation.

It would seem obvious that if you were in trouble, you would know. This is normally the case. However, it is not uncommon for the trouble to be far worse than a business owner realises. There are also those *"What if.."* events that force you into trouble with little notice. There are many examples. These are but a few.

- The lockdowns and the other dramatic responses to the COVID-19 pandemic came as a complete shock to everyone. No one could have reasonably predicted this. It saw the death of many businesses, even with government support. Businesses are still feeling the pain from this event and failures years after COVID-19 can be traced back to that time.

- Overdue taxes or taxes that exceeded what you were expecting are one of the most common reasons small business fail. The circumstance where an accountant calls to tell a small business owner their tax bill is significantly higher than expected, and is due now, is far too common.

- A slow decline in margins, a continual reduction in sales, followed by several unexpected costs, can seriously derail a small business. This could happen gradually over many months and the hole could be far deeper than the owner realised.

There could be many events or scenarios that could lead to a situation that really damages a small business. If you went through the risk assessment and scenario planning processes in earlier chapters, you will hopefully have identified those catastrophic events that could see you hit serious trouble.

If you see an ongoing slide in the cash in your bank account, if you are struggling to pay your suppliers and your staff, you need to know why and act as soon as you can.

> What are the signs you are in trouble? Cash is always the key

The hope is your accountant will give you a good idea about the tax obligations you face. Unfortunately, you can't rely entirely on your accountant to do this. If cash is already tight and you discover your tax bill is much bigger than you thought, then an already difficult situation can spiral out of control very quickly.

When the cash is really tight, your business is at its most vulnerable. It only takes a few additional shocks and things can get much worse and quickly

# Fraud — it does happen

I covered the lack of corruption and the high levels of transparency that exist in New Zealand business. We are in a country where honesty is a part of our business culture. This culture means we are also very trusting, which is how most small business owners want to run their businesses.

We want to place trust in our staff to do their jobs so that we can get on with doing our jobs. Most staff members will be totally honest, and you should have nothing to fear. Sadly, not everyone operates like this and far too many decent, trustworthy small business owners suffer the consequences of fraud.

Even the most diligent business owner can be deceived. The cash can be disappearing from the business through the actions of an individual that an owner may not pick up until it is too late.

Fraud can be devastating to a small business, both financially and emotionally. By understanding some basics of fraud and putting some simple processes in place, it is one threat to your business' survival you can remove.

## *The four factors present in fraud*

Those that have studied the common traits of fraudsters observed some common factors that are repeated in almost every case. [2]

The four factors that typically exist for people to commit fraud are:

1.  **Pressure**. There is usually some pressure or incentive the person faces that pushes them toward fraud. It may be financial hardship, gambling debts, or some other financial problem.

2.  **Opportunity**. The fraudster sees a way to carry out the fraud without detection. Usually when they get away with it once, the opportunity to grow the fraud continues.

3.  **Capability**. Fraud usually requires a level of skill and competency to pull it off without detection, especially the larger, more damaging fraud.

4.  **Rationalisation**. Fraudsters rationalise their actions, e.g. *"Everyone does it, why shouldn't I?"* or *"I deserve more so I am owed this"*.

# Common areas fraud occurs in small business

There are some common areas where fraud can occur within small businesses. Each business will be different. While you want to be trusting, and most times you can be, just pause and consider where someone might take advantage of you.

The one factor from the four factors above that you have the most control over is the second point, "*Opportunity*". If you can remove this, even a staff member who is tempted will think twice if it is likely they will get caught. With some simple processes, you can remove the temptation for people to take what is not theirs.

## 1.   Redirecting cash into bogus accounts.

Those you have delegated to pay the bills for your business each month can direct money into their own bank accounts rather than paying those who should be paid. A clever fraudster will only take small amounts each month and potentially use different bank accounts, so their actions are hidden in amongst the many payments a business may make.

The best way to prevent this is to have a different person preparing all the payments each month from the person approving the money before it leaves the business' bank account. You may decide this final transfer of money out of your bank account is your responsibility.

## 2.   Credit cards

If you issue several of your employees their own credit card there is a temptation for them to use these for personal use. The best way to prevent this is to limit who gets them to the absolute minimum.

People who have a credit card should collect receipts for every transaction and present these with the credit card statement each month. When your accounts person is reconciling the monthly expenses, they should question anything that looks out of place.

This administration is very time consuming, which is another reason to avoid issuing credit cards.

It is better to set up accounts with suppliers where people can buy what they need to do their job on the account. If they need to pay for a business item, they can use their own credit card and claim it as an expense. Make sure you pay it back quickly, or staff members will get frustrated if they spend their own money and don't get repaid.

## 3.    Fuel cards

If you have a few company cars, your staff will need to fill them regularly. It is not difficult for the less honest staff member to take the card out of the work vehicle and use it to fill their own vehicle. This is not a simple thing to detect.

There are a few things you can do.

Most fuel stations will request an odometer reading when filling the vehicle. You should encourage people to provide this information and to hand you the fuel receipts.

It is a relatively small investment to put GPS tracking in all your vehicles. This offers many advantages. If you start seeing abnormally large fuel bills, you can check them against GPS data.

Just keeping an eye on the fuel usage over time and letting everyone know you are doing it may be enough of a deterrent.

## 4.    Stock theft

If you carry a lot of stock, stationery or tools, there could be a temptation for the less honest to take from you. When they are small amounts, you may not pick them up.

Regular stock takes or robust inventory management systems will pick up missing stock. Tidy work areas can identify when equipment goes missing. Issuing tradespeople a tool allowance so they buy their own tools rather than using the business' tools usually results in the tradesperson taking much better care of their own tools.

# What to do if you are in trouble?

You need to keep a very close eye on your key financial indicators all the time, in both the good times and the bad times. When owners don't do this and rely on their bookkeeper or another person in the business, there may be serious issues developing without the owner knowing. The staff may be concerned, but you can't rely on them to understand the seriousness of the situation. They may also be afraid to pass on the bad news, or they may try to deal with it without you knowing.

If you see the problems early, there will always be something you can do. The longer it takes to find out there is a problem, the more difficult it becomes to do anything. Dealing with such issues takes time. It's extremely difficult, even for a small business, to reverse a serious situation quickly.

If you are in trouble don't wait. You need to act, and you need to act quickly.

It never hurts to get some fresh eyes to look at the business. Another experienced person may see things you can do to help you survive. These could be really unpleasant, like having to make long-standing staff redundant. Therefore, a trusted advisor could be critical to have beside you.

Assuming you catch the problems early, here are some things you can consider doing.

- Review all your expenses and remove lower priority costs. You may have to cut deeper than you previously would have done.

- Put a hold on some marketing activities, although be careful that they don't cut off much needed leads.

- If the lease allows, move into lower-cost premises.

- Put a hold on any new staff, new capital purchases, or additional overhead costs.

- Usually, a small business' biggest cost is staff, but cutting staff should not be the first step. However, it has to be considered. Start with any temporary or contract labour and then casual employees.

- If reducing staff is required, you must follow the process correctly, which takes time. You also need funds to pay all entitlements, which can be a challenge at a time you are struggling with cash.

- If you can't keep up with the tax bills, put tax payment plans in place. Your accountant can help with this.

- Talk to the bank about restructuring any debt or any other options you might have with loans.

- The bank may also offer additional working capital facilities, like an overdraft, to provide more cash.

- Sell old or slow-moving stock, even at a lower price than you want. You need the cash.

- Sell assets and downsize. If you need these assets, you could refinance them to free up cash.

- Chase aged receivables with increased vigour.

- If you have been a good payer, talk to suppliers about paying them in instalments until things improve. Most will understand. This is why you should always pay on time when you can. If you were a poor payer, you will now get no sympathy. Whatever payment process you agree to, make sure you do it.

If you can slow the haemorrhaging of cash, and feel you have stabilised the business, you can take a breath and look at other options that could bring you back to a more sustainable situation.

The one thing you need to be clear on is how you got into the situation.

From here, see how you can attract more sales. Get out there and chase more work. Approach past customers. Run some low-cost marketing campaigns. Hunt down any leads.

Can you increase sales prices without losing customers?

Basically, go back through all the above chapters and objectively re-look at your business, otherwise, you may only delay the inevitable.

If you don't act early, your bank or other funder may not want to lend you any more money to dig you out of the hole. Your suppliers may put you under significant pressure to pay or stop supplying you.

People may be less inclined to help because they know they are unlikely to get paid to help you. It is a bit like calling the fire brigade when the house is well alight.

If your cash reserves have dried up, with little immediate signs of increased sales, then all these combined factors could mean you will soon be out of options.

## *Insolvency*

If you can't regain control of your business, and the money continues to go out faster than it is coming in, your business will eventually become insolvent.

The Commerce Act defines a business is solvent when:

1. *the company can pay its debts as they become due in the normal course of business;* and

2. *the value of the company's assets is greater than the value of its liabilities, including contingent liabilities.*

If you believe you are not meeting one or both of the above criteria, you may be insolvent and you need to seek advice immediately. If you continue to trade when there is no hope you can pay your creditors, you could face legal issues as you may be trading while insolvent.

# What about just walking away?

If a small business owner has decided after a time that it's not for them, walks away, owing no one money, and has enjoyed the journey, perhaps this is not a failure. It may have been all the owner wanted to do, and they achieved all the goals they set out to achieve.

If you have lost the desire to continue in your small business, and you see no opportunities to sell the business, then walking away may be your only option. If you can do so owing no one money, and can repay all debts, including paying the IRD, then it may be a good option.

If you have a limited liability company, you can't just go on the Companies Office website and close it. You need to engage an accountant to tidy up your accounts, clear your balance sheet, and make sure your taxes are all paid, so the IRD will allow you to close the company.

If, however, you walk away from a business, closing your doors simply because things aren't great, it could be very costly. You may have unpaid taxes and loans to repay. Your lease may not allow it. You may have to sell stock and assets, typically well below what they are worth. You could end up in a much worse financial position than you realised.

If you can remain solvent, and you can brush yourself off, take a breath, and hang in there for longer, there may be other options you could consider. This might include a sale or a closure where you are in a better financial state.

## Mainzeal's failure.
## There are many lessons for small business

Mainzeal was a part of the New Zealand construction landscape since the 1960s and was involved in many of New Zealand's iconic projects.

**MAINZEAL**
Building ~~Certainty~~
UNCERTAINTY

In 1995, the Chinese company Richina acquired a majority ownership of Mainzeal. Its primary interests were in China. They recruited the former Prime Minister Dame Jenny Shipley to the board as they felt her political connections would open many doors in China.

Richina saw Mainzeal as a source of cash and took money from the construction business year-after-year. Mainzeal also lent Richina, and its related businesses, large amounts of money.

These funds were not secured against anything, were not accompanied with any formal documentation, and the Directors of Mainzeal sought no legal advice on the implications of these loans. Had they done so, they would have realised Chinese laws made returning that money to New Zealand almost impossible.

Richina was listed on the New Zealand stock exchange and the reports on its performance and its lack of transparency were not good [5][6]

Sadly, for Mainzeal, it was also performing well below expectations in New Zealand. Between 2005 and 2012, it delivered losses in four of the eight years and very meagre profits in the other four years.

It was involved in several construction projects that did not go well. This included the Vector Arena in 2003, and the high voltage electrical connection between the south and north islands.

Mainzeal treated the money owed by Richina and other related party businesses as an account receivable.

This made its balance sheet look healthy. However, remove this and Mainzeal was, under the balance sheet definition, insolvent. This situation existed for several years before the eventual demise. Even though, by this definition, it was insolvent, Mainzeal continued entering new contracts.

As time went on, the management's growing concerns were being raised in reports to the board. They were struggling to pay creditors. Richina continued making promises to return the money it owed, but Mainzeal saw very little of this.

Things came to a head in 2013 when Richina's owner, Richard Yan, saw the reality of the situation, and told the board he would not support Mainzeal any further. This triggered the inevitable collapse of the business. Receivers came in on the 6 February 2013, followed by liquidators three weeks later.

The liquidators' first report indicated over 1,500 businesses and over 400 staff could be affected by the Mainzeal collapse. After they concluded their work, $110 Million was owed to unsecured creditors.[7]

The liquidators pursued all the funding they could to ensure staff were paid and as many creditors as possible. They also pursued the directors. In their view, the directors had continued trading when it was clear the business was insolvent and the money they were using was not Mainzeal's, nor was it the parent company's money. It belonged to their creditors.

Lengthy court cases followed including to the High Court and the Court of Appeal. After the dust settled on all this, the three directors of Mainzeal, who were present through the issues, Dame Jenny Shipley, Clive Tilby and Peter Gomm, were found guilty of reckless trading and were ordered to pay $6.6 million each plus interest. Mr Yan was seen as the most culpable and ordered to pay an even greater sum.

## Mainzeal - Lessons for Small Business

While many of the lessons from Mainzeal apply to the big-end-of-town, there is a great deal small businesses can learn from this.

1. If the business borrows or lends large amounts of money to anyone else or to you, as a shareholder, formalise it and, where appropriate, get securities attached to it.

2. When doing any business deal, especially if it's risky or you are unsure of some details, get advice, whether it is legal, financial or business advice. It may be costly, but the alternative could be far worse.

3. As a shareholder, don't keep taking money out of the business, especially if it can't afford it. This includes drawings, dividends and shareholder salaries.

4. People in business can promise a lot, and trust is important, but if there is a lot at stake, a person's word may mean nothing. Get it in writing.

5. If cash is tight, and you are struggling to pay your creditors, seek help immediately. The Commerce Act applies to all of us, no matter our size, and reckless trading is reckless trading.

# Receivership

A business will often offer security against its assets when they financed them. If the business defaults on the loan, the party owed the money can appoint a **registered receiver** to collect and then sell the asset. While any party who has lent money with a security can appoint a receiver, banks are very often the most likely party that will instigate a receivership.

Often a bank will have a **General Security Agreement (GSA)** over a business. This gives them much broader control over an entire business to sell any assets to get the money back that is owed.

A business can survive a receivership. However, it is likely the business was already in serious trouble. Once the receiver sells the assets, it may be the final nail in the coffin, triggering a liquidation.

# Voluntary administration

**Voluntary administration** was introduced in New Zealand in November 2007. It is governed by the Companies Act. It provides a business the chance to pull back from a liquidation by bringing in an administrator. This person is also likely to be a liquidator.

If your business is really struggling, and you fear you are or will become insolvent, a voluntary administration may be one option to prevent complete failure. However, a voluntary administration can only be instigated if there is some chance the business could be rehabilitated, even if it is slim.

The administrator will take control of the business. The directors can only get involved if the administrator allows it. The administrator's primary focus is establishing if the business can be recovered or sold, if assets can be sold, or any other option to pay back what is owed to the creditors.

While the administration process is occurring, it prevents other parties from taking action, so it provides some breathing space to allow external expertise to review the situation.

The administrator has a defined process they must follow to inform and engage with creditors. If, after this process, a way out of the situation cannot be agreed, then liquidation is the likely next step.

# Liquidation

Out of the nearly 70,000 businesses that cease to exist each year, only about 2,000 go through liquidation. [3,4]

Liquidations are the worst-case situation for any business. The business is insolvent; it ceases operations, and all the assets have to be sold (liquidated, or turned to cash) to pay off debts.

A business owner can instigate a liquidation voluntarily. If the owner doesn't declare liquidation voluntarily, creditors may step in. The most common party to do this is the IRD. If a creditor forces you into liquidation, a liquidator will push you aside and take over.

Voluntary liquidation gives you some ability to control the process. This is where you, the shareholder, decide there is no hope of meeting all your debts and you voluntarily decide to finish operations. If there is more than one shareholder, then it would require a **special resolution**. Either way, it is the business who would engage a liquidator.

Only individuals registered as a liquidator can carry out the liquidation. You can find a list of registered liquidators on the Companies Office website. This website has a range of registers for different professions, including a register of *"Insolvency Practitioners"*.

If you are in trouble and you do not see any way out of it, you may reduce all your costs, sell off plant and equipment, lay off staff, pay off all the money you owe, and hopefully close your business without going into liquidation. Even if you feel you have met all your obligations and have effectively dodged the liquidation bullet, it may still be wise to engage a liquidator. The liquidator can ensure everything is in order and that you have done everything correctly. This may protect you if future claims arise.

Keep in mind that one of the first things a liquidator will do will inform the Companies Office in writing that they have been engaged and that your company has gone into voluntary liquidation. This is recorded on the Companies Office and will remain their indefinitely.

## The role of a liquidator

No matter how a liquidator is engaged, their role is the same.

First, they take possession of all the assets to sell for the benefit of the creditors. They will only be interested in the owners if they are also a creditor, namely the business owes them money. Otherwise, the interests of the owner are not the liquidators' concern.

The liquidator takes control of, and freezes, the business' unsecured assets, which are then sold to repay the creditors.

The liquidator will also:

- Communicate with creditors and call creditors meetings.

- Investigate all the financial affairs of the business.

- Establish the cause of its failure.

- Assess if any illegal activities took place and report them.

- Prepare regular reports.

The liquidator has significant powers to contact and deal with anyone they need to, including the business' shareholders, accountants, lawyers, and employees.

# What personal risks do you face if your business is liquidated?

If your business is liquidated, the emotional and financial impact may only be the start of your problems.

You could face serious legal implications if you knowingly continued to operate your business when it was clear you could not pay your creditors. This is called *"trading while insolvent"* or *"reckless trading"*.

When you are struggling to pay the bills, it could be a short-term issue you are confident you can overcome. However, if this continues, and you cannot see this turning around, you may be insolvent. If you continue to trade and the liquidator establishes there was no chance you could recover, and you owed creditors money, you could be *"trading while insolvent"*. If this is the case, the penalties could be severe, depending on how much you owed.

With Mainzeal, the courts found four directors were guilty of reckless trading. The courts ordered three to pay over $6 million and the fourth over $30 million.

The other risk is what you could lose, personally, following the liquidation of your business. Therefore, you need to fully understand the extent of your liabilities when running your business. The business structure you have chosen is also critical. Re-look at the discussion on family trusts and the separation of assets. If you own a limited liability company, and you have given no personal guarantee over any of your personal assets, your liabilities are likely to be limited to your company.

If, however, your bank or other supplier secured what they have borrowed with a personal guarantee, then they may attack your personal assets to recover their money.

If you are a sole trader, you are legally liable for everything and could have your assets seized to pay off debts.

## Who gets what?

The liquidator will decide if the business could continue trading and be sold as a going concern. This is likely to attract the most money to repay creditors. More often, there is no realistic way the business can trade, even with a new owner and needs to be shut down and all assets sold.

The first funds a liquidator will pay will usually be their own fees, and the legal costs of the creditors who instigated the liquidation through a court order. After that, secured creditors have priority, then preferential creditors, and lastly unsecured creditors. Preferential creditors could include unpaid wages and benefits to staff, and the IRD.

Invariably, if you are liquidated, there may not be enough to pay secured creditors, let alone unsecured creditors.

The process will feel a little like vultures are picking at the carcass of what was your business. It's unlikely any of those you owe money will feel the slightest concern for you. In fact, it is possible people who won't get money through the process will be angry and upset. They have their own lives and businesses to run, and you owe them money.

# Phoenix laws

If your business fails, there is nothing stopping you from starting another business. However, you need to be careful if the new business has the same or a similar name to the failed business.

It can be distasteful for creditors to see a person whose business was liquidated starting a new business doing the same thing. There is no law preventing a former director starting out again, even with an essentially identical business.

A new company can buy the failed company's assets from the receiver or liquidator. In this situation, the new directors must write to all creditors of the old company, advising them of the new company's formation to ensure there is no confusion.

However, if the new company deliberately hides the fact that it has failed, and continues to trade as though nothing had changed, this could mislead or confuse suppliers. This puts creditors in an awkward position when they ask for payment from the new company, only to be told it is the former company that owes them money.

A **phoenix situation** is an effort by directors to avoid their liabilities and prevents suppliers from making an informed decision about the new company's creditworthiness. This is an illegal activity under the Companies Act and is called Phoenixing.

An example of **phoenixing** would be where a company who owes its creditors money sets up a new company. It sells the assets from the old company to the new company. This will typically be below the market value of the assets. They will also ignore goodwill. They transfer their staff onto new IEAs in the new company and continue trading as though nothing had happened.

# The personal price of business failures

The cost of business failures is significant, as was the case in all the examples we've discussed in the book. Pumpkin Patch, South Canterbury Finance, Mainzeal, finance companies, and Solid Energy. These companies owed many small businesses and contractors money. These failed businesses owed the banks and/or the government millions. Thousands of people lost their jobs. The courts prosecuted, fined, and even jailed directors. No one wins when a large company fails, but these failures happen and will continue to happen.

> *"Remember that failure is an event, not a person".* - **Zig Ziglar,** American author, salesperson, and motivational speaker.

If, through all your best efforts with the support of others, you're unable to keep your small business going, how will you feel? It will not have the sweeping effects that these large corporate failures may have, but the impact on a small business owner can be devastating.

This is the situation where you will be least able to see any success. While you are unlikely to see it when it occurs, with time, I hope you see you can come back and try again.

You need to remember that just because the business *"failed"*, it does not mean you are a failure.

This is where the resilience you have built up and the relationships you have carved out will be most critical. No matter how strong you think you are, these can be extremely tough times. Hang in there. Seek the support of those close to you. Talk about it. There is always light at the end of the tunnel.

---

### *It's bloody tough – but you can come back*

No one wants to fail in anything we take on in life. No small business owner goes into business to fail. Sadly, small business can be tough, and failures happen. When it happens, it is devastating, humiliating, and something many of those who have experienced want to forget. Sharing these experiences is not easy.

The following small business story is true and compelling, but the scars, even after nearly 25 years, have not fully healed. William, not his real name, wanted to share his story as he went from liquidation and personal bankruptcy to owning large, successful Kiwi businesses operating throughout New Zealand.

I thought we could all learn from this story.

William fell into his trade by chance when he was 17. Before his 21st birthday, he had started his own business. Like all those new to small business, William *"didn't-know-what-he-didn't-know"*. He had no one to mentor or support him but he knew his trade and he just got on with it.

William was buying the gear he needed, getting the jobs done, but payments weren't coming and running the business and monitoring the numbers was not his strength.

The challenge of paying his large suppliers grew, and, as with any supplier, they wanted to be paid. No matter his efforts, William found himself in an ever-deepening hole and was alone in dealing with the challenge. His accountants advised him he could not ignore the inevitable.

---

In September 2001, he went into voluntary liquidation. William was young, had no assets and no money, but his creditors didn't care and were not walking away without getting their pound of flesh.

They wanted what he owed them.

William was desperate to meet his commitments but had nowhere to turn. He was sinking under the pressure, and he had no more to give. He walked into the High Court just before Christmas 2001 and declared himself bankrupt.

While bankruptcy clears your debts, it comes at a significant price. Your bankruptcy status is recorded and is publicly available. As a bankrupt, you cannot be a director or own a company for a period. In William's case, this was seven years. You can't borrow money. Many employers don't want to employ someone who is bankrupt. Utility companies may not want to sign you up for their services for fear you won't pay. You may also be prevented from leaving the country.

While these are tough, nothing is worse than the stigma and mental anguish that goes with being bankrupt.

William turned to friends in business and was prepared to do anything he could to recover. He worked hard and grasped any opportunity that came his way and made the slow journey back. He met and married his wife and started a family. In 2009, the company who gave him a chance asked if he'd become a director. It was a major step back to business ownership.

William wanted to be his own man and start his own business again. He registered a new company in 2009. With 10 years' experience under his belt, he now knew how to run and grow a business and the consequences of getting this wrong. By 2024, he had grown several businesses. Together, they were generating healthy sales, and he was employing over 40 staff.

# CHAPTER 28

## CONCLUSION AND SUMMARY

The size of this book shows how much you might need to know to own and run a small business. There is a lot to absorb. Not all or this may apply to your business. Your business might be very small and very simple.

Let's summarise some of the key points. If any of these really stand out for you, revisit those chapters. Hopefully, this might demystify the complexities.

1.   Doing business in New Zealand has its challenges – but there are many success stories and it's one of the best places on earth to do business.

2.   Take care of yourself. Your wellbeing is so important.

3.   You can get into business by starting a business from scratch.

4.   You can get up into business by buying a business.

5.   Your business needs a strategy – why you exist, your values and goals. You need to know where it's heading.

6.   Business involves making decisions - but know your limitations. You are human and we are all imperfect.

7.   Without customers you have no business – understand the basics of how to market to your ideal customers.

8.   Establish how to reach your customers – how will you advertise? There is unlimited options but you have a very limited budget and little time.

9.   How will you sell your products or services? Sales is about listening and helping people.

10. Work on developing excellent systems, processes, and getting your operations right. It's about the details.

11. If you want to grow you need people. Employ the right people, set expectations and look after them.

12. Leadership - know yourself, accept yourself, then forget yourself.

13. Business involves risk. Understand your risks but don't be paralysed by them.

14. Every business needs money. Understand what you need and where to source it. Most importantly, establish how you will pay it back.

15. Growth is a common goal. It's a process and needs planning and close monitoring. Don't let it get out of control.

16. Don't discount the option to export. The world is a big place and many Kiwi business have done it successfully.

17. The Health and Safety of your staff is paramount. Start by focusing on looking after them. Then make sure you are compliant.

18. You need to meet your legal requirements. Start by doing the right and honest things.

19. You need to understand the financial basics, including your profit and loss statement and balance sheet.

20. Make sure your accountant informs you what tax you owe and make sure you pay it on time.

21. If you lose control of your cash, you'll lose control of your business. Cash is critical.

22. It's worth knowing what your business is worth, even if you don't want to sell it.

23. You may want to back out of the day-to-day running of your business at some stage. If you do, plan for this as it is not easy and takes time.

24. The best time to sell a business is the best time to keep it. A sale takes time, so plan for it well ahead.

25. Most business will face tough times. If things are not good, seek help and act quickly.


Owning your own business may be the most rewarding thing you do in your working life. The most rewarding things we pursue are not always the easiest things we would do. This is very much the case with owning and running your own small business. There will be great days. There will be really tough days. However, if it's a passion and you want it to work you can join the many thousands of kiwis who are doing it, loving it, and who would never choose any other career path.

**Good luck, and all the very best to you.**

# Appendix 1

## Traditional Advertising.

## Pros and cons of the different options

| Advertising | Advantages | Disadvantages |
|---|---|---|
| **Television (analogue and digital)** | • Highly engaging.<br>• While declining, it still has a huge reach.<br>• Those who use TV do see conversion into sales.<br>• Uses audio, video, images, colour and movement<br>• Can use specific times slots to target audience.<br>• While traditional TV is declining streaming and digital services are increasing.<br>• Digital TV options are significantly cheaper.<br>• Digital TV can be more highly targeted to specific audiences.<br>• Ai tools are lowering production costs, especially for digital television. | • Expensive and outside the reach of most small businesses.<br>• Advertisements for analogue TV are complex to develop, and expensive, requiring production capabilities.<br>• Adverts are very short and difficult to portray all information.<br>• Advertisements need to be repeated many times.<br>• Traditional television is very difficult to assess who has seen it, who can recall it and who has taken action as a result, without additional market research.<br>• Digital TV advertising is in its infancy in NZ and trying to catch up with other digital offerings. |
| **Radio** | • Lower cost than television.<br>• Can be produced quickly.<br>• Allows targeting through different stations and time slots.<br>• Can be focussed on specific locations<br>• Repetition can embed messages in people's minds | • While lower cost than TV it is still out of the reach of many small businesses.<br>• People cannot easily refer back to an advertisement.<br>• Radio is often background noise for listeners.<br>• Radio tends to interrupt entertainment and can frustrate listeners. |

| | Pros | Cons |
|---|---|---|
| | • If well thought out, it can drive people to online marketing platforms (websites).<br>• Still widely used while driving<br>• High listener numbers during peak hour driving times. | • Advertisements need to be repeated many times for the message to sink in.<br>• This repetition means campaigns need to run for longer, often months, to be effective, which becomes expensive.<br>• It is very difficult to assess who has heard the advertisements, who can recall them and who has acted on them, without additional market research.<br>• Customers may hear the radio but then go online and find your competitors – if the radio campaign is not matched with a digital campaign. |
| **Billboards** | • They will be seen as they are placed in strategic locations.<br>• Some billboard companies use smartphone data to track car movements<br>• Most locations will have good information on the number of vehicles that pass the point (usually supplied by NZTE).<br>• You can place your advertisement in a location that best aligns with your business.<br>• Billboards have the potential to be seen numerous times by a potential customer<br>• Digital billboards allow regular updates. | • Messages must be brief.<br>• You may be required to post your advertisement for a minimum time period even if it is not working.<br>• Billboards use stationary images with no sound or movement.<br>• It is difficult to assess who has seen an advertisement, who can recall it and who has taken action as a result, without additional market research.<br>• Typically fixed monthly payment. The better the location, the more you'll pay. |
| **Mailbox Flyer Drops** | • Low cost to produce and deliver.<br>• Can be very specific on the geographical area you wish to target.<br>• Easy and quick to read and establish the message. | • Difficult to assess who has seen it, who can recall it and who has acted as a result.<br>• Easily dismissed by customers (often thrown out without even reading it). |

| | | |
|---|---|---|
| | • Easy to produce and reproduce.<br>• Cost effective, as only a small number of successful responses are needed to cover the costs (e.g., real estates drop thousands of flyers; they only need one house sale to cover all costs). | • Many people won't even let you drop off "*Unaddressed/Junk*" mail<br>• Limited long-term impact.<br>• What you are selling needs to be what a homeowner wants at exactly the time they read the flyer. If not, they are thrown out and forgotten.<br>• Difficult to establish the demographics within a household.<br>• Very low conversion to sales so each sale must be worthwhile. |
| **Cinema Advertising** | • Captive audience.<br>• Allows sound and movement of a very high quality.<br>• Big screen can enhance a lower-budget advertisement.<br>• The advertisements can narrow in on target audiences, based on the movie and its rating.<br>• Usually cheaper than TV advertising. | • Difficult to assess who has seen it, who can recall it and who has acted as a result without additional market research.<br>• People know that advertisements before movies can be long and can stay outside the theatre and fail to see the advertisement.<br>• Fewer people are going to cinemas choosing to stream. |
| **Newspapers** | • One advertisement can access a very large readership.<br>• Can align your message with the appropriate readership and sections within the newspaper.<br>• Relatively simple to produce.<br>• More newspapers are going online with high readerships, allowing the normal online tracking.<br>• The top New Zealand newspapers have some of the highest online hit rates of all websites. | • Difficult to assess who has seen it, who can recall it and who has acted as a result without additional market research.<br>• A medium that has seen significant competition and declines in readership.<br>• Static image.<br>• Short life span.<br>• Low younger readership. |
| **Magazines** | • The variety of magazines allows very targeted | • Difficult to assess who has seen it, who can recall it and |

|  | campaigns, across a wide demographic. <br>• Readership numbers are usually well known. <br>• More magazines are going online. <br>• Able to access a very wide geographical readership. <br>• Much longer shelf-life than a newspaper. | who has acted as a result without additional market research. <br>• Market flooded with a huge variety of magazine titles. <br>• Typically, monthly prints so there could be a long time between deciding to advertise and reaching print. <br>• Can be expensive. <br>• A medium that has seen significant competition and declining readership. <br>• |

# Appendix 2

## Cash flow forecast

Let's produce a sample cash flow forecast to guide you in developing your own forecast.

| | Oct | Nov | Dec | Jan |
|---|---|---|---|---|
| Sales (inc GST) | $14,000 | $12,000 | $9,000 | $7,500 |
| Purchases (inc GST) | $10,500 | $9,000 | $6,750 | $5,625 |
| Gross Profit | $3,500 | $3,000 | $2,250 | $1,875 |
| %Gross Profit | 25% | 25% | 25% | 25% |
| Accountancy Fees | $680 | $0 | $0 | $0 |
| Insurance | $0 | $0 | $0 | $250 |
| Light, Power, Heating | $20 | $20 | $20 | $20 |
| Marketing | $15 | $15 | $15 | $15 |
| Motor Vehicle Expenses | $250 | $250 | $250 | $250 |
| Office Expenses | $25 | $25 | $25 | $25 |
| Telephone & Internet | $10 | $10 | $10 | $10 |
| Total Expenses (GST applies) | $1000 | $320 | $320 | $570 |
| GST Out | $0 | $0 | $0 | $3,390 |
| GST in | $0 | $0 | $0 | $2,715 |
| Net GST | $0 | $0 | $0 | $675 |
| Wages, Salaries & PAYE | $500 | $500 | $750 | $500 |
| Bank Charges | $5 | $5 | $5 | $5 |
| Interest - on Loans | $20 | $20 | $20 | $20 |
| Total Expenses (no GST) | $525 | $525 | $775 | $525 |
| Loan repayment | $500 | $500 | $500 | $500 |
| Drawings | $550 | $550 | $550 | $550 |
| Tax Payments - Provisional | $0 | $0 | $0 | $400 |
| Tax Payments - Terminal | $0 | $0 | $0 | $0 |
| Total Non-Operating Expenses | $1,050 | $1,050 | $1,050 | $1,450 |
| Net Cash | $925 | $1,105 | $105 | -($1,345) |
| Forecast Bank Balance | $925 | $2,030 | $2,135 | $790 |

## GST calculation

One of the tricky parts of the cash flow forecast is working out how much GST you have to pay. In the above example, the GST is due in January but is based on the sales and expenses for the months of October and December.

It requires some maths.

### GST on Sales

Let's take the sales first to work out what the dollar amount of GST you should pay. We know the two following formulae apply.

1.  (Sales without GST) x 1.15 = Sales with GST

2.  Sales with GST – Sales without GST = GST

Substituting the first formula into the second results in:

$$GST = Sales\ with\ GST - (Sales\ with\ GST)/1.15$$

and then

$$GST = Sales\ with\ GST \times (1 - 1/1.15)$$

giving us

**GST = 0.1304 x (Sales with GST)**

In our example the GST on the sales in October and November is:

**GST = 0.1304 x ($14,000 + $12,000)**

Therefore, the GST owed is **$3,390**

### GST on Costs

As the table shows, some of the money you spend does not include GST, such as wages, bank fees and interest on loans. These have been separated out of the GST calculation. Expenses and costs of sales in October and November need to be included.

$$GST = 0.1304 \text{ x } (\$10,500 + \$9,000 + \$1000 + \$320)$$

Therefore, the GST coming in is **$2,715**

### *Use cash amounts not invoiced amounts*

All the sums in a cash flow forecast need to reflect when you believe money will hit the bank account or leave the bank account, not when invoicing occurs. Use the cash flow from the previous year as the starting point.

### *Provisional and terminal tax*

This table includes an allowance for provisional tax, purely for illustrative purposes. It is not possible to calculate it from this table. If you are not comfortable estimating these taxes, talk to your accountant but make sure you include them in the forecast. They will appear after the GST lines as they exclude GST.

### *Accounts receivable and payable*

Over time, you are likely to get a feel for how often you get late payments. Hopefully everyone pays you on time so you can pay everyone on time. If not, you may want to move cash out into later months to account for this.

For example, if you find about 5% of your payers are always late, the $14,000 of cash you expected to receive in October will only be $13,300. Assuming you will get paid, this will push out into later months.

While this may not seem worth doing, assuming the money will come in, if things are tight, it could leave you short in months.

## Does Gross Profit apply?

Typically, Gross Profit and %GP are used in a profit and loss statement but not cash flow. However, it can be helpful to establish your purchases if you have an estimate of your gross profit.

## Stock and purchases

Another complication with cash flow forecasting is assessing changes in stock and purchases.

If you don't hold stock, or you turn it over very quickly, you can simply use your estimate of %GP to approximate the cash you will spend on purchases each month. This is what is assumed in the example above.

If, however, you buy stock in large quantities, which is not turned over quickly, you may need to add a separate line item to account for the cash involved in these stock purchases. In this case the %GP won't be relevant

## Expenses

In this example I have made the expenses even across months. This is unlikely to be the case in a real business. Find out when large bills are due and enter them in the correct months. If you aren't sure what the expenses might be, start with the cash flow from the previous year.

## Wages and salaries

I have made the assumption that December in this example has an extra pay period, so the wages bill is higher.

## Negative cash

You will notice that the cash in January is negative. This is not uncommon in New Zealand. For most small businesses, January is the slowest month as there are numerous public holidays and many businesses close their offices, so sales are well down. Unfortunately, it is also a month when tax is due. If this applies to your business, you will need to plan for this before you finish up for the Christmas/New Year break.

## Update the forecast with actuals

If you want the forecast to remain accurate, you need to update the forecast numbers with actual numbers at the end of each month so the forecast updates.

# Run some scenarios

As this is a forecast of the future, it is a best guess. No one will ever predict the future with certainty. However, you can run some scenarios from your base case. For example, what if your sales are down by 10% from this scenario? Where might you be placed and, should that situation start to eventuate, what might you do?

Here are two scenarios.

## a.    Reduction in forecast sales

The following forecast reduces sales by 10%. Keep in mind, this will mean you have less purchases and less GST to pay. If you use a spreadsheet, build these calculations into the forecast so any change at the sales line will automatically update the forecast.

| | Oct | Nov | Dec | Jan |
|---|---|---|---|---|
| Sales (inc GST) | $12,600 | $10,800 | $8,100 | $6,750 |
| Purchases (inc GST) | $9,450 | $8.100 | $6,075 | $5,062 |
| Gross Profit | $3,150 | $2,700 | $2,025 | $1,688 |
| %Gross Profit | 25% | 25% | 25% | 25% |
| Total Expenses (GST applies) | $1000 | $320 | $320 | $570 |
| GST Out | $0 | $0 | $0 | $3,051 |
| GST in | $0 | $0 | $0 | $2,461 |
| Net GST | $0 | $0 | $0 | $590 |
| Total Expenses (GST doesn't apply) | $525 | $525 | $775 | $525 |
| Total Non-Operating Expenses | $1,050 | $1,050 | $1,050 | $1,450 |
| Net Cash | $575 | $805 | -($120) | -($1,447) |
| Forecast Bank Balance | $575 | $1,380 | $1,260 | -$(187) |

In this scenario, you are **about $1000 worse off** than the original forecast after four months.

---

## b.  Reduction in %Gross Profit from 25% to 22%

What happens if your purchase prices go up, but you can't increase sales prices? This will reduce your %Gross Profit.

| | Oct | Nov | Dec | Jan |
|---|---|---|---|---|
| Sales (inc. GST) | $14,000 | $12,000 | $9000 | $7,500 |
| Purchases (inc. GST) | $10,920 | $9,360 | $7,020 | $5,850 |
| Gross Profit | $3,080 | $2,640 | $1,980 | $1,650 |
| %Gross Profit | 22% | 22% | 22% | 22% |
| Total Expenses (GST applies) | $1000 | $320 | $320 | $570 |
| GST Out | $0 | $0 | $0 | $3,051 |
| GST In | $0 | $0 | $0 | $2,817 |
| Net GST | $0 | $0 | $0 | $235 |
| Total Expenses (GST doesn't apply) | $525 | $525 | $775 | $525 |
| Total Non-Operating Expenses | $1,050 | $1,050 | $1,050 | $1,450 |
| Net Cash | $505 | $745 | -($165) | -($1,130) |
| Forecast Bank Balance | $505 | $1,250 | $1,085 | -$(45) |

This scenario is not quite as bad as a 10% drop in sales, but you are **still down over $800.**

# About the Author

Bob spent the first 25 years of his career in the power industry in Australia, Africa, Europe, Asia and New Zealand. As a qualified engineer he was involved in the construction and commissioning of power stations around the world. After taking on management roles, he led a wide variety of teams including engineering, trades, administration and human resources. He led industrial relations negotiations with multiple unions.

His final role in the corporate world, before leaving the industry, was as General Manager accountable for the operation of all the power stations and hedge and financial trading activities in one of the large New Zealand power companies. He reported to the CEO and board, had approximately 400 staff reporting to him and multi-million-dollar budgets.

Since leaving the corporate world and starting Pinpoint Business in 2012, Bob has advised hundreds of small businesses in almost every industry and at all stages of the business cycle – from startup to sale or closure, including not-for-profits, charities and commercial businesses. Bob has sat on many boards as a trustee, advisor, director and chair.

He and his wife purchased a landscape supply business in 2017, doubling its turnover before selling it in 2023.

Bob was recently the General Manager of a New Zealand wide HVAC wholesale and distribution business. He is also still advising other small businesses.

Bob has a degree in Engineering, an MBA in Finance, is a graduate of the Columbia Business School in New York and has completed psychology papers at the Waikato University.

He has written several other books, including "Success Made Small", used by Te Wananga O Aotearoa in its business courses, "Why Businesses Fail" and a history book on the journey of Irish immigrants to Australia in the 19th century (including his ancestors) called "Mullingar to Byron Bay".

Bob remains passionate about helping small business owners. He would love to hear your story. You can contact him on his website.

www.pinpointbusiness.co.nz

# Index

| | | | |
|---|---|---|---|
| Joseph Luft (Johari Window) | 242 | Loss aversion (bias) | 105, 106, 111 |
| Just-in-Time | 196 | Mailchimp | 158 |
| Kaizen | 190 | Mark-up (vs Margin) | 382, 383 |
| Keirsey Temperament Sorter | 246 | Martin Lindstrom | 134 |
| Kenneth Lay (ENRON) | 11 | Maslow's hierarchy of needs | 215, 216, 223 |
| Kenneth Rogof | 109 | McDonald's (restaurant) | 56 |
| Key performance indicators (KPIs) | 187 | Mediation (employment matters) | 236, 237 |
| Key personnel insurance | 265 | MediaWorks | 163 |
| Keywords (Web searches) | 133, 144, 148, 154, 155, 163, 164, 350 | Medici family | 405 |
| KiwiSaver | 229, 376, 420 | Michael LeGault | 123 |
| Labour hire businesses | 216 | Michael Mauboussin | 254 |
| Lean manufacturing | 43, 191, 192, 197 | Michael Porter (five forces) | 86, 90, 91 |
| Lean Start-up (Eric Ries) | 39, 43 | Michael Singer | 29 |
| Leasing (plant and equipment) | 198, 199, 448 | Michelangelo | 250, 405 |
| Lehman Brothers | 241 | Mike Tyson | 81 |
| Less than a Container Load (LCL) | 195 | Mindfulness (being mindful) | 28, 36, 37 |
| Liabilities | 393, 394, 398, 403-406, 467, 470, 510, 516, 518 | Minimum hourly rate | 19, 228, 229 |
| Life insurance | 262 | Minimum Order Quantities (MOQ) | 195 |
| Limited liability company (LLC) | 47, 48, 270, 335-339, 346, 376, 499, 510, 516 | Minimum Viable Product (MVP) | 276 |
| Link business brokers | 55 | Minimum wage | 19, 228, 229 |
| LinkedIn | 149, 151, 161-164, 190 | Mobile devices | 155, 157 |
| Liquidation | 11, 248, 259, 270, 322, 346, 415, 441, 477, 513-519 | MOZ.com (keyword searches) | 155 |
| Liquidator (registered) | 346, 441, 512, 513-517 | Multiplier ("The Multiplier") | 461-466, 487, 489, 539 |
| Liquidity | 396, 400, 405 | Multi-tasking | 189 |
| Liquidity ratio | 98, 379 | Myers Briggs Type Indicator (MBTI), | 246 |
| Living wage | 228 | myIR | 419 |
| Loan protection insurance (and mortgage) | 262 | MYOB | 203, 414 |
| Loans from shareholders | 401 | Namelix.com | 133 |
| Long-term loans | 401 | Napoleon (and strategy) | 69 |
| Looka.com | 164 | Naturalistic Decision Making | 123 |

# Resource Material and References

## About this Book

1.  Reuters News. *"Fannie Mae accounting scandal, earnings restatement"* 2007. https://www.reuters.com/article/markets/factbox-fannie-mae-accounting-scandal-earnings-restatement.
2.  Mike Lindert *"Whatever happened to Jim Collin's "Good to Great' Companies?"*. 2023. https://www.exitplanningexchange.com.
3.  Graeme Codrington. "Good to Great...to Gone!". Dec 2011 https://tomorrowtodayglobal.com/.

## Chapter 1

1.  Transparency International *"Corruptions Perceptions Index"* https://www.transparency.org/.
2.  Institute of Economics and Peace *"Global Peace Index -2023"* http://visionofhumanity.org/resources .
3.  World Economic Forum, *"Global Gender Gap Report 2023 – Insight Report June 2023"* https://www.weforum.org/publications/.
4.  The World Bank Group *"Doing Business 2020"* https://archive.doingbusiness.org/en/rankings.
5.  World Justice Project *"Rule of Law Index 2023"* https://worldjusticeproject.org/rule-of-law-index.
6.  The World Bank Group. *"Ease of Doing Business Rankings"* https://archive.doingbusiness.org/en/ranki. gs and see spreadsheet
7.  Helen Clark. Twitter Post 4 Aug 2019. Ref: https://www.thecoast.net.nz/trending-now/eye-opening-map-shows-just-how-big-new-zealand-is-compared-to-europe/
8.  *"Largest Companies by Market Cap"* SEMRUSH https://companiesmarketcap.com/
9.  Ministry of Business, Innovation & Employment (MBIE) *"Small Business in 2022"*

## Chapter 2

1   Keller A et al. *"Does the Perception that Stress Affects Health Matter?* The Association with Health and Mortality. University of Wisconsin-Madison. 2012.
2   Bob Weir *"Success Made Small – A Step-by-Step Guide to Small Business Success"* 2017.
3   Michael Singer *"The Untethered Soul"* 2007. New Harbinger Publications and Noetic Books.

4   Jenkinson, et. al (2013). *"Is volunteering a public health intervention? A systematic review and meta-analysis of the health and survival of volunteers"* BMC Public Health

5   Elizabeth Dunn and Michael Norton. *"Happy Money: The Science of Smarter Spending"*. (2013).

6   Russell Foster, *"The neuroscience of sleep: Russell Foster at TEDGlobal"* (2013).

7   Yasmin Anwar, *2007 "Sleep loss linked to psychiatric disorders"* UK Berkley News.

8   Gemma Paech (2014) *"Explainer: how much sleep do we need?"* Centre for Sleep Research, University of South Australia.

9   Viktor Frankl, (1946). *"Man's Search for Meaning"*

10  Aldridge and Lavender. *"The Impact of Learning on Health"*. Education, Resources and Information Centre (ERIC). 2000.

11  John Field (2012), *"Is Lifelong Learning Making a Difference? Research-Based Evidence on the Impact of Adult Learning"* University of Stirling

12  Russ Harris. *"The Happiness Trap"*. 2008.

13  Marmot et. al. (1991) *"Health inequalities among British civil servants: the Whitehall II study"*. National Library of Medicine.

## Chapter 3

1.  Eric Ries. *The Lean Start-up: How Relentless Change Creates Radically Successful Businesses*. 2011.

2.  *"US NASDAQ listed company buys Christchurch-based. Seequent for US$1.05 billion."* NZ Herald. 12 March 2021.

3.  Figure.nz *"Business survival rates in all industries in New Zealand"* https://figure.nz/chart/

4.  Stats NZ *"New Zealand business demography statistics: At February 2023"* https://www.stats.govt.nz/information-releases.

5.  Stats NZ. *"Homeownership rate lowest in almost 70 years"*. https://www.stats.govt.nz/news/homeownership-rate-lowest-in-almost-70-years

6.  Geoff Laurent *"The History of SHOOF"* (2015) Shoof International Limited

7.  NZBN – New Zealand Business Number. *"About the NZBN"* https://www.nzbn.govt.nz/whats-an-nzbn/about/.

## Chapter 4

## Chapter 5

1.  Willie Pietersen. *"Strategic Learning. How to Be Smarter Than Your Competition and Turnkey Insights into Competitive Advantage"* (2010). John Wiley and Sons.

2.  Simon Sinek. *"Start with Why - How Great Leaders Inspire Everyone To Take Action"* Penguin Books (2011)

3.  Infometrics *"NEET rate, 2024"* https://rep.infometrics.co.nz/new-zealand/employment/neet
4.  Ministry of Business, Innovation & Employment (MBIE) *"Maori Employment Action Plan"*
5.  Te Ao – Maori News *"Waikato rangatahi filled with new confidence about future"* 11 January 2021
6.  Stats NZ. Māori population estimates: At 30 June 2024. https://www.stats.govt.nz/
7.  NZ Herald *"Oho Mauri gives college leavers second chance"* July 2022. https://www.nzherald.co.nz/
8.  Michael Porter. *"Competitive Strategy: Techniques for Analysing Industries and Competitors"* (1980)
9.  Eva Corlett *"Blow to New Zealand media as two main outlets announce programme closures and job cuts".* (2024) The Guardian News. https://www.theguardian.com/world/2024/apr/10/new-zealand-warner-bros-discovers-closes-newshub-tvnz-programs-bulletins-cuts.
10. Ben Fahy. *"Want to reach Kiwis? NZ On Air media consumption study shows the old dogs are still dominant, but digital is nipping at their heels"* (2014). https://stoppress.co.nz.
11. Te Ara – Encyclopedia of NZ *"Channel Ratings, 2000-2012"* https://teara.govt.nz/en/interactive/45678/channel-ratings-2000-2012
12. Myllylahti et. al. *"Trust in News Aotearoa New Zealand 2024"* AUT Research Centre for Journalism, Media and Democracy.

## Chapter 6

1.  Harari, Yuval Noah (2011). *"Sapiens – A Brief History of Humankind".* Penguin Random House.
2.  Boyd, Dr Lara (2015). *"After watching this, your brain will not be the same".* TEDx Vancouver
3.  Ariely, Dan (2008). *"Predictably Irrational – The Hidden Forces that Shape Our Decisions"* Harper Collins. New York.
4.  Kahneman, Daniel (2011) *"Thinking, Fast and Slow"* Penguin Books.
5.  Reinhart, Carmen M. and Rogoff, Kenneth S. (2009) *"This Time is Different – Eight Centuries of Financial Folly"* Princeton University Press. New Jersey.
6.  Zajonc, R. B. (1980). *"Feeling and thinking: Preferences need no inferences".* American Psychologist, 35, pp151-175.

## Chapter 7

1.  Nee, Victor; Snijders, Tom; Wittek, Rafael. (2014). *"The Handbook of Rational Choice Social Research"* Stanford University Press pp 33 to72.
2.  Ariely, Dan (2008). *"Predictably Irrational – The Hidden Forces that Shape Our Decisions"* Harper Collins. New York.
3.  Lerner, Jennifer S.; Li, Ye; Valdesolo, Piercarlo; Kassam, Karim; (June 2014*). "Emotion and Decision Making*" Annual Review of Psychology.
4.  Lerner, Jennifer S.; Li, Ye; Valdesolo, Piercarlo; Kassam, Karim; (June 2014*). "Emotion and Decision Making*" Annual Review of Psychology.

5.	Kahneman, Daniel (2011) *"Thinking, Fast and Slow"* Penguin Books.
6.	Klein, Gary (1998). *"Sources of Power – How People Make Decisions"*. The MIT Press. Cambridge Massachusetts.
7.	LeGault, Michael (2006). *"Think – Why Crucial Decisions Can't Be Made in the Blink of an Eye"*. Threshold Editions. New York.
8.	Shai Danziger, Jonathan Levav, and Liora Avnaim-Pesso *"Extraneous factors in judicial decisions"* (2011).

## Chapter 8

1.	Michael E. Gerber. *"The E Myth Revisited -Why Most Small Businesses Don't Work and What to Do About It"*. (1995).
2.	Chris Malone and Susan T. Fiske. *"The Human Brand: How We Relate to People, Products, and Companies"*. (2013).
3.	John Costello et. al *"Choosing the Best Spelling: Consumer Response to Unconventionally Spelled Brand Names"* Harvard Business Review Edition October 2023 pp24-25.
4.	Edmund Jerome McCarthy *"Basic Marketing -A Managerial Approach"* (1960)
5.	Martin Lindstrom. *"Buyology -How Everything We Believe About Why We Buy is Wrong"*. (2008).
6.	Jeanna Pool. *"Marketing for Solos -The Ultimate How to Guide for Marketing Your One Person Small Business Successfully"*. (2011)
7.	Oxford Reference *"Overview AIDA"* https://www.oxfordreference.com/.

## Chapter 9

1.	*"New Zealand Advertising Standards annual turnover reports"*. https://www.asa.co.nz/resources/asa-advertising-turnover-report/
2.	Digital Boost website. https://digitalboost.business.govt.nz/
3.	Simon Kemp *"Digital 2024 : New Zealand"* Data Portal February 2024 https://datareportal.com/reports
4.	SEO.AI https://seo.ai/blog/how-many-websites-are-on-the-internet.
5.	Digital Boost website. https://learn.digitalboost.co.nz/media/1051/view
6.	*"Smartphone market in New Zealand – statistics & facts"* https://www.statista.com/topics/9745/smartphone-market-in-new-zealand/ and *"Digital 2024: New Zealand"* by Simon Kemp. Data Portal February 2024 https://datareportal.com/reports
7.	David Chaffey *"Global social media statistics research summary May 2024"* https://www.smartinsights.com/social-media-marketing/social-media-strategy/new-global-social-media-research/
8.	Ani Petrosyan *"Worldwide Digital Population 2024"* https://www.statista.com/statistics/617136/digital-population-worldwide/
9.	*"Digital 2024 : New Zealand"* by Simon Kemp. Data Portal February 2024 https://datareportal.com/reports
10.	Tamara Biljman *"The Top Social Media Trends for 2024 that you Need to Pay Attention to"* https://www.sendible.com/insights/latest-social-media-trends-report and *"50+ Social Media Video Marketing Statistics*

*for 2024"* by Mahnoor Sheikh https://sproutsocial.com/insights/social-media-video-statistics

11. *"New Zealand Digital Advertising Grows by 4.3% Year-on-Year"* The Interactive Advertising Bureau (IAB) New Zealand https://www.iab.org.nz/news

12. Mathew Gibbons. *"18 Best Paid Advertising Platforms "*. https://www.webfx.com/blog/marketing/paid-advertising-platforms/

13. Eckstut, Ariell and Joann *"What is Color? 50 Questions and Answers on the Science of Color"* 2020 Abrams and *"Color Psychology – Profit from the Psychology of Color"* Richard G. Lewis2014 Riana Publishing

14. Advertising Standards Authority (ASA). https://www.asa.co.nz/decisions/.

## Chapter 10

1. George Miller. *"The Magical Number Seven, Plus or Minus Two: Some Limits on Our Capacity for Processing Information"*. March 1956.

2. Sheena Iyengar. *"The Art of Choosing"* (2010)

3. Ecommerce Data Collection Agency (ECDB). Germany https://ecommercedb.com/markets/nz/all.

4. *"E-commerce in New Zealand – Statistics and Facts"* January 2024. https://www.statista.com/

5. Stats NZ. *"Retail sales plummet in lockdown"* August 2020. https://www.stats.govt.nz/news/retail-sales-plummet-in-lockdown/.

6. Ecommerce Data Collection Agency (ECDB). Germany https://ecommercedb.com

7. Ministry of Business Innovation & Employment (MBIE) *"Consumers know their rights, but confidence in protection regime falls"* May 2023 https://www.mbie.govt.nz/about/news/consumers-know-their-rights-but-confidence-in-protection-regime-falls

8. Digital Boost website. https://digitalboost.business.govt.nz/

## Chapter 11

1. Daniel Markovitz. *"A Factory of One"*. (2011)

2. Global Edge *"New Zealand Trade Statistics"*. https://globaledge.msu.edu/countries/new-zealand/tradestats.

## Chapter 12

1. Ministry of Business, Innovation & Employment (MBIE) *"Small Business in 2022"*

2. Guy Whitcroft (2022) *"Company Culture Impacts Business Strategy"* The Maverick Paradox Magazine. https://themaverickparadox.com/

3. Nevid J (2013). *"Psychology: Concepts and Applications"*. Wadsworth, Cengage Learning, Belmont CA p288.

4. Mackay, Hugh (2010). *"What Makes Us Tick – The ten desires that drive us"*. Hachette Australia.
5. Maslow, A. H. (1943). "A *theory of human motivation"*. Psychological Review, 50(4), 370-396.
6. Business govt.nz.
https://eab.business.govt.nz/employmentagreementbuilder/startscreen.

## Chapter 13

1. *"Inquiry into finance company failures – Report of the Commerce Committee"* Forty-ninth Parliament (Lianne Dalziel, Chairperson) October 2011
2. American Psychological Association *"APA Dictionary of Psychology"* https://dictionary.apa.org/
3. David Keirsey. *"Please Understand Me II"*. (1998).
4. Daniel Goleman. *"Emotional Intelligence -Why It Can Matter More Than IQ."* (1995).

## Chapter 14

1. Mauboussin, Michael J. (2012). *"The Success Equation — Untangling Skill and Luck in Business, Sports, and Investing"*. Harvard Business Review Press, Boston.
2. Gladwell, Malcolm (2008). *"Outliers — The Story of Success"*. Little Brown and Company.
3. Rodenberg, Jarno (2016). *"100 Richest People in World History — How Wealth is Created and Destroyed"*
4. Kahneman, Daniel (2011) *"Thinking, Fast and Slow"* Penguin Books.
5. Sir Richard Branson, *"Losing my Virginity"* (2011). Random House.

## Chapter 15

1. Bob Weir. *"Why Businesses Fail – and the journey through our irrational minds"* (2018).
2. Eric Ries. *"The Lean Start-up: How Relentless Change Creates Radically Successful Businesses"*. (2011).

## Chapter 16

1. Franchise Consultants (NZ) Ltd. *"How to use the Advantage – What you should know about starting a franchise system"* 5th Edition 2008.
2. Dr Callum Floyd. Franchise Consultants (NZ) Ltd. *"40 Ideas for a better Franchise"* (2019).
3. Bob Weir. *"Why Businesses Fail – and the journey through our irrational minds"* (2018).

# Chapter 17

1.  Dairy NZ. *"Solid foundations - Report highlights dairy's economic contribution"* September 2023
2.  Global Edge *"New Zealand: Trade Statistics"* https://globaledge.msu.edu/countries/new-zealand
3.  New Zealand Foreign Affairs and Trade *"Trade and Small and Medium Enterprises"* https://www.mfat.govt.nz/assets/Trade-agreements/UK-NZ-FTA/Trade-and-small-medium-enterprises-.pdf.
4.  Ministry of Business, Innovation & Employment (MBIE) *"Small Business in 2022"*
5.  Stats NZ. *"New Zealand International Trade"* https://statisticsnz.shinyapps.io/trade_dashboard/
6.  New Zealand Foreign Affairs and Trade. *"All for Trade and Trade for: Inclusive and productive characteristics of New Zealand goods exporting firms"* MFAT Working Paper. February 2022.
7.  The Informed Investor *"Export Success Stories"* https://www.informedinvestor.co.nz/export-success-stories/
8.  The New Zealand Treasury *"Success Stories"* https://exportcredit.treasury.govt.nz/success-stories
9.  New Zealand Trade and Enterprise – myNZTE. https://my.nzte.govt.nz/article/how-i-used-networks-to-build-my-export-business.

# Chapter 18

1.  WorkSafe. *"Fatalities"*. https://data.worksafe.govt.nz/graph/detail/fatalities.
2.  ACC *"Work Injury Statistics"* https://www.acc.co.nz/newsroom/media-resources/work-injury-statistics/
3.  Clive Lloyd. *"Next Generation Safety Leadership: From Compliance to Care"* (2020). CRC Press
4.  WorkSafe *"Meatworks death brings consequences for AFFCO"* https://www.worksafe.govt.nz/about-us/news-and-media/meatworks-death-brings-consequences-for-affco/
5.  Safe Work Australia *"Managing psychosocial hazards at work"* Code of Practice. July 2022.
6.  High Court of Australia. *"Kozarov v State of Victoria"*. 2022.
7.  Jared Savage & George Block. *" Auckland businessman Ron Salter to pay $4m to settle 'proceeds of crime' case after workplace death of Jamey Bowring"* NZ Herald. 21 Oct 2024.

# Chapter 19

1.  Sharp Tudhope Lawyers. *"Your business and the law"* October 2018 https://sharptudhope.co.nz
2.  Consumer Protection. *"Obligations under the Consumer Guarantees Act"* https://www.consumerprotection.govt.nz

3. WorkSafe *"Further action on Serene bathroom heaters"* 17 April 2024 https://www.worksafe.govt.nz/
4. Letter to Justin Sollitt from Honourable Iain Lees-Galloway 20 December 2019.
5. New Zealand Gazette *"Electricity Regulations (Prohibition of Serene S2068) Notice 2024"* https://gazette.govt.nz/notice/id/2024-au1706
6. Justin Sollitt. *"A Lot of Hot Air – Serene Fan heaters and the largest appliance recall in New Zealand history"* 2024 Unicorn Books
7. The Commerce Commission. *"Agreements that substantially lessen competition"*
8. Ian Young *"Katie Perry vs. Katy Perry: Singer loses trademark battle"* 28 April 2023 www.bbc.com
9. Joel Guinto *"Katie Perry vs. Katy Perry: Singer wins right to use name in Australia"* 22 November 2024. www.bbc.com
10. Katie Perry's website. www.katieperry.com.au
11. Kayleigh Werner *"Australian designer Katie Perry says she's 'lost everything' after Katy Perry wins trademark dispute"* 22 November 2024. www.independent.co.uk
12. Anna Kaufman *"Katy Perry wins appeal over designer Katie Perry to use her name in Australia"*. 22 November 2024. www.usatoday.com

## Chapter 20

## Chapter 21

1. ACCA Global *"The history of how humans invented accounting"* www.accaglobal.com
2. Adum Smith Ovunda. " *Luca Pacioli's Double-Entry System of Accounting: A Critique"*. Research Journal of Finance and Accounting. 2015
3. University of South Australia. *"The History of Accounting"* http://www.library.unisa.edu.au

## Chapter 22

1. The Treasury. *"Interim Financial Statements of the Government of New Zealand - For the eleven months ended 31 May 2024"* https://www.treasury.govt.nz/
2. Inland Revenue Department. *"Overdue tax debt statistics"* https://www.ird.govt.nz/about-us/tax-statistics/statistics-on-tax-debt
3. *"Consumption Tax Trends 2022 VAT/GST and excise, core design features and trends"* OECD https://www.oecd.org.
4. Tom Raynel *"Sole traders purposely earning less to avoid GST threshold"* NZ Herald. 16 September 2024. https://www.nzherald.co.nz/business/sole-traders-are-purposely-earning-less-to-avoid-gst-threshold/
5. *"IR240 Penalties and interest - What you need to know if you don't complete a return or pay on time"*. https://www.ird.govt.nz

6. *"Cut your excuses and sort your tax"* 08 April 2024.
   https://www.ird.govt.nz/media-releases
7. *"IRD Media Releases".* https://www.ird.govt.nz/index/media-releases.

## Chapter 23

1. *"Progress payments terms and e-invoicing"* Beehive.govt.nz
   https://www.beehive.govt.nz/release/progress-payment-terms-and-e-invoicing
2. Biegelman, Martin T. *"Faces of Fraud – Cases and Lessons from a Life Fighting Fraudsters"* Audio Book. From www.audible.com.

## Chapter 24

## Chapter 25

1. *"NZ Business Demography Statistics: At February 2023".*
   https://www.stats.govt.nz/information-releases/new-zealand-business-demography-statistics-at-february-2023/
2. *"Liquidations by year, 2001-2023"* Waterstone
   https://waterstone.co.nz/media-insights/insolvency-statistics.

## Chapter 26

## Chapter 27

1. *"Business survival rates in all industries in New Zealand"* Figure NZ.
   https://figure.nz/chart
2. *"NZ Business Demography Statistics : At February 2023".*
   https://www.stats.govt.nz/information-releases/new-zealand-business-demography-statistics-at-february-2023/
3. *"NZ Business Demography Statistics : At February 2023".*
   https://www.stats.govt.nz/information-releases/new-zealand-business-demography-statistics-at-february-2023/
4. *"Liquidations by year, 2001-2023"* Waterstone
   https://waterstone.co.nz/media-insights/insolvency-statistics
5. Anne Gibson *"Red ink reins in builder Mainzeal".* New Zealand herald 5 March 2006
6. Milford Assets. *"Richina Pacific"* 8 September 2007.
7. Andrew Bethell, Liquidator, BDO. *"First Report to Creditors and Shareholders..."* March 2013

## Chapter 28

www.ingramcontent.com/pod-product-compliance
Lightning Source LLC
Chambersburg PA
CBHW081757200326
41597CB00023B/4056